JESUS
THE
MAGICIAN

JESUS
THE
MAGICIAN

MORTON SMITH

Ph.D., The Hebrew University; Th.D., Harvard;
Professor of History, Columbia University

1817

HARPER & ROW, PUBLISHERS, San Francisco
Cambridge, Hagerstown, Philadelphia, New York
London, Mexico City, São Paulo, Sydney

First Harper & Row paperback edition published in 1981.

Library of Congress Cataloging in Publication Data

Smith, Morton, 1915-
   JESUS THE MAGICIAN.

Bibliography: p. 211.
Includes indexes.
1. Jesus Christ—Miscellanea.   I. Title.
BT304.93.S63   1977   232.9'01   76-9986
ISBN 0-06-067413-X

81 82 83 84 85 10 9 8 7 6 5 4 3 2 1

Contents

Preface   vii

1. Suppressed Evidence and Perennial Problems   1
2. The Historical Framework   8
3. What the Outsiders Said—Evidence in the Gospels   21
4. What the Outsiders Said—Evidence Outside the Gospels   45
5. What the Outsiders Meant   68
6. The Marks of a Magician   81
7. The Evidence for Magical Practices   94
8. What the Evidence Shows   140

Appendix A. The Pharisees in the Gospels   153
Appendix B Jesus vs. the Prophets   158
   Notes   165
   Chapter 1   165
   Chapter 2   166
   Chapter 3   169
   Chapter 4   177
   Chapter 5   184
   Chapter 6   187
   Chapter 7   190
   Chapter 8   207
   Appendix A   208
   Appendix B   209
   List of Scholarly Works and Editions Cited   211
   Abbreviations   221

Preface

? pagan
Jewish · *Magus*

"Jesus the magician" was the figure seen by most ancient opponents of Jesus; "Jesus the Son of God" was the figure seen by that party of his followers which eventually triumphed; the real Jesus was the man whose words and actions gave rise to these contradictory interpretations. "Jesus the Son of God" is pictured in the gospels; the works that pictured "Jesus the magician" were destroyed in antiquity after Christians got control of the Roman empire. We know the lost works only from fragments and references, mostly in the works of Christian authors. Hence modern scholars, trying to discover the historical Jesus behind the gospel legends, have generally paid no attention to the evidence for Jesus the magician and have taken only the gospels as their sources. The bias of their work is understandable.

This book is an attempt to correct this bias by reconstructing the lost picture from the preserved fragments and related material, mainly from the magical papyri, that New Testament scholarship has also generally ignored. Beginning with an account of the destruction of the evidence and consequent problem (chapter 1), it sketches the historical framework of Jesus' life—the facts that can be established, even from the gospels, with relative confidence (chapter 2)—and then collects the reports about Jesus the magician from the gospels (chapter 3) and from Jewish and pagan sources (chapter 4). Chapters 5 and 6 explore the implications of these reports—what the terms for "magician" meant in the ancient world—and in chapter 7 the gospels are reexamined for evidence that accords with the picture they oppose. Such evidence indicates the common core from which both legendary pictures—"Jesus the magician" and "Jesus the Son of God"—developed. Chapter 8 investigates the sources and implications of this core material.

This book has been written in the belief that advanced research on the life and teaching of Jesus is a matter of legitimate concern and possible interest to educated men and women in all walks of life, as well as to professionals in New

Testament studies. The attempt to produce a text that may interest both groups of readers has necessitated some concessions to each. Most of these concessions will be obvious and should justify themselves, but a few need comment: References to evidence and discussion of details will be found in the *Notes.* To avoid breaking up the text with footnote numbers, the notes have been divided by references to the pages to which they refer, and each note begins with a capitalized word or phrase indicating the point to which it refers. Works are cited by author and brief title; full titles, etc., will be found in the list at the end of the book. There, too, is a list of abbreviations (not exhaustive; abbreviations of biblical books and the like are omitted as familiar). Economy has prohibited discussions of collateral questions, reviews of previous work, etc. In citation of synoptic gospels, "p." refers to the parallels of the one text cited; these will be found in any "synopsis" or "harmony" of the gospels. All material from works in foreign languages has been translated, and all translations are by the author (except those from Ethiopic and Egyptian, including Demotic and Coptic). The attempt has been, not to render the original word for word, but to give accurately the sense of the passage. In translations, pointed brackets ⟨ ⟩ frame words added to make the sense clear, square brackets [ ], words I think interpolations, parentheses ( ) are used, as usual, for punctuation. I have not usually thought it necessary to mention inaccuracies in translations by earlier scholars, most often Conybeare and Preisendanz. Capitalization in a work of this sort presents peculiar problems. For example, compare "a son of a (pagan) god" and "the Son of God," the Christian title. These are conventional; but before the title was fixed some of Jesus' followers thought him a son of the (Jewish) God, and he may have thought himself either "a son of god" (an Aramaic phrase meaning "a god") or "the Son" (a deity who appears in the magical papyri and is hereinafter capitalized for clarity). Other complications will appear in course. In general, capitalization has been kept to a minimum; occasionally, however, it has been used, inconsistently, for emphasis; for instance, "Name" is capitalized in discussion of the role of the Name of God in magic. "Law," when capitalized, commonly refers to the Mosaic Law. Citations of the Old and New Testaments give the verses according to the Hebrew and Greek texts; these sometimes differ slightly from the English.

Finally, a note about some sources: The gospels were written in the last quarter of the first century A.D., but are known to us mainly from manuscripts of the third century A.D. and later. Similarly, the major magical papyri are manuscripts dating from the third century A.D. and later, but containing works some of which were written at least as early as the gospels. Occasional references to Jesus in the papyri no more prove Christian origin or inspiration than the quotations of Aratus and pseudo-Epimenides in Acts (17.28) and

Titus (1.12) prove those works basically pagan. The notion that Philostratus' *Life of Apollonius* (another third century composition) was modeled on the gospels, has been refuted by the study of Petzke, *Traditionen* 129–137.

My thanks are due to Harper & Row for their willingness to publish a book that attempts to bridge the gap between scholarship and the literate laity. Mr. John Shopp and Mr. John Loudon in particular have been extraordinarily patient and understanding of the delays and details resultant from research. Mr. Levon Avdoyan typed and proofread the manuscript; I owe much to his helpfulness and efficiency. Most of the first draft was read by Professors H. D. Betz, James Robinson, and a number of their colleagues and students at The Institute for Antiquity and Christianity of the Claremont Graduate School. The present text has profited equally from the kindness of their consideration and the frankness of their criticisms; for both I sincerely thank them. Finally, it is a pleasure to conclude the revision of this work where Strauss' *Life of Jesus* was written, in the Evangelisches Stift of the University of Tübingen. I thank the authorities of the University and of the Stift, and especially Professor Dr. Martin Hengel, Dean of the Theological Faculty, for their generous hospitality.

MORTON SMITH

Tübingen
August, 1977

~ 1 ~

Suppressed Evidence and
Perennial Problems

"O wad some Pow'r the giftie gie us
To see oursels as others see us!"

ROBERT BURNS, *To a Louse*

I

"There are always two sides to an argument." If we want to know what really happened, we had better hear both sides. If we want to understand a man, we had better hear not only what is said by those who believe his claims but also what is said by those who do not.

This rule should hold for Jesus as for everyone else, but when we ask what people who did not believe in Jesus had to say about him, the answer is hard to come by. Almost everything we know about him is found in the works of his believers, mainly in the gospels, a little in the rest of the New Testament and other early Christian texts.

His believers not only wrote these texts, they also formed an organization, "the Church," that became strong enough three hundred years later to get the support of the government of the Roman Empire and use it to suppress the works of anyone who did not agree with them. We are told that in A.D. 326 the emperor Constantine ordered that the books of "heretics" (Christians who held minority opinions) should be hunted out and destroyed. He evidently did the same for pagan works about Jesus, since he refers to the destruction of some of them in the following edict of A.D. 333:

Constantine, Victor, Greatest Augustus, to bishops and laity: ⟨The heretic⟩ Arius, having imitated wicked and impious men, deserves to suffer the same loss of privileges as they. Therefore, just as Porphyry, that enemy of piety who put together various illegal works against religion, got his just deserts, so that he was made contemptible forever after and filled full of ill fame, and his impious books have been obliterated, thus, too, we now order that Arius and those who agree with him shall be called Porphyrians . . . and besides this, if any book written by Arius be found, it is to be consigned to the fire, so that not only his corrupt teachings may vanish, but no memory of him at all may remain.

This decree was one of a series issued by Constantine and his successors ordering that works contradictory to the teachings of "the universal Church" be hunted out and destroyed.

The Church did not have to rely wholly on imperial action to get rid of unwanted data. Its bishops were given judicial authority by Constantine and his successors; they could and did act on their own. Thus Theodoret, Bishop of Cyrrhus in Syria, about 450, wrote of a "heretic" named Tatian:

This (fellow) also composed that gospel called "By the Four," cutting off the genealogies and such other things as show that the Lord was, as for his body, a descendant of David. Not only the adherents of his party used this (gospel), but also those (Christians) who followed the apostolic teachings (i.e. were of my party), but who did not recognize the rascality of the composition, but simply used the book as a compendium. I myself found more than two hundred such books revered in the churches of my own (diocese), and collecting them all, I did away with them and introduced instead the gospels of the four (canonical) evangelists.

Such pious efforts to suppress other people's opinions were not wholly successful. In spite of Constantine's commands, Porphyry is remembered as one of the chief neo-Platonic philosophers; but, thanks to Constantine, his work *Against the Christians* has come down to us only in fragments. Tatian's gospel can be reconstructed—approximately. M. James' *The Apocryphal New Testament* prints fragments of some twenty lost works about Jesus and references to many more of which only titles are known. Many such titles appear in a list dubiously attributed to Pope Gelasius (A.D. 492–496) that ends with a typical blast, "We declare that these and similar works which Simon Magus . . . and all heretics and disciples of heretics or schismatics have taught or written . . . are, not only repudiated, but indeed purged from every Roman Catholic church, and, with their authors and the followers of their authors, in the unbreakable chain of excommunication, eternally damned."

Little by little, through the past two centuries, scholars have collected fragments of reports and opinions about Jesus that contradicted the dogmas of the branch of the Church that finally triumphed. We cannot recover the destroyed evidence, but we can piece together enough remains to show the variety of beliefs that Jesus' followers held, and even something of what the majority of his contemporaries—those who did not become his followers— thought of him. It begins to become possible to hear the many other sides of the case.

II

In the case of Jesus we particularly want to hear the other sides, because the side presented by the gospels has produced many perennial problems. For hundreds of years scholars have been studying the gospels with minute attention; they have thus arrived at general disagreement about the gospels' central character.

Yet Jesus should be one of the better known figures of antiquity. We have at least half a dozen letters from Paul, who perhaps knew Jesus during his lifetime (II Cor. 5.16) and joined his followers within, at most, a decade after his death. We have four accounts of Jesus' public career—the canonical gospels—written anywhere from forty to seventy years after his death; these are generally thought to rest, in part, on earlier written material. Few public figures from the Greco-Roman world are so well documented, but none is so widely disputed. This suggests that there is something strange about the documents, or about the scholars who have studied them, or both.

Probably both. Most of the scholars have not been historians, but theologians determined to make the documents justify their own theological positions. This has been true of liberals, no less than conservatives; both have used "critical scholarship" to get rid of theologically unacceptable evidence. But not everything can be blamed on the scholars. They could not have performed such vanishing acts had there not been something peculiar in the evidence itself.

In the first place, the gospels repeatedly contradict each other, even as to the course of events. Did Jesus disrupt the temple market at the beginning of his preaching career (Jn. 2.13–16), or at the end of it (Mk. 11.15–17), or, as some apologists would say, at both times? Was he crucified on the day before the passover meal (Jn. 18.28), or on the day after it (Mk. 14.16), or on both? There are hundreds of such specific, factual differences.

In the second place, the gospels were written, not merely to record events, but also to produce and confirm faith in Jesus the Messiah (that is, "the Christ"), the Son of God—not a historical figure, but a mythological one: a god who came down from heaven, assumed a human body, went about doing miracles and teaching, was crucified, died, was buried, rose from the dead, went back to heaven, and is now sitting up there, awaiting the time set for his return to raise the dead, judge all men, destroy this world and produce a new one. Since this mythological figure is incompatible with the known world, liberal New Testament scholars have tried to distinguish as sharply as possible between "the Christ of faith" and "the Jesus of history." "The Christ of faith" was commonly said to have resulted from "the resurrection experience" of "the primitive Church," in other words, from the psychological inability of Jesus' followers to accept his death, their subconscious resistance to it, and the hallucinations this resistance produced in them. Since the gospels reflect this "resurrection experience," they present "the Christ of faith." The task of liberal criticism was to get behind the gospels to "the Jesus of history" who was expected to be a non-mythological figure, a simple preacher of "the great truths on which the Church was founded." These "great truths" would be readily recognizable by the critic, since they would be the ones he himself believed.

When this "critical" program was carried through, almost everything in the gospels turned out to belong to "the Christ of faith"; next to nothing was left of "the Jesus of history." This result was convenient for preachers (it minimized the historical obstacles to homiletic developments), but is indefensible as the outcome of a historical study of four ancient documents. Moreover, the fundamental antithesis, that between "the Christ of faith" as a mythological figure and "the Jesus of history" as a preacher free of mythological presuppositions, is anachronistic. Where in ancient Palestine would one find a man whose understanding of the world and of himself was *not* mythological?

The picture of the world common to Jesus and his Jewish Palestinian contemporaries is known to us from many surviving Jewish and Christian documents. It was wholly mythological. Above the earth were heavens inhabited by demons, angels, and gods of various sorts (the "many gods" whose existence Paul conceded in I Cor. 8.5, and among whom he counted "the god of this age," II Cor. 4.4). In the highest heaven was enthroned the supreme god, Yahweh, "God" *par excellence,* who long ago created the whole structure and was about to remodel, or destroy and replace it. Beneath the earth was an underworld, to which most of the dead descended. There, too, were demons. Through underworld, earth, and heavens was a constant coming and going of supernatural beings who interfered in many ways with human affairs. Sickness, especially insanity, plagues, famines, earthquakes, wars, and disasters of all sorts were commonly thought to be the work of demons. With these demons, as with evil men, particularly foreign oppressors, the peasants of Palestine lived in perpetual hostility and sporadic conflict, but the relations were complex. As the Roman government had its Jewish agents, some of whom, notably the Herods, were local rulers, so the demons had their human agents who could do miracles so as to deceive many. The lower gods were the rulers of this age, and men who knew how to call on them could get their help for all sorts of purposes. So could women, whose favors they had rewarded by teaching them magic and other arts of civilized life. On the other hand, Yahweh, like the demons, was often the cause of disasters, sickness, etc., sent as punishments. He sometimes used angels, sometimes demons, as agents of his anger, and his human agents, his prophets, could also harm as well as help. Most Jews believed that in the end he would destroy or remodel the present world, and create a new order in which the Jews, or at least those who had followed his law, would have a better life. However, as to the course of events and the actors in the coming catastrophe, there was wide disagreement; any number of contradictory programs circulated, with various roles for one or more "messiahs"—special representatives of Yahweh—anti-messiahs, and assorted mythological monsters.

This was the picture of the world *common* in first century Palestine. Even Herod Antipas, the Romans' puppet prince in Galilee, is said to have thought Jesus was John the Baptist raised from the dead. Even Josephus, a Jew of the priestly aristocracy who as a young man was sent on a mission to Rome, held beliefs of this sort: he was proud of the Jews' control of demons; he claimed to have prophetic powers himself and to have prophesied that the Roman general, Vespasian, would become emperor and rule all mankind; and he saw Vespasian as a messiah foretold by at least some biblical prophecies. His own prophecy was famous; the Roman historians Suetonius and Dio Cassius reported it. Suetonius and Tacitus say that such messianic prophecies were common throughout the Near East. We should presume that almost all Palestinian Jews of Jesus' time thought themselves involved in the mythological cosmic drama. That Jesus did so is not merely a matter of presumption; it is supported by the unanimous evidence of the gospels.

For these reasons the antithesis between "the Christ of faith" and "the Jesus of history" is a gross exaggeration, and often a misleading apologetic device. Both general probability and specific evidence require us to recognize the possibility that "the Christ of faith" originated in the lifetime, if not in the mind, of "the Jesus of history" and that one of the first to believe in "Jesus the Christ" was Jesus himself. Consequently, we cannot suppose that all gospel elements reflecting "the Christ of faith" must be unhistorical. Some may be, but others may be true. Granting that the stories about Jesus and his sayings have come down to us through, and often from, the early churches, that they have been preserved by memory, recast in more memorable forms, simplified, harmonized, adapted to new purposes, and supplemented by invention; even so, they remain evidence, not only of the sort of churches that preserved them, but also of the sort of man from whom those churches arose. No matter how much we discount their historical value as records, there can be no question of their historical value as results, as symptoms. Whatever else Jesus may or may not have done, he unquestionably started the process that became Christianity. We have therefore to ask: What sort of man and what sort of career, in the society of first century Palestine, would have occasioned the beliefs, called into being the communities, and given rise to the practices, stories, and sayings that then appeared, of which selected reports and collections have come down to us?

Trying to find the actual Jesus is like trying, in atomic physics, to locate a submicroscopic particle and determine its charge. The particle cannot be seen directly, but on a photographic plate we can see the lines left by the trajectories of larger particles it put in motion. By tracing these trajectories back to their common origin, and by calculating the force necessary to make the particles move as they did, we can locate and describe the invisible cause. Admittedly, history is more complex than physics; the lines connecting the original figure to the developed legends cannot be traced with mathematical accuracy; the intervention of unknown factors has to be allowed for. Consequently, results can never claim more than probability; but "probability," as Bishop Butler said, "is the very guide of life."

III

This brings us back to the question of the suppressed evidence. If the historical Jesus be defined as the common cause and starting point of the movements that took their rise from him, then the more movements we can see, the more lines we can trace back, the more accurate the result. Therefore, scholars are now searching the gospels for evidence of the many early beliefs about Jesus that may once have been held separately by different groups of his followers, beliefs now fused into the gospels' composite picture: teacher, divine man, prophet, suffering servant of God, son of man, son of God, angel/ word/power/wisdom of God, and so on. But these various beliefs present only one side of the material. They show only the lines followed by those men attracted to the new element. What about those it repelled? How did they interpret it?

By some amazing oversight, New Testament scholarship says almost nothing about them. For instance, the recent book *Jesus as Seen by His Contemporaries,* by Professor E. Trocmé of the University of Strasbourg, one of the foremost European students of the gospels, brilliantly reviews the history of the study, and goes on to characterize the different notions of Jesus reflected by the gospels' sources—"the Jesus of the 'sayings of the Lord,' the Jesus of the stories about sayings, the Jesus of the biographical stories, the Jesus of the parables, the Jesus of the miracle stories"—with little consideration of the Jesus of Jesus' opponents. Only when he comes to "Jesus as a Public Figure," and has to account for the crucifixion, does he give considerable attention to materials other than those used as propaganda by the gospels, and here he devotes most attention to the gospels' reports of the enthusiastic reception of Jesus by the crowds. This public acclaim, and inaccurate reports of some of his sayings, supposedly occasioned his opponents' "misunderstandings" (which are not discussed) and caused the jealousy and fear that led to his death. A picture of Jesus based on such a selection of the material has about as much historical value as a portrait of Charles de Gaulle or Mao Tse Tung drawn exclusively from Gaullist or Maoist publications. We must try to hear the other side too.

cosmologia

Nazarene!

mandaeans

~ 2 ~

The Historical Framework

No myth ô history

No interpretations of Jesus will show us the man as he saw himself. All are outside views. This is inevitable. How many of our friends do we know as they know themselves? None. Even our knowledge of ourselves is mostly incommunicable. Personality is so complex and changeable that even a good autobiography is a high-speed photograph of a waterfall: it imposes a fixed form on a process falsified by fixation. *persona · bethlehem*

An individual, like a waterfall, must be identified by external data—location, action, effects. If we ask these questions about Jesus, reasonably reliable answers are available. He was born in Palestine, probably within eight or ten years of the beginning of the present era. He grew up in Galilee, was baptized by John the Baptist, formed a band of his own followers, and went about with them mainly in Galilee, but at least once visited Jerusalem and there was arrested and crucified—on these matters the gospels agree; we have no reason to question their reports. *historical* *for persons*

Nor is there any reason to question their unanimous report that Jesus attracted attention as a miracle worker. Rationalists long assumed that miracles do not occur and that the gospel stories of Jesus' miracles were legendary outgrowths of the basic, historical material, to be pruned away by the critic in search of "the historical Jesus," unless they could be explained as misunderstandings or exaggerations of normal events. Then came the discovery that blindness, deafness, loss of speech, paralysis, and the like might occur as hysterical symptoms and be "cured" instantaneously if the hysteria suddenly ceased. It also appeared that certain individuals were amazingly successful in quieting hysterical patients. Hence Jesus' "exorcisms" and "cures" are now commonly thought to have resulted from the sudden cessation of hysterical symptoms and cognate psychological disorders. Almost nobody thinks the preserved stories are accurate in all details, but few scholars would deny that at least some of them probably derive from reports of "cures" that actually occurred in Jesus' presence and were understood by the patients, the observers, and Jesus himself, as miracles performed by him.

Such cures made Jesus famous. To understand their importance, we must remember that ancient Palestine had no hospitals or insane asylums. The sick and insane had to be cared for by their families, in their homes. The burden of caring for them was often severe and sometimes, especially in cases of violent insanity, more than the family could bear—the afflicted were turned out of doors and left to wander like animals. This practice continued to the present century; I shall never forget my first experience in the "old city" of Jerusalem in 1940. The first thing I saw as I came through the Jaffa Gate was a lunatic, a filthy creature wearing an old burlap bag with neck and armholes cut through the bottom and sides. He was having a fit. It seemed to involve a conversation with some imaginary being in the air in front of him. He was pouring out a flood of gibberish while raising his hands as if in supplication. Soon he began to make gestures, as if trying to protect himself from blows, and howled as if being beaten. Frothing at the mouth, he fell to the ground on his face, lay there moaning and writhing, vomited, and had an attack of diarrhea. Afterwards he was calmer, but lay in his puddles of filth, whimpering gently. I stood where I had stopped when I first saw him, some fifty feet away, rooted to the spot, but nobody else paid any attention. There were lots of people in the street, but those who came up to him merely skirted the mess and walked by. He was lying on the sidewalk in front of a drugstore. After a few minutes a clerk came out with a box of sawdust, poured it on the puddles, and treated the patient with a couple of kicks in the small of the back. This brought him to his senses and he got up and staggered off, still whimpering, rubbing his mouth with one hand and his back with the other. When I came to live in the "old city" I found that he, and half a dozen like him, were familiar figures.

Such was ancient psychotherapy. Those not willing to put their insane relatives into the street, had to endure them at home. Also, since rational medicine (except for surgery) was rudimentary, lingering and debilitating diseases must have been common, and the victims of these, too, had to be cared for at home. Accordingly, many people eagerly sought cures, not only for themselves, but also for their relatives. Doctors were inefficient, rare, and expensive. When a healer appeared—a man who could perform miraculous cures, and who did so for nothing!—he was sure to be mobbed. In the crowds that swarmed around him desperate for cures, cures were sure to occur. With each cure, the reputation of his powers, the expectations and speculations of the crowd, and the legends and rumors about him would grow. Such crowds and their needs, *not* the later Christian communities, were the earliest matrices of gospel stories and continue, even now, to produce similar stories, for example, see the *New York Times* (Oct. 10, 1977, p. 31, col. 1):

A Lebanese monk was proclaimed a saint by Pope Paul VI. Sharbel Makhlouf, a hermit who died in 1898 at the age of 70, thus became the first Lebanese to be canonized by the Roman Catholic Church. . . . Thousands of the faithful went to the rocky peak of Annaya on Mount Lebanon to pay homage to the peasant monk who was canonized in Rome. Many thousands had trudged the steep 17-mile road from the ancient port of Byblos. Religious fervor reached a peak when onlookers said they had seen the bronze statue of Saint Sharbel bless the crowd, after which several paralytics had risen and walked and a blind girl had regained her vision.

From this social and medical background of the Near East we can understand why the gospels represent Jesus as attracting attention primarily as a miracle worker, and winning his followers by miracles. The gospels do so because he did so. These facts have been neglected as unedifying by liberal exegesis; we must look at the evidence.

Mark is generally said to be the oldest gospel. According to Mark (1.16–20) Jesus' miracles in Galilee began with the calls of the first four disciples: "Passing by the sea of Galilee, he saw Simon and Andrew, Simon's brother, casting ⟨a net⟩ into the sea, for they were fishermen. And Jesus said to them, 'Come after me and I shall make you be fishers of men.' And at once, leaving their nets, they followed him. And going on a little, he saw James the son of Zebedee, and John his brother, and they too were in their boat, mending their nets. And at once when he called them, leaving their father Zebedee in the boat with the hired servants, they went after him." Mark has no introduction to these stories; he wants the reader to believe that Jesus had never seen these men before. Their immediate responses to his unexpected and unexplained summons are miracles that testify to his supernatural power. The same power ("authority") is the important thing revealed by his teaching, and is immediately manifested by his "casting out a demon" (quieting a lunatic, 1.23–26). Consequently "the news of him went out everywhere into all the Galilean countryside," (1.28) and as soon as the Sabbath was over, "they brought him all the sick and those possessed by demons, and the whole city was assembled at the door ⟨of the house where he was staying⟩. And he cured many sick with various diseases and cast out many demons" (1.32ff.). Understandably when he left the city early the next morning, everybody hunted for him (1.37). When he cured a leper and the leper spread the news, the crowds became so great that he could no longer publicly enter a city, but stayed in the countryside, "and they came to him from everywhere" (1.45). When he went back into Capernaum the crowd that assembled was so large that some men bringing a paralytic had to go up on the roof and lower the sick man, on his bed, into the healer's presence (2.1ff.). Again when he went out by the sea, crowds came from as far away as Jerusalem and Sidon, "hearing the things he did" (3.8) "for he healed many, so that all who had afflictions fell on him, trying to touch him, and ⟨those possessed by⟩ unclean spirits, when they saw him, fell before him and cried out, saying, 'You are the Son of God.'" (3.10f.). These stories set the theme for the gospel of Mark; from here on it frequently refers to crowds or individuals coming to Jesus or wishing to see him because of his miracles. Even his enemies, while he is being crucified, declare his miraculous deeds—"He saved others, but he cannot save himself" (15.31).

Written about A.D. 75, Mark was used in the 80s or 90s by both Matthew and Luke. They also used another early source or sources, now lost, from which they have in common a good deal of material not found in Mark. This material is called Q. The source, or sources, are matters of endless dispute, but most scholars would agree that they were earlier than Matthew and Luke. The preserved material consists chiefly of sayings attributed to Jesus, but also contains stories of his miracles and represents people as coming to him because of them. A centurion, "having heard about Jesus," sent or came to him, asking him to heal a valuable slave. Clearly, what he had heard were stories of a man who could do miracles, and he was not disappointed. (The story of this healing was famous; John knew it in a different form—4.46-54). In another Q story Jesus cast out a mute demon (cured a case of hysterical aphasia); "the crowds marveled, but some of them said, 'He casts out demons by Beelzebul, ruler of the demons.'" The accusation indicates the reason for his fame. It circulated widely. Mark and Matthew have it in different contexts. An answer for it is given in Q: Jesus said, "If I cast out demons by Beelzebul, by whom do your boys cast them out? . . . But if I cast out demons by the finger of God, then the kingdom of God is in touch with you." Q material also contains Jesus' defense of doing miracles on the Sabbath—a defense that appealed to Jewish oral law—and it presents his miracles as the reason for believing his message: If the miracles done by Jesus in the towns of Galilee had been done in Tyre and Sidon, those pagan cities would long ago have believed him; therefore the Galileans, who did not believe, will get their just deserts on the day of judgment. Another Q story shows that the early churches appealed to Jesus' miracles as proof that he was the Messiah, against rival claims by the followers of John the Baptist. The Baptist demonstrates his ignorance by sending messengers to Jesus to ask whether or not he is "the coming one." Jesus demonstrates his identity with a display of miraculous cures and an implicit argument from them: "Go tell John what you have seen and heard. Blind see, lame walk, lepers are cleansed, deaf hear, dead are raised, good news is proclaimed to the poor, and lucky is ⟨the man⟩ who is not scandalized by me." Why should anyone have been "scandalized"—the verb means, "made to stumble," that is, prevented from believing—by a man who did such miracles? The answer to this question will become clear later on.

Matthew has some material, peculiar to his gospel, that appears neither in Mark nor in Q. So does Luke. How much of this peculiar material they got from earlier sources, how much they invented, we cannot tell. We do know that the material peculiar to each portrays Jesus as a miracle worker and says he attracted his following by his miracles.

Matthew gives us an initial description of his work, "He went about in all Galilee, teaching in their synagogues and preaching the good news of the kingdom and healing every disease and every infirmity in the people. And the news of him went out into all Syria, and they brought him all the sick, those in the grip of various diseases and afflictions, those possessed by demons, the moon-struck and the paralytic, and he healed them. And many crowds followed him, from Galilee and the Decapolis and Jerusalem and Judea and Transjordan." This may be a reworking of various verses in Mark; if so, Matthew believed Mark's account, took it over, and developed it. Accordingly, almost all the Markan passages noted above are also found in Matthew. Besides these, Matthew on his own finds an Old Testament verse to prove that Jesus was sent to do miracles, "to fulfil the ⟨word⟩ spoken by Isaiah the prophet, who said, 'He himself took our infirmities and carried off our diseases.'" Matthew also says that when Jesus cured a blind and deaf man the crowd thought him "the son of David" (the Messiah, 12.22f.; compare 21.14f.). Matthew adds a cure of two blind men with the conclusion that "they, going out, spread word of him through all that land" (9.27–31). Summarizing Jesus' work, Matthew repeatedly says, he "cured every disease and every affliction" (4.23; 9.35; cp. 10.1). For Matthew it was Jesus' walking on the water (and enabling Peter to walk on it, a miracle only Matthew reports) that persuaded his disciples to prostrate themselves and say, "Truly, you are the Son of God" (14.23–33). Another Matthaean summary, towards the end of Jesus' work in Galilee, reads, "And crowds upon crowds came to him, bringing with them their lame, deformed, blind, mute, and many others, and they laid them at his feet and he cured them, so that the crowd marveled, seeing the dumb speaking and lame walking and blind seeing, and they praised the God of Israel" (15.30f.). We should not suppose that such summaries are wholly reflections of Mark; Matthew knew stories from other sources, and summarized in these passages the picture he found in much of Christian tradition.

A similar picture of Jesus as miracle worker appears in the material peculiar to Luke. Luke takes over most of the Markan and all of the Q material outlined above, and also makes Jesus begin his public career by proclaiming himself the fulfilment of the messianic prophecies of Isaiah, including prophecies of miraculous cures—"recovery of sight for the blind"—probably metaphoric in Isaiah, but, as the sequel shows, understood literally by Luke as referring to Jesus' miracles (4.16–30). Luke underlines the miraculous nature of the call of the first disciples (5.1–11). He adds explicit statements declaring that crowds came to Jesus to be healed. He augments the testimony of the demons to his divinity (4.41), and reports the growth of his reputation and spread of his fame that followed individual miracles (7.16f.; 9.43). He says that the women who followed and financed Jesus were some of those "healed of evil spirits and illnesses," and singles out among them "Mary, called the ⟨woman⟩ of Magdala, from whom seven demons had been cast out" (8.2). He has Jesus describe his work with the words, "I cast out demons and perform cures" (13.32). He repeatedly says that the crowds rejoiced at his miracles and reports that even Herod Agrippa wanted to meet Jesus in the hope of seeing him do some miracle (23.8).

Even more important is the role of Jesus' miracles in John, for John emphatically makes them the proof of Jesus' supernatural status. First, Nathaniel recognized him as "Son of God" and "King of Israel" because Jesus told him what he had been doing before they met (1.48f.). Jesus welcomed the belief and promised to show him greater wonders (1.50f). Next, he turned the water at Cana into wine and by "this beginning of the signs". . . "revealed his glory, and his disciples believed in him" (2.11). Soon many in Jerusalem "believed in his name, seeing his signs that he performed" (2.23). A Pharisee, Nicodemus, came to him secretly saying, "Rabbi, we know you are a teacher come from God, for no one can do these signs that you do, unless God is with him" (3.2). Miracles not specified as "signs" also call forth faith; the woman of Samaria, like Nathaniel, was led to think Jesus the Messiah because, "He told me everything I had done," and other Samaritans believed because of her report of this miracle (4.39). Specified as signs are, besides the Cana miracle, the healing of the royal official's son, the feeding of the 5,000, probably the healing of the man born blind, and the raising of Lazarus. There are also many references to performance of unspecified signs, and these signs are regularly represented as the reason for which his disciples believed and the crowds followed him. John himself thinks them the proper reason for believing him the Messiah and the Son of God. That Jesus did signs, but the Baptist did not, proves Jesus the Messiah, the Baptist merely his prophet (10.41). In its original form the gospel probably concluded with the words, "Now Jesus did many other signs in the presence of the disciples, signs which are not reported in this book. But these have been reported in order that you may believe that Jesus is the Messiah, the Son of God, and that, believing, you may have life in his name" (20.30f.).

In sum, all major strands of gospel material present Jesus as a miracle worker who attracted his followers by his miracles. All of them indicate that because of his miracles he was believed to be the Messiah and the son of a god. Anyone who wants to deny the truth of these reports must try to prove that within forty to sixty years of Jesus' death all the preserved strands of Christian tradition had forgotten, or deliberately misrepresented, the most conspicuous characteristic of the public career of the founder of the movement.

Moreover, there is yet earlier and more important evidence for Jesus' role as a miracle worker. The cited passages have mostly been comments by the evangelists, since these make clear what was understood to be the effect of the miracles—the following they attracted, and the beliefs they occasioned. These comments are consistent, plausible, fit the historical situation, and (except for their naive exaggerations) present no excuse for doubt. Behind them however stand the miracle stories themselves. They appear in every branch of the tradition and must be prior (in substance, if not in present form) to the comments they occasioned. In their present form they are usually complex, showing multiple layers—original narrative, introduction, expansion, comment, and conclusion. The original narratives must therefore be older than the developed forms. Whatever their individual historicity, they prove that Jesus was remembered as a miracle worker in the earliest Palestinian churches.

There is one piece of evidence in the gospels that might seriously be cited against the notion that Jesus was a miracle worker, but this evidence turns out, on examination, to indicate that he was one. It is the little group of stories reporting that, when asked to give a (miraculous) sign, he refused to do so. The stories are apologetic —their purpose is to justify his refusal—therefore their core (the refusal) must be historical; it is not a thing his followers would have invented. Nor is it a thing they would have reported unless it was remembered and thrown in their faces, as an argument against their claims. The preservation of these stories is evidence of the claims: Jesus' followers must have presented him as a miracle worker, or the argument, that when challenged he could not perform a miracle, would have been worthless. Nobody thought it was worthwhile to report that the great Rabbi Akiba could not perform miracles—in his own time he was not expected to do so. The report about Jesus indicates the expectation. It also indicates that the gospel grew up in an atmosphere of polemic involving appeals to remembered, historical facts of Jesus' career. One of these facts was that, on at least one occasion, when challenged to display his miraculous powers, he either could not or would not. This is to be expected of a faith healer whose power depends to some extent on the patients' belief in him. That Jesus recognized the importance of the patients' belief is indicated by his often repeated saying, "Your trust has healed you," and others like it. Accordingly, the psychological plausibility of the story strengthens the case for its basic historicity, and consequently for a picture of Jesus as a man who might be thought to claim miraculous powers and be challenged to display them.

Similar apologetic motivation and psychological plausibility appear in Mk. 6.1ff:

He comes into his home town . . . and on the Sabbath he started to teach in the synagogue. And the crowd, hearing, were astonished, saying, "Where does this ⟨fellow⟩ get such ⟨stuff⟩?" and "What wisdom was given to this ⟨guy⟩?" and "⟨What⟩ kind of miracles are done by his hands? Isn't this the carpenter, the son of Mary, and brother of James and Joses and Judah and Simon? And aren't his sisters here with us?" And they were scandalized ⟨prevented from believing⟩ by ⟨their knowledge of⟩ him. [And Jesus said to them, "A prophet is not without honor, except in his own home town, and in his own family, and in his own house."] And he could not do any miracle there [except, laying his hands on a few sick, he cured ⟨them⟩]. And he marveled because of their unbelief.

Again the theme of "scandal" (as above, pp. 11f.). Notice the difference from Paul: For Paul the "scandal"—the stumbling block that prevents the Jews from believing—is Jesus' crucifixion. In Mark and Q it is Jesus himself. The report in Mark and Q is probably the earlier. Paul's claim appears to be an apologetic attempt to explain most Jews' rejection of Jesus: they did not reject him because of his practices, but only because of his fate. On this point, however, Paul cannot be believed. The fate—the crucifixion—was the result of a prior rejection which must have had a prior cause.

Why would the worshipers of a supernatural saviour have made up a story like the one in Mk. 6.1ff? Surely not to explain the saying, "A prophet is not without honor, except in his own home town!" On the contrary, this saying is clearly intrusive. We know that it circulated independently; an older, simpler form appears in Jn. 4.44, "A prophet has no honor in his own country." Yet another is found in the Oxyrhynchus Papyri (no. 1, recto). This saying was probably invented in some congregation outside Palestine to "explain" the comparative failure of Christianity in Jesus' "own country." Mark saw that it could also be used to "explain" Jesus' own failure in his home town; he tacked on the dangling phrases about family and house to make it seem appropriate for his purpose, and inserted it in the home town story. But the added phrases spoil the original epigrammatic form, and the insertion interrupts the story in which, "They were prevented from believing," should be followed by its consequence, "He could not do any miracle." No Christian making up a frame for the saying would have invented the report that Jesus could not do miracles when rejected. The report was an embarrassment, as shown by Matthew's alteration of it ("He did not do *many* miracles there," 13.58), Mark's gloss on it ("except, laying his hands on a few sick, he cured ⟨them⟩"), and Luke's replacement of the whole story by a less embarrassing version made up largely from other sources—which version, however, tried to "explain," without specifying, the awkward fact (4.16–30). Since the report was embarrassing, its preservation in Christian material means it was something the Christians had to concede; therefore, it was probably true. It also fits the psychological facts: A faith healer cannot heal when he finds no faith. Moreover, the story contains other family information, some of which was also embarrassing—its description of Jesus as "the carpenter" and "the son of Mary," its knowledge of the names of his brothers and the location of his sisters. In the ancient world manual labor was thought degrading, so Matthew changed "the carpenter" to "the son of the carpenter" (13.55); Luke and John omitted it. None of this would be explicable if the story were a mere frame for the saying; nor are the embarrassing details explicable as Christian invention. Evidently these are **historical recollections that Jesus' followers did not treasure for their own sakes, but had to admit, and tried to explain, because they were being used against them by other Jewish groups who also remembered these facts. The** primary thrust of the Christian defense is to represent this incident as wholly exceptional. Everywhere else, Jesus was not rejected—and could do miracles.

A man who can do miracles is thought to have some sort of supernatural power. If his miracles are beneficial (cures, etc.), his power is thought holy. So is his person. As a holy man his sayings and actions will be remembered, and men will follow him to benefit from his holy power, hear his sayings, and imitate his way of life. If his followers begin to think him the Messiah, and if **they become so numerous and enthusiastic as to frighten the civil authorities, he will soon be in serious trouble. Thus the rest of the tradition about Jesus can be understood if we begin with the miracles. But the miracles cannot be understood if we begin with a purely didactic tradition. In this respect the** contrast between the gospels and the early rabbinic traditions about the Pharisees—almost wholly devoid of miracles—is decisive evidence. Teachers of the law were not, in this period, made over into miracle workers. Neither were the authors of apocalyptic prophecies; we have a dozen, and their authors are wholly anonymous. But a miracle worker could easily come to be thought a prophet and an authority on the Law.

From all this evidence it seems that Jesus attracted attention and followers as a miracle worker, especially as an exorcist and healer. Why then was he crucified? The reason just suggested, on grounds of pure probability, is in fact the one reported by the gospels. His miracles attracted enormous crowds and led many to think him the Messiah. Both the crowds and the messianic speculations worried the priests who controlled the temple and city of Jerusalem. The temple was a center of national, as well as religious feeling; a long series of riots, revolts and wars had been, and would be, set off by attempts to control it. The Romans, ruling central and southern Palestine at this time, watched it as a possible center of trouble, and kept an eye on the rest of the country, intervening with military force to disperse assemblies they thought dangerous. If the temple were to become the center of a general Jewish uprising they might close or even destroy it. (It did so in A.D. 66, and was destroyed in 70.) Consequently, the problem posed for the priests by Jesus, his followers, and their enthusiasm is perfectly summed up by John when he represents the high priests, after Jesus' raising of Lazarus, calling a meeting of the "sanhedrin"—the Jerusalem city council—and saying, "What shall we do? This fellow is doing many miracles. If we let him go on like this everybody will believe in him, and the Romans will come and take away from us both this ⟨holy⟩ place and ⟨the leadership of⟩ the people" (11.47f.). The story is fictitious in detail, but true in essence to the situation. It does not rule out the possibility that other factors, which the gospels were less willing to report, were also involved. However, there is no reason to question the essential historicity of the passion story, told in the four gospels from at least three different sources, with considerable differences in details, but unanimous agreement as to the main events: The city authorities had Jesus seized and handed him over to Pilate; Pilate had him crucified as a would-be messiah, "the King of the Jews." Since Pilate was governor of Judea from about A.D. 26 to 36, the crucifixion is to be dated within that decade.

Thus the external framework of Jesus' life—the what, when, and where —is reasonably certain. Beyond these facts lie difficulties. For instance, some of his disciples thought he rose from the dead. Without that belief Christianity would be inexplicable. But how shall we explain the belief? Certainly not from rabbinic Judaism; no such belief is known to have been held about any rabbi of his time. Why then about Jesus? Again, he was executed as a messianic pretender; but the charge may have been false. Did he really claim to be a messiah, and if so, what did he mean by the claim? Yet again, the gospels represent him as a teacher, but what did he teach?

On these and similar questions the evidence of the gospels is always suspect and often self-contradictory. As to what it signifies, contemporary scholars are in utter disagreement. Their disagreement results not only from the contradictions in the material, and from those between the theological positions now being defended, but also from the method now prevalent in the study—uncontrolled structural analysis of selected New Testament passages, to discover their components, and equally uncontrolled conjecture as to the social matrices from which these components might have come. Since very little is known of the social forms and milieux of Christianity during the century from 30 to 130, and the little known is commonly neglected by specialists in the study of the New Testament, their conjectures, if taken together, would yield a chaos valuable only to discredit the method that produced it. In contrast to such conjectures, what *can* historically be determined, beyond the general character of Jesus' career, are the social types current in his world, by which such a career could have been interpreted at that time. These provide parameters of the possible, and from them we can estimate with somewhat more confidence the reliability of reported details.

Since our hope is to determine Jesus' social identity we must deal with what psychologists call an "identity problem." In our own society the most familiar form of such a problem is that posed by the awful question, "What do you want to be when you grow up?" The question supposes that you will be a nameable something —an example of one of the types known and named in your society. A boy who replied simply, "A man," would be dismissed as a dummy, or instructed by further questions: "But what do you want to *do?*" (Instruction: you must "do," in the main, some one "thing," perform some socially approved function, and therefore be describable by one or another of your society's terms for its functionaries: butcher, baker, or candlestick maker.) The question is common nowadays because family ties have loosened, opportunities for employment have proliferated, and even a lower-class child has a wide range of choices. In antiquity, family ties were strong, vocational training schools uncommon, opportunities for employment few, and choices therefore limited. The average boy became what his father had been before him. This made cultural diversification difficult, but it also made for social and psychological stability. "Identity crises" were rare.

They did occur however, usually as the result of something extraordinary in the child. In ancient Greece, for example, a boy of extraordinary strength might become a professional amateur athlete—a type still familiar, but less honored. One fellow from Thasos won 1200 (some say 1400) victories, was worshiped as a god throughout Greece and even beyond Greek territories, was credited with miracles of healing, and was said to have been fathered by a god. A boy of extraordinary beauty would also have extraordinary opportunities: Philip of Croton was worshiped as a hero after his death because he had been the most beautiful man in Greece. Extraordinary intellectual abilities also might give the boy a choice. Lucian, the famous lecturer, has left an account of his own "identity crisis": His father, to save money, took him out of school in his early teens and gave him to his maternal uncle to be trained in the family trade as a stonemason. On his first day he broke a stone slab, his uncle whipped him, he came home in tears and had a dream in which he saw two women contending for his adherence. One was the goddess of stonecutting, the other, of rhetoric. The latter lady, and the life she offered, were more attractive, so he turned to her; her competitor turned to stone, and he mounted a chariot drawn by winged horses in which he was taken up to the heavens. The reader is to suppose this revelation persuaded Lucian's father to let him go on with his studies. Extraordinary psychological gifts could also yield an unusual career: A slave girl in Philippi was subject to fits, supposedly seizures by a prophetic spirit; her owners set her up as a prophetess and got a substantial income from her customers. When Paul cured her by casting out the spirit they brought him to court (Acts 16.16f.).

These cases, a handful from many, show the essentials. Some extraordinary endowment or event may release an individual from routine succession to a recognized role in life. This extraordinary element is commonly thought to be somehow "divine" or "demonic" (terms often almost equivalent). The person in whose life it occurs is therefore different, and may also be called "divine" or "demonic." His inner identity crisis, and his unconventional solution of it, pose an outer "identification crisis" for his society. How can it identify this new figure? How can it categorize the extraordinary man? The categories used by ancient society reflected its notion of the world and were therefore mainly mythological, as the terms "divine" and "demonic" indicate.

Accordingly, the social types recognized by men of antiquity are not closely similar to modern ones except in cases where both are determined by some common, objective function. Butcher, baker, fisherman, and farmer are of course common to the ancient and the modern worlds. Besides these, each society has social types defined by functions peculiar to itself—only Rome, for instance, had tribunes and lictors. Finally, each society has some peculiar categories shaped by its peculiar mythology. By these it tries to explain abnormal types and the persons who deal with them—as we recognize hysterical, paranoid, and manic-depressive types, and psychiatrists and faith healers, they recognized demoniacs of various sorts, divine men, prophets and magicians. As we (depending on our sympathies) speak of "freedom fighters," "brothers," "communists," "rabble rousers," and so on, men of first-century Palestine (depending on their sympathies) spoke of "messiahs," "prophets," "deceivers," "brigands," "charlatans." Jesus was located in these two ranges of variation—he won attention as a miracle worker, and was executed as a messiah, a would-be "King of the Jews." This was recognized even by Jesus' followers. Acts 5.34ff. says that after the resurrection, when the apostles were arrested while preaching in the Temple, and were brought before the sanhedrin, one of its members, the famous Pharisee Gamaliel, advised his colleagues as follows:

Watch yourselves ⟨in dealing⟩ with these men, ⟨and consider well⟩ what you will do. For in times past Theudas arose, saying he was Somebody, and to him some four hundred men attached themselves. He was killed, all who believed in him were scattered and ⟨the movement⟩ came to nothing. After him Judas the Galilean arose in the days of the census and led off ⟨into revolt⟩ the people who followed him. And he perished and all those who believed in him were scattered. So as regards the present ⟨case⟩ I should say, keep ⟨your hands⟩ off these men and let them go, because if this plan or undertaking is ⟨merely⟩ human it will go to pieces, but if it is from God you will not be able to destroy them and you might, also, turn out to be resisting God.

This is Christian propaganda. There is no likelihood that the Christians had reliable reports of what was said in the sanhedrin, and there is every likelihood that Luke (the author of Acts) is following the custom of ancient historians and making Gamaliel say what he thought Gamaliel should have said. The Christian argument is clear: The other movements broke up and disappeared because they and their founders were merely human. Christianity has not broken up and disappeared; therefore it was founded by God. This argument depends on the reader's knowledge that, long after Gamaliel's death, Christianity is still going strong, so the probable date for the passage is about the time when Luke wrote, roughly in the 80s or 90s, and the speech is probably his own work.

Even this Christian progaganda shows that the Christians themselves expected Jesus to be seen as a figure *of the same social type* as Judas and Theudas. Judas was a legal teacher who started a resistance movement against Roman control, and whose descendants, if not he himself, assumed royal dignities probably indicative of messianic claims; comparison with him places Jesus in the category of revolutionists and/or messiahs. Theudas, by contrast, was a *goes*—the word means primarily "magician," and by extension, "deceiver"—who persuaded people to follow him to the Jordan, which he promised to divide so as to give them passage —presumably to the Kingdom of God. It is not clear whether they were headed from Palestine back to the desert (Yahweh's traditional domain), or from Transjordan to Jerusalem, but it is clear that Theudas claimed to be a miracle worker and the comparison with him reflects Jesus' reputation for similar powers.

Thus, Luke's story of Gamaliel's speech shows us how the Christians thought an intelligent but pious contemporary, who was not of their party, would place Jesus among the social types of his time—a teacher and pretended miracle worker who might have messianic claims and whose followers might be involved in revolutionary activities. We now must try to place him more precisely within the ancient spectra of these two types. Just what terms were used to explain him, and why? In answer to this question the gospels give us some of his followers' opinions. These are the familiar statements of faith, repeated and reinterpreted in every book on Jesus, to suit the author's creed. We shall try to supplement and control them by going back to our original question and asking, What did those who were not his followers have to say about him?

～ 3 ～

What the Outsiders Said—
Evidence in the Gospels

I. COMMON OPINION

"Who do men say that I am?" The question arose in Jesus' mind too—at least Mark says it did (8.27–30p.), and Matthew and Luke take over the story. The disciples answer, "John the Baptist, and others Elijah, and others, one of the prophets." This is the early Christian account of outside opinions, by contrast to the inner circle's belief, here expressed by Peter, "You are the Messiah" (Matthew, "the Messiah, the Son of the living God" 16.16). Of course the disciples report only the nicer forms of the outside opinions; one does not tell one's master bluntly that men think he "has a demon." Nor does one needlessly report to others such opinions of one's master; so when Mark summarizes what Herod had heard about Jesus, we get the same list (6.14p.). Less flattering opinions may be indicated by implication or even stated directly when they have to be refuted, or when they serve to explain the course of events.

Reviewing the evidence, we find it of two sorts. Some judgments are presented as mere observations of fact or as notions commonly held, others are attributed to specific groups. We shall begin with the former. What did people generally think of him?

He was reportedly thought a Jew (Jn. 4.9) and a Galilean (Jn. 7.41), as was Peter (Mk. 14.70p.). To be a Galilean was a reproach in Jerusalem where the north-country accent was noticeable. Some of his enemies said he was a Samaritan (Jn. 8.48—and had a demon; there were famous magicians in Samaria, Acts 8.9ff.). That such stories could circulate indicates that he was not of distinguished ancestry; some of his critics claimed, "We don't know where he comes from" (Jn. 9.29), and wondered that, although he had no for-

mal education, he could read (Jn. 7.15). The beginning of his career as a public figure was generally admitted to have been his baptism by John the Baptist.
Apparently this was an embarrassment to his disciples, so it probably figured
in the polemic against him. In contrast to John who was conspicuously ascetic,
he practiced no observable abstinence and was accused of being gluttonous
and a drunkard (Mt. 11.19p.). Such reports, whether true or not, do nothing
to explain his importance. The important thing was his power to do miracles.
If we piece together the evidence about this, we get the following picture:
Jesus' miracles produced primarily astonishment, "all the people marveled."
Fame immediately followed; so did fear. All these facts appear mainly in the
evangelists' comments and show us what they thought the consequences of the
miracles would be. They knew their society; we have no reason to doubt their
judgment. The fame, at least, is necessary to explain the course of events. Both
Jesus' career and the success of his followers after his death would be inexplicable had he not become conspicuous.

    The evangelists say his miracles and teaching won him not only devoted
followers, but general admiration. Mark even claims that his enemies were
afraid to attack or arrest him in public. From one of Jesus' adherents this report
is suspect, but not improbable. Authorities then, as now, may have preferred
to act inconspicuously. The chief reasons for questioning Jesus' popular following are the reports that, in spite of their initial hesitations, the Jerusalem
authorities did seize him at the beginning of Passover, and the Romans had
him crucified on either the day before the feast or the first day of it. Further, the
crowds turned from him after his arrest, petitioned for the release of another
prisoner, demanded that Jesus be crucified, and mocked him on the cross.
However, these reports may not disprove his previous popularity. That the
mob should have turned against him after his arrest is not improbable if he had
formerly won its support by a reputation, which his arrest discredited, for
miraculous powers. The reports of the mocking presuppose expectation of
miracles and attest disillusionment. Was such ridicule invented by Jesus'
worshipers? Hardly.

    A further reason for opposition to Jesus is commonly supposed to have
been his legal teaching, but the evidence for this opinion is inadequate. It is
true he was sometimes called "teacher" or "rabbi," but the terms, roughly
equivalent and equally vague, were commonly mere expressions of respect like
"Doctor" in modern English. They do suggest that Jesus, during his lifetime,
was thought by persons other than his own disciples to be an authority on legal
questions, but other evidence of this is scant.

    There are only two stories of lawsuits brought to him for adjudication.
Both are dubious, and in one Jesus is said to have refused to act, on the ground
that he was not an authorized arbitrator. There are a dozen reports of general

legal questions being asked him, but half of these questions were merely attempts to embarrass him, not genuine requests for information, and the rest occur in stories that seem to have been made up by his followers so that they could attribute to him their own instructions for converts. Significantly, several questions concern not Jesus' actions, but those of his (later?) disciples, while others are asked of the disciples, not of him. Finally, the earliest forms of most of these stories are found in four sections of Mark that contain little else and seem to have come from a single source, quite different from the bulk of the material used in the gospels. If reliable, this peculiar source indicates that the beginning of these disputes was not Jesus' teaching, but his practice (or that of his followers). His opponents take offense at his practice and question it. He then answers the question by some brilliant saying or miracle. If his answer is a saying, it may be a legal teaching, but is more likely to be an evasion of the question. (For a breakdown of the evidence see the notes.)

In sum, the bulk of the questions about Jesus' legal teachings are of dubious historicity, and, for what they are worth, indicate that such legal teaching as he did was mostly *ad hoc*, in attempts to answer objections that arose primarily from his and his disciples' libertine practice. There is no reason to suppose the practice derived from legal theory, and no consistent legal theory is attributed to him in the gospels or in any other New Testament books. Moreover, none was remembered by his disciples, who differed violently about legal observance, nor by rabbinic tradition, which should have been interested in the question. Accordingly, we conclude that for outsiders, Jesus' legal teaching was less important than his illegal practices. Even the opposition to his practices is attributed mainly to members of pietistic groups, not to the common people.

The many stories of Jesus' popular following are complemented by the fact that in the synoptic gospels prior to the arrest there are only two stories in which action turns on mass hostility, and both of these are told as exceptional. They seem to have been so.

This suggests that the sayings in which Jesus speaks of himself or his disciples as sheep among wolves, innocent outcasts in an evil generation and a wicked world destined for destruction, are probably products of his followers' reflection on his fate. The probability is clearest in sayings based on the crucifixion, for instance, that anyone who would be saved must "take up his cross." But the rest are suspect too, because there is no reliable evidence that he or his followers suffered any significant persecution before his last days in Jerusalem. Moreover, the sayings consigning most of mankind to damnation are contradicted by another series of sayings that speak of salvation here and now (without cross) for a chosen few, while those of yet another series promise it hereafter to the great majority—all the poor and the lowly, *ex officio*—as the result of a general reversal of social positions. All three sets of sayings can hardly be genuine. Which set accords with the popular following reported by the stories and required to explain the course of events? We return to the basic facts that unless Jesus had a large following he would not have been crucified, and the preaching of his resurrection would not have found such ready and wide acceptance. The course of events presupposes a popular following, the following accords with the miracle stories, both stories and following authenticate the sayings promising salvation to the poor, and these contradict the threats of general damnation. Accordingly, the sayings hostile to the world cannot safely be used to prove that the world was hostile to him. Some groups were hostile, and some sayings (discussed below) reflect their hostility; but for general hostility there is no adequate evidence, against it there is adequate evidence, and the sayings that presuppose it are probably spurious.

This conclusion is supported by the fact that Mark consistently, and John inconsistently, contrast Jesus' following by the people with the opposition to him by small, specified groups. The contrasts are supported by many passages peculiar to Matthew and to Luke. While these are suspect as apologetic exaggerations, the basic contrasts are plausible. In the light of the evidence reviewed, we can reasonably accept them and identify Jesus' opponents as members of the groups thus specified.

II. FAMILY AND TOWNSPEOPLE

In the crisis before the end of the world, according to a saying Matthew attributes to Jesus, "a man's enemies shall be those of his own household" (10.36). If Jesus did say this, he may have been speaking from experience. We have seen that his townspeople rejected him (above, pp. 15f.). As for his family, Mk. 3.21 says, "Those connected with him came out to put him under restraint, for they said, 'He is out (of his mind).'" Of course Matthew and Luke suppressed this. Mk. 3.31–4 says that once, when a crowd was sitting around him, his mother and brothers came and could not get through to him. When somebody told him they were outside, he indicated his disciples and said, "These are my mother and my brothers." In Jn. 7.3ff. his brothers say to him in Galilee, "Go to Judea so that your disciples too can see what works you are doing. For no one does things in secret and tries, himself, to be open. If you do such things, reveal yourself to the world." John's comment on this is, "For neither did his brothers believe in him." Jesus tells them that he will not go up to Jerusalem for the feast, and then, after they had gone, he goes up secretly. Whatever lies behind this amazing episode, its picture of hostility between Jesus and his brothers is clear. This picture is not contradicted by the fact that his brothers later appear in the Church. They had no choice. He was executed as a would-be "Messiah," that is, an anointed king. The title was hereditary, and he was childless, so his brothers found themselves saddled with his claims. (More than half a century later some of their descendants were rounded up and interrogated by the Romans, and only then dismissed as harmless.) Moreover, the Church, once it began to prosper, offered Jesus' brothers unusual opportunities. James eventually became head of the congregation in Jerusalem; others travelled about with their wives, almost certainly at the expense of the communities they deigned to visit. Eventually they appeared in Christian tradition among the earliest witnesses for the resurrection, revered figures to whom two New Testament forgeries, the Epistles of James and Jude, are falsely attributed. Their success in the Church is substantiated by the rarity of stories hostile to them, and this rarity argues in favor of the authenticity of the few stories that do show hostility. They are less likely to have come from later invention, when the brothers were among the "pillars" of the Church (Gal. 2.9), than from memories of the facts of Jesus' lifetime—memories that opponents of the Christians may have helped to keep alive.

The stories of Jesus' relations with his mother present a similar picture. We have already mentioned Mark's stories of Jesus' snub to her and of his rejection by his townspeople (3.31ff.; 6.1ff.); these are the only passages in which Mark clearly refers to her. Matthew and Luke give her a prominent role in the birth stories, but thereafter add nothing to Mark; she is not mentioned in Q. John's stories about her are typically ambiguous: She and Jesus' brothers were with him in Cana, where she told him the wine was running out and was told to mind her own business—though he did provide more wine, 2.1–11. From Cana they went to Capernaum (2.12). Thereafter, during Jesus' lifetime, his brothers appear only in Nazareth for the scene already reported (7.3ff.), and his mother, although mentioned as known to those who reject him (6.42), appears only at the crucifixion where she stands at the foot of the cross. There Jesus commits her to the care of "the disciple whom he loved" (19.25ff.). It is not said that Jesus loved her. Any hero who speaks to his mother only twice, and on both occasions addresses her as "Woman," is a difficult figure for sentimental biographers. Even those willing to accept this evidence find it difficult to evaluate, not only because of its built-in ambiguities, but also because: (1) the scene at the foot of the cross is almost certainly fictitious (Mark and Matthew mention no Christians near the cross, only a few women "watching from a long ways off," and his mother is not said to have been among them); (2) the Cana story is probably also a fiction; it has been shown to have been modeled on a Dionysiac myth; (3) "mother" and "brethren" are symbolic figures in the allegorization of the events of Jesus' life attempted by at least one editor of the gospel of John. Perhaps we may conclude that the Johannine tradition knew Jesus' relations with his mother were on the cool side, and used this fact for its own purposes when creating legends about him.

To explain this coolness we may recall that in Mark's story of the rejection the townspeople refer to Jesus as "the son of Mary" (6.3). In Semitic usage, to refer to a man as the son of his mother was to indicate that his father's identity was uncertain. Matthew (12.55) recast the reference to avoid the implication, Luke (4.22) replaced "Mary" with "Joseph. Another version of the saying, in Jn. 6. 42, also has Joseph. The common explanation, that Mark wrote "son of Mary" because he believed in the virgin birth, is contradicted by the fact that Mark says nothing of the virgin birth, while Matthew and Luke, who both tell stories about it, both refer in this passage to Jesus as the son of his father. Besides, we have already seen Matthew and Luke making other changes in Mark's story to get rid of embarrassing details (above, pp. 15f.). Finally, it is incredible that an ancient editor, so sensitive that he wanted to get rid of "the son of Joseph," should have substituted for it "the son of Mary," which was certain to be understood in a pejorative sense. This is proved by the history of the text: a long string of Christian copyists (who surely believed in the virgin birth) changed "the son of Mary" into "the son of the carpenter and of Mary," or just "the son of the carpenter," but not a one changed Luke's "the son of Joseph" or Matthew's "the son of the carpenter" into "the son of Mary." Mark's phrase was offensive; the others were not.

These facts make it probable that Jesus was not the son of Joseph; had he been so, "the son of Mary" would never have appeared in a Christian text. The probability is confirmed by a number of curious details: (1) Matthew's genealogy of Jesus (1.2–16) refers to only four women besides Mary: they are Tamar, whose children were born of incest; Rahab, the madam of a brothel; Ruth, a non-Israelite, who got her second husband by solicitation, if not fornication, and so became the great-grandmother of David (Ruth 4.21f.); and Bathsheba ("the wife of Uriah"), whose relations with David began in adultery, though she became the mother of Solomon. That the author of a genealogy for a Messiah should have chosen to mention only these four women requires an explanation. The most likely one is that Matthew wanted to excuse Mary by these implied analogies. (2) Each man in the genealogy is said to have begotten his son, until Joseph, of whom it is said, he was "the husband of Mary, from whom Jesus was born" (1.16). (3)The genealogy in Luke says that Jesus was, "as was believed," the son of Joseph (3.23).

These latter details are commonly explained as adaptations to the theory of the virgin birth, but how is the theory to be explained? Most critics think it was produced to fulfil the prophecy in Isaiah 7.14 which read, in a Greek translation, "Behold, the virgin shall conceive and bear a son." But if the theory was invented to fulfil this text, why is this text not cited in Luke's account of its "fulfilment"? The only New Testament author who knows anything about the fulfilment of Is. 7.14 is Matthew (1.23). This is not surprising, because Is. 7.14 is the beginning of a prophecy conspicuously unsuited to Jesus' career, and in the original Hebrew it says nothing about a virgin birth— the Hebrew has "young woman" instead of "virgin." But Matthew (or the school he drew on) is notoriously unscrupulous in ripping Old Testament verses out of context to make them prophecies of gospel stories. In such cases the starting point was commonly the story; the editor's problem was to find a text that could be forced to fit it. Therefore, we can be almost certain that the story of the virgin birth was also given to him by tradition, not invented from the text he twisted to suit it. If so, where did the tradition come from? Why was the story invented? Perhaps because some of Jesus' followers wanted to make him a match for hellenisitic "divine men" who often had divine fathers. Perhaps also because the irregularity of his birth had to be explained. The motives may have coexisted.

If Jesus' birth was in fact irregular, he would have been a ridiculed child in the small country town where he grew up, and we could easily imagine the reasons for his leaving Nazareth, for his visions, conversations with demons, and so on. We could also understand the surprising lack of material about his family in the gospels, and the cool or even hostile tone of what little there is. To judge from the evidence just reviewed, the saying, "If anyone . . . does not hate his father and mother and wife and children and brothers and sisters, and himself too, he cannot be my disciple" (Lk. 14.26), reflects Jesus' own attitude to his family better than that of his followers.

If so, how are the hostile stories and their preservation to be explained? And how, in any event, can we explain the preservation of details discreditable to Jesus, but of no apparent importance to anyone in the later churches? Who in the churches of Rome, Egypt, or Asia Minor knew anything about the peasants of Nazareth? Who, even in the Jerusalem church, cared anything about them? Yet here are details preserved in the gospels to tell us that Jesus was the son of Mary (his father uncertain), was a carpenter in Nazareth where his family lived, went back for a visit after he had set up as an exorcist, but was regarded with contempt by the townspeople and could do no miracles there. Even his brothers did not believe him, and once, at the beginning of his career, his family and friends tried to put him under restraint as insane. For his part, he rejected them, said that his true family were his followers, and had nothing to do with them through all his later career. This coherent and credible account is broken up by the gospels into half a dozen fragments and presented in different lights and different contexts so that only when the details are picked out and put together does the coherence and credibility of the picture become

clear. Once it does, the fragments are recognizable as fragments, and the reason for the gospels' preservation of them also becomes clear. They were preserved because they were parts of the polemic that was circulated by Jesus'
enemies and the opponents of the early churches.

The different gospels tried to meet this polemic in different places and in
different ways— with stories of a virgin birth, with lists of ladies in the holy
family who were not wholly holy, with the claim that his relation to his family
was transcended by that to his disciples, and, if nothing else could be done, by
concession of the charges when concession was necessary—presumably at an
early period when the facts were still common knowledge. Mk. 6 tells of the
rejection and associated charges because they were known; it tries to deal with
them simply by putting them into the framework of the author's faith. Mark
says, in effect, "Yes, it is true, after all his miracles, after raising the dead
(chapter 5), Jesus came to his own village (chapter 6), and because they did not
know the source of his wisdom and his miracles, but did know the facts (which
our enemies keep repeating) of his obscure birth and humble origin, they
rejected him and thereby made it impossible for him to help them. They shut
the door in the face of the mercy of God." This is aimed at Mark's fellow Jews
who were still repeating the same stories to justify a similar rejection, but it
was also written for Mark's fellow believers who, because they shared his faith,
would see the tragedy and be able to use the story in their arguments.

III. HERODIANS AND PHARISEES

Having established the existence of a polemic tradition that preserved the
stories of Jesus' townspeople and family and forced Christians to refer to them,
we have now to ask what group or groups propagated this polemic, and what
they added to it. The gospels mention many adversaries, but some are
mythological, others appear only once or twice, and of others who may have
had some importance in shaping opinions—for instance, the followers of John
the Baptist—we are given only glimpses, not adequate information. Sometimes too, the information we are given can be proved anachronistic and is
useful only to trace the growth of the Christian tradition—it shows at what
periods certain elements developed. A good example are the references to the
Herodians, whom Mark introduces in Galilee, where the Pharisees plot with
them to encompass Jesus' death (3.6). Throughout Jesus' work in Galilee the
plot has no reported consequence and we never hear of the Herodians again
until Jesus reaches Jerusalem, where they reappear, again with the Pharisees,
and try to trap him into forbidding payment of tribute to the Romans
(12.12ff.)—a prohibition that could have been cited in a charge of sedition.
Many scholars think the Herodians were agents of the Herods—a Jewish

family of which various members, with Roman support, held various Palestinian princedoms from 37 B.C. to the end of the first century A.D. If so, this cooperation with the Pharisees during Jesus' lifetime is unlikely, for the most prominent Herod in Jesus' later years (Herod Antipas) had an unsavory record, was following policies of which the Pharisees disapproved, and reigned only in Galilee. What were Herodians doing in Jerusalem? If we look for a time when the Pharisees were vigorously pro-Herodian and when a Herod was active in the persecution of Christians in Jerusalem, we find it a decade *after* the crucifixion, in the reign of Herod Agrippa I, who held Jerusalem from 41 to 44. Accordingly, we may conjecture that the Herodians in Mark are a minor anachronism. This enables us to date one of Mark's sources, the peculiar collection of embarrassing questions in two parts of which they appear—it was evidently put together in or after the 40s.

The case of the Herodians has a far more important analogue—that of the Pharisees, the group most often mentioned as Jesus' opponents. Almost all gospel references to the Pharisees can be shown to derive from the 70s, 80s and 90s, the last years in which the gospels were being edited. The evidence for this is so full and many-sided that it must be treated separately in Appendix A. From that evidence it appears that some Pharisees may have had some differences with Jesus, but the serious conflict between Christians and Pharisees grew up in Jerusalem after Jesus' death, soon became acute, when Paul and (probably) other Pharisees were active in persecuting the new sect, reached a crisis in 41–44 when the Pharisees had the support of Herod Agrippa I (Acts 12), and subsided after the flight of Peter, the death of Herod, and the accession of James, Jesus' brother, to leadership of the church. When Paul visited Jerusalem in the late 50s he found that the church under James was on excellent terms with its Pharisaic neighbors, from whom there were many converts (Acts 21.20); when he was tried there, the Pharisees in the sanhedrin defended him (Acts 23.9); later, about 62, when James was executed by a Sadducean High Priest, the Pharisees seem to have protested the execution and secured the High Priest's deposition. We hear no more of hostility between them and the Christians until after the Jewish revolt of 66–70, culminating in the fall of Jerusalem, in which the older leaders, both of the Pharisees and of the Christian community in Jerusalem, were probably displaced or destroyed. After 70 a profoundly reorganized Pharisaic group with Roman support took the lead in forging a new, "amalagamated," rabbinic Judaism, but deliberately excluded Christians from the amalgam. This resulted in a period of sharp conflict between the sects, and the conflict is reflected by most of the references in the gospels. Some however (mainly in Mark), reflect the earlier persecution in Jerusalem (roughly A.D. 33–44), a few, the period of good relations begun by James (roughly 44–70).

IV. THE SCRIBES

Eliminating the Pharisees and the minor groups leaves only one class that could both have known the facts about Jesus' parentage and background and have kept repeating them in anti-Christian polemic that Christians tried to answer in the way we have seen. This group was the scribes. They appear both in Galilee and Jerusalem, and, although never mentioned by John, are frequent in all the synoptics and were probably mentioned in one source of Q. Although there is no Q saying in which both Matthew and Luke refer to them, Matthew makes favorable references to them in two of his Q sayings, and since most of his references to them elsewhere are unfavorable, it seems likely that these favorable ones came from his source, not himself. An isolated, favorable saying that does occur in his peculiar material (13.52) probably came to him from an earlier source; his own attitude is shown by his repeated application to them of the savage sayings he collected in chapter 23, and his remodeling of the friendly story in Mk. 12.28ff. to make it a hostile one (22.35ff.). Luke, when using Mark, often deleted Mark's references to scribes, so he probably also deleted them from those Q sayings that refer to them in Matthew. When he refers to them in his peculiar material, the reference probably stood in his sources. One of his sources tried to hellenize the scribes by calling them "lawyers." Besides Matthew's dislike and Luke's omissions, we have to reckon with the tendency, demonstrated in Appendix A, IV, to replace "scribes" with "Pharisees." It seems that they played a larger role in earlier Christian tradition than they do in the present gospel texts.

All this evidence makes us wish we knew more about the scribes as a professional class. They were almost certainly a professional class, not a party (in contrast to the Pharisees and Sadducees), nor a small, distinct social group (in contrast to the high priests). What the members of this profession did is not completely clear. They were authorities on the Pentateuch, and probably on most of the rest of the books now in the Old Testament—there was not yet a "Bible"; the question, which books should be considered sacred, would not be settled in any sect for half a century. Many scribes may have made their living as upper-school teachers, others perhaps gave legal advice, and some were professional drafters and copyists of documents. Precision is impossible for lack of reliable evidence from this period; moreover, the limits of the group probably were not precise; but we may suppose that for the most part its members were the middle and lower-middle-class schoolteachers, lawyers, and notaries of the Galilean towns, dependent for their status on their limited knowledge of "the Law," and therefore devoted to "the Law," proud of their knowledge, and pillars of local propriety. When rabbinic Judaism developed, the great scholars were often contemptuous of them (*M. Sotah* IX.15); their replacement by Pharisees in the later gospels may perhaps represent a social upgrading of Jesus' milieu as well as the introduction of opponents more important to the later Church. The great scribes attached to the Jerusalem temple were a different class of beings, so another way to upgrade Jesus was to specify that the scribes who dealt with him had "come down from Jerusalem." Perhaps some did. Class feelings and professional connections can be taken for granted, so this group seems the one most likely to have served in Jesus' lifetime as the hostile communication network by which small-town, Galilean stories of his family background, rejection, and the like reached Jerusalem and became parts of the persistent polemic the gospels had to recognize and tried to answer.

As for the scribes' notion of Jesus, Matthew speaks of some who became his followers (13.52), and Mark says that one praised his emphasis on the great commandments (12.28ff.). But the hostile references are more frequent. The hostility centers on three themes. The first is Jesus' transgression of the Law: he eats with publicans and sinners; his disciples do not wash their hands before eating; he heals on the sabbath. The Christians reply to these criticisms with a flood of attacks on the scribes for picayune and heartless pedantry in legal observance. The second theme of scribal attack is Jesus' pretension to supernatural power: he assumes divine prerogatives by forgiving sins; a prophet should give a sign, he offers none; he does not claim to be sent as a prophet; his power is unexplained; he does not rebuke his followers when they hail him as the Messiah; and he teaches that the Messiah is the son of a being greater than David (i.e., God). We may connect with these the Christian claim that he taught "with authority, and not as the scribes," that is, with supernatural power to command both men and spirits, and consequently, to do miracles. This is also the Christian's reply to the scribes' final charge—that Jesus is a magician, "has" the demon Beelzebul, and does his miracles by his control of demons.

This last charge is most important because it tells us how these opponents understood him. Take it away, and all that remains is a collection of unrelated complaints, most of them not very serious; introduce it, and these complaints can be seen as component elements of a comprehensible structure. Such a structure must be supposed. To observe a man objectively, without trying to conjecture some explanation for his actions, calls for extraordinary training not to be expected of the rustics in ancient Galilee. The phenomenon of Jesus confronted them with an "identification crisis." They had to explain him in their own terms. They had to explain the miserable background, the baptism by John, the disappearance into the desert, the miracles, the devoted disciples and thronging crowds, the neglect of the holy Law, the failure to conform to the prophetic pattern, the rumors of messianic and more-than-messianic claims. How, in their terms, could all these be explained? Simply: his background and baptism prove him an ordinary man and a sinner; therefore, the miracles, success, impious behaviour, and supernatural claims prove him a magician. He "has," not merely has control of, but is united with, indeed, he *is* the demon Beelzebul (Mt. 10.25—an unmistakably Palestinian demon, impossible to attribute to "the hellenistic church"). Hence the powers of this lower-class nobody, hence his miracles, his following, his hold over his disciples, their visions, his supernatural claims, his failure to conform to the prophetic pattern, his inability to say, "Thus saith the Lord," his transgression of the Law, and his teaching on his own authority. "I say unto you," he says to his dupes; and who is "I"? Beelzebul!

That this interpretation seemed plausible to Jesus' contemporaries is proven by its success. We find reflections of it in all our major sources—Mark, Q, John, and the material peculiar to Matthew and to Luke. The tradition is rich enough to show some of the forms taken by the charge, and by the Christians' attempts to answer it. Most important is Mark 3.20–30, adapted by both Matthew and Luke. After reporting Jesus' success as an exorcist, the enormous crowds that followed him, the sick falling over each other to touch him, prostrating themselves and hailing him as "son of God," and Jesus' consequent appointment of twelve assistants, Mark says,

And he goes into a house, and the crowd assembles again, so that they don't even have time to eat. And hearing ⟨all this⟩ his family came out to seize him, for they said, "He's out ⟨of his mind⟩." And the scribes come down from Jerusalem said, "He has Beelzebul," and "He casts out demons by the ruler of the demons." So, calling them together, he said to them in parables, "How can Satan cast out Satan?" ⟨etc.⟩ . . . "Nobody can go into the house of a strong man and plunder his property unless he first ties up the strong man . . . I tell you for sure that men will be forgiven all ⟨other⟩ sins and blasphemies . . . but ⟨anyone⟩ who blasphemes against the holy spirit has no forgiveness forever." . . . ⟨This⟩ because they said, "He has an unclean spirit."

From this it seems that Jesus' exorcisms were accompanied by abnormal behavior on his part. Magicians who want to make demons obey often scream their spells, gesticulate, and match the mad in fury. This connection between magic and mania recurs in other forms of the charge against Jesus: in Jn. 7.20 and 8.52 for instance, when the crowd says to him, "You have a demon," they mean, practically, "You're crazy"; but compare Jn. 10.20 where they distinguish the states, "He has a demon and ⟨consequently⟩ is insane." Identification of the two conditions lies behind Lk. 4.23, where Jesus is made to anticipate that his townspeople, ridiculing his claim to be a healer, will tell him, "Doctor, cure yourself."

The variety of the demonological diagnoses in Mk. 3.20–30, suggests they come from good tradition. Later invention would have said only, "He has an unclean spirit," as the evangelist does in his explanatory note at the end (3.30), but this was not enough for the actual situation. Anyone who wanted to subdue that spirit (as did those who wanted to put him under restraint) would want to find out its name, or at least its title. It was thought that demons, like dogs, would obey if you called them by their names. In this case, the scribes from Jerusalem say the name is Beelzebul, the title, "the ruler of the demons "; the two are presented as if they referred to the same being, but elsewhere we find, "He casts out demons by the ruler of the demons," without any mention of Beelzebul (Mt. 9.34). In other situations, people are said to have called Jesus "Beelzebul" (but not "the ruler of the demons," Mt. 10.25). Jesus' question, "Can Satan cast out Satan?" suggests that others identified Jesus' demon as Satan. The argument about "the strong man" was probably intended to refute the charge about "the ruler of the demons," since he is the power to whom the persons seized by his servants would belong; he would have to be tied up before they could be carried off and set free, and Jesus implicitly claims the power to "tie" him (as did many ancient magicians whose spells for this purpose have come down to us, see chapter VII). On the other hand, a Q saying that both Matthew and Luke attach to this passage (Mt. 12.27f.; Lk. 11.19f.) takes us back to Beelzebul: "If I cast out demons by Beelzebul, by whom do your boys cast them out?" Particularly interesting is the final saying attributed to Jesus, that blasphemy against "the holy spirit" is unforgiveable. "The holy spirit" is the spirit by which some Christians thought Jesus did his miracles, the blasphemy is calling it a demon, and the saying shows that at least some Christians were willing to admit that Jesus did "have a spirit," but insisted that it was a (or "the") holy one.

These arguments and counterarguments, as well as blunt accusations ("You are a Samaritan and have a demon," Jn. 8.48), enable us to recognize the same implications behind a number of ambiguous charges. Jesus, for instance, is accused of being "one who leads astray"; the term might mean merely "deceiver," but it might also refer to one who advocates the worship of alien gods (which was part of magic), and Fr. Samain has persuasively argued that in the gospels it means "magician." In John the Jews accuse him before Pilate of being "a doer of evil" (18.30). This would seem too vague to be a legal accusation did not the Roman law codes tell us that it was the vulgar term for a magician. When Pilate is reluctant to have him executed, they return to the charge, saying, "He made himself a son of a god" (19.7) which would seem equivalent to "He made himself a god" (cf. 10.33ff.). This was what many magicians claimed to do, so we shall have to consider the accusation more closely later on.

These accusations explain a famous puzzle—the well-attested report that many people thought Jesus "was" John the Baptist. This stands first in Mark's account of what people said about him, and again in the disciples' answers to Jesus' question, "Who do men say that I am?" But what does it mean? The gospels agree in representing Jesus and the Baptist, before the latter's arrest, as associated, observably distinct figures. How then could the crowds think him the Baptist? The opinion Mark reports, "the Baptist has been raised from the dead, and therefore the powers work by/in him," must answer this question. Origen, the greatest of ancient Christian commentators, saw the difficulty and tried to resolve it by conjecture: "⟨The⟩ supposition was something like this, that the powers which had worked in John had gone over to Jesus." He compares this to the Christian belief that the Baptist was Elijah, which he understood as meaning that the Baptist was possessed by the same spirit and power (the same supernatural beings) that had worked in Elijah.

This is a plausible interpretation of "the powers work in him," but does not explain the reference to the Baptist's having been raised from the dead. The powers could have shifted their domicile to Jesus regardless of the Baptist's demise. The wisest commentators said nothing about this difficulty until the study of ancient magic led Kraeling to the right track: Jesus was called "John" because it was believed that he "had," that is possessed, and was possessed by, the spirit of the Baptist. (In the form given by Mk. 6.14, this belief could have arisen only after the Baptist's execution, but that seems to have taken place relatively early in Jesus' public career.) We have seen that, in the same way, Jesus was called "Beelzebul" by those who thought he "had" the demon so named (Mt. 10.25). It was generally believed that the spirit of any human being who had come to an unjust, violent, or otherwise ultimely end was of enormous power. If a magician could call up and get control of, or identify himself with such a spirit, he could then control inferior spirits or powers. (In third-century Smyrna, Christians were believed to do their miracles by using just such necromantic control of the spirit of Jesus, because he had been crucified.) More frequent are spells by which spirits of the dead are themselves given assignments. Particularly interesting in relation to Mk. 6.14 is a prayer to Helios-Iao-Horus to assign to the magician, as perpetual "assistant and defender," the soul of a man wrongfully killed. This would establish approximately the sort of relation Jesus was believed to have with the soul of John. In the light of these beliefs it seems that Mk. 6.14 should be understood as follows: "John the Baptist has been raised from the dead ⟨by Jesus' necromancy; Jesus now has him⟩. And therefore ⟨since Jesus-John can control them⟩ the ⟨inferior⟩ powers work ⟨their wonders⟩ by him ⟨that is, by his orders⟩." A little later, after Jesus had been executed, the Samaritan magician, Simon, was similarly thought to "be" Jesus. The Christians, of course, maintained that the spirit by which Simon did his miracles was not Jesus, but merely a murdered boy.

We need not appeal to the elusive figure of Simon for an example of the supposed relationship between Jesus and the Baptist. One of the greatest figures of antiquity, a man of incalculable influence on the thought and history of the western world, himself claimed to be possessed by, and identified with, the spirit of an executed criminal, and to do whatever he did by the power of this indwelling spirit. By its power he could even hand over his opponents to Satan. This man and his claims are known from his own correspondence—he is Saint Paul, who asserted, "I live no longer I, but Christ lives in me" (Gal. 2.20), and "I dare speak of nothing save those things which Christ has done through me, by word and deed, by the power of signs and miracles, by the power of ⟨his⟩ spirit, to make the gentiles obedient" (Rom. 15.19). He wrote the Corinthians about a member of their church that, "Being absent in body, but present in spirit, I have already judged ⟨the offender⟩ . . . uniting you and my spirit with the power of our Lord Jesus, to give this fellow over to Satan for the destruction of his flesh" (I Cor. 5.3ff.). If Paul thus proves the possibility of ancient belief in such a relationship as that supposed to have existed between Jesus and the spirit of the Baptist, he also provides the strongest evidence that this was not, in fact, the source of Jesus' power. For Paul's letters are full of allusions to Jesus (mostly as "Christ"); his own belief in his dependence on Jesus' spirit comes to expression, somehow or other, on almost every page. If Jesus had thought himself to have any such relationship with the Baptist there would be more signs of it in the tradition—at least in attempts to answer claims of opponents (including the Baptist's other followers). That the gospels refer to the charge rarely and almost casually, as a popular misunderstanding, is conclusive evidence that it was groundless, not only in fact, but also in Jesus' belief.

The opinion reported by John, that Jesus had "made himself a god" (10.33ff.,19.7), may help to explain another elusive figure in the gospels' background, the man about whom the disciples reported to Jesus, "Teacher, we saw a fellow exorcising demons by ⟨use of⟩ your name . . . and we forbade him, because he did not go along with us." Jesus reportedly replied, "Do not forbid him, (for no one who does a miracle in my name can soon speak evil of me), for anyone not against us is for us." One of the commonest forms of exorcism was to order the demon out "by the name of" some more powerful being, usually a god whose "true name" or "true" title or function the magi- cian knew. Use of this true name and designation not only enabled the magi- cian to call effectively for the god to come and enforce his orders; it also was effective by itself, for the name both was an independent power and united the magician with the god he named. Thus it gave him, at least momentarily, both the god's power and its own. Such use of the name of course depends on the supposition that the person named is a supernatural power. We have here another form of the notion of Jesus presupposed by the exorcism stories—the notion that he is, or is united with, a supernatural being, so that even his name is a power. That the story is authentic seems likely. By authorizing persons other than the apostles to use Jesus' name, it undermines the disciplinary authority of the congregational leaders of early churches who claimed to be the successors of the apostles; therefore, they and their adherents would hardly have invented it. (In fact, Matthew omitted it, probably for this reason; he was strong on church discipline.) Besides, the saying with which it concludes, "Whoever is not against us is for us," fits the enthusiastic days of Jesus' lifetime, but not the persecutions after the crucifixion.

V. "High Priests"

With the following, opposition, and reputation that we have traced, Jesus came to Jerusalem, and there encountered a new set of opponents, the Jewish authorities who ran the city—under Roman supervision. The Romans kept a garrison there, but seem to have taken little part in the day to day administration. The Jewish authorities are described in the gospels as "the high priests, elders, and scribes," but the "high priests" evidently were in control; they commonly appear first whenever two or three of these groups are named together. The term "high priests" in the plural seems to refer to those who held, or had held, the high priestly office and also to influential men of the families from which high priests were commonly chosen. The gospels say they arranged for the arrest of Jesus, interrogated him, handed him over to the Romans, and secured his execution. Reportedly, they stirred up the crowd to demand the crucifixion, though a number of passages shift the guilt to "the crowd," "the people," and in John, to "the Jews." The stages of this change reflect the progressive separation of Christianity from the other branches of Judaism, concluding in John with its loss of Jewish identity. Accordingly, these passages are not reliable evidence as to Jesus' actual opponents.

Even the reliable passages reveal little. In the gospels the high priests never appear outside Jerusalem. Jesus is said to have prophesied while yet in Galilee that they would reject him, but the prophesies (most of which foretell—and precisely date!—the resurrection) are either spurious or heavily doctored and give no clue of the priests' reasons for the rejection. When the priests themselves come on the scene, they at once plot to seize and destroy him, and are restrained only by their fear of his popular following. Mark does not state the reason for their hostility, but first refers to it shortly after his account of Jesus' attack on the temple market (11.18). Hence it is often supposed to have resulted from the attack, and may have. However, Jn. 2.13ff. locates the attack early in Jesus' career and says nothing of any consequent plot against him (though Jn. liked to report such plots), while Mt.

21.14ff. represents the attack as followed by miraculous cures in the temple, whereupon Jesus is hailed as "the son of David" (the Messiah) and the high priests object to the title, not the attack.

They next appear in the synoptics to ask, "By what authority do you do these things?" (Mk. 11.27f.)—an amazingly mild question if "these things" refers to the attack on the market. This reference is commonly conjectured because the question is asked by the high priests whom the attack would concern. But in Mark and Matthew the question does not immediately follow the attack; instead it follows a miracle. If we suppose the "authority" referred to is the authority that enables him to do miracles, that is, power to command supernatural beings (and this is the meaning "authority" commonly has in Mark), we can understand the mildness of the question. Jesus seems to have been a figure capable of shaking the confidence even of an established clergy.

The main reason for thinking the question authentic is Jesus' refusal to answer it. The refusal has been elaborated into a "game story" demonstrating Jesus' cleverness. He counters the question by asking his opponents one they cannot safely answer, and then says, implicitly, "Since you won't answer my question, I won't answer yours." So he wins, that is, he escapes the embarrassment of a blunt refusal to answer. But why refuse at all? No classical Israelite prophet of Yahweh ever hesitated to declare, "Yahweh has sent me"; but Jesus is never said to have said so—not in so many words. The synoptics put the claim in his mouth, but only indirectly. John, of course, remedied the oversight— repeatedly! Since the later tradition developed the claim, a story reporting Jesus' refusal to make it is probably early. But again, why refuse? Whoever told the story showing his cleverness in avoiding an answer must have thought he had something to conceal. What did they think his secret was? Or what did he think it was, that made him unwilling to declare it? And why did he *never* say, "Thus saith the Lord"?

The gospels report that outsiders thought him a prophet because of his miracles, but they insist that the outsiders were wrong; he was more than a prophet, he was the Messiah and the Son of God. Whatever we may think of the positive part of this claim, the negative part seems correct. If judged by the standard of the "classical" prophets of the Old Testament prophetic books, Jesus was not a prophet. By that standard a prophet is a messenger of Yahweh sent to declare to king or people "the word of Yahweh." Not so Jesus. In the synoptics he does not represent himself as a messenger, he never claims to declare "the word of Yahweh," and he is distinguished from the Old Testament prophets by many other traits (itemized in Appendix B). What then was the source of his miraculous power? The story not only leaves this question unanswered, but also says nothing of the conjectures with which the high priests must have tried to answer it when Jesus refused to reply. Some answer must have been conjectured; the miracles demanded one, and Jesus' refusal to give it was sure to provoke unfavorable suspicions of which we soon find traces.

Between the uncertainty of Jesus' power and the certainty of Roman power the high priests hardly hesitated long. We have seen that the fear of a messianic uprising and consequent Roman intervention, which Jn. 11.48 puts in their mouth, is completely credible. That they bribed Judas to betray Jesus' whereabouts and provided the force that seized him is equally credible; more dubious is Luke's unique report that some of them were present at the arrest (22.52). The accounts of interrogations and trials—by night before the sanhedrin, and before the high priests Annas and perhaps Kaiaphas, by day before the sanhedrin, Pilate (repeatedly), and Herod—are unscrupulous dramatizations of uncertain events. The composition of speeches to present dramatically what an author thought might have been said in historic situations was a common practice among ancient historians, one defended and exemplified by Thucydides himself (1.22). However, Thucydides insisted that when events were concerned he would report only what had actually happened. Luke's story of a trial before Herod was probably invented to fulfil Ps. 2.1ff; cp. Acts 4.27. Another such invention was the nocturnal trial before the sanhedrin (on Passover night, when leaving one's house was prohibited! Ex. 12.22). We have just seen that the passages shifting the blame for Jesus' conviction from the high priests, by degrees, to "the Jews" are polemic misrepresentations; they are matched by many apologetic elements representing Pilate as convinced of Jesus' innocence, anxious to release him, and yielding only reluctantly to the high priests' ("crowds'" "Jews'") demand for his execution—all these are incredible inventions to show that Christianity and its founder were really innocent in the eyes of the Roman judge: Jesus was not a deservedly condemned criminal, but the victim of a political deal. When such propaganda, and the novelistic elements—cleverness stories, and so on—are set aside, little reliable information remains.

Among the elements discrediting the stories of the trials before the sanhedrin is their suggestion that the high priests were in doubt as to what to do with Jesus, whereas they were previously said to be plotting to destroy him. Now they "seek testimony against him." Whom did they want to convince? The story was made up to discredit the charges attributed to "false witnesses"—that he threatened to destroy and miraculously rebuild the temple. John says he did make this threat (or offer?). Matthew and Mark say it was one of the taunts flung at him during the crucifixion, and it recurs in Acts where the first martyr, Stephen, is charged with repeating it. Evidently it was an important cause of the hostility toward the early Jerusalem church; yet it plays no part in the proceedings before Pilate, nor in any recorded events except the cases of Jesus and Stephen. It is a reminder of how little we know.

The climax of the nocturnal trial is Jesus' admission that he is "the Christ, the Son of the Blessed" (so Mk. 14.61f.; Mt. 26.63 has, "the Son of God"), and also "Son of Man." The High Priest declares this blasphemy and all the members of the sanhedrin condemn Jesus to death. From the point of view of Jewish law the proceedings are impossible—claiming to be the Messiah does not constitute blasphemy; a condemnation for blasphemy would have to be punished by the penalty legally prescribed (stoning), not by handing the offender over to the Romans; etc., etc. Such considerations, with historical difficulties of the sort already mentioned, leave no doubt that the stories are fictitious; their true function seems polemic—to make Jesus' death result from the Jewish authorities' rejection, as blasphemous, of the formal statement of his true nature and rank. This statement is what Mark's church was preaching; the rejection of this triple title and the consequent charge of blasphemy by the high priest and sanhedrin are the retrojected reactions of the Jews opposing the church in which this tradition was formed.

This explains why it is only here (14.61f.) in the whole gospel of Mark that we find united, in a single question and answer, Jesus' three "official" Christian titles: Christ (Messiah), Son of Man, and Son of God. Each one usually appears by itself. This suggests that they came from different traditions, perhaps originally from groups that had different notions of Jesus' nature. When they are brought together, it is by editorial revision or invention, theologically motivated as here. The difference between the traditions is particularly clear in the case of the title "Son of God," which in the synoptics almost always appears in miraculous contexts. The only exceptions are this passage (Mk. 14.61f. with its parallels) and Mk. 1.1 (the title of the gospel). On the other hand, "Son of God" very rarely appears in messianic contexts. The likelihood is that the term came from a tradition in which it designated not a messiah, but a supernatural being, both worker and subject of miracles. By contrast, "Son of Man" indicated not an ordinary messiah, but a supernatural, apocalyptic figure destined to preside over the end of the world (with which the "Son of God" never has anything to do, except when editorially equated with "Messiah" or "Son of Man"). Thus the purpose of Mk. 14.61f. is to give the most dramatic possible presentation of the doctrine of Mark's church, that Jesus was not merely Messiah, *but also* Son of Man *and* Son of God, and to represent the rejection of this doctrine as the basis for the rejection of Jesus by the Jewish establishment, and as the reason for the accusation of blasphemy brought against him and his followers.

That this doctrine and this dramatization of it were not peculiar to Mark's church is indicated by the fact that Luke, who here follows a different tradition and reports a trial, not at night, but in the daytime, has a different version of the dialogue but makes it come to somewhat the same point—Jesus is the

Son of God (Lk. 22.66–71). Such diversification of what is clearly the same story suggests that the common source lay a good ways back. The supposition of a trial before the sanhedrin doubtless dates from a time when the actual course of events had been forgotten, but the confrontation between Jesus and the High Priest must have been imagined shortly after his arrest. Priestly rejection of his claims to one or another of the titles Messiah, Son of God and Son of Man could—if he claimed them—have begun in his lifetime.

John, who seems here to have better historical information, says nothing of a trial before the sanhedrin. He has Jesus taken to the house of Annas, a senior member of the high priestly group. Questioned by Annas about his teaching, Jesus replied that he had always and only taught in public—"Why ask me? Ask the people who heard me" (18.19–21). He was slapped for impertinence and sent on to Kaiaphas, the High Priest at that time, from whom, next morning, he was sent to Pilate. In John's account of the trial before Pilate, when "the Jews" are pressing for Jesus' execution, they advance the argument, "We have a Law, and according to the Law he ought to die, because he made himself a son of God" (19.7). According to John, Pilate was terrified by this statement, took Jesus aside and tried to get out of him some account of his origin, got only a pretentious enigma that did nothing to relieve his fear, therefore proposed again to release him, and consented to his execution only when "the Jews" argued that he had claimed to be a king, that to make such a claim was an act of rebellion against the emperor, and that to release such a rebel was a treasonable act—which Pilate could be sure they would report. Faced with this threat, Pilate consented to the execution and took what advantage he could of the situation by presenting Jesus as "your King," thereby forcing "the Jews" into a public declaration of loyalty, "We have no King but Caesar." Content with that, he paid their price and ordered Jesus crucified (19.7–16).

The scene is brilliantly contrived to: (1) contrast the ignorant ruler of this world with the heavenly King who knows the secret, (2) exonerate Jesus, (3) make "the Jews" testify to Jesus' claim to be a son of God, (4) make this claim responsible for his death, (5) make "the Jews" publicly renounce their messianic hope—by their public, legal pronouncement they henceforth have no claim to the messianic promises of the Old Testament, to which the Christians are now heir. It is amazing that a scene so loaded with theological motives should fit the actual situation so well and correctly dramatize (though it could not accurately report) the political conflict going on between Roman rulers and Jewish priesthood. Particularly interesting for our purpose is the suggestion that Pilate immediately understood "son of God" in terms of pagan mythology. So he would have.

Thus three widely variant traditions, those of Mark (followed by

Matthew), Luke, and John, all represent Jesus' claim to be a son of God as a (more often, as *the*) principal reason for the high priests' determination to have him executed. If the present accounts of the trials were completely independent inventions their similarities would be astounding. It is better to suppose that the three stories are different reflections of a charge made by the high priests against Jesus. If this charge figured in the trial before Pilate it must have been phrased in different language: claiming to be the son of a god was not an actionable offense in Roman law, but, as already mentioned, magicians often claimed to be gods or sons of gods, so the claim could have been an important point (and could have been remembered by Christians as the all important point) in the evidence brought to prove the actual charges, which were those of political subversion and practicing magic. The charge of practicing magic is made bluntly in Jn. 18.28ff. where Pilate asks, "What accusation do you bring against this man?" and the priests reply, "If this fellow were not a 'doer of evil' we should not have handed him over to you." "Doer of evil," as the Roman law codes say, was common parlance for "magician." Whether or not used before Pilate, the charge may have been brought against Jesus during his lifetime; its role in the gospels proves that it was important in the hostility between the high priests and the early Jerusalem church.

The synoptics' trial scenes are surprisingly taciturn. Perhaps the evangelists found it difficult to think of what a son of God should say in such a situation. Jesus may have experienced that difficulty too. Having nothing to say is an excellent reason for taciturnity. His opponents presumably had plenty to say—but his followers did not choose to report the more disgraceful or specific and damaging points. There is no hint of the damning facts that he was arrested at a secret, nocturnal assembly in which some of his men were armed (Luke elsewhere insisted they had only two swords, 22.38), and one of the High Priest's servants was wounded (Mk. 14.47; Luke said Jesus healed him, 22.51; Matthew said Jesus forbade armed resistance, 26.52—admirable advice for a Roman subject, but a trifle too late). The stories agree that the high priests took Jesus to Pilate, but only Luke allows them to present charges: "We found this fellow perverting our people, and prohibiting the payment of tribute to the emperor, and calling himself 'Christ' ⟨that is⟩ 'King.'" (23.2). (Then as now, to be executed as a political leader and pretender to a throne was no social disgrace, but the other presumable charges were less respectable.) In the other synoptics, Pilate, without any explanation, questions Jesus as to his royal claims (Mk. 15.2p.). When Jesus is enigmatic and Pilate inclines to release him, it is again Luke who lets the accusers speak, "He stirs up the people, teaching through all Judea and beginning from Galilee down to here" (23.5). Next, the people demand a prisoner's release (allegedly customary at the festival) and Pilate offers to release Jesus; the high priests in Mark and

Matthew stir up the people to ask for one Barabbas, and to demand Jesus' crucifixion (Mk. 15.11p.). In Luke they do so themselves (23.18ff.). No arguments are given.

In Luke the high priests do not appear at the crucifixion; in Mark and Matthew they are among those who mocked Jesus while on the cross. The taunt assigned to them is, "He saved others, he could not save himself. Let the Christ, the King of Israel, now come down from the cross, that we may see and believe" (Mk. 15.31p.). To this Matthew makes them add, "'He trusted in God, let God deliver him now if He wants him,' for he said, 'I am a son of God.'" Since it seems from Mark's story that there were no disciples of Jesus present at the crucifixion, except for some "women watching from a long way off" (15.40), we may suppose the conversations at the cross fictitious, and take the taunts as evidence of the anti-Christian propaganda of the groups to whom they are attributed.

John omits the mocking, but makes the high priests complain to Pilate about the sign on the cross stating the charge against the culprit. For Jesus' cross Pilate had written, "The King of the Jews." The high priests asked him to write, "He said, 'I am the King of the Jews,'" but Pilate refused to change the sign. Behind this plausible legend lies not only the surprising political sensitivity already noticed, but also the ancient belief in omens. Any chance sign or utterance might be an omen and thereby shape the course and nature of the world. So Pilate's thoughtless—or politically shrewd?—sign was the final, official confirmation by the ignorant ruler of this world that Jesus was indeed the promised Messiah.

The final appearance of the high priests in the gospels is in Matthew. They tell Pilate, "That magician, while yet alive, said, 'After three days I shall arise,'" and they ask that a guard be set at Jesus' sepulchre to prevent the disciples from stealing the body and spreading the report that he had risen as he prophesied. Pilate gives them some watchmen; they seal the sepulchre and set the watch. After the resurrection, the watchmen report to them what has happened and they bribe the men to say that while they were asleep the disciples stole the body. "And this story has been spread among the Jews down to the present time" (Mt. 27.62–66; 28.11–15).

When we review these reports about the high priests, we find an account of their historical actions that is brief, clear, and credible: They asked Jesus the source of his miraculous power and, when they got no answer, bribed one of his followers to betray his whereabouts, seized and handed him over to Pilate with charges that probably included the practice of magic, criminal assembly, armed resistance, and a plot to destroy the temple, and certainly included allegations that he claimed to be King of the Jews, forbade payment of tribute to Rome, and was stirring up the people to revolt. If there was a chance that he would be freed, thanks to the practice of releasing a prisoner at the festival, they may have used their influence to help secure that favor for Barabbas. The picture they had formed of Jesus is reasonably clear.

VI. SUMMARY

The authors of the gospels tried to answer the attacks on Jesus being circulated by opponents of the Church. Their answers enable us to identify the opponents, to distinguish earlier from later groups, and to ascertain the notions of Jesus formed by the earlier groups during his lifetime. But care is necessary to weed out anachronistic elements. New Testament apologetics have been shaped by the beliefs and needs of the two or three generations between the crucifixion (A.D. 30?) and the composition of the gospels (A.D. 75–100?). Some of the opposition they report is wholly imaginary (that of the demons), more is put into the mouths of groups that had little or nothing to do with Jesus (Herodians and Pharisees).

With allowance for such misleading material a reasonably clear picture can be recovered. Jesus, by his miracles, attracted a large and enthusiastic following. His followers, and perhaps some outsiders, called him "rabbi" or "teacher" when they addressed him politely in Hebrew, Aramaic, or Greek (he probably understood and spoke all three), and he doubtless did some preaching, but there is no evidence that he was accepted as a legal authority by any save his disciples, nor that his legal *teaching* aroused any popular opposition. Even his libertine *practice* (eating with sinners, neglect of fasts, sabbaths, and purity rules) got him into trouble mainly with the "scribes"—the schoolteacher-lawyer-notary class of the Galilean towns. Their hostility and their local connections soon made common knowledge of his dubious parentage, lack of formal education, humble trade, rejection by his townspeople and family, and inability to perform any miracles when he returned to his home town. They also spread the word that his family had tried to put him under restraint as insane, that he was possessed, that he had a demon, and that his miracles were done by magic. In Galilee, after the Baptist's execution, many believed that he had raised from the dead and called into himself the spirit of the Baptist, and by him controlled the demonic powers. This is said to have been common opinion; the scribes, who pretended to learning, identified him with a demon whom they called *Beelzebul.* More favorable outside opinion thought him a prophet, most often Elijah, the famous Old Testament miracle worker, whose return was expected to precede the end of the world; but he made no claim—in fact, he reportedly refused to claim—that he was a prophet sent by "the Lord" (Yahweh), or that what he said was "the word of the Lord." The pagans (a minority in the Galilean population, but not absent and not to be forgotten) seem to have thought him a god or the son of a god, as did some of the people from whom he cast out demons. Some of these people became his followers and others among his followers may have shared their opinions; others thought him the Messiah, and others "the Son of Man," a supernatural being expected to preside over the end of the world.

Spread by scribes and pilgrims, the penumbra of malicious gossip, popular opinion, and rumors of his followers' beliefs accompanied him to Jerusalem. There the attention of the high priests was drawn to him by the enthusiasm of his followers when he entered the city, by the story—if not the spectacle—of his miracles, and by his interference with the temple market. Convinced that he was not a prophet, and fearing the consequences of a messianic uprising, they interpreted the supernatural claims made either by or for him as blasphemy. They turned him over to Pilate with charges of magic and sedition.

These early elements, wholly compatible with, and explicable from, Jesus' Palestinian environment, account for the great majority of the apologetic material in the gospels. That material is intended to counter the polemic begun and carried on by the scribes, taken up by the high priests, and at two later periods, first from about A.D. 30 to 44 and again from about 70 to 100, vigorously pushed by the Pharisees. The addition of references to the Pharisees in stories and sayings that originally lacked them is a good indication that the original forms of such stories and sayings antedated the rise of Pharisaic influence after 70. Hence we may reasonably suppose that the outsiders' picture of Jesus discernible in the gospels is mainly that of the scribes and high priests of Jerusalem, but carries on considerable elements derived from the scribes of Galilee and from Jesus' lifetime.

Whatever their origins, these are the things his opponents said about him. Whatever their inaccuracies, they cannot be dismissed as the inventions of Christian propaganda. We know of them because they were charges the authors of the gospels wanted to answer. There may also have been some charges they did not want to answer. We shall investigate that possibility, and also try to fill out the figure that has emerged from the gospel material by next considering the reports about Jesus in early non-Christian works and in the hostile material of which early Christian writers tell us.

～ 4 ～

What the Outsiders Said—
Evidence Outside the Gospels

I

The earliest non-Christian work that refers to Jesus is Josephus' *Antiquities*. Its last sections, where the references occur, were written in the 90s of the first century. By that time Josephus was in his fifties. He was born in 37/38 of a priestly family in Jerusalem, one of importance to judge from his career: at thirty he played a leading role in the Jewish revolt in Galilee. With such a background he should have been well informed about early Christianity. Since he barely mentions it we may suppose he did not think it of much importance.

Of his two references to Jesus, one (*Ant*. XX.200) is merely in passing; he speaks of "the brother of Jesus, the so-called Christ, James was his name" as one of the persons illegally brought to trial and executed by a Sadducean High Priest in 61/62. Since Josephus' works have been preserved by Christian copyists and no Christian would have forged a reference to Jesus in this style, the text has generally been accepted as genuine.

The other reference however (*Ant*. XVIII.63f.) is a brief account of Jesus himself that, in its present form, declares flatly, "This ⟨man⟩ was the Christ" and goes on to assert that his resurrection was foretold by "the holy prophets." Obviously Josephus—by this time a vigorous supporter of rabbinic Judaism—never wrote such statements. Scholars are still divided as to whether the whole passage is spurious, or a genuine passage has been Christianized by alterations to the text. In general, opinion inclines to the latter view especially because the passing reference to Jesus in XX.200 implies that he had been already identified. If we suppose the alterations to the text were minimal, the original was something like this (my insertions and changes are marked by pointed brackets; for the words changed, see the notes):

At this time ⟨in the middle of Pilate's governorship, about A.D. 30⟩ there lived Jesus, a man ⟨who was a sophist⟩, if it is proper to call him a man. For he was a doer of miracles, a teacher of men who receive ⟨impiety⟩ with pleasure. And he led ⟨astray⟩ many Jews and many of the Greeks ⟨who said that⟩ this⟨fellow⟩ was the Christ. And when, on accusation by our leading men, Pilate condemned him to the cross, those who formerly loved ⟨him⟩ did not cease ⟨to do so⟩ , for ⟨they asserted that⟩ he appeared to them on the third day, again alive, while ⟨pretended⟩ prophets kept saying these and ten thousand other incredible things about him. And to the present ⟨time⟩ the tribe of Christians, named after him, has not disappeared.

Messiah and miracle worker, with a claim to be more than man—the combination is just what we should have expected.

II

From about the same time as Josephus' *Antiquities* or a bit later come the earliest rabbinic stories about Jesus and his followers. One distinguished rabbi, Eliezer, of the generation that flourished from about A.D. 70–100, is said to have been arrested as an old man on the charge of being a Christian. Reportedly, he submitted his case to the Roman governor's discretion, was therefore pardoned, and later explained his arrest by the admission that once in Sepphoris, a city of Galilee, a Galilean had told him some heretical teaching "in the name of Jesus the son of Panteri" to which he had assented. The story goes on to make him confess his guilt in transgressing the rabbinic ordinance prohibiting any intercourse with heretics. This is suspicious; the ordinance may be later than the confession. Subsequent versions of the story cite the saying attributed to Jesus: "From filth they came and to filth they shall return," and a legal conclusion is drawn from it: the wages of a prostitute, if given to the Temple, may be used for building privies. The saying may be early—it resembles many of the Q sayings in being antithetical, vague, and pompous—the legal conclusion was probably drawn by some second-century rabbi, to discredit the principle by an obscene implication.

For our picture of Jesus the story is most important as the first appearance of Pantera (and its variants), the name generally given by Jewish tradition to Jesus' father. Christian scholars have commonly supposed it an abusive deformation of *parthenos*, the Greek word for "virgin," and have taken it as evidence for Jewish knowledge of the Christian doctrine of the virgin birth. However, it seems unlikely that the doctrine was widely current, least of all in Galilee, at this early date. Moreover, that form of it which emphasizes the word *parthenos* is found in the gospels only in Matthew (1.23), and is one of the latest elements of the gospel—a clear gloss. Besides, it depends on a Greek translation of Isaiah 7.14; it cannot be derived from the Hebrew with which the rabbis were more familiar. Jesus is never referred to as "the son of the virgin" in the Christian material preserved from the first century of the Church (30–130), nor in the second-century apologists. To suppose the name *Pantera* appeared as a caricature of a title not yet in use is less plausible than to suppose it handed down by polemic tradition. It was not a very common name, but we do know of a Sidonian archer, Tiberius Julius Abdes Pantera, who was serving in Palestine about the time of Jesus' birth and later saw duty on the Rhine. It is possible, though not likely, that his tombstone from Bingerbrück is our only genuine relic of the Holy Family.

If Rabbi Eliezer approved of any other teachings of Jesus ben Pantera, no trace of the fact has been preserved in the tradition. Even the teaching he reportedly approved was one he had not known until a Christian (?) told him of it. However, he probably did refer, in a discussion of Sabbath law, to Jesus' magical practices. The question was whether one who cuts (tatoos?) letters on his flesh during the Sabbath is guilty of violating the law prohibiting labor on that day.

Rabbi Eliezer declared him guilty, but most scholars innocent. Rabbi Eliezer said to them, "But is it not ⟨the case that⟩ Ben Stada brought magic marks from Egypt in the scratches on his flesh?" They said to him, "He was a madman and you cannot base laws on ⟨the actions of⟩ madmen." Was he then the son of Stada? Surely he was the son of Pandira? Rabbi Hisda ⟨a third-century Babylonian⟩ said, "The husband was Stada, the paramour was Pandira." ⟨But was not⟩ the husband Pappos ben Judah? His mother was Stada. ⟨But was not⟩ his mother Miriam ⟨Mary⟩ the hairdresser? ⟨Yes, but she was nicknamed *Stada*⟩ as we say in Pumbeditha, "*s'tat da* ⟨i.e., this one has turned away⟩ from her husband."

The concluding comments are a good example of the confusion produced in rabbinic material by several factors. First, the rabbis are generally ignorant of chronology and constantly guilty of absurd anachronisms. Second, they habitually refer to their enemies by abusive nicknames and puns, usually bad. Third, in the case of Jesus particularly, this practice of concealed reference has been carried to the extreme by manuscript copyists to avoid censorship. The original Ben Stada seems to have been a Jew who advocated some cult involving the worship of deities other than Yahweh. He was entrapped by Jews in Lydda, condemned by a rabbinic court, and stoned. Since Jesus also was accused of introducing the worship of other gods—notably himself—he was nicknamed Ben Stada. Hence it is often difficult to tell to whom the passages on "Ben Stada" refer.

The dispute about the tatooing almost certainly refers to Jesus because similar charges are specified by second-century pagan and Christian writers as elements in the Jewish account of him. (Magicians did write spells and the like on their flesh; directions for doing so are given in the magical papyri, e.g., *PGM* VII.222–232; VIII.65ff. Moreover, Paul claimed to be tatooed or branded with "the marks of Jesus," Gal. 6.17—most likely, the same marks that Jesus had carried.) These charges witness to the survival of elements from the home town stories that we saw the gospels trying to answer. "He was a madman" reflects the reported opinion of his relatives who "went out to take him because they said, 'He is out ⟨of his mind⟩.'" (Mk. 3.21) and also the repeated charge that he was possessed. The charge of practicing magic is now familiar. The accusation that he had been in Egypt and learned magic there, though it now appears for the first time, was probably the reason for Matthew's story of the flight into Egypt (2.13–21) —a story known only to Matthew and implicitly contradicted by Luke (who keeps the Holy Family near Jerusalem for forty days to have Jesus presented in the temple, and then sends them back to Galilee). But if Matthew's story is false, why was it invented? Matthew says, "In order to fulfil that which was spoken by the Lord through the prophet, saying, 'From Egypt I have called my son.'" This is another of Matthew's discoveries of a prophecy to justify what he wanted to say. The reference of the prophetic text to the people of Israel is so clear from its context that it would never have been pressed into this unlikely service had Matthew not needed it to justify the story. The story therefore needs another explanation and the likeliest one is to be found in its apologetic utility— "Yes," it says in effect, "Jesus did spend some time in Egypt, but only when he was an infant. He could not possibly have learned magic at that age." Eliezer's discussion and Matthew's gospel were roughly contemporary— somewhere about A.D. 90. On Jesus' learning magic in Egypt, see p. 58.

Wherever Jesus learned his magic, his fame as a healer lived on. From the generation after Eliezer (about 100–130) we have the following story, told as an illustration of the general rule that one must have nothing to do with heretics:

A case ⟨in point was that⟩ of Rabbi Elazar ben Dama. A snake bit him and one Jacob of the village of Sama ⟨in Galilee⟩ came to cure him in the name of Jesus ben Pantera, but Rabbi Ishmael would not allow it. He said to ĥim, "You are not permitted, Ben Dama." He said to him, "I will give you a proof ⟨that it is permissible⟩ for him to cure me," but before he could finish his proof, he died. Rabbi Ishmael said, "You are lucky, Ben Dama, that you departed ⟨this life⟩ in peace and did not break through the scholars' fence ⟨around the Law⟩."

That even a rabbi was willing to employ a Jewish Christian healer shows that Christianity was still alive in the Jewish population of Galilee in the early second century. This was the time when the rabbis put the curse against heretics into their daily prayer to keep Christians from attending synagogues.

Nevertheless, a century later the same sort of incident still occurred in Galilee; the grandson of a distinguished rabbi was healed by a magician who "whispered ⟨a spell⟩ to him in the name of Jesus ben Pandera," and his grandfather said he would have done better to die. Yet rabbinic literature knows almost nothing more of Jesus than the little indicated by the preceding passages. An "early" (but nameless) tradition in the *Babylonian Talmud* reports that he was "to be stoned ⟨!⟩ because he practiced magic and incited ⟨Jews to worship alien gods⟩ and ⟨as a false prophet⟩ led Israel astray." This combines three legally distinct charges. The combination recalls the three opinions about Jesus set forth in Mt. 16.14ff.; "John the Baptist" (called up from the dead by magic); "Elijah   or one of the prophets"; and "the Son of the living God." The charges may come from historical tradition; the rest of the passage connected with them is a tissue spun out of later legal prescriptions and bad puns.

The notion that the statement of charges comes from good tradition is supported by the fact that it turns up independently— once with the addition, "He led Israel into sin"   at the end of a different story, two versions of which are found in the *Babylonian Talmud*. Here again, while the report of the charges may be correct, the story is pure fantasy: Jesus was a pupil of Joshua ben Perahya, but was excommunicated by him for noticing that their hostess, at an inn, was blear-eyed. He repeatedly besought ben Perahya to take him back, was repeatedly rejected, and at last in desperation set up a brick and worshiped it. All this nonsense happened in the time of the Maccabean King Alexander Jannaeus, that is, about 80 B.C.! Moreover, the same story is told in the *Jerusalem Talmud* about another teacher of that time and a nameless pupil. The Babylonians have taken over a Palestinian story and used it to slander Jesus. The one fact of historical interest is that they not only identified the disciple, but changed the teacher to Joshua ben Perahya, who was particularly famous in Babylonia as a magician. Thus they went out of their way to make Jesus a magician's pupil. This indicates what they thought of him—even his forte, magic, he learned from one of their ancestors.

Both the story of the magician's disciple and that of Jesus' being stoned probably date from the third or fourth century A.D. From the middle years of the third century comes an obscure curse by a Palestinian rabbi, "Woe on him who makes himself alive by the Name of God." This may reflect the belief (later widespread) that Jesus did his miracles and even raised himself from the dead by magical use of the divine Name, the greatest of all spells. About the same time another rabbi advised his pupils as to biblical verses they might use for refutation, "if the whore's son tells you there are two gods"—the second god being Jesus himself. A generation later another Palestinian, Rabbi Abbahu, said, "If a man tells you, 'I am a god,' he is a liar; 'I am the Son of Man,' he will regret it; 'I go up to the heavens,' he promises, but he will not perform." Here the reference to Jesus is unmistakable; evidence that he claimed to be able to go up into the heavens is also found in the New Testament. A blessing of the late third or early fourth century concludes with the assurance that you shall have no sons or disciples who publicly disgrace themselves "like Jesus the Nazarene."

These passages are the only ones in rabbinic literature that can confidently be presented as evidence of independent Jewish traditions about Jesus. A few more, especially some about Balaam, may have referred to him, but both the references and the contents are so dubious that no reliable information can now be extracted from the texts. This silence is the more surprising since we know from Christian complaints that a colorful Jewish tradition about Jesus did exist. We hear of it chiefly from the Jewish diaspora outside Palestine and the Jews who spread it were probably not, at first, of the rabbinic party. Granted that much rabbinic material may have been lost to censorship, and more suppressed from fear of it, yet if there had been major disputes between Jesus and the Pharisaic teachers of his time, some echoes should have been preserved in rabbinic tradition. The lack of any trace of direct contact goes to confirm the conclusions reached from the gospels: that Jesus' original opponents were the scribes, that the Pharisees first came into conflict with the members of the Jerusalem church after the resurrection, and that they were introduced into stories about Jesus during the middle and later years of the first century.

III

While rabbinic Judaism was turning its back on Jesus and his followers, repeating old accusations and indulging in new fantasies, the cult of "the Messiah, the Son of God" was spreading through diasporic Judaism.

With it spread the opposition. The report that Claudius expelled the Jews from Rome in A.D. 41 because they were, "at the instigation of Chrestus, repeatedly rioting," probably refers to some local troublemaker. But when Paul arrived in Rome shortly after A.D. 60, the leading men of the Jewish community there are said to have told him, "as for this sect ⟨of the Christians⟩ we know that people are talking against it everywhere." The people in Rome were, that is certain. Just a few years later, when much of the city burned in the fire of July, 64, the Christians were sufficiently notorious for the imperial government to pick them as scapegoats. But why were they chosen?

We have reports by two Roman historians, Suetonius and Tacitus, who wrote early in the following century. Suetonius is brief: "Penalties were imposed on the Christians, a kind of men ⟨holding⟩ a new superstition ⟨that involved the practice⟩ of magic"—this appears as one item in his list of Nero's *praiseworthy* reforms. Tacitus' dislike of the Christians was outweighed by his hatred of the emperor. The result was the following:

⟨After the fire there arose a rumor that Nero had planned it.⟩ To abolish the rumor, Nero provided scapegoats and subjected to extreme tortures ⟨those⟩ whom the mob called Christians and hated because of ⟨their⟩ crimes. The founder of this movement, Christus, had been executed in the reign of Tiberius by the procurator Pontius Pilate. Repressed for a moment, the deadly superstition broke out again, not only throughout Judea where the disease had originated, but also throughout Rome where, from everywhere, all things atrocious or shameful flow together and are practiced. Accordingly, those admittedly ⟨Christian⟩ were first seized, then, by their information, a huge multitude were convicted, not so much of arson as of hatred for the human race.

He then goes on to describe the tortures by which they were put to death and concludes:

As a consequence ⟨of these tortures⟩ , although ⟨they were used⟩ against malefactors who deserved the most extreme measures, compassion was aroused, as if ⟨the convicts⟩ were being executed not for the public good, but to ⟨gratify⟩ one man's cruelty.

Tacitus' opinion, written shortly after 115, carries weight. He was long a member of the imperial commission on religious affairs and, besides, was a man of outstanding intelligence with a passion for accurate information. It is a pity therefore that he did not specify the crimes of which the Christians were found guilty. His generalization, "hatred of the human race," is most plausibly understood as referring to magic. The common explanation, that it is an application to the Christians, who were still a Jewish group, of the Roman belief about Jews in general, is derived from Tacitus' comment on the Jews in *Histories* V.5, "among themselves they scrupulously keep their promises, and are quick to pity and help ⟨each other⟩, but they hate all outsiders as enemies." This opinion probably was a factor in Tacitus' estimate of the Christians, but does not suffice to explain it. He did not think the Jews' hatred of outsiders an offense sufficient to make their total extermination a matter of public interest, but he did think this of the Christians' "hatred of the human race." The difference of proposed policy indicates a different notion of what the group was doing. Nor can "hatred of the human race" be explained as a reference to political subversion. Roman historians were familiar with political subversion, had no hesitation about referring to it, and had a rich vocabulary to describe its varieties. Therefore, had political subversion been in question, Tacitus would not have been so vague. Also, there is no evidence that after Jesus' crucifixion any sizeable body of Christians in the early Roman empire harbored any thoughts of practical, political revolution. The coming of the Kingdom was left to God; "Messiah" was translated into "Christ"; and "Christ" was not a political term. It is practically certain that the Roman Christians of A.D. 64 were not charged with plotting a revolution.

On the contrary, hatred of the human race is a charge appropriate to magicians as popular imagination conceived them. Lucan, a Roman poet who conspired against Nero and was forced to commit suicide in 65, the year after the fire, has left a lurid picture of the witch who will not worship the gods, but devotes her life to the cult of the powers of the underworld (to whose company Jesus, an executed criminal, was thought to belong). An important element of this cult was cannibalism. Lucan's witch is not content to call up a soul from the underworld, she forces it to reënter and revivify its dead body so that the entire man is raised from the dead (as the Christians claimed Jesus had been). In her prayers at the beginning of this rite, addressed to the gods of the underworld, and among them the nameless "ruler of the earth" (a role often assigned to the Jewish god in gnostic documents), she makes much of her cannibalism as a meritorious service by which she has deserved attention, "If I call on you with a mouth sufficiently evil and polluted, if I never sing these hymns without having eaten human flesh . . . grant ⟨my⟩ prayer." She was not unique; accusations of cannibalism and related, equally revolting crimes are frequent in Roman descriptions of witchcraft, and even the gods of the magicians were charged with cannibalism. We shall presently see explicit evidence that the same charge was brought against the Christians.

Tacitus' opinion is the more surprising because, just before he wrote, an equally distinguished Roman official had investigated the Christians and found them innocent simpletons. This was Pliny "the younger" who in A.D. 110–111 was governor of Bithynia in northwest Turkey. Many persons were brought to trial before him, accused of Christianity. He wrote the emperor Trajan (*Letters* X.96) asking what to do about the cases, and saying that he had inquired into the beliefs and practices of the accused, had tortured two serving women to test the truth of what was told him, and had found nothing but a "depraved and extravagant superstition" and an apparently harmless association: they meet on stated days before dawn, "sing a hymn to Christ as to a god," and bind themselves by an oath—to commit no crime. Later they reassemble to partake of food, "but common and harmless." Nevertheless, although Pliny dismissed the cases of those who denied they had ever been Christians and supported their denial by invoking the gods, offering incense and wine to the statue of the emperor, and cursing Christ ("none of which things, it is said, those who are truly Christians can be forced to do"), he executed those who admitted they were Christians and refused to desist. As for those who admitted they had once been Christians, but claimed to be so no longer, he suspended judgement until he could learn the emperor's opinion.

This is an amazing letter; it declares that an organization is foolish but innocent, and inquires whether or not all persons who have ever been members of it should be put to death! To investigate this paradox would lead us too far afield. If we take the letter as it is usually taken, at face value, we can discern the questions Pliny asked and the answers he received:

> What's this I hear of nocturnal meetings?
> We're working people, so we have to meet before dawn. Like all working people, we've got to be at work by sunrise.
> What are the spells you sing?
> They aren't magical spells, they're hymns.
> Do you evoke, as a demon, that crucified criminal?
> No, we worship him as a god.
> What is the oath you take at your meetings?
> We only swear not to commit any crime.
> Do your secret meals take place at your nocturnal meetings?
> No, we come back later—at the end of the day, like everybody else.
> What's the menu?
> Mostly just bread and a little wine; we're poor.
> What about eating a body and drinking blood?
> That's a lie! That's what our enemies say. We never do anything like that.
> Very well. Have her racked and see if she sticks to her story. Where's the other one?

These questions clearly show what opinion the Roman authorities had formed of Christianity; they thought it was an organization for the practice of magic. The difference between the result of Pliny's investigation and the opinions of Tacitus and Suetonius is understandable. Christianity at Rome in 64 was a different thing from the Christianity practiced in Asia Minor in 111 after half a century of imperial surveillance. Even in the 60s the forms of the religion in the two areas probably differed. Asia Minor had been the theater of Paul's greatest success and Paul's brand of Christianity was peculiar—he represented a moralizing interpretation, as opposed both to the legalism of the Jerusalem community under Jesus' brother James and to the libertine, magical tradition of the original apostles.

IV

Jesus' Palestinian opponents did not limit the presentation of their case to the officials of Rome. When they learned of the success of Christian missionaries in the diaspora, they organized a counter-mission to publicize their version of what had happened. We may reasonably suppose that version was put into writing almost as soon as the Christian one. The earliest preserved reference to the gospels dates from about 135, and we first hear of the Jewish anti-gospel from the Christian apologist Justin Martyr, writing in Rome between 150 and 165. In his *Dialogue with Trypho* (an imaginary Jewish interlocutor) he reproaches his opponent as follows,

⟨You Jews⟩ have sent chosen men into every part of the empire as official representatives ⟨of the High Priest and the sanhedrin⟩, proclaiming, "A godless and libertine heresy has arisen from a certain Jesus, a Galilean magician. We had him crucified, ⟨but⟩ his disciples stole him by night from the tomb where he had been put ⟨when⟩ taken down from the cross, and they deceive people, saying he has risen from the dead and ascended into heaven." ⟨You also slander Jesus,⟩ saying that he taught those godless and lawless and unholy things that you report to every race of men ⟨in your attacks⟩ against those who confess Christ ⟨as⟩ both ⟨their own⟩ teacher and ⟨the⟩ Son of God.

The "godless and lawless and unholy things" included the practice of nocturnal orgies in which, after human flesh had been eaten, the lights were put out and a group grope, enlivened by indiscriminate and possibly incestuous intercourse, ensued.

Here we can be sure that Justin is answering charges spread from Jerusalem since some of the same charges are already referred to by Matthew in a story found only in his gospel, and certainly intended (and probably invented) to answer them. After the crucifixion "the high priests and the Pharisees met with Pilate, saying . . . 'That magician said, while ⟨he was⟩ yet alive, "After three days I shall arise." Order, therefore, that the tomb be made secure till the third day, lest his disciples come, steal him, and say to the people, "He is risen from the dead."'" So Pilate gave them soldiers to guard the tomb. After the resurrection the guards reported to the high priests (not to the Pharisees!) what had happened, and were bribed to say that "His disciples, coming by night, stole him while we were asleep." So, Matthew concludes, "They, taking the money, did as they were told, and this story has been spread among the Jews to the present day."

"To the present day" shows that the story is late, but the fact that the Pharisees were added only to the first half shows that it was first told about the high priests only, and this indicates that it originated before 70 while Christians were still in Jerusalem and the high priests were the main source of trouble. Justin also dates the origin and dissemination of the Jewish account to the years before 70. After the passage quoted above he goes on to say, "Besides all this ⟨the anti-Christian propaganda he had described⟩, even after your city has been taken and your land desolated you do not repent, but you dare to curse him ⟨Jesus⟩ and all those who believe in him," (*Dialogue* 108.3). "All this" was therefore prior to the fall of the city. The cursing to which Justin often refers found its chief expression in the ritual curse added to the daily prayer, but also in teaching. Justin urges his hearers "not to abuse the Son of God nor ever, persuaded by Pharisaic teachers, ridicule the King of Israel, ⟨repeating⟩ such things as the heads of your synagogues teach you after the ⟨daily⟩ prayer." (*Dialogue* 137.2).

As to the content of this teaching, Justin gives us only glimpses. An astute apologist, he had no intention of presenting his opponents' case. Trypho is little more than a straw man, set up to ask the questions that enable Justin to make his own points. Embarrassing questions—like those about Jesus' parentage—are not asked (though we have seen from the gospels and rabbinic literature that they played an important role in Jewish polemic). Sometimes however, Justin refers to them by asides in his own comments. He used this same technique in the two *Apologies* he addressed to the Roman government. If we put together these asides, and the few questions of Trypho that do seem to reflect Jewish tradition about Jesus, we get the following picture: Jesus was an unscrupulous teacher ("sophist," *I Apology* 14.5), "a man born of men, who performed those ⟨feats⟩ we call miracles by magic art and therefore was thought to be a son of God." Actually, he was "a magician who led the people astray" and the miracles were "magically produced hallucinations."

This last charge had exercised an earlier apologist, Quadratus, who wrote about 125. We have only a fragment of his text, arguing that, "The ⟨mighty⟩ works of our saviour were permanent because they were true—those healed, those risen from the dead, who did not only seem to be healed or risen, but were always present, not only when the saviour was present, but also after his departure . . . so that some of them came down into our own times." The implied contrast was with magically produced hallucinations that supposedly lasted only so long as the magician was present.

The charge of magic implies rejection of the Mosaic Law, and rejection of the Law was presumably the basis for the charges of "lawlessness," "unholiness," and immorality that Justin says the Jews brought against Jesus. The statement that they called his teaching "godless" probably summarizes their criticism of his claim to be in some sense divine, the criticism being that such a claim denies the unique divinity of the creator. In any event, the Jews concluded that his claims, whatever they were, had been refuted by his crucifixion which put him under the curse of the Law (*Dialogue* 32.1). The stories of his resurrection were explained as we have seen above.

It is clear that this Jewish account, as reconstructed from Justin, substantially agrees with the picture of Jesus given by his opponents, as reported in the gospels. However, this agreement does not prove it derived from the gospels. We should not suppose that the Jews of the second century got all their information about Jesus from books they were forbidden to read, or that Justin was so ignorant of the actual Jewish claims that he had none to refute, and therefore made up imaginary ones by drawing on gospel material. On the contrary, it is clear that we have to do with different reflections of a continuing case, one first made by Jesus' scribal opponents in his lifetime, carried on and developed until 70 by the high priests and the Pharisees in Palestine, and by the opponents of the early Church in the diaspora, and initially accepted by the Roman government.

V

The peculiarity of this continuing, primitive tradition becomes clear as soon as we can compare its content with the remarks about Jesus made by pagans who derived their information from diasporic Christian communities and so, indirectly, from the gospels. Such a pagan is Lucian.

Born about 120, he lived until about 185, a famous essayist and lecturer and a brilliant man of the world who wrote of fanaticism, fraud, and superstition with contemptuous amusement. When in 165 a Cynic philosopher named Peregrinus burnt himself alive as a demonstration of indifference to pain, Lucian wrote a *Life of Peregrinus* representing him as a charlatan who so imposed on successive patrons that in the end he had no other way out. This satire gives us a picture of some Palestinian Christians, said to have been among Peregrinus' dupes.

"They still reverence that man who was put on a stake in Palestine because he introduced into ⟨human⟩ life this new initiation" (Chapter 11). Consequently, "these poor creatures have persuaded themselves that they shall be completely immortal and live forever . . . Besides, their first lawgiver persuaded them that they all are brothers of one another when, once having gone over ⟨to the sect⟩, they deny the Greek gods and worship that crucified sophist himself and live according to his laws. Accordingly, they have equally little regard for all things and think them all common ⟨property⟩, taking them over ⟨from the common fund⟩ without ⟨giving⟩ any accurate guarantee" (Chapter 13).

The difference from the preceding material is clear. Jesus is primarily a teacher who introduced a new "initiation" which Lucian probably thought the distinctive rite of a "mystery cult." Like most founders of cults, he was also the giver of the cult law. Lucian thinks the law foolish and perhaps a bit wicked— the verb translated "having gone over" is most commonly used for transgressing a law; here it is used to suggest that Christians sin by denying the Greek gods. But Lucian is more amused by their credulous communism than angry at their impiety. This is the first non-Christian reference to Jesus as a "lawgiver" or to Christians as living according to his laws. Nothing is said of miracles or magic. The notion of Jesus is that which would be formed by an intelligent, but unsympathetic, outside observer of the everyday life of a Christian community like that pictured in the early chapters of Acts. The great difference between this picture and the others we have seen—those given by Josephus, rabbinic literature, Roman officials, and the Jewish sources of Justin—indicates that the others did not derive their notion of Jesus from observation of the Christian communities around them. That they derived it from the gospels is equally incredible since it shows no trace of the legal discussions and sermons that make up so large a part of the gospels and would be easy to ridicule. It is only explicable from a tradition based on observation of Jesus himself as he appeared in Palestine to those who were not his followers.

Lucian may not have been ignorant of this tradition. Perhaps he even parodied it in one of his attacks on superstition, by making a pseudo-philosopher tell of

. . . the Syrian from Palestine who is an expert ⟨in exorcism, and⟩ how many ⟨demoniacs⟩, falling down moonstruck and rolling their eyes, their mouths full of foam, he takes in hand and stands them up and sends them off in their right mind, ridding them of their great troubles—for a huge fee. For when, standing over ⟨his⟩ prostrate ⟨patients⟩, he asks ⟨the demons⟩ whence they came into the body, the sick man himself is silent, but the demon answers, either in Greek or in some foreign tongue, ⟨telling⟩ where he comes from and how and whence he came into the man. And ⟨the exorcist⟩, resorting to conjurations and, if the demon does not obey, also threatening ⟨it⟩, drives it out.

All this is put in the mouth of a credulous fool who concludes, "And indeed I saw one going out, its color black and smoky" (*Philopseudes* 16).

It is possible that this parody was inspired by some gospel story like Mk. 5.1–19; but it is equally possible and more likely that both Lucian and the gospel drew on common knowledge of the common dramaturgy practiced by exorcists. In any event, Lucian's exorcist is not represented as Jesus, but as a contemporary of Lucian himself. The only trait that suggests a parody of Jesus is the man's identification as "the Syrian from Palestine." This is not much to build on since Jews were famous for their skill in exorcism. The probability therefore is that Lucian was caricaturing a type, not a man. If any reference to Jesus was intended, it makes more striking the fact that Lucian kept this tradition wholly separate from the other. There is no trace of the miracle man in his account of the founder of the sect, or vice versa. This would confirm our conclusion that the Palestinian tradition and the picture derived from Christian communities were distinct.

VI

Not all pagan philosophers were so contemptuous of Christianity as Lucian. Some thought it a serious threat and therefore were not content to base their opinions about it on superficial impressions derived from contact with a few Christians. A dozen years after Peregrinus' death an otherwise unknown

Platonist named Celsus made a study of the cult and wrote a treatise attacking it. When Christianity triumphed the treatise was destroyed, but before that, about A.D. 247, the Christian apologist Origen wrote a reply to it and quoted a good deal of it, almost sentence by sentence. Much of the text Origen answered can be dissected from his reply, and the content of some passages that he did not quote can be made out from his comments. What he passed over in silence—presumably the most embarrassing points—we shall never know.

The popular picture of Jesus that Celsus knew was primarily one of a miracle worker. Accordingly, Celsus seems to have begun his attack by saying Jesus did his miracles by magic. To this familiar charge he adds, "And since ⟨Jesus⟩ foresaw that others too, having learned the same arts, would do the same, boasting that they did so by the power of God, he orders that such men shall be expelled" (*Against Celsus* I.6). This seems to reflect a "saying of Jesus" that has not come down to us, presumably one of the sort dealing with church discipline that first become conspicuous in the later strata of Matthew; it more likely belonged to the Christians' tradition about Jesus than to the outsiders', so the fact that it appears first in Celsus is a reminder that he drew his material from both sides and that he must be used with caution.

Insisting that Jesus, though believed by the Christians to be the Son of God, had taught only a short while before his own time (a short while that is, in comparison with the span of human history I.26), Celsus presented the things he thought a Jew of Jesus' time might have said to him, putting them in the mouth of an imaginary Jewish interlocutor (I.28). This procedure suggests he was drawing on what he believed to be early Jewish tradition; the content of "the Jew's" remarks proves the suggestion correct. He accused Jesus of having made up the story of his birth from a virgin, whereas actually he came from a Jewish village and from a poor country woman who lived by her spinning. She was thrown out as an adulteress by her husband, a carpenter. Wandering about in disgrace, she secretly gave birth to Jesus, whom she had conceived from a soldier named Panthera. After growing up in Galilee, Jesus went as a hired laborer to Egypt. There he learned some of those magical rites on which the Egyptians pride themselves. He came back (to Palestine) hoping for great things from his powers and because of them proclaimed himself a god (I.28, 38).

From this, according to Origen, Celsus' Jew went on to attack first the story that the holy spirit had descended on Jesus after his baptism in the form of a dove, then the application to him of the Old Testament prophecies of a saviour, and finally, the story of the star and the magi (I.40)— all of this must have been based on Christian material. The report that Jesus had only ten disciples presumably rests on independent tradition, since Celsus knew the gospel of Matthew and would not have laid himself open to the charge of error had he not had some other evidence he preferred. Ten instead of twelve as the chosen number recalls a tradition in *B. Sanhedrin* 43a (end) that Jesus had five disciples, but the present form of the talmudic tradition is unreliable. As for Celsus' report that the ten were "tax collectors and sailors of the worst sort, not even able to read or write, with whom he ran, as a fugitive, from one place to another, making his living shamefully as a beggar"; this is typical ancient polemic and may have come from any opponent, including Celsus himself, though the picture given may be correct. The Christian references to the sins of the apostles, cited by Origen to demonstrate Jesus' power as healer of souls (I.63), are theologically motivated and no more reliable than the polemic.

The following attack on the story of the flight into Egypt (I.66) is almost certainly based on Matthew, but the charge that Jesus could give no sign to prove himself the Son of God (I.67), may have come from that hostile tradition which the gospel parallels were intended to answer. So may the charge that the miracles were done by control of a demon (I.68); it is here presented in a form that shows no verbal relation to the gospel accounts of the same accusation.

Strong evidence for Celsus' use of independent tradition is the fact that he represented his Jew as speaking to Jewish, not Gentile, believers (II.1). Origen was quick to point out that this was inappropriate; his correct observation indicates that Celsus was using a Jewish source. The indication is confirmed by the fact that the speaker not only addresses Jews, but also uses arguments chosen to appeal to them. Finally, at the beginning of Book III Celsus dismisses both Jewish attack and Christian defense with the Greek proverb, "a fight about the shadow of an ass," on the ground that since the messianic expectations on which both parties rely are absurd, it is a waste of time to follow their dispute as to whether or not Jesus fulfilled these expectations.

How closely Celsus followed his Jewish source from I.28 to the end of II is uncertain. He probably left out much that he thought was of exclusively Jewish interest, and he may have added arguments to appeal to his gentile readers. Then Origen, in turn, omitted, abbreviated, or misrepresented points he thought likely to obscure Christian truth. Consequently there is no chance of recovering the original. We shall try only to pick out the traits of Jesus' life that seem to have come from it, rather than from the gospels, and supplement these with occasional remarks made by Celsus in the later sections of his work where he once or twice used data from Jewish polemic.

That Jesus "followed all the Jewish customs, even ⟨those⟩ about the sacrifices" (II.6), comes from an argument directed against Jewish Christians who kept some elements of the Law, but abrogated others. "Liar" and "braggart" (II.7) may come from any polemic; "profane" we have already noticed. In VI.75 Celsus says that Jesus' body was, "as they say, small and ugly and undistinguished." Origen finds an unlikely source for "ugly" in Isaiah 53.1–3, but knows of no evidence for "small and undistinguished," yet "they say" indicates that Celsus had some source. His statement that Jesus claimed to be a god (II.9, etc.) is explicable from Christian texts, but is also attributed in the gospels to Jesus' opponents. That he was thought an "angel" looks like a reflection of an early Jewish Christology not represented by the gospels. "Deserted and betrayed by his associates, hid, fled, and was caught" (II.9–12) all *might* have come from the gospels; but "hid" and "fled" could better have come from a different account of the same events, and Celsus said he was betrayed by "many" disciples (II.11). Origen denies that Jesus "hid" and "fled," and objects that there was only one traitor, but nevertheless derides Celsus' claim that he "had many true things he could say about . . . Jesus that bore no resemblance to those written by his disciples," but he "left these out ⟨of the argument⟩."

Coming to the events of the trial and passion we find that in II.44 Celsus compared Jesus to a "bandit." This is the first time the term has been applied to him. It may be an example of guilt by association—Matthew and Mark say he was crucified between two "bandits"—but the word is one commonly used by Josephus for "revolutionaries" and in Celsus' source its use may have reflected the charge that Jesus was stirring up resistance to Rome. Another peculiar trait is Jesus' "rushing with his mouth open to drink" (II.37) at the crucifixion. That "he persuaded no one so long as he lived" (II.39,46) is, as Origen said, mere malice, therefore undatable. Celsus wrote, "With his own voice ⟨Jesus⟩ clearly proclaims, as you yourselves have written, 'Others, too, will be with you, doing similar miracles, evil men and sorcerers,' and he names one 'Satan' as devising these things"(II.49). This is not from the gospels, so Origen claims it is false. He also argues: the men of whom Jesus warned us to beware would claim to be Christ, sorcerers make no such claims, therefore Jesus was not a sorcerer. (A bad argument, stronger when reversed: The men of whom Jesus warned us to beware were sorcerers, therefore sorcerers did make such claims, therefore Jesus may have been a sorcerer.) The resurrection, according to Celsus, was witnessed by "a hysterical woman and perhaps some other ⟨man⟩ of those from the same coven" (II.55), but the variance from the gospels cannot be relied on—he may have cut down the number of witnesses to strengthen his case for doubting the event.

VII

That many elements in Celsus' work came from Jewish sources is suggested by the references in later Christian writers to the same elements as things that the Jews say. Eusebius, about 300, tried to explain "their" Panthera story as a misunderstanding of scripture, and Epiphanius, a century later, actually gave Panthera a legitimate place in the Holy Family—he became the Saviour's "paternal" grandfather! Later Christian writers found other places for him in the same genealogy. These uneasy adjustments prove "son of Panthera" was so firmly attached to Jesus that Christian writers thought they had better "explain" rather than deny it. Tertullian, about 200, sums up the Jewish account of Jesus as he knew it:

Son of a carpenter or a prostitute, profaner of the Sabbath, a Samaritan and one who had a demon . . . bought ⟨by the high priests⟩ from Judas . . . beaten with a reed and slapped, disgraced with spittle, given gall and vinegar to drink . . . ⟨ a man⟩ whom his disciples spirited away ⟨from the tomb⟩ so they could say he had risen, or whom the gardener hauled off, lest his lettuces be damaged by the crowd of sightseers (*De spectaculis* 30).

The gardener is a figure new to us. Had he long been a part of the tradition, or was he newly invented on the basis of Jn. 20.15? We cannot tell.

The course and content of the Palestinian tradition hostile to Jesus have been traced down to the late second century. From here on it is so contaminated by elements from the gospels, and from invention, that none of its later traits can safely be used as evidence of how Jesus' contemporaries saw him. Other traditions about Jesus that might have preserved early elements prove similarly unreliable. The Mandaeans, a sect in southern Iraq and thereabouts, claim descent from the followers of the Baptist and have some stories about Jesus—according to them he was a magician and representative of the power of evil. Jesus was in contact with the Samaritans and was sometimes identified with the Samaritan magician Simon, but Samaritan and Mandaean traditions, and the scraps of Simonian polemic that may be reflected in early Christian literature, yield nothing useful. This is not to say that they may not contain old elements, but there is no way to be sure which of their elements are old.

Ancient magical material is a bit more reliable because it is archaeologically datable. We have seen that already in Jesus' lifetime magicians began to use his name in their spells. Acts 19.13 shows that the practice was continued, even by Jewish magicians, after his death. Accordingly, of the three oldest representations of the crucifixion, two are on magical gems and the third probably refers to Christian magical beliefs.

Of the gems, one, a brown jasper formerly in the Pereire collection, shows Jesus hung by his wrists from the cross and seated on a bar that projected from the upright to carry the weight of the body. His legs are dangling and slightly spread. (These traits correspond to Roman practice.) Around the figure, and on the reverse of the stone, is a magical inscription: "One Father, Jesus Christ, *soa mnoa moa*" etc.—a long screed of mumbo jumbo. This probably dates from about A.D. 200. Another stone, an orange jasper in the

Graffito in the Imperial Palace on the Palatine, Rome.
Late second century A.D.

Magical gem with crucifixion. British Museum G. 231.
Third century A.D.(?).

The raising of Lazarus as represented on a gold glass plate
of the fourth century A.D., now in the Vatican Library
(No. 31 in the catalogue by C. Morey, *Catalogo del Museo
Sacro* IV, Vatican City, 1959, p. 9 and pl. V).

British Museum (G 231), is probably somewhat later. It shows the crucified figure but no cross. The torso is twisted and the haloed head is turned to the (viewer's) left; the hips and legs are also in profile, the legs bent slightly backwards at the knees; on the whole it suggests a flying figure and may be intended to represent a vision. Below the extended arms are two small figures, one on either side, kneeling in adoration. Above the head a damaged inscription may perhaps have read in Hebrew or Aramaic, "Jesus, M(essiah)." The reverse of the stone is covered with Greek letters and magical signs of uncertain significance.

Perhaps the earliest of all representations of the crucifixion is a graffito, a picture scratched on the plaster of a schoolroom on the Palatine hill in Rome. It shows a crucified figure seen from behind. The feet rest on a small crossbar, the head is turned to one side. On that side, slightly below, stands a young man, one hand raised in reverence. A misspelled Greek inscription reads "Alexamenos reveres God." The date is about 200, possibly a bit before. So far so good. But the head of the crucified figure is that of a donkey.

There was a long standing legend that the god of the Jews was a donkey, or donkey-headed. The legend probably arose from the fact that the donkey was the sacred animal of Seth, the villain in the Egyptian pantheon, who was commonly thought by the Egyptians to be the god of foreigners. He was also, being a villain, given a large role in magic, and often appears as a donkey-headed figure on magical gems. The Jews were among the largest groups of foreigners in Egypt, so their god, Iao, was identified with Seth. *Io* or *Eio* in Coptic means "donkey," so the identification was almost predetermined. Moreover, the Jews had a great reputation as magicians; this confirmed the identification. Therefore the donkey-headed Seth on magical gems is identified as Iao (= *Yah* or *Yahweh*, the personal name of the Israelite god). The Palatine graffito shows a further identification of Seth-Iao with the crucified Jesus. Alexamenos is accused of (or praised for?) practicing either Christianity or magic or both, most likely both. Another such graffito (this one certainly abusive) was drawn in Carthage a little before A.D. 197 by a nonobservant Jew. It showed a figure "with donkey's ears and a hoof ⟨instead of⟩ one foot, carrying a book and wrapped in a toga." The accompanying inscription read "The god of the Christians ⟨is⟩ a donkey who beds ⟨with his worshipers⟩." Bestiality was associated with demonic possession. A little bone crucifix, to be worn as an amulet, was found about 1945 in Montagnana (about midway between Mantua and Padua). It shows a donkey crucified on a living tree at the bottom of which an ape is crouching. There was no archaeological context and the date is uncertain.

Whatever may or may not have been the magical connotations of these two graffiti and the crucifix, there is no question that Jesus' name continued to be used in magic as that of a supernatural power by whose authority demons might be conjured. From the late first or early second century we have a lead curse tablet from Greece (Megara) conjuring Althaia Kore (i.e. Persephone), Hecate, and Selene to put a curse on the victims' "body, spirit, soul, mind, thought, sensation, life, heart." The goddesses are conjured "by the Hecatean words and Hebrew conjurations . . . ⟨Jes⟩us, Earth, Hecate, ⟨Jes⟩us." (The text of the tablet has been damaged, so the readings of Jesus' name are not sure; they were proposed and defended by Wünsch in his critical edition and have been generally accepted.)

Another lead tablet from a grave in Carthage is about a century later. It reads, "I conjure you, whoever you are, demon of the dead, by the god who created earth and heaven, Iona; I conjure you by the god who has authority over the subterranean regions, *Neicharoplex* . . . by . . . holy Hermes . . . *Iao* . . . *Sabaoth* . . . the god of Solomon, *Souarmimoouth* . . . the god having authority over this hour in which I conjure you, Jesus".

This tablet is roughly contemporary with three of the oldest of the major surviving magical papyri, all of them pagan, but here and there containing spells in which Jesus is invoked, thus: *PGM* III, line 420 (in Coptic): "A spell to improve one's memory" contains the comment, "The name of the soul of the god is 'I am Kou, Bou . . . Jesus.'" *PGM* IV, line 1233 (also Coptic): "Be blessed, God of Abraham. Be blessed, God of Isaac. Be blessed, God of Jacob. Jesus Christ, holy spirit, son of the Father, who art under the Seven and in the Seven, bring Iao Sabaoth. May your power increase . . . until you drive out this evil demon, Satan." Again in *PGM* IV, line 3020 in another exorcism, this time in Greek: "I conjure you by the god of the Hebrews, Jesus, *Iaba*, *Iae*, *Abraoth*, *Aia*, Thoth," etc. (Line 2929 of the same papyrus may contain an anagrammatized reference to Jesus in an invocation of Aphrodite for a love charm.)

PGM XII, line 192: "A spell to get ⟨a revelation in⟩ a dream, ⟨to be said⟩ to ⟨the god of the⟩ pole star. . . Jesus, Anou(bis?)" . . . (the text has been lost because of damage to the papyrus).

These uses of Jesus' name in pagan spells are flanked by a vast body of material testifying to the use of his name in Christian spells and exorcisms, and to the practice of magic by Christians of various sects (including the self-styled "Catholic Church"). Exorcism became a regular ritual of the Church; other magical practices are often attested by conciliar legislation against them and by "Catholic" writers (primarily Irenaeus, Hippolytus, and Epiphanius) against "heretics". The attestations are confirmed by a multitude of Christian amulets, curse tablets, and magical papyri in which Jesus is the god most often invoked. After Christianity gained official status in the fourth century, this side of the religion was gradually driven underground, but the change was slow. Thus Jesus long continued to be represented in Christian art as a magician, complete with magic wand, as he appears on a fourth-century gold glass plate in the Vatican library, reproduced on the cover of this volume. This Christian cult of Jesus the magician must be left aside in our effort to determine the content of the *outsiders'* traditions about him, but it does strengthen the case for those traditions by showing that they were not peculiar to outsiders nor solely the product of malicious misrepresentation. On the contrary, some of their most important elements were accepted by hundreds of thousands of believing Christians through the first millennium, and more, of Christian history.

VIII

Reviewing the non-gospel evidence for the outsiders' image of Jesus, we find it dominated by the memory of his miracles, the inference of his magic, and the suppositions based on that inference and on rumors of Christian practice, especially of the eucharist. When we compare this material with the gospel reports of what outsiders said, we find ourselves dealing with two stages of the same tradition—the same themes and patterns run from one to the other, but there are also significant differences; subjects important to the opponents in the gospels are dropped by those in the later documents, and topics that the gospels barely hint at become conspicuous later on.

As we should expect, matters of local Palestinian interest generally disappear. We hear no more, for instance, of Jesus' necromantic identification with John the Baptist, or his possession by Beelzebul. (Loss of such discreditable details indicates that the outsiders did not usually rely on the canonical gospels, which preserved them). The notion that he was Elijah disappeared; the belief that he was a prophet lived on in some branches of Christian tradition, but apparently not in circles outside Christianity, though rabbinic Judaism continued to apply to him some terms appropriate for a false prophet.

As to his life, the stories of his rejection in his home town and by his brothers are forgotten—nobody in the great world cared what those Galilean peasants had thought about him. But the great world was a world of snobs, so the tradition of his humble background and, above all, his illegitimate birth, was perpetuated and developed. As we have seen, the stories of his birth, his stay in Egypt, and the theft of his body from the tomb were known to Matthew, who tried to discredit the first two by indirect contradictions, and attacked the third directly. Consequently, the silence of the gospels does not always discredit material that first appears explicitly in the outsiders' tradition. Some details that the authors of the gospels would certainly have suppressed—for instance, the name of Jesus' father, Panthera—are traceable back to the time of the gospels themselves and have an equal claim to reliability.

Along with stories of his relations to his townspeople and family, the stories of his arguments with representatives of the various Jewish sects have generally disappeared. For the Christians it was important to have "Jesus'" teaching on these disputed matters, so their own arguments were put into his mouth. For the outsiders no such interest existed. Nor were they interested in his legal teaching. Josephus may have been an exception in this matter, textual corruption makes his attitude uncertain. Rabbinic literature reported a saying Rabbi Eliezer may have heard from a (second generation?) Christian (?), and another third-century story about a second-century Christian who cited one legal saying of Jesus from Matthew and invented another *ad hoc*. These traces show that the thought of Jesus as a legal authority was not wholly unknown to rabbinic circles, but was of little importance to them. The Roman authorities knew nothing of it. The tradition of the Jewish diaspora as it appears in Justin and Celsus, knew Jesus as a teacher, not of the Law, but of magical and libertine practices. Only in the latter half of the second century do pagans who think of Christianity as a mystery cult begin to speak of Jesus as its "lawgiver."

Finally, Jesus' claim to be the Messiah became a comparatively minor matter. Josephus knew of it, but the rabbis do not mention it until the end of the third century, by which time Christianity had made it famous. It was remembered in diasporic Judaism, but does not play the leading role in pre served answers to Jewish polemic. Justin appeals to Trypho not to be "persuaded by Pharisaic teachers" to "ridicule the King of Israel." Presumably Jesus' messianic claim appeared in Jewish accusations to the Romans, but there is no sign that the Romans ever took it seriously. They had no reason to do so. As a practical matter the claim had died with Jesus. Celsus knew that Christians and Jews were still arguing over the question and he drew much of his polemic material from a work produced for the Jewish side of the argument, but he contemptuously dismissed the claims of both sides as absurd. Evidently Jesus' Messiahship was not a matter of importance for the pagans he hoped to deter from conversion to Christianity.

In contrast to these neglected themes, references to Jesus' miracles, and those done by disciples "in his name," are plentiful—in Josephus, in rabbinic literature, in Justin and Celsus—they are the (unmentioned) reason for the continued appeals to his name in the magical material, and they may be the source of Lucian's parody. From this accumulation of evidence it is clear that he was remembered primarily as a miracle worker.

His miracles were commonly explained as works of magic; he was therefore also remembered as a magician. Contributing factors in shaping this picture of him and developing it far beyond the hints in the gospels were the secrecy of the early Christian communities, the Christians' talk of mutual love, their habit of referring to each other as "brother" and "sister" (which led to charges of promiscuity and incest), their ideal of having all things in common (which some Christian practice, and much ancient gossip extended to wives and husbands), and above all their practice of the eucharist. Reports of the formula "this is my body, this is my blood" leaked out and were taken as evidence of cannibalism. Cannibalism, incest, and sexual promiscuity were reported of magicians. Therefore, the Christians were persecuted as magicians, and Jesus was conceived as the founder of their association. His magical reputation and theirs confirmed each other.

Only as Christianity gradually spread and became better known (and as its lunatic fringe died out) was this picture discredited. A rationalist like Lucian, who no more believed in magic than he did in the gods, could already in the 160s ignore the legend and picture the Christians as amiable simpletons. On the other hand, a century later the philosopher Porphyry was still scandalized by Jesus' saying, "Unless you eat my flesh and drink my blood, you have no life in yourselves." "This," he said, "is not truly beastly or absurd, but absurd beyond all absurdity, and bestial beyond every sort of bestiality, that a man should taste human flesh and drink the blood of men of his own genus and species, and by so doing should have eternal life . . . What sort of saying is this? Even if allegorically it have some more hidden and beneficial ⟨meaning⟩, yet the stench of the wording, coming in through the hearing, sickens the very soul." And so on, through a solid page of rhetoric.

It was generally believed that Jesus' magical powers had been the basis for his claim to be a god. That he was thought an angel is a related tradition reported by Celsus and confirmed by scattered Christian evidence. Against such claims and beliefs, the Jewish tradition emphasized the details of his life that demonstrated his humanity: his natural (and discreditable) birth and death. It also tried to discredit the Christian story of the empty tomb by claiming that the disciples had stolen the body. And it seems to have perpetuated a sort of counter-gospel, an extended story of Jesus' birth, education, public career, and passion, that differed from the canonical gospels in many details—sayings condemning magicians; ten disciples, mostly uneducated, forming with Jesus an itinerant, mendicant group; Jesus' observance of Jewish customs, including sacrifice; his "small, ugly, and undistinguished" body; an attempt to escape before the arrest ("hiding and flight"); betrayal by several disciples; execution as a "bandit"; and "rushing with his mouth open to drink" at the crucifixion. For most such fragments of the counter-gospel we are dependent on Celsus, and because Celsus chose them for his purpose of denigrating Jesus they all can be represented as inventions intended to serve that purpose. But some are not the sort of thing that would have been made up for that purpose—why, for example, ten disciples instead of twelve? A non-canonical source, and one with Palestinian roots (whence the Panthera story) seems more probable.

IX

Now at last, putting the data from the gospels and from the other sources together, we can sketch the life of "Jesus the magician" as it was pictured by those who did not become his disciples:

The son of a soldier named Panthera and a peasant woman married to a carpenter, Jesus was brought up in Nazareth as a carpenter, but left his home town and, after unknown adventures, arrived in Egypt where he became expert in magic and was tattooed with magical symbols or spells. Returning to Galilee he made himself famous by his magical feats, miracles he did by his control of demons. He thereby persuaded the masses that he was the Jewish Messiah and/or the son of a god. Although he pretended to follow Jewish customs, he formed a small circle of intimate disciples whom he taught to despise the Jewish Law and to practice magic. These he bound together and to himself by ties of "love," meaning sexual promiscuity, and by participation in the most awful magical rites, including cannibalism—they had some sort of ritual meal in which they ate human flesh and drank blood. Surrounded by this circle he travelled from town to town deceiving many and leading them into sin. But he was not always successful. The members of his own family did not believe him; when he went back to Nazareth his townspeople rejected him and he could do no miracle there. Stories of his libertine teaching and practice leaked out and began to circulate. The scribes everywhere opposed him and challenged his claims. Finally, when he went to Jerusalem the high priests had him arrested and turned him over to Pilate, charging him with the practice of magic and with sedition. Pilate had him crucified, but this did not put an end to the evil. His followers stole his body from the grave, claimed he had risen from the dead, and, as a secret society, perpetuated his practices.

Such was the picture formed by outsiders, but how did they understand it? We have, throughout, been using "magician" as if its meaning were clear. But what did Jesus' contemporaries mean when they said "magician"?

~ 5 ~

What the Outsiders Meant

I

To say that most of his contemporaries thought Jesus a magician begs the question, What did they think a magician was? This question is hard to answer because the meaning of "magician" differs from one cultural tradition to another, and in Palestine during Jesus' lifetime a number of different cultural traditions were mingled. Scholars commonly talk of "Jewish" and "Greco-Roman" elements, but this antithesis oversimplifies the situation. The Semitic-speaking people of the land were by no means wholly Jewish. The ancient Israelites had never controlled, let alone settled, the whole country, and although the Jews had overrun most of it during the half century from 125 to 75 B.C., and had forcibly "converted" to Judaism many of the groups they conquered, their control even during this brief period had never been complete and their skin-deep conversions (to which Jesus' family may have owed its Judaism—Galilee was one of the areas overrun) had done as much to strengthen the pagan elements in popular Judaism as they had to establish Jewish beliefs in the converts. Therefore, to picture Jesus' environment we have to reckon with a strong strain of native, Palestinian, Semitic paganism. Besides this, the country had long been influenced by Phoenician and Egyptian beliefs (Egyptian amulets are frequent in archaeological finds). Persian influence had been important in the development of both monotheism and demonology (it provided the notion of a counter hierarchy of demons organized under their own ruler), and in the shaping of beliefs about the coming end of the world. Finally, Greek beliefs and practices were familiar everywhere. Of about 360 years from Alexander's conquest to Jesus' baptism, Galilee had been ruled by Greeks, Romans, and Roman agents (including Hyrcanus II and the Herods) for about 320.

All these cultures shared the belief that this world has an enormous supernatural population—gods, angels, demons, spirits of the dead, and so on. "Orthodox" Jews, it is true, thought there was only one god, but they believed in as many angels and demons as did their neighbors, and for practical purposes gods, angels, and demons were much the same. Whatever forms they were thought to have, all were conceived as being psychologically like ordinary people. Each had his own tastes and could be angered, placated, persuaded, bribed, and so on. Like people, they differed in status. Each culture had its own establishment of great gods who were honored publicly by official cults in the great cities, while the minor beings depended on petty shrines or private devotions, and spirits of the dead were often practically beggars, pleading from their tombs for the passerby to give them a word of greeting and a little wine. Even the least however had supernatural powers that could be formidable if brought into action, and even the greatest could be reached—a man who knew how to deal with them could get them to intervene on his behalf in all sorts of ways.

The Jews' god, Yahweh, was no exception. In fact, he was particularly famous for his usefulness in magic. In the magical papyri (which contain a sprinkling of Jewish spells, but are mainly pagan documents) his name outnumbers that of any other deity by more than three to one. Widespread ancient reports of Jewish magic involving worship of angels and demons, as well as Yahweh, have now been confirmed by the recovery of *SHR* (*Sefer ha-Razim*, "The Book of Secrets"), a Jewish magical text of late Roman times that gives directions for such worship, prescribing the prayers and sacrifices to be made to these minor powers.

Such private dealings with supernatural beings make up most of what we call "magic" as well as what we call "private religion." There is no clear line between the two. When we compare avowedly religious texts and reports of religious practices with the texts of the magical papyri and the practices they prescribe, we find the same goals stated and the same means used. For instance, spells for destruction of an enemy are commonly supposed to be magical, but there are many in the Psalms. The cliché, that the religious man petitions the gods while the magician tries to compel them, is simply false. The magical papyri contain many humble prayers, and the black mass was an outgrowth of Christian beliefs that credited a priest with the power practically to compel his god to present himself on the altar. Consequently, we shall not try to define "magic" abstractly, but shall look at some of the sorts of magicians that circulated in Jesus' world to see what they were supposed to do.

II

The common Greek word for "magician" in Jesus' time was *goes* (plural *goetes*). It was usually, but not necessarily, abusive. Plato, writing in praise of the demon Eros as the intermediary between men and the gods, had said in the *Symposium* (202e), "Through him all divination is made possible, and the science of the priests and of the specialists in sacrifices and initiations and spells, and all prophecy and *goeteia*." Here *goeteia* (what *goetes* do) is one special technique like the others named, a recognized and legitimate function. It seems to have been a sort of Greek shamanism, a form of mourning for the dead in which the *goetes* became ecstatic and were thought to accompany the dead on their journey to the underworld. Such *goetes* were evidently popular—their ability to "charm" their hearers (perhaps with songs of mourning, perhaps with descriptions of what they "saw") was such that deceitful but persuasive speakers were called both "sophists" and *goetes*. (This may account for the use of both terms to describe Jesus.) *Goeteia* could also refer to physical magic. According to Herodotus, men thought to turn themselves into wolves may be *goetes* (IV.105). The followers of Euripides and Socrates, who detested sophistry no less than superstition, came to use *goeteia* as a general term for "deceit," and to equate *goes* with "beggar," "deceiver," and "impertinent scoundrel." A passing reference in the *Meno* (80b) indicates that by Plato's time, in some cities *goetes* were liable to arrest. Plato as an old man (when his feeling for Eros, song, and ecstasy was no longer what it had been when he wrote the *Symposium*) put into his *Laws* a penalty for men who "are so bestial as to . . . say that they can lead about the souls of the dead and . . . persuade the gods, pretending they can charm them by sacrifices and prayers and spells"—these were to be imprisoned for life. As to poisoning, he recognized that the Greek term had two meanings, one, the damage done by a physical substance, the other, that done by "tricks and spells and enchantments" which persuade men that they are harmed by others who thus practice *goeteia*. He ruled that the latter type of "poisoning" should be punished by death if the offender were a prophet or interpreter of portents; but by a penalty proportionate to the damage if an amateur (*Laws* 932eff.).

These passages indicate the scope of *goeteia* in classical times: accounts of the underworld, practice as mediums, necromancy, charms, curses, and therefore, by extension, any deceitful persuasion. By New Testament times we find Josephus describing as *goetes* men who do or promise to do miracles—divide the Jordan, make the walls of Jerusalem fall down, overpower the Romans, and give the people "salvation and rest from troubles." Here Josephus' use of *goetes* is abusive. The word had lower class connotations and was widely used of political orators and the like to mean approximately "spellbinder", or just plain "fraud." Josephus means more than that, for he distinguished these "magicians" from the ordinary revolutionists (whom he commonly calls "brigands"), and the distinction seems to be based on the "magicians'" claim to be able to perform miracles.

III

A step above *goes* was *magos* (plural *magoi*, Latinized and thence Anglicized as "magus" and "magi"). The real magi were a priestly clan of Media who came on the Greek scene in the 540s B.C. when Cyrus, King of the Medes and Persians, conquered the Greek cities of Asia Minor. Herodotus, writing a century later, tells us they were interpreters of dreams, omens, and portents. Also, whenever a Persian wanted to sacrifice, he had to have a magus stand by and sing an account of the birth of the gods (I.132). The magi not only supervised private sacrifices, but also conducted public ones, especially those required on special occasions. For instance, when the Persian invasion of Greece in 480 was held up by a great storm, the magi tried to still it. "Offering victims to the dead and singing spells with loud outcries to the wind, and, besides, sacrificing to ⟨the Greek sea goddesses⟩ Thetis and the Nereids, they stopped ⟨the storm⟩—on the fourth day; or, in other words, it blew itself out" (VII.191).

Herodotus' sarcasm was typical of the developing rationalism of his time. In the drama of the later fifth century *magos* can mean "quack;" "the arts of the magi" can be equated with "the use of drugs" and "the deceits of the gods." The word "magic" (*mageia*, what magi do) first appears at this time. "Two arts have been discovered ⟨by men, that⟩ of *goeteia* and ⟨that⟩ of *mageia*, which are ⟨the arts of causing⟩ errors of the soul and deceptions of the opinion." This neat distinction probably owed more to the author's antithetical style than to his perception of the facts. Insofar as there was a real differentiation, it was due to the continued prestige of the magi as an important priestly caste of a great country. They were a powerful, ancient, mysterious, and oriental caste about whom strange and scandalous stories circulated.

Herodotus observed that "the magi differ in many respects from other men" and reported a few of the differences: they pride themselves on killing noxious animals; they will not bury a human body until a bird or dog has torn it (I.140). More famous was their practice of endogamy; a younger contemporary of Herodotus reported that "the magi have intercourse with their mothers, and it is legitimate for them to have intercourse with their sisters and daughters, and they have their wives in common." Endogamy and peculiar purity rules helped to keep them a group apart, which enhanced the reputation of their secret doctrines. Pliny "the elder" reports of Nero that,

Not even his love for the lyre and the songs of the tragedies was greater ⟨than his madness for magic⟩. As he hurled himself from the highest human good fortune into the deepest vices of the mind, he conceived, above all, a desire to command the gods . . . No art was ever, by anyone, more passionately patronized. For this he never lacked funds, nor strength, nor intelligence to learn . . . The magus Tiridates came to him, bringing enough attendants for ⟨the celebration of⟩ a triumph over Armenia, and therefore a heavy burden to the provinces ⟨through which he passed⟩. He was unwilling to go by sea since they think it improper to spit in the sea or pollute its nature by other human necessities. He brought magi with him and even initiated Nero in magical meals; however, although Nero gave him a kingdom, he was not able to learn this art from him. Accordingly, we can be sure that it is incapable of producing evidence, is without effect, empty, but nevertheless does have some shadows of truth. In these however it is the poisoning arts that are effective, not the magical.

Pliny probably practiced law in Rome through the latter years of Nero's reign; he knew what he was talking about, but his judgment of the teaching of the magi was too sensible for the temper of the times. Legends of their wisdom had been circulating almost as long as reports of their nonsense. One generation later, at the end of the first century A.D., Plutarch, using hellenistic sources, gave the following account of them:

Most of the wisest men . . . think there are two gods, rivals as it were, one the maker of good things, the other of bad. But others call the better power a god, the other a demon, as does Zoroaster who . . . called the god "Ahura Mazda," the demon, "Ahriman." . . . Moreover, he taught ⟨his followers, the magi,⟩ to offer sacrifices of petition and thanksgiving to Ahura Mazda, and give to Ahriman apotropaic and sorrowful offerings. Accordingly, pounding a certain herb called *omomi* in a mortar, they call on Hades and darkness, and then, having mixed it with the blood of a slaughtered wolf, they take it to a sunless spot and scatter ⟨it there⟩. Moreover, they think some plants are ⟨creations⟩ of the good god, some of the evil demon, and animals ⟨likewise⟩ . . . and they think fortunate the man who kills the most ⟨evil animals⟩.

Stories of the magi offering human sacrifices to the gods of the underworld had already appeared in Herodotus, VII.114. Plutarch goes on to attribute to them teachings about the approaching end of the world, destruction of the wicked, and an age of peace and happiness for the righteous. Such Persian ideas have become familiar to us through Jewish adaptations of them preserved in several Old and New Testament books. How much else may have come from the Magi into Judaism and so into Christianity remains uncertain.

One reason for the uncertainty is the fact that, besides the genuine magi, a large crop of imitators flourished along the eastern Mediterranean coastlands throughout the Roman period. Acts (13.6–12) gives us a brief picture of one of them, a Jew temporarily patronized by the Roman governor of Cyprus about A.D. 48. He illadvisedly tried to discredit Paul, who turned out to be a more powerful competitor and struck him blind. We glimpse another similar character in a sentence of Josephus: "At this time Felix, ⟨who⟩ was administering Judea, saw ⟨the new Queen of Emesa⟩ and . . . conceived a desire for the woman, and sending one of his friends, (a Jew named Atomos, a Cyprian by race, who pretended to be a magos) he persuaded her to leave her husband and marry him." (*Antiquities* XX.142). Such individuals probably passed off as "teachings of the magi" many elements of Mediterranean magic that we now find attributed to their masters. For instance, Philo of Byblos, a contemporary of Plutarch, quotes "Zoroaster, the magus" as saying, "God has the head of a hawk. This is the first ⟨god⟩, incorruptible, eternal, unbegotten, ⟨etc.⟩ . . . **and wise, the sole discoverer of holy magic." This hawk-headed god is identified by Philo with lion-headed and snake-bodied deities like those conspicuous on magical amulets of about the same time and region.** Similarly Origen writes on one occasion that "no magus can involve the omnipotent God nor his son . . . Jesus Christ . . . but . . . those who invoke Beelzebub are magi" (*Homilies on Numbers*, XIII.5); but on another occasion that not only Jews "in their prayers to God and when they are invoking demons use ⟨the phrase⟩ 'the god of Abraham and the god of Isaac and the god of Jacob,' but so do almost all those who practice spells and magic rites, for this sort of title for God is found very often in the books of the magi" (lit. "magic books," *Against Celsus* IV.33). **This latter statement is true.**

The magi are credited with teaching on moral questions, but also with cannibalism and with the practice of techniques to send men alive into the world of the dead and bring them back again. These last were parodied by Lucian whose story is the best picture we have of a bogus magus at work. Lucian puts it in the mouth of one Menippus, a pretended initiate, who tells how he tried all schools of philosophy, found their doctrines false and their teachers corrupt, despaired of learning the truth by rational means, and therefore "decided to go to Babylon and beseech one of the magi, the disciples and successors of Zoroaster," for a revelation (ch. 6, end):

Arriving, I attached myself to one of the Chaldaeans, a wise man of more than human skill, with long grey hair and a very reverend, trailing beard— his name was Mith-robarzanes. With entreaties and supplications I hardly succeeded in persuading him to lead me down the road ⟨to the underworld⟩—for whatever fee he chose. Taking me on, the man first washed me ⟨daily⟩ for twenty-nine days, beginning with the new moon. He would take me down at dawn to the Euphrates, ⟨turn me⟩ towards the rising sun, and say over me some long formula I couldn't well make out, for he ran it all together and didn't pronounce clearly . . . but it seemed to call on various demons. Then, after the charm, he would spit three times in my face and go back ⟨to the city⟩ without looking at anybody who met us. And our food was nuts, our drink milk, and a mixture of honey and milk, and Choaspes water, and we slept outdoors on the grass.

When he had enough of this preparation, he took me about midnight to the Tigris, cleansed me, wiped me off, sanctified me all around with a torch and a squill and many other things, at the same time muttering that charm. Then, having completely magified me and circled around me so I might not be harmed by the phantoms, he brought me back to the house, just as I was, walking backwards, and at last we prepared for the voyage. He himself put on some magic vestment which looked much as if it were Median, and he fixed me up . . . with a cap and lion skin and lyre besides, and ordered me, if anybody asked my name, not to say Menippus, but Hercules or Ulysses or Orpheus. . . . He had prepared a skiff and animals for sacrifice, and milk mixed with honey, and the other things needed for the rite. Putting all these into ⟨the boat⟩ . . . we too got in . . . and for a while were carried down stream . . . then we sailed into the marsh and the lake in which the Euphrates loses itself. Crossing this we came to a deserted, wooded, and sunless place where we got out, Mithrobarzanes leading, dug a pit, slaughtered the sheep and sprinkled the blood around it. The magus meanwhile, holding a burning torch, no longer spoke quietly, but cried out as loud as he was able. Shouting, he called on all the demons at once, and the Punishers and the Furies and nocturnal Hecate and awesome Persephone, mixing in at the same time some barbaric, unintelligible and polysyllabic names. At once the whole place rocked, and the ground was split by the spell, and the barking of Cerberus could be heard . . . (This led to a guided tour of the underworld.)

Such is the range of meanings available for "magus" in the early Roman empire. It might mean anything from a genuine Median priest or potentate to a fellow who peddled amulets or poisons to superstitious or jilted serving girls. In general however the term was pretentious. A man's enemies would probably call him a *goes*, though they might refer to his practices as *mageia*, but there was no fixed rule. Even "magus" was often used contemptuously, like the English "swami." And just as "swami," even when used to describe a native of Brooklyn practicing in southern California, has Indian connotations, so "magus" continued far into Roman times to carry a suggestion of Persian prestige.

IV

Nevertheless, the friends of a higher class practitioner would be apt to claim that he was not a magus, but rather, a "divine man." The "divine man" was a god or demon in disguise, moving about the world in an apparently human body. He could do all the beneficent things a magus could, and he could also curse effectively—though of course he would curse only the wicked. He did his miracles by his indwelling divine power and therefore did not need rituals or spells. This was the critical test by which a divine man could be distinguished from a magician—so at least his adherents would argue. The magical papyri describe a number of rites by which one can obtain a spirit as a constant companion. A magician who has such a spirit at his service can also dispense with rites and spells, he need only give his orders and they will be obeyed. Moreover, there were some magical rites that were supposed to deify the magician, either by joining him with some god in a permanent and perfect union (as Paul claimed to be joined with Jesus), or by changing the form, nature, or power of his soul so as to make it divine. A magician who had been so deified would thereafter be a divine man and would perform miracles by his own power, not by a spirit's. While the theoretical differences between magus and divine man were thus blurred, there remained important practical differences. The term "divine man" carried none of the unpleasant connotations attached to "magus"—nothing of membership in a secret society, incest, worship of evil demons, human and other repulsive sacrifices, cannibalism, or barbarism. Consequently—and best of all —it did not make the man who bore it a criminal.

Fortunately we have a full length account of one divine man, Apollonius of Tyana, who was probably a younger contemporary of Jesus, though he outlived him by a long time. Even better, we have a Christian's attack on Apollonius, an attempt to prove him a magician, that parallels Celsus' attack on Jesus. These we shall discuss in the next chapter and they will adequately illustrate the ancient notion of the divine man.

V

In contrast to such exalted daydreams, the definition of "magician" implied in Roman law was dreadfully down to earth, though surprisingly vague. The decisive criterion seems to have been common opinion. As in Greece, the law on poisoning also covered maleficent magical acts. The formulation it was given in the legal revision of 82–81 B.C. remained valid to A.D. 529. We do not have the exact wording, but the commentary attributed to the jurist Paulus, who worked in the early 200s, reads as follows:

Any who perform, or procure the performance of, impious or nocturnal sacrifices, to enchant, curse, or bind anyone with a spell, are either crucified or thrown to the beasts ⟨in the arena⟩. Any who sacrifice a man, or make offerings of his blood, or pollute a shrine or temple are thrown to the beasts or, if people of position, are beheaded. It is the prevailing legal opinion that participants in the magical art should be subject to the extreme punishment, that is, either thrown to the beasts or crucified; but the magicians themselves should be burned alive. It is not permitted for anyone to have in his possession books of the magic art. If they are found in anyone's possession, when his property has been expropriated and the books burned publicly, he is to be deported to an island, or, if he is of the lower class, beheaded. Not only the practice of this art, but even the knowledge of it, is prohibited.

This is obviously a collection of several opinions. How many were prior to Paulus and collected by him? How many were added to his text before it was declared authoritative by Constantine about 327? In any event, the passage is evidence for an extension of the criminality of magic from specific noxious acts to the whole of "the magic art" (*ars magica*) that now appears for the first time as a recognized legal concept. Nevertheless, even in Paulus' time this "magic art" did not contain everything we should now regard as "magic". Its extension was probably limited by the persistent Persian connotations of the term *mageia*. In any case, we find other opinions that treat of actions we commonly think magical, but say nothing of "magic." A good example is Paulus', "On prophets and astrologers" which runs as follows:

Prophets who pretend that they are filled with the god are to be expelled from the city to the end that public good behavior should not be corrupted by human credulity for the hope of some promised event, or, in any case, that the peoples' minds should not be disturbed by this. Therefore, they are first lashed, ⟨then⟩ expelled from the city. But if they persist, they are thrown into public prison, or deported to an island, or, at all events, sent elsewhere. Those who introduce new sects or religious observances unknown to reasonable men, things by which peoples' minds might be disturbed, are to be deported if upper class, executed if lower. Anyone who consults astrologers, soothsayers, readers of entrails, or diviners about the life expectancy of the emperor, or the stability of the government, is to be executed, as is the one who gives the response. One had better avoid not only ⟨the act of⟩ divination, but the science itself, and its books. But if slaves consult about the life expectancy of their masters, they are to be subjected to the extreme penalty, that is, the cross. And any persons consulted ⟨by them for this purpose⟩, if they give answers, shall be either condemned to the mines or banished to an island.

The uncertainty as to the definition of "magic" resulted from the variety of purposes and practices covered by the Roman legal term. This was shown by the embarrassment of the imperial legislators when they had to recognize the universal use of spells and amulets in medicine and agriculture. Constantine unhesitatingly sacrificed consistency to convenience in a ruling issued about 318:

If any are discovered to have been using magic arts so as to threaten men's safety or pervert modest persons to libidinous practices, their science is to be punished and deservedly penalized according to the severest laws. However, no accusations are to be heard against remedies sought out for human bodies or, in rural districts, to protect the mature grapes from fear of rains or from being crushed by the pounding of hailstones.

This is almost a return to the old position that only harmful acts were to be punished. Nevertheless, the reversal was soon reversed. Within fifty years even an old woman's singing charms to cure fever, or a young man's recitation of the seven vowels as a remedy for stomach trouble, would be punished by death.

VI

The figures thus far discussed —*goes,* magus, divine man—were familiar in the Greco-Roman and Persian sides of the Palestinian culture of Jesus' time. If we look at the Semitic side we see a somewhat different picture. In the centuries following Jesus' lifetime magic continued to be closely associated with madness. The rabbis define "a madman" as "one who goes out by night alone and spends the night in a graveyard and tears his clothes and destroys whatever is given him," and they note that this condition may occur in transient fits; they also distinguish between such a madman and a magician who "spends the night in a graveyard so that an unclean spirit will come upon him." The distinction was however a matter of dispute, and the dispute probably reflected common uncertainty as to whether one who "had a spirit" was possessor or possessed.

We have met this uncertainty before in the gospels, where the opponents' charges that Jesus "had" a demon seemed sometimes to mean that he was himself possessed, sometimes that he had control of a demon and could make it do miracles (above, pp. 32, 47f.). This alternation of meanings may be a sign that the tradition, in this respect, is accurate, since a corresponding alternation of states is actually observed in primitive magicians. Thus Eliade, describing shamanism, writes,

The Yakut shaman's power and prestige derive exclusively from his capacity for ecstasy . . . just as in the case of the Altaic shamans. . . . It is . . . to his mystical capacities that the shaman owes his ability to discover and combat the evil spirits that have seized the patient's soul; he does not confine himself to exorcising them, he takes them into his own body, "possesses" them, tortures and expels them. All this because he shares their nature, that is, he is free to leave his body, to transport himself to great distances, to descend to the underworld, to scale the sky, and so on. This "spiritual" mobility and freedom, which are fostered by the shaman's ecstatic experiences, at the same time make him vulnerable, and frequently, through his constant struggling with evil spirits, he falls into their power, that is, he ends by being really "possessed."

Another difference of opinion that appeared in the gospels may also be explicable from Semitic material. We saw in chapter 3 that the identification of Jesus with the Baptist indicated that some people thought he had practiced necromancy and so got control of the Baptist's spirit. On the other hand, the Beelzebul stories and their like suppose his demon was not that of a dead man, but an independent supernatural power. A third interpretation is reflected in the miracle stories in most of which there is no mention of any spirit; the miracles are done by Jesus himself, by his own divine power. Like God at creation, he simply commands and things happen. Whoever shaped these stories thought him a god. Yet these three implicit opinions (necromancy, control of a demon, divine nature) are presented side by side. A similar confusion appears in the Old Testament passages that refer to the *ba'al 'ob*, the "master of a divining spirit." The *'obot* (plural of *'ob*) are a mysterious class of beings, commonly said to be "spirits of the dead," but probably some sort of underworld deities. Although they are in the realm of the dead, and speak from the earth in whispering voices (Isaiah 8.19; 29.4), they are associated with deities and are referred to as objects of worship to whom Israelites sometimes turn, abandoning Yahweh. These *'obot* can enter men and live in them, evidently for a long time, so that the man possessed is known as "one who has an *'ob*" (I Sam. 28.7), more specifically, "one who has in him an *'ob*." The priestly law said such persons were to be stoned (Lev. 20.27). The most famous of them is "the witch of Endor" to whom King Saul went when Yahweh refused to speak to him (I Sam. 28.8). Saul said to her, "Do magic for me with the *'ob* and bring up ⟨the spirit of⟩ the man I shall name." Evidently her permanent, personal *'ob* was not the same as the spirit who was to be brought up just this once.

The witch assented to Saul's request. When he told her to call up Samuel she did so forthwith. Apparently, one who had an *'ob* could command spirits of the dead without any extended ritual, but the silence of the story on this point may be due to artistic economy and cannot be trusted as an account of what the storyteller thought would have happened (let alone what actually would have happened had the meeting ever occurred). As the story stands, the similarity to what was believed of Jesus is striking, but so is the difference. Jesus' power during his lifetime is connected with the dead only by his identification with the executed Baptist, that is, with the demon of a dead man, not with an underworld deity. Perhaps the distinction should not be pressed. The *'obot* were enough like spirits of the dead to mislead most lexicographers, but they were classed with gods by Leviticus and Isaiah, and the witch of Endor, when she saw Samuel's spirit, said, "I see ⟨a⟩ god rising from the earth." Thus, if Jesus was believed to have either an *'ob* or the spirit of a dead man, he might have been thought to have or be a kind of divinity. Belief in *'obot* or similar powers seems to have lived on in Palestine to at least the third century A.D., when it is attested by some of the rabbinic passages with which this section began.

("The man who has a spirit," or his equivalent, is a figure who appears in most societies and is differently identified in many, according to the categories available. In ancient Israel the most important of such persons had been identified as "prophets." By Jesus' time the Jewish upper classes had long ceased to take living prophets seriously, but persons believed by the lower classes to be prophets continued to appear and, as the gospels report, Jesus was one of them. The identification is not strictly germane to this chapter, of which the purpose is to describe the various notions of "magician" that were current in first-century Palestine so as to show what may have been meant by the charge that Jesus was a magician. However, "false prophet" and "magician" were often used almost as synonyms. Prophecy, conceived as foretelling the future, was one of the main goals of magic, and prophets were thought to do miracles of the sorts magicians claimed to perform. Consequently, the question of Jesus' relation to the legendary Israelite prophets would have some relevance here. However, it would interrupt the argument for too long a time. It is therefore relegated to Appendix B. We return to the magicians.)

The most prestigious magical figure from the Jewish legends of Jesus' time was Solomon, son of David, King of Israel and great master of the demons. Solomon's control of demons was a matter of pride for Josephus (*Antiquities* VIII. 45–49), is often reported in Rabbinic literature, and is the subject of a romance preserved in several Greek versions, *The Testament of Solomon*. In this romance he has one demon who serves as his agent to introduce and direct the others; a similar figure, though with a different name, appears in some of the rabbinic stories (e.g., *B. Gittin* 68a–b). Solomon's control of the demons was due to his possession of an amulet, the famous seal engraved with the secret name of Yahweh. In the romance this seal was given him by "the Lord, the highest god, Sabaoth." Ancient amulets bearing divine titles, including these three and various Greek forms of Yahweh, are well known. A Jewish exorcist who demonstrated his powers before the emperor Vespasian used one of these seals and backed it up with a herb prescribed by Solomon, and spells written by him (Josephus, *Antiquities* VIII.46ff.). Solomon had meanwhile been made the author of a whole literature of forgeries. The legend also took advantage of the Biblical reports of Solomon's corruption by his wives to make him fall into the power of the demons (the alternation of possessor and possessed that has been noticed above.) None of these developments had any adequate basis in the Old Testament reports about the real ruler. Therefore, it is clear that by Jesus' time the Solomon legend had been shaped by popular stories about magicians' powers and to some extent by knowledge of actual magicians, their practices and their perils. This illustrates the importance of magic in Jesus' environment and helps to explain why Jesus' powers were similarly interpreted. Moreover, that Solomon was not only a magician, but also King of Israel and son of David, may have helped some of those who thought Jesus a magician to believe that he might also be the Messiah, the promised son of David and King of Israel. Those of his followers who did think him the Messiah could easily draw on the Solomon legend to justify his dealings with demons, and to extend the story of his powers. Conversely, as time went on, the notion of Solomon as ancestor and antecedent of Jesus led Christians to attribute to him miracles taken from Jesus' repertory. Precision about this give-and-take relationship is made difficult by the relative lack of evidence for the content, in Jesus' lifetime, of the legend about Solomon's magical powers. However, the fact of the relationship is important as evidence that even in Jewish priestly circles of the first century like those of Josephus, to be thought a magician was not necessarily discreditable, and in other Jewish circles it might be taken as a messianic trait.

IN CONCLUSION: We have now seen some of the notions of magicians that were current in first-century Palestine—*goes,* magus, divine man, *ba'al 'ob,* (false) prophet, and Solomonic ruler. These were not the whole troupe. Chaldeans have been mentioned only in passing. Nothing has been said of Egyptian magicians because very little is known of them in this period, but they were plentiful and of great repute. What if the story that Jesus learned his magic in Egypt should happen to be true? At any rate, we must beware of supposing that the figures reviewed exhaust the range of possibilities. Moreover, now that these figures have been distinguished, it must be added that they were generally confused. In common usage the lines between *goes*, magus, and divine man shifted according to the sympathies of the speaker. The same is true for the distinction between true and false prophets and the Greek translations that might be chosen for *ba'al 'ob*. Therefore, we cannot make an exact list of traits that always characterized any one of these types. We must again look at particular cases, especially that of Jesus, and try to see what points were actually alleged as evidence for the charge of magic.

～6～

The Marks of a Magician

I

What then were the marks of a magician? First of all, he had to do miracles. He was primarily a miracle worker. In the synoptic gospels it is Jesus' exorcisms that lead the scribes to say, "He has/is Beelzebul," and, "He casts out demons by the ruler of the demons." This was apparently the charge answered by Quadratus (though we have only his reply to it) and was the point of departure for the real opponents of Justin, as it was for his imaginary Trypho. It was certainly fundamental in Celsus' explanation of Jesus' career: "Having been brought up in obscurity, he went as a hired laborer to Egypt and there acquired experience of some ⟨magical⟩ powers. Thence he returned, proclaiming himself a god on account of these powers." "Powers," in Greek means both the powers and the miracles done by them.

Celsus' statement clarifies the connections between Jesus' claim to divinity and his miracles and the charge of magic brought against him by his enemies. This connection can already be seen in Justin who makes his opponent say, "Why is it not possible that your so-called Christ, being ⟨actually⟩ a human ⟨born⟩ of humans, did what we call "powers" by magical skill, and *on account of this* was thought to be a son of a god?" Thus, in popular thought "son of god" and "magician" are alternative titles for the miracle man. This is why in the synoptics, the title "Son of God" is almost always used in connection with miracles, and in the fourth gospel Jesus' claims to be from God, and to be able to die and come to life again, and to make his followers immortal are met with the charge, "you have a demon." In Jn. 8.48 this is expanded: "You are a Samaritan and have a demon." Why a Samaritan? Because in Samaria there was a famous miracle worker, Simon, still remembered as "Simon *Magus*," which means "Simon the magician." Simon like Jesus was thought to "be" or "have" a "great power of God." He had some sort of connection with Jesus—perhaps they had both been disciples of the Baptist—and he had an enormous success both in Samaria and in Rome. When the gospel of John was written he was the outstanding example of the miracle working magician who claimed to be a god, so John made the Jews reply to Jesus' claims of deity and miraculous powers with the accusation, "You are a Samaritan ⟨like Simon the magician⟩ and ⟨like him⟩ have a demon."

Even when not directly connected with miracles the claim to be divine is, by itself, taken as evidence that he was a magician, and it is by virtue of this latent claim that charges against his life and teaching are also taken as evidence of magic. "Impiety," "shameful" or "harmful teachings," infamous life and shameful death would not of themselves be grounds—as Celsus makes them—for the charge of practicing magic; they become so primarily because they refute the claim of divinity (the alternative explanation of the miracles), and secondarily because they locate Jesus in the society of vagabonds, quacks and criminals to which magicians—especially *goetes*—were supposed to belong.

Some more specific evidence for connection with the magi may have been found in the tradition reported by Celsus that Jesus and his followers taught a sort of dualism,

. . . making some sort of opponent to God and calling this ⟨opponent⟩ "devil" and, in Hebrew, "Satan." . . . so that when the greatest God wants to help men in some way, he has this being who works against him and he is not able ⟨to carry out his plan⟩. Likewise the Son of God is defeated by the devil and, by him, made to suffer, and teaches us to be contemptuous of the sufferings that the devil inflicts. ⟨Moreover,⟩ he ⟨Jesus⟩ foretells that Satan himself, appearing in the same way ⟨as Jesus⟩, will perform great and marvelous works ⟨miracles⟩ and claim for himself the glory due to God. But we should not be deceived by these ⟨miracles⟩ nor desire to turn away to Satan, but should believe in him ⟨Jesus⟩ alone. These ⟨Celsus says⟩ are obviously the teachings of a man who is a *goes,* a trickster trying to discredit in advance his rival claimants and rival beggars.

Celsus had good information; his picture of the Antichrist is paralleled in Paul but is not characteristically Pauline; Paul probably got it from even earlier tradition. Moreover, it is typical of early Christianity in representing the Antichrist as a miracle worker, an evil magician, vis à vis Christ. This antithesis, and also the eschatological expectations and the role of Satan as opponent of God, recall the teachings of the magi as reported by Plutarch; but if Celsus made this point, Origen was too wise to try to refute it.

A more damaging point that Origen had to counter was the similarity of Jesus' miracles to those of the common, lower-class magicians. He says Celsus reviews the stories about Jesus,

. . . and immediately puts them on a level with the works of the *goetes* on the grounds that they too promise marvelous things, and with the tricks done by those who have learned from Egyptians, who sell their revered teachings in the middle of the market for a few obols, and drive demons out of people and blow away diseases and call up spirits of ⟨long dead⟩ heroes and produce appearances of expensive dinners, ⟨complete with⟩ tables and pastry and non-existent entrées, and make objects not really alive move as if alive and seem to be so, as far as appearance goes. And he says, "Then, since these fellows do these things, will you ask us to think them sons of God? Should it not rather be said that these are the doings of scoundrels possessed of evil demons."

Notice again the implication that Jesus' claim to be a son of a god was based on his miracles. Origen tries to evade this in his reply. He says,

You see that by these ⟨arguments Celsus⟩ practically grants that magic ⟨*mageia*⟩ is ⟨effective⟩. . . . And the things told of Jesus would be similar ⟨to those done by the magicians!⟩ if ⟨Celsus⟩ had first shown ⟨that Jesus⟩ did them as the magicians ⟨do⟩, merely for the sake of showing off ⟨his powers⟩. But as things are, none of the *goetes*, by the things he does, calls the spectators to moral reformation, or teaches the fear of God to those astounded by the show.

This argument attracts our attention to an interesting fact—that the miracle stories in the synoptics are *not* usually connected with Jesus' teaching, and when they are, the connections are usually secondary. Evidently the traditions were originally separate; this suggests that the activities were.

Other Christians, forced like Origen to concede that Jesus' miracles resembled those of other magicians, found other claims to distinguish them: Jesus' miracles and those of his disciples were real, the others' only appearances; permanent, the others' did not last; not done like the others', by trickery, spells, or invocation of demons; not idle shows, but helpful to men, yet performed gratis; greater than the others' and confirmed by the greatest miracle of all, his resurrection from the dead; foretold by the prophets, as was his whole career; the cause of innumerable conversions, they brought into being the new nation of his disciples who still perform similar miracles—even resurrections!—by the mere invocation of his name. These arguments to prove Jesus was not a magician enable us to reconstruct, by reversing them, the concept of "magician" they imply: a miracle worker whose wonders are illusory, transient, produced by tricks or by the help of demons controlled by spells, sacrifices, and magical paraphernalia. Such a man is primarily an entertainer whose feats are trivial, performed for money, and of no practical value. He is not a figure in any respectable religious tradition; no prophets foretold him, no converts follow him; he has no message and no disciples, but at most a spiel and an apprentice.

This figure is easy to imagine and completely credible; there must have been many such marketplace magicians in the ancient world and any traits of this picture in the tradition about Jesus served the purpose of his opponents. The picture is however a caricature. It represents only the lowest type of ancient magician. We have seen other types; the word covered a social range that ran from guttersnipes to the teachers of Nero. This range could accomodate men attached to major religious traditions—the primary reference of *magos* was to such men. Since the magi had distinctive ethical and eschatological teachings, the fact that Jesus had similar teachings would not have prevented his being thought a magus. He certainly had disciples, and those who accused him of being a magician must have known this; therefore, by "magician" they meant a figure who could appear as a teacher and attract a following. The Christians attempted to refute the accusation by reducing "magician" to its lowest possible meaning and arguing that *this meaning* did not match Jesus. By this maneuver they misrepresented the sense of the accusation. Why? Perhaps because, properly understood, it would have seemed true. What then was its proper sense? What evidence did Jesus' contemporaries have in mind when they declared him a "magician"?

II

Fortunately we can control and complete the Christian material on this question with a similar case in which we know something of both sides.

Apollonius of Tyana was born of a well-to-do Greek family in the south-central Anatolian town of which his name preserves the memory. His parents sent him for higher education to the Greek city of Tarsus on the south coast about the same time as the Jewish parents of Paul, in Tarsus, sent their boy to Jerusalem for his education. Both boys came down with incurable religiosity: Paul first became a Pharisee and then was converted to Christianity; Apollonius became a Pythagorean (a holier-than-thou, ascetic, vegetarian type) and after some years set out for Babylon where he studied with the magi, and then for India to find the Brahmans and learn their teachings. He came back claiming to have done so, formed a circle of disciples, and lived with them as an itinerant philosopher, holy man, and miracle worker, going from temple to temple along the coasts of northern Syria, Anatolia, and Greece, where Paul, shortly before, had gone from synagogue to synagogue. From Greece, in the last years of Nero, Apollonius went to Rome (where Paul had already been executed). A brush with the police may have persuaded him to push on to Spain where one of the Roman governors was plotting a revolt. After the revolt and Nero's suicide in 68 he returned to Sicily and Greece, then visited Alexandria where in 69 he is said to have been consulted by Vespasian at the beginning of his revolt. Vespasian went to Rome, Apollonius to the "naked sages" in upper Egypt, a community of ascetics with pretensions to supernatural powers. Thence he returned to the eastern Mediterranean where he continued his itinerant life until 93 when he went to Rome to face charges of magic and sedition; he was accused of having sacrificed a Greek boy to divine from his entrails the fate of a conspiracy to kill the emperor Domitian. He reportedly vanished from the courtroom in Rome, returned to Greece, and continued his life there and in Asia Minor undisturbed until his death—some said, his ascent to heaven—shortly after Domitian's assassination in 96. He is also said to have appeared after his ascension or death to a young man who did not believe his teachings.

Like Jesus, Apollonius is a figure of indubitable historicity. He is referred to and cited by classical and Christian authors; fragments of his treatise on sacrifices and his letters have been preserved; the main outlines of his life, as sketched above, are not seriously questioned in spite of their legendary elements. Whether or not he reached the Brahmans, what ascetics he found in upper Egypt, how he escaped from his trial, and how he died will always be dubious, but his figure and general career are known.

The historical similarities between Apollonius and Jesus are clear: both were itinerant miracle workers and preachers, rejected at first by their townspeople and brothers, though the latter eventually became more favorable. An inner circle of devoted disciples accompanied each. Both were credited with prophecies, exorcisms, cures, and an occasional raising of the dead. As preachers both made severe moral demands on their hearers. Both affected epigrammatic utterances and oracular style; they taught as if with authority and came into conflict with the established clergy of the temples they visited and tried to reform. Both were charged with sedition and magic but tried primarily for sedition.

Given these basic historical similarities, it is not surprising that similar opinions and legends grew up about the two of them. Both were said to have been fathered by gods and to have been amazingly precocious youths. Both at early stages in their careers went off into the wilderness and there encountered and worsted demons. The similarities between their reputed miracles have already been mentioned. At the ends of their lives, Apollonius escaped miraculously from his trial; Jesus, executed, rose miraculously from the dead; both then lived for some time with their disciples, were said finally to have ascended to heaven, and were credited with subsequent appearances, even to unbelievers.

Most important for our present purposes are the facts that both were believed by their followers to be sons of gods, beings of supernatural power, and both were accused by their enemies of being magicians. For Apollonius, as for Jesus, most of our information comes from his believers and is preserved in documents put together some generations after his death. The preserved *Life of*

Apollonius was written by one Flavius Philostratus at the behest of the empress Julia Domna in the early years of the third century and was completed only after her death in 217.

Philostratus tells us he got his information from the cities and temples where Apollonius had worked—presumably these were centers of oral tradition—from Apollonius' own letters and his will, and from earlier works about him of which he mentions three. One, by Moiragenes, otherwise unknown, represented Apollonius as a magician; Philostratus says no attention should be paid to this since Moiragenes was ignorant of many of the facts about Apollonius. A second work was by Maximus of Aegae, a little town east of Tarsus. Apollonius spent some years in Aegae at the beginning of his career and Maximus' work seems to have dealt mainly with the events of these years. The third work was a record kept by Damis of Nineveh, Apollonius' most faithful disciple, who became his follower when he set out to visit the Brahmans and stayed with him almost until his death. He was Apollonius' Boswell but his work remained unknown until a *soi disant* relative brought it to the empress. We can be sure he was well rewarded; Julia's son, the emperor Caracalla, worshiped Apollonius as a hero, financed his shrine at Tyana and built him a temple. We may suspect Damis' "relative" had concocted the "memoirs" to interest these imperial patrons: Apollonius was a hero of the Pythagoreans who produced many literary forgeries, and the travel stories that Philostratus got from "Damis" are full of fantasies that resemble Pythagorean fictions. But this does not prove they were pure fabrications. Apollonius undoubtedly had disciples whose stories about him survived in Pythagorean circles; pseudo-Damis may also have used some documents; indeed, it would be surprising if he had not.

Thus, the *Life of Apollonius* presents a literary problem much like that of the gospels. It also resembles them in literary form—after praise of the hero's family and legends about his birth, his childhood is almost wholly passed over and his adult life is presented in a series of anecdotes connected merely by a geographic frame (references to his travelling and the places where this or that happened); the narrative becomes more coherent towards the end of the life with trial, escape, and later adventures, only to blur again when it comes to the death and subsequent appearances. These similarities add weight to another: like the gospels the *Life* is in part an apologetic work, written not only to glorify its hero, but also to defend him against the charge of practicing magic.

On this point Philostratus is explicit (*Life* I.2), and he indicates some of the reasons for which Apollonius was thought a magician. First, because he had lived with the magi in Babylonia, the Brahmans in India, and the "naked sages" in Egypt. Second, because he foresaw and foretold many things; this gave him the reputation of being "wise in supernatural things." This referred primarily to his ability to interpret prodigies, but the other miracles with which he was credited, particularly his ability to recognize and exorcise demons, must have been major causes for the belief in his magical powers. Whether the sexual irregularities of which he was accused had anything to do with the charge of magic is not clear. The hierophant at Eleusis who refused to initiate him is said to have called him a *goes* and "a man impure as to supernatural things," without further explanation; the former charge, similarly unexplained, is attributed to the priests at the oracle of Trophonius, and to the watchmen of the temple of Dictynna in Crete. The accusation brought against him before Domitian was specific: he had sacrificed a boy in a magic rite to read in his entrails the future of the plot against the emperor. His eccentricities in dress and diet—long hair, linen garments, vegetarianism, etc. —and the fact that some people worshipped him as a god, were also alleged, as was his giving of oracles.

Some further characteristics of magicians are indicated by the things Philostratus, in trying to clear his hero of the charge of magic, insists that Apollonius did *not* do, thereby telling us that magicians were thought to do them. He would not sacrifice living creatures nor even be present when they were sacrificed (*Life* I.31; VIII.vii.12 end). When he called up the soul of Achilles from the dead, it was not by the Homeric sacrifices standard in necromancy, but by pure prayers (IV.16). He commanded demons as he would evil men, solely by his spiritual authority (IV.44). The accusation of magic brought against him by the philosopher Euphrates was a slander consequent on his exposure of Euphrates' avarice, and the fact that Euphrates did not strike him when they quarreled was not due to his magical skill, but to Euphrates' last minute self-control. That the owner of a ship carrying statues of the gods refused to take him aboard was not due to his reputation as impure or ill-omened, but to the man's superstition; most people wanted to ship with Apollonius because they thought his presence would prevent storms and assure safe passage (V.20 vs. IV.13). He is contrasted with the Egyptians and Chaldaeans who went about the cities organizing expensive sacrifices to avert earthquakes and the like—he got the desired results with cheaper offerings (VI.41). Unlike magicians he was not out for money, or fame—when he stopped the plague in Ephesus he gave the credit to Hercules the Averter (VIII. vii.9). Unlike magicians he did his miracles without sacrifices, prayers, or spells—by the power of his own divine nature (VII.38 end). Finally, he had official approval; he was consulted by the emperor Vespasian who would never have consulted a magician (VIII.vii.2).

III

If we think of Philostratus' *Life of Apollonius* as the "gospel" of that Pythagorean cult of him which won the backing of Julia and Caracalla, we may

now look at the "outsiders" opinions about him, as we did at those about Jesus.
(The ones reported by Philostratus we have already considered.)

Lucian who about 165 cast Peregrinus as a Christian, presented another
pretentious fraud—a fellow named Alexander—as a disciple of a friend of
Apollonius. In passing, he treated Apollonius' circle much more roughly than
he did the Christians. He wrote (*Alexander* 5):

When Alexander was yet a boy and very beautiful . . . he was an uninhibited whore
and went for pay with any who wanted him. Among the others, one lover who had him
was a *goes* of those who claim to use magic and supernatural incantations to secure
favors in love affairs and send ⟨evil spirits⟩ on enemies and turn up treasures and secure
bequests. This fellow, seeing a well grown boy more than ready to be serviceable in his
affairs, and in love with his rascality not less than he himself was with the boy's beauty,
gave him a thorough training and continually used him as helper, servant and assistant. He ⟨the *goes*⟩ himself in public passed as a doctor and knew . . . ⟨to quote a
Homeric verse⟩ "Many good compounds of drugs—and many bad." Of all these skills,
Alexander became heir and legatee. Moreover, this teacher and lover was a native of
Tyana who had been one of those associated with the notorious Apollonius of Tyana
and a party to all his pretentious performance. You see the sort of school from which
the man I am describing ⟨came⟩.

The man he was describing, Alexander, passed himself off as a prophet inspired
by the god Asclepius-Glycon and started a famous oracle and mystery cult of
this god.

At the beginning of the third century when Philostratus was writing in
Apollonius' defense, the historian Dio Cassius told as the greatest of marvels
the story of how Apollonius in Asia Minor saw the murder of Domitian in
Rome while it occurred, and cheered the murderer on. Yet ten books later Dio
says of the emperor Caracalla, "He was so fond of magicians and *goetes* that he
even praised and honored Apollonius the Cappadocian, who flourished in
Domitian's time and was a *goes* and *magos* in the strict sense of the words. Yet
Caracalla built a temple for ⟨those who worshipped⟩ him as a hero."

After Philostratus' time however Apollonius' reputation improved. The
Severan dynasty probably continued its support of his cult; about 230 the
emperor Alexander Severus is said to have had in his private chapel statues of
"deified emperors, but also chosen, outstanding, and holy men, among whom
was Apollonius and, according to a writer of his time, Christ, Abraham,
Orpheus, and suchlike." Origen, writing after 245, thought Apollonius both
magus and philosopher and referred to his ability to win over distinguished
philosophers, who at first had thought him a *goes,* as proof that philosophy gave
no security against the power of magic (Christianity did). In the latter half of
the century the philosopher Porphyry, in his *Life of Pythagoras,* cited Apollonius as authority for a number of details—among others, that Pythagoras

was the natural son of the god Apollo (chapter 2). Porphyry also seems to have been the first to compare Apollonius and Jesus, presumably to Jesus' disadvantage: Apollonius, like Jesus, did miracles, but when arrested he neither stood dumb nor submitted himself to indignities, but lectured the emperor as a philosopher should, and then vanished.

Philosophic patronage did not suffice to rescue Apollonius from the magical tradition. Like Jesus he was remembered by magicians as a magician. A magical papyrus (*PGM* XIa) preserves directions to secure the services of the demon thought to have served him. To the end of the Middle Ages he was credited with the preparation of many "talismans"—objects of permanent magical power to protect a city or frontier from a specified peril. Nevertheless, Porphyry's influence prevailed in literary circles. By the end of the third century an epic poet had done a *Life of Apollonius,* and about 304 a high imperial official, Sossianus Hierocles, wrote an attack on Christianity in which he included a comparison between Apollonius and Jesus as basis for the argument that the pagans, who in spite of Apollonius' miracles revered him merely as a man pleasing to the gods, were more sensible than the Christians, who because of Jesus' miracles thought him a god.

After Christianity triumphed Hierocles' work was destroyed, but we know something of it from replies that it drew from two Christians — Lactantius, a professor of Latin rhetoric, and Eusebius, Archbishop of Caesarea in Palestine, the famous Church historian. Both replies attacked Apollonius as a magician and tried to defend Jesus from the same charge; they necessarily appeal to the popular criteria and thereby clarify them.

Lactantius, being a rhetorician, did not add much to the intellectual content of the case. He argues that "⟨If you say⟩ Christ was a magician because he did miracles, then Apollonius was a more capable ⟨magician⟩" because he escaped, but Christ was caught and crucified (*Div. Inst.* V.3.9). Again, because Apollonius was a mere magus he could not persuade men to worship him under his own name; the best he could get was identification with "Herakles, the averter of evil," but Jesus, since he was not a magus but a god, was worshiped accordingly. Finally,

. . .we do not think ⟨Jesus⟩ a god because he did miracles, but because we see that in him have been fulfilled all those things which were announced to us by the divination of the prophets. So he did miracles? We should have thought him a magus, as you now think and as the Jews thought in his lifetime, had not all the prophets with one spirit predicted that he was to do these very miracles. Therefore, his marvelous deeds and works do no more to make us think him a god than does that very cross . . . because it too was prophesied at the same time. Not therefore from his own testimony—for who can be believed if he speaks about himself—but from the testimony of the prophets . . . has he won credence for his divinity, a testimony that . . . can never be given to Apollonius or to Apuleius or to any of the magi.

Eusebius was more thorough. He replied to Hierocles in a long pamphlet, first accusing him of plagiarism from Celsus (chapter 1), then briefly arguing for the incomparable superiority of Jesus to Apollonius—Jesus had been prophesied, had won more, more devoted and more devout followers, had ultimately converted the Roman empire, and was still effective in exorcism (chapter 4). From this preface Eusebius went on to lay down the following set of dogmas: The natural limits of human powers are providentially fixed; therefore, no man can do miracles. Admittedly, to help men the supreme god might send one of his closest companions as a "divine" messenger in human disguise but with supernatural powers. Such a messenger, however, would stir up the whole human race and enlighten the entire world. Apollonius did not do so; therefore, he was not such a messenger; therefore, he could not do miracles; therefore, if he did not pretend to do miracles he may have been a philosopher, but if he did pretend to, he was a *goes*—a fraud (chapters 5–7). Eusebius himself pretends that he would prefer to think Apollonius a virtuous philosopher (chapter 5), but then goes through Philostratus' *Life of Apollonius* and picks out the details he thinks useful to prove either Philostratus a liar or Apollonius a *goes*—now in the sense of *magician*.

The inconsistency was deliberate. Apollonius was a man of high reputation in some philosophic circles and honored by a cult that had enjoyed imperial patronage. He could not be dismissed in the way Celsus had dismissed Jesus—as a mere streetcorner magician, nor could his claim of divinity (or the claim his followers made for him) be taken out of hand as evidence that he was a magician (as Celsus had taken the similar claim in Jesus' case). Apollonius had behind him the philosophic tradition of "divine men," a tradition supported, for instance, by legends about Pythagoras. Moreover, Apollonius came too close to Jesus for comfort. Eusebius had to admit the possibility that a supernatural being might appear in human form; he could only take refuge in the argument outlined above, that one who did appear would attract the attention of the whole world.

On this shaky argument he based his initial alternative: *either* a philosopher with no supernatural claims *or* a fraud. "Magician" was carefully omitted from consideration—it also came too close to home; to present it as a third possibility would evoke the common opinion of Jesus and almost demand a damaging comparison. On the other hand it was too plausible an explanation to be omitted; indeed, Eusebius himself almost certainly thought it the correct one. Despite his philosophic talk about the natural limits of *human* powers he of course believed, like everyone else, that magicians could get the assistance of demons and make the demons use their supernatural powers for the magicians' purposes. His problem was to introduce this explanation without spoiling his fine initial antithesis between Jesus, the world-shaking, divine messenger from the heavens, and all mere men of merely human powers. He solved the problem by taking advantage of the ambiguity of *goes:* "fraud"/"magician." Beginning with the antithesis, Apollonius was either a misrepresented philosopher or a deliberate *goes* (= fraud), he introduced little by little the evidence to prove him a *goes* (= magician) and quietly dropped Jesus out of the picture.

Consequently he has a double set of criteria to prove Apollonius a magician. One group are those that prove him a mere man: inconsistency, ignorance, the fact that he did no miracles before visiting the Brahmans, and his use of flattery and deception. These merely disprove the claim that he was of divine nature and therefore necessitate some other explanation for his miracles. The other group are those that actually indicate magical practice: the use of uncanny materials for unnatural purposes, association and studies with *goetes* and magi, recognition and control of demons, necromancy, charges of magic made by his contemporaries, predictions, cures, other miracles, the attribution to him of magical devices, and the fact that he was especially accused of magic while others who had studied with eastern sages were not.

IV

If we now compare the criteria used for the charge of magic by the opponents of Apollonius and those of Jesus, and against it, by their defenders, basic similarities and particular differences become clear. Fundamental for the accusation in both cases are the miracles with which the accused are credited and the fact that many of these miracles—notably exorcisms, cures, predictions—resemble those of common magicians. A second major grievance was the claim of divinity, or at least the fact of being thought divine. Although Eusebius could not make much of this, he, like the other opponents of Apollonius and of Jesus, gave close attention to those traits in the character and career of the accused that disproved the claim of divinity and therefore necessitated some less favorable explanation of the miracles. For this the opponents of Jesus could use the major facts of his career: disreputable origin, life as a vagabond, violation of the law, lower-class associates, legal condemnation and crucifixion. Nothing like these was available to the opponents of Apollonius. (Domitian was remembered as a tyrant; to have been jailed by him was creditable.) Therefore, they had to do what they could with minor details unworthy of a deity—ignorance, inconsistency, flattery, deception, and stories of early sexual irregularities. To support their attacks both sides fell back on common report—both Apollonius and Jesus had been accused of magic by their contemporaries, therefore the charges were true. In both cases they were supported by claims that the accused had studied with magicians: Jesus had gone to

Egypt and learned his magic there; Apollonius not only to Egypt, but also to Babylon and India to learn of the magi and the Brahmans. Apollonius' ascetic practices and eccentric dress were made grounds for additional charges against him; no such traits are reported of Jesus, but his ordinary manner of life, neglect of fasting, and fondness for food and drink were used to discredit his claim to supernatural powers.

To these similar charges the defenders of both Apollonius and Jesus made similar replies. They asserted that their heroes were truly divine, and to support these assertions they tried to distinguish their deities from magicians. Magicians used animal sacrifices, strange materials, and elaborate spells often containing barbarous words and names of demons. They were out for money and were commonly cheats, their miracles usually illusory, commonly trivial, and sometimes harmful. They had no moral teaching, were often themselves conspicuously immoral, and could not offer men a way to salvation. In contrast therefore the traditions about Apollonius and Jesus minimize the ritual aspect of their miracles, represent them as indifferent or hostile to money, emphasize the reality, importance, and beneficence of their cures, emphasize their moral teaching, and represent them as bringing salvation. Finally, the Christians insisted that, unlike any magician, Jesus and his career had been foretold by the prophets of the Old Testament and his claims had been confirmed by his resurrection from the dead, post-mortal appearances, and ascension to heaven. The followers of Apollonius had no prophecies to adduce, but did have the great miracle of his escape from death and claimed an ascension and appearances after death.

All these apologetic motifs must be kept in mind as we turn to the last and most important step of our investigation, the question: What evidence did the Christian tradition, as presented in the gospels, have in common with the picture of Jesus the magician? Since the authors of the gospels wished to defend Jesus against the charge of magic, we should expect them to minimize those elements of the tradition that ancient opinion, as seen in this chapter, would take to be evidence for it, and to maximize those that could be used against it.

This expectation is, in the main, confirmed. The evangelists could not eliminate Jesus' miracles because those were essential to their case, but John cut down the number of them, and Matthew and Luke got rid of the traces of physical means that Mark had incautiously preserved (e.g. of 7.33f.; 8.23ff.). They could not eliminate the claim that Jesus was the Son of God because that was also essential to their message, but the synoptics make him keep it a secret until the High Priest compelled him to admit it (Mk. 14.61f.p.). Until that time he did not himself make the claim; it was made for him by voices from heaven, demons, his disciples, the crowds, and so on. This is apologetic modesty. His connections with Samaria have almost entirely disappeared from the synoptics. If he had any contact with magicians, or ever went to Egypt, Mark and Luke say nothing of either, and Matthew has located both in his infancy. Accusations of magic made against him are mentioned rarely, mainly for refutation, and some are left unexplained, like the charge that he "was" the Baptist. References to his discreditable background and human failings have been minimized. His teachings about Satan and other demons are vestigial. Moral teaching is emphasized. Money and food, that must have been constant concerns, are scarcely mentioned—money, mainly to reject it. Prophetic predictions of his career are found whenever possible (and sometimes when impossible). Pilate, and in Luke, Herod Antipas, are made to declare him innocent.

In evaluating all these points of the evidence, and others like them, the reader of the gospels must keep in mind that the gospels were written in a hostile world to present the Christian case. Consequently, the elements in them that could be used to support the charge of magic are probably only the tips of the iceberg of suppressed traditions, while elements that counter the charge must be viewed with suspicion as probably exaggerated, if not wholly invented, for apologetic purposes. We have to deal with a body of edited material.

~ 7 ~

The Evidence for
Magical Practices

I

The complex of apologetic arguments and defensive censorship as sketched in the preceding chapter was partially countered by the fact that some of Jesus' admirers thought him a magician and admired him as such (Mk. 9.38f). Lots of magic was practiced in the early churches: Acts 19.19 suggests the extent of it in Ephesus (the magical books of those Christians who could be persuaded to burn them were valued at about $320,000). In second and third-century works on heresy, when Christians are attacking each other, accusations of magic fly thick as brickbats at Donnybrook Fair. That such accusations were not just malicious inventions, but reflected actual practice, is proved by evidence from Egypt, whence we have many Christian magical papyri and amulets in Greek, and more in Coptic. Consequently, we have to reckon not only with a tradition that tried to clear Jesus of the charge of magic, but also with one that revered him as a great magician. This latter was not incompatible with belief in his divinity: the gods too practiced magic and some were famous magicians—Circe and Isis for example. Finally, we must remember that both devotion and popular storytelling tend to exaggerate the powers of their heroes and play up the marvelous.

Given these various motives the material in the gospels shows equal variety. Exaggeration of the miraculous for devotional or literary effect is commonplace. The contrary tendency—to play down the miraculous in order to avoid the charge of magic—has been demonstrated by the classic work of Fridrichsen, *La probleme du miracle*. The magicians had to operate more circumspectly, but their interests are represented by many details useful for magical purposes. For instance, the advice to exorcists in Mk. 9.28f.—after Jesus' exorcism of a demoniac boy, "When he came indoors, the disciples asked him privately, '⟨Why⟩ couldn't we cast out this ⟨demon⟩?' And he said to them, 'This kind cannot ⟨be made⟩ to leave by anything but a ⟨secret?⟩ prayer.'" (Clement of Alexandria commented that "the prayer" of the gnostic is more powerful than faith.) There is another encouragement to miracle workers in the saying, variously reported, that all commands given with perfect confidence will be obeyed. Further, there is the preservation in a few miracle stories of details reporting Jesus' techniques; thus Mark claims to give the exact Aramaic words used for the raising of Jairus' daughter—*talitha koum* (5.41). Mark translates these words ("Girl . . . get up") as the Greek magical papyri sometimes translate Coptic expressions. However, *talitha koum* also circulated without translation as a magical formula: a partial misunderstanding of it became the basis of another phrase—if not an entire story—preserved in Acts 9.36ff. where Peter raises a dead woman conveniently named Tabitha by saying to her in Greek, "Tabitha, get up." (*Tabitha* is a mispronunciation of *talitha*, which the storyteller mistook for a proper name.)

These evidences of continuing magical interest in the Christian communities which produced the gospels complicate the evaluation of the gospel reports. Because of their interest in magic those who transmitted the material may have noticed and preserved the reports of Jesus' practice. More significant stories may have been kept secret, as magical texts commonly were. On the other hand, the interests of those retelling the material may have led them to invent magical details, and even entire stories.

When these contradictory tendencies are taken together with those previously noticed—to minimize the miraculous in order to avoid the accusation of magic, and to exaggerate miracles for edification and literary effect—the one clear thing to emerge from the tangle is the difficulty of trying to determine the authenticity of particular details. Fortunately, that is not at present our problem. We have instead to look at the tradition *as preserved* and ask what elements accord with the opinions formed about Jesus by those who were not his followers. To see even the followers' tradition as the outsiders saw it will enable us to recognize those general traits in Jesus' life that must have been the main bases of the conflicting opinions about him. Details can never be guaranteed, but those general characteristics of a tradition that accord with and explain *both* the opinions of a man's adherents, *and* those of his opponents, have a claim to authenticity far stronger than that which can be advanced for supposedly idiosyncratic sayings.

II

Matthew's story that Jesus was fathered by a god is potentially antimagical; it belongs to the "divine man" theology and is closely paralleled, as we have seen, by a story told about Apollonius (*Life I.4*)—both would make it possible to explain their heroes' miracles as works of "inherent divine power," not of magic. But after the birth come the magi. Their story was inspired by the visit of Tiridates and his train to Nero that culminated in their reverencing him as a god. Matthew's tale belongs to a body of material that attributes to Jesus titles and claims characteristic of the emperors and their cult. People said that Tiridates and his magi had initiated Nero in their mysteries and secret meals; the gospel story implies that Jesus needed no initiation: he was the predestined ruler of the magi, as well as of the Jews; but unlike the ignorant Jews, the magi knew this. They understood the star that signaled his coming and came themselves to meet him, make their submission, and offer the gifts due their ruler. Moral: all magicians should do the same; Jesus is the supreme magus and master of the art. Matthew also used the story for other purposes: to reconcile the biblical prophecy that the Messiah should be born in Bethlehem with the known fact that Jesus came from Nazareth, and to explain away the report that Jesus went to Egypt and learned magic there (above, p. 48)— the magi's coming occasions Herod's plot, which occasions the flight into Egypt.

Like most ancient biographies the gospels and the *Life of Apollonius* had nothing to say about their heroes' childhood and adolescence except a story or two attesting precocious powers and probably derived from the divine man cycle, though similar stories of precocity turn up in the lives of unquestionaly human heroes (Josephus, *Vita* 8f.). They have no clear connection with magic.

III

The report of Jesus' baptism (Mk. 1.9) with which our knowledge of his mature life begins is a simple statement of historical fact, but the story that follows is mythological: "And then, coming up from the water, he saw the heavens split open and the spirit as a dove coming down to him, and a voice from the heavens, 'You are my beloved son, I am much pleased by you'" (1.10f.). No gospel says anything of any ritual, though the baptism must have been accompanied by prayers and thanksgivings (possibly also by hymns) and effected with some regular form of actions and formula of words. The omission of such elements here—in spite of their importance to the event—should warn us that elsewhere the absence of reference to ritual does not prove that none was used. We have seen that rituals and formulae were apt to be taken as evidence of magic, and therefore to be deleted (above, pp. 83, 87, 92).

Even without reference to ritual the story of the coming of the spirit is surprising because the event it describes is just the sort of thing that was thought to happen to a magician. Essentially, it admits the charge that Jesus had a spirit and, as told by Mark, it takes for granted that the reader will know this is a good spirit, not a bad one. (This is one of many passages indicating that Mark's gospel was written for readers who were already Christian or about to become Christians.) Luke and Matthew identified the spirit as "holy" and "of God"—surely to refute the charge of magic. Jesus' spirit had led him to crucifixion; the case for supposing it a demon that deceived and destroyed him must have been plausible. Why should any of his followers have included a story that could so easily be used to justify the charge of magic? John, for whose theology of incarnation the story was an embarrassment, turned the whole thing into a vision reported by the Baptist (1.32ff.), but his remodeling shows that he knew a version like Mark's (though probably independent of Mark) and did not dare omit it, even though it did not suit his theology.

This story seems to have been important in the tradition from which both Mark and John drew. Evidently it was the accepted account of the beginning of Jesus' work. It identified that beginning as the baptism, followed by the descent of the spirit on Jesus, and it described that descent as an objective fact: the heavens split open, the spirit came down as a dove. This description may be a complete fiction, or may report as fact an hallucination experienced by Jesus himself, but in either event we should like to know its source. What could have led Jesus to have had such an experience, or his followers to make up such a yarn? No Old Testament prophets had birds roost on them. Rabbinic literature contains nothing closely similar.

This leads us to consider the extant accounts of how magicians got spirits as constant companions and servants whom they could order about at will so as to perform miracles without elaborate rites or spells. These accounts derive not only from the abnormal experiences of magicians, but also from their neighbors' experiences of the extraordinary powers of suggestion that certain individuals possess and use to heal or cause sickness, excite love or hatred, instill convictions, or even produce hallucinations and dispel them. Such powers were thought magical, but the "magicians" were known to exercise them without any magical rites. This was "explained" mythologically by analogy from slavery: such magicians "had" spirits as slaves, always on call. Hence grew a thicket of stories about ways to get spirits as servants.

These stories can be classified by the sorts of servants promised. One familiar form is that in which a ghost, "the demon of a dead man," is evoked as Jesus was thought to have evoked the Baptist. Most often such demons were employed for single assignments, usually to harm enemies or to bring women to would-be lovers, but the opinion reported by the gospels and the example of Paul indicate that they were also thought to be available as constant attendants and to do miracles like those of Jesus, mainly exorcisms.

This indication is confirmed by the papyri. The "Magical Papyrus of Paris" (*PGM* IV. 1930–2005) prescribes a prayer to the sun god, "Give me the authority over this spirit of a murdered man, ⟨a part⟩ of whose body I possess

. . . so that I may have him with me as helper and defender for any affairs in which I need him." The following section (lines 2006ff.) gives more elaborate rituals for calling up such a spirit when one is desired, but concludes, "However, most magicians take the equipment ⟨objects inscribed with spells, etc.⟩ home, put it away, use the spirit as a servant ⟨always in attendance⟩, and so accomplish whatever they want with all possible speed. For ⟨this method⟩ effects its purposes immediately, with complete convenience and without any wordiness" (that is to say, spells). After this come two short recipes and then a long rite including the conjuration of a dead man's spirit to be the servant of an amulet, one of whose many powers will be to drive out demons. Directions of the same sort are given in *SHR* I.5 and some early Christians said that the Samaritan magician, Simon Magus, did his miracles by such control of the spirit of a murdered boy.

Thus the notion that Jesus "had" the Baptist was not, by ancient standards, an impossible explanation of his powers. Nevertheless, it seems to have been dropped rather early. It did not fit the facts well—Jesus' miracles had probably begun before the Baptist's death and therefore could not all be explained by use of the Baptist's spirit. In any case spirits of the dead were mainly used for harmful magic, while Jesus was mainly a healer. Moreover, important groups of Jesus' followers, and of his opponents, maintained that his miracles were not done by a ghost, but by a supernatural being of a higher order than men. His followers called it "the holy spirit," his opponents "the ruler of the demons" (Mk. 3.22 p., 29 p.).

Directions for getting such a spirit were available in magical texts. Here is one from *PGM* I.54ff: *a spirit ally*

Having sanctified yourself in advance and abstained from meat (?) and from all impurity, on any night you wish, wearing pure garments, go up on a high roof. Say the first ⟨prayer of⟩ union when the sunlight is fading . . . having a black Isiac band over your eyes . . . When the sun rises, greet it . . . reciting this ⟨hereafter specified⟩ holy spell, burning uncut frankincense ⟨etc.⟩ . . . While you are reciting the spell, the following sign will occur: A hawk flying down will stop ⟨in the air⟩ in front of you and, striking his wings together in the middle ⟨in front of his body⟩, will drop a long stone and at once fly back, going up into heaven. You take up that stone and having cut . . . engraved and pierced it . . . wear it around your neck. Then at evening, going up to your roof again and standing facing the light of the ⟨moon⟩ goddess, sing the hymn ⟨specified⟩, sacrificing myrrh ⟨etc.⟩ . . . And you will soon have a sign, as follows: A fiery star, coming down, will stand in the middle of the roof and . . . you will perceive the angel whom you besought, sent to you, and you will promptly learn the counsels of the gods. But don't you be afraid. Go up to the god, take his right hand, kiss him, and say these ⟨specified spells⟩ to the angel. For he will respond concisely to whatever you wish ⟨to ask⟩. You, then, make him swear with this ⟨specified⟩ oath that he will remain inseparable from you and . . . will not disobey you at all . . . And you set forth

⟨these⟩ words for the god ⟨to agree to⟩: "I shall have you as a dear companion, a beneficent god serving me as I may direct, quickly, with your power, already while I am on earth; please, please, show ⟨grant⟩ me ⟨this⟩, O god!" And you yourself speak . . . in accordance with what he says, briefly . . . But when the third hour ⟨of the night—about 9 P.M.⟩ comes, the god will leap up at once. Say "Go lord, blessed god, whither you eternally are, as you wish," and the god will become invisible. This is the holy ⟨rite for⟩ acquiring an attendant ⟨deity⟩. *spirit ally "*

Know therefore that this god, whom you have seen, is an aerial spirit. If you command, he will perform the task at once. He sends dreams, brings women or men . . . kills, overthrows, raises up winds from the earth, brings gold, silver, copper, and gives it to you whenever you need; he frees from bonds . . . opens doors, makes invisible . . . brings fire, water, wine, bread and whatever foodstuffs you want . . . he stops ships ⟨in mid voyage⟩ and again releases them, stops many evil demons, calms wild beasts and immediately breaks the teeth of savage serpents; he puts dogs to sleep or makes them stand voiceless; he transforms ⟨you⟩ into whatever form you wish; . . . he will carry you into the air; . . . he will solidify rivers and the sea promptly and so that you can run on them standing up; . . . he will indeed restrain the foam of the sea if you wish, and when you wish ⟨he is able⟩ to bring down stars and . . . to make hot things cold and cold hot; he will light lamps and quench them again; he shakes walls and sets them ablaze. You will have in him a slave sufficient for whatever ⟨tasks⟩ you may conceive, O blessed initiate of holy magic, and this most powerful assistant, who alone is Lord of the Air, will accomplish ⟨them⟩ for you, and the ⟨other⟩ gods will agree to everything, for without this god nothing is ⟨done⟩.   *spirit ally*

Communicate this to no one else, but hide it, by Helios, since you have been thought worthy by the Lord God to receive this great mystery. . . . ⟨Here follow the spells to be used in the preceding ceremony.⟩ . . . And when you send him away, after he goes, sacrifice to him . . . and pour an oblation of wine, and thus you will be a friend of the powerful angel. When you travel he will travel with you; when you are in need he will give you money; he will tell you what is going to happen and when and at what time of night or day. If anyone ask you, "What do I have in mind?" or "What happened to me?" or "⟨What⟩ will happen?" ask the angel, and he will tell you *sotto voce,* and you say it to the inquirer as if from yourself. When you die he will embalm your body as befits a god, and taking up your spirit will carry it into the air with himself. For an aerial spirit ⟨such as you have become⟩ having been united with a powerful assistant will not go into Hades. For to this ⟨god⟩ all things are subordinate. So when you wish to do something, say into the air only his name and "Come," and you will see him, and standing right beside you. Then tell him, "Do such and such" —the work ⟨you want done⟩—and he will do it at once, and having done it, will ask you, "Do you want anything else? For I am in a hurry to go back to heaven." If you have no other orders at the moment, tell him, "Go, Lord," and he will go. Now this god will be seen only by you, nor will anyone hear his voice when he speaks, except you only. When a man ⟨is sick⟩ in bed he will tell you whether he will live or die, and ⟨if the latter⟩ in which day and which hour . . . He will also give you wild plants and ⟨tell you⟩ how to perform cures; and you will be worshiped as a god, since you have the god as a friend.

Compare Jn. 15.15. Here and throughout this chapter gospel parallels to magical terms and phrases are given in the text only when they are isolated and can be cited briefly; when, as often happens, there are large groups of them, or they require some comment, they are given in the notes. The reader interested in the general relation of the New Testament to magical material should therefore be careful in this chapter to keep an eye on the notes.

The preceding rite resembles the gospel story in five points: (1) It is an account of an initial purification followed by reception of a spirit come down from heaven. (2) The first manifestation of the supernatural power is a bird. (3) The spirit enables the recipient to perform miracles and (4) leads to his being worshiped as a god. (5) The rite, like the gospel story, is a mythological attempt to explain the origin of a social figure like the Jesus of the gospels. As the miracles this magician is enabled to perform include most of those with which Jesus is credited, it would seem that the social types behind these two myths are similar if not identical. ("Myth" should not be taken to imply that nothing of the sort was experienced. It refers solely to *objective* reality. Objectively there is no more likelihood that the Lord of the Air came down to a magician than there is that the Holy Spirit came down to Jesus. But it is just as likely that many magicians tried to carry out rites resembling the one described as it is that Jesus "was baptized in the Jordan by John." And it is equally probable that many magicians persuaded themselves that they had made friends with deities, and that Jesus thought the spirit had come down on him when he came up from the water. One terrible trait of mythological thought is its power to produce corresponding experience.)

The magical papyri contain several such rites to get spirits as assistants and belief in this sort of relationship was widespread—for instance, St. Irenaeus, in about 180, explained the miracles of the heretic Marcus by supposing he had "some demon as an assistant." But all these stories, and this type of theory, fall short of the gospel myth in one respect: In them the spirit is merely acquired as an assistant, in the gospels its descent is followed by a voice from heaven declaring Jesus "my beloved son." The story strongly suggests that the sonship is a result of the descent of the spirit. But what is the sonship?

Many would say, the messiahship. Mark equated "Messiah" (="Christ") with "Son of God" and "Son of Man" (14.61f.). From then on the equation has been customary. But "Son of God" was not, in Judaism, a customary messianic title, nor a common way of referring to the Messiah. Nor is it often connected with the messiahship in the synoptic gospels. Instead it almost always appears with miracles. As "Son of God" Jesus casts out demons (Mk. 3.11; 5.7p.; Lk. 4.41), walks on the sea, and knows the Father (Mt. 11.27p; 14.33). Because he claims to be "Son of God" the devil demands miracles from him (Mt. 4.3,6 p.) and the Jews mock him when he is unable to perform them (Mt.

Jewish Kabbalah: dove

27.40,43). Because he was "a son of god" miracles attended his death (Mk. 15.38f.p.). By contrast, the gospels rarely attribute Jesus' miracles to "his spirit" or to "the holy spirit"; this sort of attribution is most conspicuous in their reports of the charges of his enemies (who of course say "demon," not "spirit"). In most miracle stories no explanation at all is given; Jesus simply speaks or acts and the miracle is done by his personal power. This trait probably reflects historical fact, but why did this fact result in Jesus' being called "Son of God"? The existence of a title implies a conceptual type—in this case, to judge from the usage, a supernatural being in human form who performs miracles by his own divine power. (Accordingly, Christians predicted that the Antichrist, when he appears and claims to be a son of a god—that is, a god—will be a miracle worker, II Thess. 2.3–10; *Didache* 16.4).

Where did this figure come from? Why is he only a son of a god and not a god? To answer these questions scholars have looked to Greek and Latin material; their findings have not been satisfactory. Sons of gods are plentiful in mythology, but in real life the title "son of god" was rarely used except for Roman emperors. While its use for Jesus may have been influenced by the gospels' tendency to apply to him the imperial attributes, this is wholly inadequate to explain the gospel figure. (For example, emperors rarely did miracles.) Consequently, we must look elsewhere, in this case to the Semitic-speaking paganism of first-century Palestine, and the semi-pagan Palestinian cult of Yahweh from which Christianity sprang. In Hebrew and Aramaic "son of" is commonly used to mean "member of the class of"; hence, "the sons of god" is a regular way of saying "the gods," just as "the sons of men" (commonly translated "the children of men") is a regular way of saying "men." Thus in Genesis 6.2—"the sons of god saw the daughters of men" means "the gods saw women." A few other examples are scattered throughout the Old Testament. Isolated survivors of monotheistic censorship, they indicate the popular basis of the usage and justify us in supposing that when a Palestinian demoniac said "Jesus, son of god" he meant "Jesus, god." The evangelists took such expressions of Semitic paganism as portents and adjusted them to their own monotheistic belief: this is why Jesus moves through the gospels as a deity doing miracles by his own divine power, but in the synoptics is never explicitly called a god. It also explains why the title "Son of God" appears before and independently of the legends of divine paternity. The legends were apologetic, but the title preceded the apology and determined the line it was to take.

Thus "son of god" is explicable; it means "god." But the gospel story still has to be explained: It tells of a man made a god by a rite of purification followed by the opening of the heavens and the coming of a spirit. Where do we find such stories? In the magical papyri. For instance, *DMP* X. 23ff., where a magician says, "Open to me, heaven! . . . Let me see the bark of Phre descending and ascending . . . for I am Geb, heir of the gods; I make intercession before Phre my Father ⟨for⟩ the things proceeded from me . . . Open to me, mistress of the spirits, . . . primal heaven!" Innumerable spells identify the magician with the god invoked and reach their climax with the words "for I am" followed by the name of the god. For example, *PGM* VIII. 2ff.: "Come to me, Lord Hermes, as infants in the wombs of women ⟨Gal. 4.19⟩ . . . For you are I and I am you ⟨Jn. 17.21⟩; your name is mine . . . I am your image . . . I know you Hermes, and you me. . . . Do all ⟨I ask⟩" (II Cor. 9.8–15). Witness also an invocation of the world ruler, the Good Demon (*PGM* XIII. 784ff. = XXI):

But Thou, Lord of life, King of the heavens and the earth and all those that dwell therein ⟨III Macc. 2.2⟩, whose righteousness is not turned aside, . . . who hast irrefutable truth, whose name and spirit ⟨rest⟩ upon good men, come into my mind and my vitals for all the time of my life and accomplish for me all the desires of my soul. For you are I and I am you. Whatever I say must happen . . . For I have taken to myself the power of Abraham, Isaac, and Jacob and of the great god-demon Iao Ablanathanalba.

Two magical texts of this sort in the "Magical Papyrus of Paris" are of special interest because of their resemblance to the gospel story. One—*PGM* IV. 475–830—preserves the beginning of a rite to attain immortality by ascent into the heavens. After seven days of rituals and three of purity, begin by saying the following spell:

First beginning of my beginning, a ĕ ē i ŏ u ō, first source of my source . . . spirit's spirit, first ⟨element⟩ of the spirit in me . . . fire . . . first ⟨element⟩ of the fire in me . . . ⟨etc. water, earth⟩ . . . perfect body of me ⟨name⟩ molded by a powerful arm and incorruptible right hand in a world dark and enlightened, lifeless and enlivened . . . may it seem right to you . . . that I should participate again in the immortal beginning . . . . . . that I may be reborn in thought ⟨Jn. 3.3ff.⟩ . . . and *that the holy spirit may breathe in me* . . . that I may marvel at the holy fire . . . that I may behold the abyss of the east, the fearful water . . . and may the lifegiving ether poured around me hear my ⟨voice⟩ . . . since I—a mortal born of a mortal womb, strengthened with immortal spirit . . .—shall behold today with immortal eyes the deathless Aeon and Lord of the fiery diadems—I, hallowed by holy rites, a holy power having replaced briefly my human, psychic power which I shall afterwards receive back . . . undiminished, I, ⟨name⟩. . . . Since it is not within my power while a mortal to ascend with the golden rays of the immortal luminary . . . be still, ⟨my⟩ corrupt mortal body, ⟨while I leave you⟩, and again ⟨receive⟩ me safe after ⟨I have satisfied⟩ this unavoidable and pressing need, *for I am the Son,* I surpass the limit of my souls ⟨?⟩, I am ⟨meaningless letters⟩.

With this the magician inhales the rays of the sun, leaves his body behind, and rises into the heavens.

Here we have deification by the gift of the holy spirit which transforms the recipient into "the Son," a supernatural being who by declaring his identity is able to work a miracle, specifically, to ascend into the heavens—a miracle with which Jesus was credited after his death and perhaps before. Holy spirits, with and without the definite article, are familiar in the magical papyri. "The Son" as a distinct supernatural being is rarer, but does appear again in a Demotic papyrus where a spell concludes, "Let ⟨that which I have asked⟩ come to my hand here today; for I am he who is in the seven heavens, who standeth in the seven sanctuaries; for I am the son of the living god."

Compared to the gospel story the most conspicuous element lacking in the preceding rite is the bird, but even that appears in a similar text, *PGM* IV. 154–221, which reads (beginning from line 170):

At any dawn you wish, when it is the third day of the moon, going to the roof of a high building, spread on the earthen ⟨floor of the roof⟩ a clean sheet. Do this with an initiated expert. Then you yourself, wearing a wreath of black ivy, after eleven o'clock, when the sun is in the midst of the heaven, lie down naked on the sheet, looking upward, and order that your eyes be covered with a black band. Then, wrapping yourself up like a mummy, closing your eyes and keeping your face toward the sun, begin the following prayer: "Powerful Typhon, sovereign and ruler of the realm above, God of gods, King . . . thou who scatterest the darkness, bringer of thunder, stormy one, who dazzlest the night, who breathest warmth into the soul, shaker of rocks, earthquake-destroyer of walls, God of foaming waves and mover of the deep. . . . I am he who searched through the whole world with thee and found the great Osiris, whom I brought to thee a prisoner. I am he who fought as thine ally . . . against the gods. I am he who locked the double doors of heaven, and put to sleep the invisible dragon, who stayed the sea, the tides, the streams of the rivers, until thou mightest subdue this realm. I, thy soldier, have been defeated by the gods. I have been cast down because of vain wrath. Raise up, I beseech thee, thy friend, I entreat thee, and do not cast me on the earth, O King of gods . . . Fill me with power, I beseech thee, and grant me this grace, that, when I shall order one of those gods to come, he shall at my spells come and appear to me quickly." . . . When you say these things thrice the following sign of your union ⟨with the god⟩ will occur, but you, armed with your magic soul, should not be terrified. For a sea hawk, flying down, will strike you with his wings on your body, by this very sign indicating that you should arise. You, therefore, arise, clothe yourself in white garments, and burn uncut frankincense in drops on an earthenware altar, saying as follows, "I have been united with thy sacred form. I have been empowered by thy sacred name. I have received the effluence of thy goodness, Lord, God of gods, King, Demon". . . When you have done this, descend, having attained that nature equal to the God's which is effected by this ritual union.

Here not only the bird as messenger of the god, but also the notions of salvation as resurrection from death, of the believer as the god's soldier and friend, doorkeeper of the heavens and at war with the gods of this lower world, of union with the god in form, of the gift of power by the god's name, and of the believer's achieving a nature like the god's are all paralleled in New Testament texts.

From this evidence (and from the lack of any evidence nearly so similar from any other source) we conclude that the story of how a spirit descended on Jesus and made him a "son of god" resembles nothing so much as an account of a magical rite of deification. The ritual details and spells (prayers and hymns) have been omitted, as in the preceding story of the baptism, but the essential acts and result are there. While John's baptism and Jesus' subsequent experience can hardly *in fact* have constituted such a rite, the story shows how they were understood in the very early Palestinian Christian circles from which Mark derived his material. Whoever thus understood them had an imagination shaped by stories, if not by actual experience, of magical rites.

IV

After Jesus' baptism and deification Mark says, "And at once the spirit drives him out into the wilderness. And he was in the wilderness forty days, being tempted by Satan, and was with the wild animals" (Mk. 1.12f.).

This fits the pattern of a magician's life, especially a shaman's. Compare Eliade's report that a shaman, at the beginning of his career, commonly "withdraws into solitude and subjects himself to a strict regime of self-torture." He is supposed to be tested, subjected to terrible ordeals, or even killed by evil or initiatory spirits, but is helped by friendly spirits who appear in the forms of animals. The statement that the spirit *drove* Jesus into the wilderness accords with rabbinic reports of demonic compulsion and suggests that Jesus was "possessed," although elsewhere it is claimed that he "had" the spirit. We have noticed in other stories about him this alternation between "possessing" and "being possessed," and have remarked that it is characteristic of shamans in general.

What purpose such potentially discreditable material served in the life of Mark's church, and what value Mark found in it that decided him to include it, the text does not indicate. It looks like a plain statement of historical facts as interpreted by a man who believed in spirits, and as reported by one who wanted to give an outline of Jesus' career beginning with his baptism. Critics who find Jesus' career embarrassing, and therefore want to minimize Mark's interest in history, incline to suppose that these verses are "the rudiment of an originally more extended ⟨temptation⟩ legend" of unknown function. They may be right: there is independent evidence that Mark intended his stories to be supplemented by instruction based on his church's oral tradition and perhaps on documents kept secret from the ordinary believers. If so, the temptation legend must be much older than the Gospel according to Mark.

Jesus passed Shamanistic temptations to magic

Matthew and Luke do supplement Mark's report with a long Q story of Jesus' temptations (Mt. 4.1–11; Lk. 4.1–13), but it would be risky to suppose that this story is what Mark knew and left out. The Q story is apologetic—told to show why Jesus did not perform the miracles expected of a messiah. Why did he not come flying through the air, turn stones into bread, provide food for everyone, and conquer the world? The gospels imply an answer. These things could have been done only by a magician. This world is the realm of the devil (Lk. 4.6) and anyone who wants to rule over it must worship the devil, in other words, become a magician. Since Jesus did not rule over it, he was not a magician, *Q.E.D.*

Flying through the air and turning stones into bread were typical feats of magicians. This was pointed out by the great Norwegian scholar, Eitrem, who first recognized the purpose of the story. He also pointed out that Psalm 91, quoted by the devil to persuade Jesus to jump from the temple and fly through the air (Mt. 4.6 p.), was famous for its magical use (here discredited by attribution to the devil). Further, the report that after the temptation the angels served Jesus attributes to him the success magicians strove for—to be served by supernatural beings—but makes the additional point that magicians are served only by demons, Jesus, because he rejected magic, was served by angels.

Eitrem also interpreted the report of Jesus' fasting and the offer to give him "all the kingdoms of the world" as traits derived from magic, but for these he had no close parallels. The Greek magical papyri mention "fasting" only as a condition for eating, drinking, or doing something, as we speak of "fasting communion." Rabbi 'Aqiba' (martyred in 134) thought one could get an "unclean spirit" (demon) by fasting and sleeping in a graveyard (*B. Sanhedrin* 65b). Presumably the fast involved lasted overnight. This is interesting because Jesus' rejection of fasting was one of the points in which he most conspicuously differed from the Baptist, and for which he was most criticized (Mt. 11.19p.). His disciples began fasting only after his death (Mk. 2.20). Mark says nothing of his fasting in the wilderness. The forty-day fast before the temptation was modeled on those of Moses and Elijah and was probably invented to put Jesus in their class and distinguish him from magicians. In fact, by rejection of fasting, he resembled magicians more closely than this storyteller liked to remember. Furthermore, the Greek magical papyri contain no spell by which a man can become a king, and they never promise a magician an earthly kingdom. The devil's offer to give Jesus "the kingdoms of this world" comes from the Jewish messianic tradition. Its appearance here is an apology for Jesus' failure to satisfy the demands of that tradition—to have done so, to have accepted an earthly kingdom, would have been tantamount to the practice of magic, the worship of "the god of this aeon." Jesus' kingdom was "not of this world" (Jn. 18.36. Compare Lk. 17.20).

Son was highest shamanic runs but offer to he devil's son!

That the offer of the kingdoms had a different background than the other two temptations is shown by the fact that unlike the others it is not presented as a challenge to prove himself the Son of God. The challenges in the other stories are refused. The storyteller knew the tradition that represented Jesus as a miracle working "son of god" (i.e., a god); he wanted to discredit it. The miracles this (son of) god was expected to work come from the magical tradition. This fact confirms what the evidence in the previous section

No suggested: "the Son" was a miracle working deity in magical mythology, and it was thought possible for a magician on whom "the Holy Spirit" descended to become or be united with "the Son." From these considerations it seems clear that the Q temptation story, as found in Mt. 4 and Lk. 4, was intended to discredit the picture of "Jesus the magican." The picture must therefore have been earlier than the source of Q.

V

After his shamanic session in the wilderness Jesus came, Mark says, to Galilee (1.14), and miracles began to happen.

Curiously, the first miracles reported are of the most credible sorts, and occur in the most plausible succession: winning disciples, exorcisms, and cures. We should expect a miracle worker to get his start in this way: making a few disciples, developing a reputation and self-confidence, demonstrating in public his power to control hysteria, and eventually curing objective, psychosomatic ailments—fever, paralysis, and so on. Mark however is completely oblivious to psychological plausibility; he describes these events as miracles without explanatory precedents. Therefore, the plausible sequence cannot be due to his invention. If not accidental, it may result from historical recollection: we have here again a beginning—the first disciples, exorcisms, and cures—and beginnings (first love, first job, first combat experience) are apt to be remembered when their many successors have long been forgotten or confused. Witness Mrs. Bloom in *Ulysses.*

Whatever their historicity, these miracles are all familiar feats of the magician's repertory. Apollonius, like Jesus, was famous for his attraction of followers. Love charms promise to make the beloved, or anyone whom the magician may touch, follow him everywhere. That the men whom Jesus called "left their father" and boat and servants to follow him (Mk. 1.20p.) is a trait of Christian conversion emphasized in the gospels: Jesus later speaks of followers who have "left home or brothers or sisters or mother or father or children or lands for my sake." Such conversion is promised by love spells: "Let her forget father and mother, brothers, husband, friend; let her forget all of these, except only me"—whom of course she is to follow, as Jesus was followed about by his male disciples and by a company of women from many of whom he had "cast out demons." The Pied Piper is a legendary example of similar power.

Spells and amulets for exorcism are frequent in the papyri and in literary collections of magical material; Apollonius and the Indian sages were credited with exorcism and Lucian and Celsus make fun of it in their accounts of popular credulity. Like the Indian sages Jesus was said to be able to exorcise at long distance, and like Lucian's Palestinian magician, to speak to "the demons" and make them give information about themselves.

Cures are also a major concern of magic. They stand first among the miracles for which *The Book of Secrets* (I.1) gives instructions; spells and recipes for them in the magical papyri are numerous, amulets for them are innumerable, and they are prominent in literary collections of magical material and in stories about magicians. Jesus' first reported cure (as distinct from exorcism) is of a fever (Mk. 1.30p.); cures for fever are particularly frequent in the magical material cited; the condition often has psychological causes and responds readily to suggestion. Our distinction between "cure" and "exorcism" however may be unjustified in this instance. Mark says, "taking her hand he raised her, and the fever left her." Luke understood this as an exorcism and made it more vivid, "he rebuked the fever and it left her" (Mk. 1.31; Lk. 4.38f.). The magical tradition has preserved an appropriate rebuke: "Plague and fever flee from the wearer of this amulet." That fevers are caused by demons is often supposed in the magical papyri; the notion that diseases actually *are* demons appears already in Sophocles. It is found again in Philostratus' story that Apollonius stopped the plague in Ephesus by recognizing it—a demon disguised as an old beggar—and having it stoned. The magical material cited above contains prescriptions or stories of cures for most afflictions cured by Jesus—fever, blindness, lameness, paralysis, catalepsy, hemorrhage, and wounds. In Lk. 10.19 Jesus gives his disciples the "authority" (i.e. power, as usual) "to walk over snakes and scorpions . . . and nothing will hurt you;" the postscript to Mark made the risen Jesus promise his believers immunity from snakes and poison. Spells against snakes, scorpions, and poison are frequent in the magical material and there were rites and amulets that promised protection from everything. Panaceas are perpetual.

Thus the miracles with which Mark represents Jesus as beginning his career in Galilee are drawn entirely from the magician's repertory. This should not be taken as discrediting their claim to historicity; rather the contrary: it is evidence that such "cures" did occur. The cure of Peter's mother-in-law is completely plausible: An old lady suddenly recovered from a fever when her son-in-law came back from synagogue bringing as a guest an attractive young holy man who had just healed a demoniac in the presence of the congregation and was doubtless accompanied by half a dozen of the congregation's most prominent members (who would expect hospitality and see the condition of the house). Does this "miracle" strain your faith?

Once more Mark seems utterly unaware of such a question. Therefore, the psychological and historical plausibility of his story cannot be attributed to his invention; it might be due to historical recollection, or it might be mere accident, but such accidents are becoming suspiciously frequent.

VI

Another "accident" confronts us in the structure of Mark's gospel between Jesus' first miracles in Galilee and his entry of Jerusalem. For the past half century scholars have commonly held that this structure is a collection of stories, sayings, and teaching material, mostly connected by accidental associations—catch words, similarities of form or content, and the like; Mark is thought to have added introductory expressions ("And again . . . And thereafter . . . And it happened" etc.) suggesting temporal sequence, but the suggestion is thought false. Here scholarly opinion is supported by the fact that both Matthew and Luke, when expanding Mark, felt free to rearrange his material. If this opinion be supposed correct the question arises: Why do the gospels have this curious structure? In response some scholars have cited analogies from popular literature—for instance, the collections of stories about Dr. Faustus, a Renaissance magician—others have seen, in the lack of historical coherence and causal sequence of events, evidence of the lack of historical interest in the early churches which preserved stories about Jesus' life merely as isolated anecdotes for use in sermons, instruction of converts, and the like.

The analogies from popular literature, however, beg the question: Why do popular narratives have such a structure? In fact, some popular narratives do not. The *Chanson de Roland*, for instance, is coherently (however incorrectly) constructed. Similarly, the supposed lack of historical interest in the early churches (apart from its inherent improbability) would explain why Mark found only anecdotes and sayings, but would not explain why he—who obviously had historical interests—did not try to construct out of these scraps a coherent, causally connected account.

We must seek some further explanation. Could it be that the preserved material reflects the historical facts? There *are* lives full of interesting events without clear causal connections. Such are the lives of actors. In the average autobiography of an actor one finds much the same structure as in Mark—a sequential account of the beginning of the career, then anecdotes, sayings, more anecdotes: "On another occasion . . . Sometime later . . . It happened . . . Again . . ." This similarity of structure is plausibly explained by the similarity of the lives reported. The life of an itinerant magician, like that of an actor on tour, is likely to be a picaresque novel without a plot—a string of incidents connected mainly by the central character. Mark reports these incidents with minimal framework, but even if his framework had been richer, the narrative—unless distorted—would have remained the same. Actually, poverty of style diminishes likelihood of invention and speaks for reliability of the narrative. Not that it can be wholly relied on. Lack of plot facilitated insertion of imaginary episodes, omission of embarrassing ones, and changes in order. But, granting distortions of details, the *sort* of life reflected by the central chapters of Mark, like that reflected by corresponding sections of Philostratus' *Life of Apollonius*, is the life of a recognizable historical type: the itinerant magician or holy man.

VII

Chapter VI showed that the primary characteristic of a magician was to do miracles. In this Jesus evidently excelled. Through all antiquity no other man is credited with so many. The gospels contain well over 200 items about Jesus that directly involve something miraculous—miracle stories or sayings that express or lay claim to miraculous powers. Comparable items in Philostratus' *Life of Apollonius* number about 107, in the Pentateuch's stories of Moses, 124, in the stories of Elisha in II Kings, 38.

To classify these items, we begin with those from which Jesus' fame began—the exorcisms. The magical parallels to these, already discussed, gave Jesus the reputation spread by his enemies, of being a magician who controlled "the ruler of the demons." "To drive out one demon by another" was proverbial and the philosopher Porphyry praised the god Sarapis as "the ruler of the demons who gives spells for their expulsion." So the belief attributed to Jesus' enemies is one they could easily have held. Indeed, something like it was held by some of his followers. Matthew, for instance, thought Jesus could control spirits by calling on their ruler, his Father (presumably Yahweh) who, if Jesus only said the word, would send him twelve legions of angels (72,000, Mt. 26.53). A spell to secure such an angelic bodyguard is given in *SHR* VI. By contrast, those of his followers who believed that "the holy spirit" had descended on him and made him "the Son" thought that he himself was able to control spirits, not only to order them out (exorcism), but also to send them on errands or send them into things or people. So the centurion, asking Jesus to heal his slave, says in effect "Don't bother ⟨to come yourself⟩ . . . Just say the word. ⟨I'm sure that will suffice⟩. . . . I too have a position of authority ⟨and many demands on my time, so I can't do everything myself⟩. I have soldiers under me ⟨as you have spirits⟩. When I tell one to go, he goes," and so on.

Similarly, the author of *SHR* claims in the preface that his book will teach the reader "to rule over spirits and demons, to send them so that they will go, like slaves."

Such spending of spirits and giving people over to them was often attributed to magicians and much feared. Scores of references to it occur in the magical papyri; hundreds of examples survive in "defixions"—spells usually written on lead tablets or potsherds and buried by graves or thrown into water so that they would come to the attention of the powers below to whom they gave over, for damage or destruction, the persons specified. "Eulamon, receive ⟨him—the victim⟩. Osiris, Osiris Mnevis, Phre . . . ⟨and other under-world gods⟩ inasmuch as *I give over* to you Adeodatus the son of Cresconia, I ask you to punish ⟨him⟩ in the bed of punishment . . . and bind him down from the present day and hour. Now, now! Quick, quick!" This is exactly the language of Paul: "I have already judged ⟨the offender⟩ . . . *to give* ⟨him⟩ *over* to Satan for the destruction of his flesh" (I Cor. 5.3ff.). It was repeated by the forger of I Timothy, "Some . . . have shipwrecked their faith, among whom are Hymenaeus and Alexander, whom *I have given over* to Satan, that they might be taught not to blaspheme" (I Tim. 1.19f.).

This was the blackest sort of magic, so it is not surprising that the gospels minimize Jesus' practice of it. He does not "send" the legion of demons into the Gadarene swine, he just "permits" them to enter and destroy them (Mk. 5.13p.); compare *PGM* LXI.10ff. where the magician is speaking to oil he has enchanted, "I let you loose against (so and so) daughter of (so and so) . . . lay hold of her head, blind her, let her not know where she is," etc. Even more risqué is John's explanation of the betrayal of Jesus. That he should have been betrayed by one of his own followers required explanation: If he was so good, why were his disciples not loyal to him? As Celsus would ask, if so wise, why did he choose a traitor, and why not foresee the treason? (Origen, *Against Celsus* II. 9–12). Mark had tried to answer such questions—Jesus foreknew it all; it was all a fulfilment of prophecy (Mk. 14.18ff., 41f.). John went further—Jesus not only foreknew it, he arranged it. Until the beginning of the last supper the devil had been able only to put the idea of betraying him into Judas' mind. Then Jesus, to fulfil scripture (13.18) and to glorify himself by voluntary self-sacrifice (13.31; 10.18), told the twelve that one of them would betray him and gave a piece of bread to Judas, "And after ⟨he had eaten⟩ the bread, then Satan entered into him. Accordingly, Jesus says to him, 'What you will do, do quickly,'" and Judas immediately goes out and arranges for the betrayal.

The notion that a demon can be sent into food so as to enter anyone who eats the food is common, particularly in love charms:

Spell said to the cup. Say seven ⟨times⟩, "You are wine; you are not wine but the head of Athena. You are wine; you are not wine but the entrails of Osiris, the entrails of Iao Pakerbeth, Eternal Sun o o o . . . i a a a"—To make it compulsive ⟨add⟩ "Ablanathanalba akrammachamarei e e e, the ⟨angel⟩ put in charge of compulsion, Jacob Ia Iao Sabaoth Adonai Abrasax"—"as soon as you go down in to the entrails of (so and so) let her love me (so and so) for the whole time of her life."

A theory to suit this practice was developed by theologians; we find them seriously explaining that idolatry is bad because the worshipers eat portions of the sacrificed food and so take the demons into their bodies. Accordingly, Origen is quoted as commenting on John's story, "Notice that Satan did not at first enter Judas, but only 'put into his heart' ⟨the notion⟩ that he should betray his teacher. But after the bread, he entered him. Consequently we should beware lest the devil intrude 'into our heart' any of his unrecognized weapons for, if he gets one in, he then finds a way by which he himself may enter." The edifying moral does not fit the correct observation: Satan entered only after *the bread* and the bread was the 'unrecognized weapon,' not of Satan, but of Jesus who sent Satan into the bread, and so into Judas, to make Judas carry out the prophesied program that called for the Messiah's betrayal by one who "had eaten" his "bread." Even Jesus' concluding command, "What you will do, do quickly," echoes a common conclusion of spells, "Now, now! Quick, quick!"

Closely related to the practice of sending evil spirits is that of causing hatred. This was a regular part of the magician's business. A class of spells known as "dividers" were available to cause hatred or prevent love. These were used most often in love affairs, but magic had a large place too in family quarrels. Texts tell us of "magical practice and curse and incantation and stroke and evil eye and evil spells . . . the spells of the mother and the daughter . . . the spells of the daughter-in-law and the mother-in-law," etc. Similarly, in the gospels Jesus says, "I have come to set a man against his father, and daughter against her mother, and daughter-in-law against her mother-in-law, so that a man's enemies shall be those of his own household" (Mt. 10.35f.p.). Matthew and Luke connect this Q saying with eschatological material; it is commonly explained as referring to the family divisions caused by conversions to the early churches and interpreted as signs of the coming end of the world. However, if Jesus persuaded workingmen to leave their families and follow him, the family quarrels would have started in his lifetime. Eschatological overtones are common in this sort of magic, for example: "I call on You, the terrible One in the empty wind, invisible, great God, who smitest the earth and shakest the world, lover of tumults and enemy of stability . . . Iaia Jacob Iai . . . give conflict, hostility," etc., to two men who are to be sundered "as

Typhon ⟨Set⟩ and Osiris." It is not impossible therefore that Jesus' claim to this magical power has been given a somewhat more edifying, Jewish eschatological sense by substitution of "I have come" for "I am able". (Behavior of dubious morality for a magician becomes unobjectionable when the actor is a prophet or Messiah of God.)

The obverse of causing hatred is causing love. The gospels' Jesus claims to be able to do this for individuals, here and now, without reference to the end of the world. We shall deal with this in connection with the eucharist later. At present we return to his alleged power over spirits.

In contrast to the account of Jesus' gift of Satan to Judas (or vice versa?), John was more open about the sending of good spirits. He does insist that the spirit was not given during Jesus' lifetime (Jn. 7.39)—this exculpates his hero from the charge of having practiced magic in giving it—but he makes Jesus promise that after his death he will ask the Father to send (Jn. 14.16f., 26), or will himself send "from the Father" (Jn. 15.26), "the spirit of truth" to "be in you," to "lead you into all truth," and to "foretell the things to come." These passages are paralleled by dozens of magical texts in which a magician either sends or asks a deity to send a spirit, occasionally to enter someone, more often to reveal secrets and foretell the future. A few examples:

"I conjure you (Spirit), because I wish you to enter into me" (*PGM* IV. 3205f.).

⟨After a long list of gods⟩ "I conjure these holy and divine names, that they may send me the divine spirit, and that he may do whatever I have in mind and desire . . . Send this demon in response to my holy spells . . . and let him say to me whatever I have in mind, speaking the Truth" (*PGM* I. 312ff.).

"Thou who ridest on the blasts of the air-roving winds, goldenhaired Helios . . . send from the adyta the true prophet . . . Now, now! Quick, quick!" (*PGM* VIII. 75ff. This and the preceding citation come in part from early magical hymns of which several texts are preserved.).

"Good Demon, whose power is greatest among the gods, hear me ⟨and⟩ go to (so and so), into his house, where he sleeps, into his bedroom, and stand beside him, fearful, terrifying, with the great and powerful names of the god, and say to him ⟨what I have ordered⟩" (*PGM* XII. 134ff.).

"Come to me, air-walking spirit, called by symbols and names not to be uttered, ⟨come⟩ to this divination . . . and enter his ⟨the medium's⟩ soul, that it may receive the imprint of ⟨thine⟩ immortal form, in powerful and incorruptible light, for I call on you singing . . . Come to me, Lord, borne on immaculate light, incapable of falsehood or anger, to me and to this boy who will see ⟨you⟩" (*PGM* VII. 559ff.).

The variety of these five examples may suggest the much greater variety of the many other parallels.

Besides making Jesus promise to send "the spirit of truth" into his disciples, John reported that after his resurrection he sent "the holy spirit" into them by blowing on them (20.22). This recalls Celsus' Egyptian magicians who "drive demons out of men and blow away diseases." An exorcism full of Old Testament references, but said to come from an Egyptian and invoking Egyptian as well as Israelite gods, begins, "I conjure you by the god of the Hebrews, Jesus Iaba Iae Abraoth Aia Thoth," and has a terminal note reading "I charge you, whoever may receive this conjuration, not to eat pork, and every spirit and demon of whatever sort will be subjected to you. When you exorcise, blow once, drawing the breath up to your face from the tips of your toes, and the demon will be expelled. Keep it ⟨for times when you are⟩ pure, for the spell is Hebrew and has been kept by pure men." The notion that spirits could be blown shows the popular background of this demonology. A date before the destruction of Jerusalem in A.D. 70 is suggested by the phrases, "I conjure you by Him ⟨who dwells⟩ in the pure ⟨city of⟩ Jerusalem, beside Whom burns forever the unquenched fire ⟨of the Temple altar⟩." After 70 this must have been read as a reference to the heavenly Jerusalem, but its original reference was to the earthly one—only there was the undying fire a marvel.

Jesus is pictured not only as having himself controlled spirits, but as having given twelve of his disciples the power ("authority") to expel demons and having sent them out to live as itinerant exorcists. Mark reports that they cast out many demons (6.13); Matthew and Luke say nothing of the exorcisms; but Luke has another story of some seventy disciples sent out to preach and heal who came back reporting, "Lord, the demons too are subject to us when ⟨we use⟩ your name." To this Jesus replies with assurances that Satan has fallen from power, that nothing on earth can hurt them, and that their names are written in heaven (on the list of those to be saved—10.17ff.). Such claims to knowledge of the world of spirits were often made by magicians, we shall come back to them presently; here the more important matter is the magician's ability to empower others to perform magical actions and particularly to exorcise.

There is no question about this ability—magic was a technique that could be taught (as can hypnosis, acting, and pharmacology, probably its most important ingredients). Our sources reflect this fact in different ways. Most realistic is Lucian's account of how Alexander, when "a well grown boy" was taken in hand by an experienced magician (himself formed in the school of Apollonius) and thoroughly drilled. It was not necessary to begin as a boy. The stories of Apollonius' studies with the magi and the Brahmans, fanciful as they are, presumably reflect the fact that a grown man might go to a magician for training—a fact presupposed and parodied in another one of Lucian's famous stories, a version of "the sorcerer's apprentice" (*Philopseudes* 34ff.).

In the magical papyri we sometimes see reflections of such relationships—very rarely the mention of a teacher ("Do this with an initiated expert"), occasionally a reference to an associate or advanced student ("If you wish to use a fellow initiate so that he alone, with you, will hear the words said ⟨by the god⟩, let him hallow himself with you for seven days," *PGM* IV. 732ff.), much more often reference to boys used as mediums. For the most part however the papyri neglect the need of teaching and stylize the transmission of the art in literary form as if it were purely a matter of communicating verbal information, although the spells constantly presuppose extensive knowledge of magical techniques. Thus the papyri are rather like advanced cookbooks, the sort that only an experienced cook can understand.

In the same way the gospels have stylized Jesus' communication of his powers in legal terms, as a "giving of authority." Nothing is said of training. As in the case of baptism, nothing is said of ritual or formulae, except for Luke's concluding phrase, "when ⟨we use⟩ your name" (Lk. 10.17). Nevertheless, in exorcism as in baptism, some ritual was necessary. Similarly, nothing is said of ritual in the references to the gift of healing (here joined by Q to that of exorcism) though the formula, like that of exorcism, almost surely involved the use of the name "Jesus." Consequently, after the envoys were sent out, "Herod heard, because his ⟨Jesus'⟩ *name* became famous" (Mk. 6.14). Another power Q gives the envoys is that of sending "their peace" into a house; this "peace" is a spirit—if no one in the house is worthy of it, it will return to the senders (Lk. 10.5f.p.). They can also curse. If no one in a city will receive them, they have only, on leaving, to knock the dust off their shoes in order to designate that city for special punishment in the day of judgment (Lk. 10.10ff.p.). Obviously we here have to do with Jewish magic, though exact parallels are not preserved.

Jesus' name was used in spells as the name of a god. So were the names of Adam (*PGM* III. 146), Abraham, Isaac, and Jacob, and of Moses and Solomon who were famous as magicians. It is remarkable that no names of historical persons from Greek, Egyptian, or Persian tradition are used in the papyri as names of deities in spells, although many such persons are named as authors of spells or magical books. This suggests that magical deification may have been unusually prominent in Jewish tradition (as exorcism seems to have been).

As magician and god Jesus was supposed to have or get the keys of the (kingdom of the) heavens, and he was said to have promised to give them to Peter. We have already seen that other magicians claimed to have or have used these keys. Add *PGM* III. 541, where one declares himself "Keeper of the key of the three-cornered paradise of the earth, the kingdom."

For the authors of the gospels, since Jesus controlled spirits, he also controlled men. So did other magicians—that was one goal of their art. We have noticed the magical parallels to Jesus' reported power to make men drop everything and follow him, leaving their homes and families (above, pp. 106f.). Here magical theory, like Christian theology, is an attempt to explain the extraordinary, antisocial attraction some people have for others; the absurdities of the explanations do not disprove the events reported. Such things happen. However, the credibility of the stories cannot be taken as proof of their truth. Because such things happen people are likely to invent stories about them. The truth remains uncertain. Whatever the truth of the preserved stories it seems practically certain that Jesus did attract disciples who left their businesses, homes, and families to follow him about the country.

Of Jesus' reputed powers over men, one of the most important for later history was that of forgiving their sins and empowering his disciples to do so. The notion of a god's forgiveness of sins is worldwide and not specifically magical. It played an important role in Israelite religion and was developed by the Baptist, who thought himself a prophet sent by God to introduce a new rite, a "baptism of repentance for the forgiveness of sins." Since Jesus' career began with his reception of this baptism, he may have arrogated to himself the power claimed for the rite. Whether or not he retained the rite is disputed. The synoptics represent him as forgiving sins without any rite, simply by his declaration. The Baptist's requirement of repentance is replaced by one of trust (in his power), or love (for him?—Lk. 7.47). The Markan story makes the scribes take offence at the act, interpreting it as a claim to divine power. The original storyteller intended the reader to realize that the scribes were right — this is indeed a manifestation of Jesus' power as a (son of) god. Understandably a Jewish magician credited with divine power is expected to perform the functions of a Jewish god. That Jesus claimed to do so—at least when the effectiveness of his performance could not be objectively tested—is not unlikely. Consequently the transmission of this power to his followers is represented as a consequence of his breathing into them his holy spirit (Jn. 20.23). When they are possessed by his spirit he is in them and acts through them; the proof of this is their ability to perform miracles like his (Jn. 14.10ff.; 15.4ff.; 17.20ff.). This theory presumably grew from the facts of early Christians' seizures by "the spirit," but such seizures would hardly have occurred, after Jesus' discreditable death, if his followers had not been prepared by his possession of them while he was yet alive.

Similarly, the belief that Jesus knew the minds of people he met may be founded on fact. Some people are uncannily (or cannily?) able to read the minds of others. To those who do not have the gift it looks like magic. (Calling it "mental telepathy," "extrasensory perception," or "divine omniscience" adds little to our ignorance.) This gift is almost necessary for a successful magician; therefore most of them must have had it, as the gospels say Jesus did. Legend

guru

+ trance possession

extended it to include knowledge of the futures and pasts of all concerned.
Trying to live up to their legends, magicians who believed in the efficacy of
magic produced spells to improve and extend their natural gifts:

Taking your finger, put it under your tongue ⟨in the morning⟩ before you speak
to anyone, and say the following ⟨spell⟩ with the great Name: "Make me foreknow
what is in everyone's mind today, for I am . . . Iao, Sabaoth, Iao . . . Adonai," etc.
(*PGM* III. 263ff.).

Having offered a sacrifice ⟨at sunrise⟩, pour a libation with black wine . . . say,
"Make me foreknow the nature of each woman . . . beginning with her ancestry (?)
. . . know beforehand each man and . . . what he has in his mind, and the nature of all
of them" (*PGM* III. 327ff.,; cp. Jn. 2.24f.).

PGM V.213ff. prescribes an elaborate ceremony of which the final spell
concludes,

I shall not allow any god or goddess to prophesy until I (so and so) know what is in the
minds of all men, Egyptians, Syrians, Greeks, Ethiopians, of every race and people, of
those who question me and come into my sight, whether they speak or keep silent, so
that I can tell them what has happened to them in the past, and their present
conditions, and what will happen to them in the future, and I know their trades and
lives and practices and jobs, and their names and those of their deceased ⟨relatives⟩ and
of everybody ⟨with whom they have had to do⟩, and so that I can read a sealed letter
and tell them all ⟨that is in it⟩ correctly.

Such abilities were evidently expected of magicians, hence they are also
attributed to Apollonius and to the Indian sages; they were claimed by Lucian's
archfraud Alexander, and both Lucian and the antipope St. Hippolytus wrote
exposés of magicians' tricks to discover the contents of sealed letters and give
other proofs of their abilities to read men's thoughts.

Philosophically the problem of knowing men's thoughts, and even of
knowing their forgotten pasts (which they may know subconsciously), differs
from that of knowing their futures (of which they too are ignorant). Popular
thought usually ignored this distinction. Prediction was the most valued
function of the magician —as we should expect given the practical importance
of foretelling future events and the psychological importance of anxiety. Accordingly the most common elements in magical papyri are directions for
divination, and all famous magicians are credited with prophetic powers.

As usual the gospels' Jesus follows the pattern. Like Apollonius he knows
what is happening in distant places and foretells specific events that will
happen to particular persons. He is credited with omniscience, which Apollonius and the Brahmans are made to claim; yet, like Apollonius, he is also
represented as ignorant of particular facts, under the necessity of asking questions, and liable to false expectations and disappointments. Similarly, the

magical papyri promise, like Jesus, to send spirits that will reveal everything, but side by side with these promises they give innumerable rites for evidently necessary divination of particular details. It seems that what we have in both traditions is the wishful exaggeration of similar gifts or skills.

Nevertheless, according to the gospels Jesus' prophetic powers go further. Besides personal prophecies, he also repeatedly prophesies the future of the world, its coming end, the judgment to follow, etc. Nothing like this is found in magical papyri (the customers wanted more practical, personal information) nor in the *Life of Apollonius* (as a Platonizing Pythagorean he probably thought the world was eternal), but Plutarch says magi predicted the destruction or violent remodeling of the world (above, p. 72), and Celsus claimed this side of Jesus' teaching was familiar from Syro-Palestinian prophets:

Many anonymous fellows both in temples and outside them, and some living as beggars around cities or camps, readily, from any chance cause, throw fits and pretend to prophesy. Each has the convenient and customary spiel, "I am the god," or "a son of god," or "a divine spirit," and "I have come. For the world is about to be destroyed, and you, men, because of your injustice, will go ⟨with it⟩. But I wish to save, and you shall see me again coming back with heavenly power. Blessed is he who has worshiped me now! On all others, both cities and countrysides, I shall cast eternal fire. And men who ⟨now⟩ ignore their punishments shall repent in vain and groan, but those who believed in me I shall preserve immortal" (Origen, *Against Celsus* VII. 9).

This looks like a parody of Christian preaching, and there is little other evidence for the existence of such prophets (though Celsus does twice mention beggars or magicians who claim to be "from above," but whom no respectable intellectual would believe to be "sons of god" I. 51, 68). On the other hand we have little evidence for most aspects of the popular religion of Jesus' time, and there is nothing improbable in the supposition that other Palestinian magicians said much the same sort of thing as Jesus. Eschatological prophecy was rife in his time and at least one of his contemporaries (Simon Magus) was thought, and probably claimed, to be a god. So Celsus' story may possibly be true. It is interesting that he hesitates between "god" and "son of a god." A prophet speaking Greek modeled on Aramaic would have used the terms as equivalent (above, p. 101). Celsus, ignorant of Aramaic, was uncertain whether they differed. It is also interesting that Origen (VII. 10f.) does not claim that there are no such prophets, but tries to discredit Celsus' report because he did not give their names and exact transcriptions of their prophecies! In sum, how far Jesus' eschatological prophecies were paralleled by those of contemporary pagan prophets and magi remain uncertain. That such conspicuously false predictions were peculiar to Jesus is not impossible but seems unlikely.

We come to firmer ground with the tangible miracles of which the most important, after exorcisms, were healings. Cures are conspicuous in stories about magicians generally and Jesus in particular. These stories have been discussed above (pp. 107f.). Many may be false, but as a whole it seems they were not products of completely free invention, because they mostly concern cures of conditions resulting from hysteria (fever, blindness, paralysis, etc.) which sometimes admit of "miraculous" cures. Conditions not thus curable are far less common in the stories, whether of Jesus or of other magicians. No magician was noted for cures requiring major surgery, but stories of such cures were often told about the gods, and would have been told more often about magicians, had the storytellers not been limited to some extent by knowledge of what did *not* happen. Besides curing, Jesus was probably thought able to protect people from illness or demons by laying his hands on them; the belief has many magical parallels.

Along with cures go resurrections from "death"—presumably (if any occurred) from hysterical coma. Magical papyri contain a few directions for resurrections (*PGM* XIII. 277ff.; XIXb), but these profess to make the revived body perform a specific function, in other words, they originate from exaggerations of the necromantic claim to call back and utilize the spirit of a dead man. So do the stories of such feats in Lucan's *Pharsalia* VI. 624–830, and Lucian's *Philopseudes* 26f. By contrast, Apollonius' resurrection of a dead girl (*Life* IV. 45) comes so close to Luke's story of the youth of Nain (7.11ff.) that it deserves to be quoted:

A girl seemed to have died just before marriage. The bridegroom was following the bier, crying out as ⟨men do⟩ about an unfulfilled marriage, and Rome mourned with him, for the girl had been of a counsular family. Apollonius, witnessing the grief, said, "Put down the bier, for I shall put an end to your tears for the girl." Therewith he asked what her name was. Most thought he was going to deliver a speech . . . but he merely touched her and said over her something not clearly heard, and awoke the girl from seeming death. She uttered a cry and went back to her father's house.

If a dead body is a thing and not a person, the resurrections bring us to stories of miracles involving control of purely physical objects. Since these miracles are the most clearly impossible, stories about them are the most surely false and among the most likely to be secondary developments of the tradition. Accordingly, the fact that the gospels attribute only five such miracles to Jesus may be taken as evidence of the tradition's relative reliability. Moreover, these few miracles are among those to which magical parallels are rarest and most remote:

(1) and (2): Jesus twice made food increase so that a small amount served a great company (Mk. 6.32ff.p.; 8.1ff.p.). Magical papyri and stories of magicians speak of demons supplying food, but not of increasing an initial supply.

These stories about Jesus are modeled on the close parallel in II Kings 4.42ff. where the social setting and dialogue are also similar; the magical parallels are remote and unrelated. This is a clear case in which Old Testament material has been used for secondary expansion, to prove Jesus greater than Elisha: Elisha fed only a hundred, Jesus four or five thousand.

(3) The story of Jesus' calming a storm (Mk. 4.39p.) aims higher. For this there must have been magical parallels—it was a miracle reported of ancient Greeks, Pythagoras and Empedocles. The magi had claimed to perform it in the fifth century B.C. and still did so in Pliny's time. It was so important for agriculture that in the fourth century A.D. Constantine had to except magic intended to prevent rains and hailstones from his general prohibition of the art. That there are no spells for it in the magical papyri presumably results from their origin in Egypt (where weather magic was little needed) and demonstrates the danger of supposing papyri reveal the whole range of Greco-Roman magic. Apollonius' talismans, too, were thought, even by Christians, to prevent or quiet storms. (He himself did not have to quiet storms; when he was present they would not occur, *Life* IV. 13.) Nevertheless, the gospel story may be another development of an Old Testament passage (Ps. 107.23ff.); it attributes to Jesus a miracle which in the Old Testament is one of the great works of Yahweh (Ps. 89.10; etc.), and its purpose is to indicate Jesus' divinity. Its conclusion makes this clear: "Who is this, that even the wind and the sea obey him?" (Mk. 4.41p.). Anyone who knows the Psalms knows Whom the wind and sea obey: Ps. 114.3ff.; 148.8; etc. But magicians also read the Psalms and could quote them for their own purposes, so an exorcism invoking "the headless demon" (a great figure in ancient magic) identifies him with a variety of Egyptian and magical gods, with Isaac, Sabaoth, Iao, and with the magician, and declares, "This is the Lord of the world, this is he whom the winds fear." (*PGM* V. 136f.). Thus, even attributes of Yahweh may stand in the gospels as evidence of magical associations.

(4) Jesus' withering the fig tree (Mk. 11.12ff.p., 20ff.p.) is cut from the same two faced cloth. An even stronger case can be made for deriving it from magic. Magician's powers to harm are attested by many spells. Some spells intend their victims to "wither," "consume," or "burn up." Magic has probably had some influence here. However, sudden withering of the wicked is so prominent in the Old Testament as a demonstration of Yahweh's power to punish, that the gospel story seems a demonstration that Jesus could act with no less power and severity than the Old Testament god. A good many passages in the gospels put in Jesus' mouth, or say of him, things that early rabbis put in the mouth, or say, of "the Holy One, blessed be He." These are just the claims we should expect from a Jewish magician; of course he would identify himself with the Jewish god.

(5) The Johannine story of Jesus' turning water into wine (2.1—11) was modeled on a myth about Dionysus told in a Dionysiac festival celebrated at Sidon. A first or second-century A.D. report of the festival shows striking similarities, even in wording, to the gospel material and makes its polemic purpose apparent. I do not know any close magical parallel before the practice of the Christian magician Marcus (Hippolytus, *Refutation* VI. 39f.).

In sum, of the five "nature miracles" attributed to Jesus, two unquestionably show an attempt to adjust him to Old Testament tradition; three have important connections both with Old Testament and with magical motifs; and one shows a Dionysiac interpretation of the eucharist, motivated at least in part by rivalry with a neighboring Phoenician cult. The resultant stories, however, are not incompatible with the picture of Jesus the magician, who claimed to be a god.

From the preceding list of "nature miracles" Jesus' walking on the sea, transfiguration, institution of the eucharist, and ascension to heaven were omitted because they concern his body, not the outside world. There is no suggestion that the sea or the air were changed. The eucharist, although it may have been thought to involve the alteration of external objects, is primarily conceived as a miraculous extension of Jesus' body. (The resurrection is excluded because it is usually attributed, not to Jesus, but to God the Father who "raised him from the dead," Rom. 10.9, etc. Jn. 10.18 attributes it to Jesus himself; so does *B. Sanhedrin* 106a, as an act of magic.)

Walking on water (Mk. 6.45—52p.; Jn. 6.19ff.) is one of the feats attributed to a "Hyperborean" magician by Lucian's dupes (*Philopseudes* 13). A magical papyrus promises that a powerful demon will enable its possessor to walk on water. Matthew concludes his account of Jesus' performance with the words, "Those in the boat worshiped him saying, 'Truly you are Son of God'" (14.33). This shows what he thought the point of Mark's story; his understanding was probably correct.

Akin to walking on water are Jesus' miraculous escapes and his becoming invisible or intangible. These were favorite feats of magicians: there are dozens of spells for invisibility and a generous supply for escaping from capture or from bonds. Escape tricks are still performers' favorites—as demonstrated by the Great Houdini—but the interest of the papyri in such matters suggests that there was a criminal element in the magicians' clientele. However, the most famous of all disappearances and escapes was Apollonius', from the courtroom of Domitian (*Life* VIII. 5 end).

Besides becoming invisible, magicians could transform themselves to anything they chose (*PGM* I.117; XIII. 270ff.), but Jesus' transfiguration (Mk. 9.2ff.p.; II Peter 1.17f.) should not be seen as a display of this power. It is more like the stories of gods in disguise who at length reveal themselves to their favorites in their true forms. Another magician who revealed his "true form" to his followers in initiation ceremonies was Lucian's Alexander (chapter 40). Ascent of a mountain covered by a cloud from which a deity speaks recalls Moses' ascent, with his disciples, of Sinai. But this is contrast, not indentification because: (1) The evangelists tell of the mountain in their stories about Galilee; it is not Sinai. (2) Moses saw Yahweh and received the Law; Jesus saw only Moses and Elijah, and neither received nor gave any law. If we suppose Yahweh the supreme God and the Law His supreme revelation, Jesus will be inferior to Moses—an unlikely conclusion for a Christian story. But if we suppose with Paul that the Law was "ordained by angels through an intermediary" (Gal. 3.19; cp. Acts 7.53), and that Sinai is the symbol of slavery (Gal. 4.25), we shall see the mountain of the transfiguration as opposed to Sinai, and the declaration to which the gospel story leads, "this is My beloved Son," as a declaration of deliverance from the Law into the "liberty in which Christ has set us free."

Paul opposed Sinai to the heavenly Jerusalem, not to a mountain in Galilee. So where did the mountain in Galilee come from? Probably from an event in Jesus' life. The event may have been shaped by magical tradition. Going up a mountain into a cloud to meet the gods and so be glorified was part of that tradition, it is reported also of Apollonius and of earlier magicians—for example, by pseudo Isaiah of the King of Babylon, and by Ezekiel of the King of Tyre. By Jesus' time Jewish visionaries were ascending into the heavens to meet God and be clothed with His glory. Jesus, in the transfiguration story, stays on earth. He only goes up a mountain and meets, not the supreme God Himself, but only some supernatural beings. All this suggests that the story is limited by recollection of facts. Pure mythopoeic fancy would not have been so restrained, but the facts were that three disciples did experience some such hallucinations on a mountain in Galilee.

The beings Jesus "met" on the mountain are called by the gospels "Moses" and "Elijah," to show the Law and the prophets waiting on the Son of God. But how could they serve him? Lk. 9.31 says they foretold his fate. Spells to make gods appear and foretell one's fate are plentiful; there is a fine one in *The Eighth Book of Moses*. The good magician allows or teaches his disciples to see the gods. But were "Moses" and "Elijah" gods and not prophets? The alternative is false. In the magical papyri Moses was both god and prophet. "Angelification" of Enoch and Isaiah is reported in Jewish works of about Jesus' time, and for Jewish thought of that time, as for magical thought, angels were "gods" and pagan gods were "angels." Since Elijah had been carried off to heaven by a fiery chariot (II Kings 2.11), he must have been

[handwritten marginalia: Law; chariot-palan Mysticism]

supposed a supernatural power. In the transfiguration he and Moses were thought deities by Peter, who therefore proposed to make "tabernacles" for them and for Jesus like the "tabernacle" the Israelites made for Yahweh at Sinai. Making the Sinai tabernacle was the first great act of obedience to the Law; therefore Peter's proposal is—to begin a new legal servitude to Jesus, the Law (Moses), and the Prophets (Elijah). To prevent this, the supreme God, the Father, comes down in his cloud and implicitly abolishes the Law by declaring Jesus' unique status as Son. When the cloud lifts, Law and Prophets are gone, Jesus alone remains to direct his disciples.

Of the mythical, magical, and Old Testament elements intertwined in the transfiguration story, the Old Testament elements belong to the latest layer, the theological interpretation. But what were the events interpreted? Jesus took three disciples apart; they went up a mountain and, after unspecified proceedings, saw him in glory speaking with supernatural beings; then one of the disciples spoke; a cloud blotted out the vision; they found themselves alone with Jesus, in his ordinary appearance, on the mountainside. This is the familiar story of the magical séance that ends abruptly when the spell is broken by an inauspicious act. The type was parodied by Horace (*Satires* I.8) and is found often, perhaps hundreds of times, in later literature on witchcraft. So widespread a story probably reflects common experience in hallucinative rites.

In contrast to the complex story of the transfiguration, that of the eucharist (Mk. 14.22f.p.; I Cor. 11.23ff.) is a simple report of a familiar magical operation—giving enchanted food to cause love. Often the food is identified with the body and/or blood of a god with whom the magician is identified; thus the food becomes also the body and blood of the magician; whoever eats it is united with him and filled with love for him. A good example has been quoted above, (p. 111), another is the following (*DMP* XV. 1ff.):

⟨One mingles various ingredients in a cup of wine and says over it⟩ "I am he of Abydos . . . I am this figure of one drowned that testifieth by writing . . . as to which the blood of Osiris bore witness . . . when it was poured into this cup, this wine. Give it, blood of Osiris ⟨that?⟩ he ⟨?⟩ gave to Isis to make her feel love in her heart for him . . . give it, the blood of ⟨the magician⟩ (so and so, son of so and so) . . . to (so and so, daughter of so and so) in this cup, this bowl of wine, today, to cause her to feel a love for him in her heart, the love that Isis felt for Osiris when she was seeking after him everywhere. Let (so and so, daughter of so and so) feel it, seeking after (so and so, son of so and so) everywhere . . . loving him, mad after him, inflamed by him, seeking him everywhere, there being a flame of fire in her heart in her moment of not seeing him."

There are a good many analogous rites in which the essential actions are the same but the identifications are not made explicit. One from *The Diadem of Moses* invokes Iao Sabaoth Adonai.

Nuptial mystery

These texts are the closest known parallels to the text of the eucharist. In them as in it a magician-god gives his own body and blood to a recipient who, by eating it, will be united with him in love. Next to these comes the text from the Sidonian ritual already mentioned (p. 120), a Dionysiac parallel to the eucharist, but not its source—the wine is the god's creation, not his blood, whereas "this is my body" and "this is my blood" define the eucharistic miracle. (To try to derive them from the passover ritual or any other Jewish rite is ludicrous. Strange as some rituals of Judaism may be, they do not include eating people.)

The purpose of the rite—to unite the recipients with Jesus, and thus with each other, in love—explains the discourse John substitutes for the story of the eucharist: "I give you a new commandment, that you love one another as I have loved you . . . By this all will know that you are my disciples, if you have love for (literally, "in") each other." The purpose of the rite also explains the agreements and variants of the New Testament texts. They all agree in the words "This is my body" and "this . . . my blood." In the last clause Mark and Matthew have "my blood of the covenant," Paul and most manuscripts of Luke have "the new covenant in my blood." The differences in form of the references to the covenant suggest that it is a secondary element introduced into the primary formula in different places by different Christian circles. It shows an interpretation of the rite by reference to Ex. 24.8 where Moses sprinkles the people with blood from the offerings made on their acceptance of the covenant—their agreement to keep the Law—at Sinai. This interpretation is amazing because for the Christian rite it is essential that this blood should be drunk. But one of the strongest traits of Israelite tradition is the tabu against blood; blood in food was strictly forbidden (Gen. 9.4, and often). That the blood of the sacrifice of the covenant should be drunk (!) is by traditional Jewish standards an atrocity that can have been conceived only by a circle bent on demonstrating its freedom from the Law. Therefore the apparently secondary addition of a covenantal interpretation to the original magical formula, "This is my body; this is my blood," suggest that some of Jesus' earliest followers went even further than he did in rejection of the Law—or, at least, that they adapted his magical rite of union so as to make it also a ritual expression of his libertine teaching. (The other additions to the basic formula are clearly secondary; some appear only in one group of texts, some only in another, and all are interpretive, disciplinary, or hortatory.)

Closely related to the eucharist are a number of claims attributed to Jesus, mainly in John's gospel, which assert or presuppose that he is a supernatural being whose relations to the Father and to his disciples are essentially miraculous. Thus he claims to be united with his followers so that he is in them and they in him. "Remain in me and I in you . . . remain in my love" (Jn.

15.4–9). Such is the union promised by love charms in the magical papyri, for example *PGM* XXXIIa:

Adonai, Abrasax, Pinouti and Sabaos ⟨sic⟩, fire the soul and heart of him, Amonios, whom Helen bore, for him, Serapiacus, whom Threpta bore, now, now, quick, quick! In this hour, in this day, from this ⟨moment⟩ mix together the souls of both and make Amonios, whom Helen bore, and Serapiacus, whom Threpta bore, one and the same, every hour and every day and every night. Therefore, Adonai, highest of gods, who hast the true Name, set to it, Adonai!

In the synoptics Jesus is made to promise his disciples that he will be with them wherever two or three invoke him, "always, to the end of the world" (Mt. 18.20; 28.20). Similar promises are made to the magician by and concerning his familiar spirit (in the rite quoted above, pp. 98f.). In John the promise of companionship is expressed by the metaphor of living together, "If any one loves me . . . my father, too, will love him, and we shall come to him and dwell with him" (Jn. 14.23). The magical papyri anticipate that the god will come to the magician's house and share his table and even his bed. "He will tell you all things clearly ⟨compare Jn. 14.26⟩ and will be a companion, eating with you and sleeping with you." Clearly these come from the same conceptual world.

This brings us to the risen Jesus. Of the miracles that followed his death, his post-mortem appearences to his followers, making himself unrecognizable or invisible, going through locked doors, empowering his followers to handle serpents and drink poison without being harmed, and breathing into them the holy spirit have been treated above and are without exception paralleled in magical material.

Ascent into the heavens (Lk. 24.51; Acts 1.9f.) is particularly important since it was a major concern of the time—Apollonius is made to declare it the true test of deification (the goal of magic) and we find it in the magical papyri as the means of immortalization. Consequently, it is interesting that there are traces of stories that credited Jesus with the feat during his lifetime: In Jn. 3.13 he speaks as one who has already made the ascent; in Philippians 2.5ff. *Jesus* (*not* the preexistent Word) is said to have been "in the form of God" at some time before his death; and I Tim. 3.16 says he was seen by the angels before his assumption.

To these may be added the report that Jesus promised the dying thief, "Today you shall be with me in paradise," as well as the sayings in which Jesus claims knowledge of heavenly things and of the ways of spirits: In heaven the guardian angels of children always have access to ("see the face of") the Father (Mt. 18.10); "I saw Satan falling from heaven like lightning" (Lk. 10.18ff.); "When an unclean spirit has gone out of a man, it goes through waterless

goal of yoga

places seeking rest and does not find any. Then it says . . .", and so on; not to mention the eschatological prophecies. Jesus appears in the gospels as one who knows the world of spirits. This was the age old claim of the *goetes*, and shamans were also famous for their ascents into the heavens. It was also the claim of the Jewish magician who put together *The Book of Secrets* (*SHR*). Listing in his preface the things to be learned from his book he put first, how to do miracles, second, general wisdom, and third,

To know what is necessary for ascent to the heavens; to travel through all that is in the seven heavens, to behold all the signs of the zodiac, and . . . sun . . . moon and ⟨stars⟩; to learn the names of the ⟨angelic⟩ guards of each firmament and their work and how they manage everything, and what are the names of their servants, and what libations are to be made to them, and what is the time ⟨in which each of them⟩ will consent to do whatever is asked by anyone who approaches them in purity.

We have seen (above pp. 101f. and note) the spells in the Demotic Magical Papyrus to make the heavens open and enable the magician to see the sun god in his boat and to worship the angels. Innumerable passages in the papyri make the magician claim secret knowledge of the gods' names, appearances, practices, etc.

Jesus' ascent into and acquaintance with the heavens both explain and are explained by his miraculous nature, set forth notably in statements beginning "I am." Such statements are among the most characteristic elements of magical material; they appear as the climax in many spells. Moreover, some of the things Jesus says he is, are things magicians say they are, thus:

Jn. 10.36: "I am the Son of God."
PGM IV. 535: "I am the Son."
DMP XX. 33: "I am the Son of the living God."
Mt. 26.63f.: "The High Priest said to him, 'I conjure you by the living God to tell us if you are the Messiah, the Son of God.' Jesus says to him 'You said ⟨it⟩.'"
Jn. 6.51: "I am . . . the one come down from heaven."
PGM IV. 1018: "I am the one come forth from heaven."
Jn. 14.6: "I am . . . the truth."
PGM V. 148: "I am the truth."
DMP IX. 13f.: "I am youth, the great name that is in heaven, whom they call . . . 'True.'"
Jn. 8.12: "I am the light of the world."
Lucian, *Alexander* 18: "I am . . . light for men."
PGM XII. 232: "I am Helios who showed forth light."
DMP IX. 10: "I am one shining."

PGM VIII. 50 (to Hermes): "I am you and you are I" (cp. VIII. 37; XIII. 795).

Jn. 10.30: "I and the Father are one."

Jn. 17.21 (to the Father): "You are in me and I in you."

PGM VIII. 37f.; "I am your image."

Jn. 14.9: "He who has seen me has seen the Father."

DMP V. 9: "I am . . . the . . . form of soul that resteth above in the heaven of heavens."

PGM XII. 230: "I am the god whom no one sees."

Mt. 11.27p.: "None knows the Son but the Father, and none knows the Father but the Son."

PGM VIII. 49: "I know you, Hermes, and you, me."

monarchielism

VIII

Since the stories of Jesus' miracles come mostly from the magical tradition, we expect them to be full of details found in that tradition; they should share the same notions and express them in the same words. This they do, and the wealth of such details affords further proof of the magical origin of the stories.

First, the magical and the gospel material have the same view of the world. This could be demonstrated in many points, but is not of great importance for our argument, since this view of the world is common to most documents of the times. That aspect of it which does concern us is the combination of theoretical monotheism with practical polytheism. As to this, all the following notions are common to the gospels and to magical texts. (The proof passages are cited in the notes.)

Over all is "the highest god," but below him are a vast number of supernatural beings—"gods," "angels," and/or "demons"—in one or more hierarchies: for instance, the demons are subject to a "ruler of the demons" or "of this world." Moreover, the demons are divided into classes and are characterized as causes of diseases, disabilities, etc; some of them are said to have these afflictions themselves—deafness and loss of speech, for instance, are caused by deaf and dumb demons. The basic notion that demons are the causes of insanity, disabilities, and diseases, or are themselves the diseases, is unquestioned, and is the chief reason for interest in demons. Similarly angels are of less concern as attendants of the highest god and agents in his cosmic administration than as helpers who can be called on to fight the demons.

Demons are thought to enter their victims; the remedy is to drive them out. A number of demons may enter a single individual—often they go in sevens. Once in possession of a man they may not only cause disease or loss of faculties, but also act and speak through their victims; they often make them act foolishly or criminally, sometimes hurt themselves, sometimes even commit suicide. Men are "led" or "driven" by indwelling demons, and a demon or the affliction it causes may be called a "whip." Another more frequent pair of metaphors is "binding" and "loosing." By demons men are "bound" with diseases; "binding" explains paralysis, loss of faculties, etc., and a cure may be described as "the bond" of a disease being "loosed." A helpful magician like Jesus will not only "loose" spells, afflicted persons, and "the bonds" of their afflictions, but will also "bind" the demons. And evil magicians may loose harmful demons.

This theory of possession had its hopeful side. For instance, if you could get a good spirit to enter you, it would speak through you, and, since it could speak better than you could, it might come in handy, particularly if you had to defend yourself in court. Jesus is made to promise his followers such supernatural aid; one of the spirits promised in John's gospel is "the paraclete," that is, "the speaker for the defense;" Paul's theology is mainly an extension of this notion of possession.

Jesus' ability to control the demons is described as his "power" or "authority;" both terms are also used in magical material. The "power" was thought to be in him and to work of itself, like an electric charge, without his volition—a notion probably derived from actual cures of hysterical persons who succeeded in pushing through the crowds and touching the holy healer. Nevertheless, some of his more elaborate miracles or magical rites followed periods perhaps preparatory, and certain exorcisms are said to have presupposed prayer (and perhaps fasting), as they commonly did for other magicians.

Jesus the magician's power, thus fortified, is divine and may be described as "the finger of God." The demons are sometimes aware of it as soon as—or even before— he comes in sight. They also know his true, supernatural titles ("Son/Holy One of God") and immediately call him by them, since calling a person by his true title or name is a common magical means of getting control over him. However, it doesn't always work; so with Jesus as with other magicians the demons are reduced to entreaties—"Don't torture me! Don't send us out of the country!"—and try to make terms or secure favors in return for leaving. (Jesus' permitting the legion of demons to destroy the Gadarene swine was an example of the success of such bargaining.) Sometimes it is not even necessary for the magician to be present. Jesus, Paul, and others can cure or exorcise at a distance by sending a letter, or a piece of their clothing, or by merely giving an order.

Sometimes, however, demons or diseases are recalcitrant, and then Jesus/the magician resorts to additional means to make his commands effective. (References to these additional means, scattered through the gospel stories, have been supposed mere details of dramatic invention; comparison with other magical material demonstrates their consistency and function.) First the demon may be questioned and made to declare his true name. If he resists or tries to use the magician's name or title in a counterattack, he may be silenced—the word is "muzzled." He must then be ordered out. Usually a command, "a word" is enough. Orders short and to the point, like royal commands or the orders of a master to a slave, make the best impression. (They may be particularly impressive if spoken in a foreign language, supposedly the native one of the demon. However, Greek texts that quote Coptic, Hebrew, or Aramaic formulae, as the gospels and the magical papyri do, may simply preserve the original words of the magician.) A standard form is "I command you," and the spirit who obeys is said "to be subjected" to the magician. In other cases, however, Jesus/the magician may show "anger," "snort," or "fume;" he "sighs" or "groans," and may resort to rebukes, threats, or prayers. Some of the prayers for exorcism in the magical papyri are long, elaborate compositions, but others are very brief, like the commands. Jesus' advice was, keep it short. "Don't repeat yourselves like the *goyim*."

Besides prayer, magicians might—and Jesus did—resort to physical means. Most common was touching the patient, either fingering the affected area, or taking hold of the person; Jesus/the magician's hand was his most potent instrument. Fluid could help to make the contact closer; the readiest form of fluid was spittle, and both spittle and the act of spitting were commonly believed to have magical powers; so we find Jesus, like other magicians, smearing spittle on his patients or using a salve made with spittle.

Almost as important as the command to leave the patient was the command not to return, which we find Jesus and other magicians adding to their exorcisms. That demons did return—in other words, that hysterical patients relapsed—is indicated not only by Jesus' "explanation" of the phenomena, but also by modern medical experience and by ancient spells and amulets to prevent such returns. It seems that the period right after the cure, when the new state of mind was still strange and likely to be upset by hostile contact, was particularly dangerous. This may account for Jesus' sometimes prohibiting his patients to speak to anyone, and for the same prohibition being laid on participants in magicial rites, once they have been put in a state to see or receive the god. The notion lives on in the Jewish laws prohibiting a man to interrupt his prayer in order to speak to anyone.

When a cure seemed successful, people said that the demon had "gone out from" the demoniac or "gone out out of him" (repeating "out"). Jesus, like other magicians, sometimes made the demon destroy some object as proof of his departure from the patient, and sometimes made the patient give a spectacular proof of his cure—for example, if he had been paralyzed, take up his mattress and carry it away.

These observations on the minor traits common to gospel stories and to magical material have chiefly concerned cures and exorcisms because the obvious magical character of these attracted the attention of those scholars from whose works much of the above data has been drawn. But we have seen that many other stories came from magic, and we shall now see that much of the teaching attributed to Jesus did so.

IX

We should not expect the teaching that the gospels attribute to Jesus to be so consistently connected with magic as were the miracles. Like other magicians he was represented both as holy man and as incarnate god; as both he was expected to teach on all religious subjects, from the wishes of gods to the practices of men. Similar variety of teaching was attributed to Apollonius, Alexander the false prophet, and their like. Accordingly, pronouncements on topics he omitted were apt to be supplied by his followers. Paul's arguments show that Jesus' teachings were revered as authoritative, but that Christian communities facing new circumstances often needed new authoritative teaching on new topics. Their needs were met partly by the spirit of Jesus, which early Christians thought was living in them, partly by visions in which the risen Lord spoke to the visionaries (Apoc. 1.9ff., etc.) and partly by Christians themselves, confident of being guided by the divine spirit (e.g. I Cor. 7.40). The scrupulous sometimes tried to distinguish between the teachings of the living Jesus, those of the spirit of Jesus, and those of Jesus' inspired followers, but the possibilities of confusion, to say nothing of fraud, are obvious. Moreover, much of Jesus' teaching was preserved in bare collections of barely connected sayings and this form facilitated interpolation of new sayings to meet new needs. Many such spurious sayings have been identified in the gospels, and many such identifications are probably correct. Another factor that contributed to the growth of Jesus' posthumous teaching was the tendency of storytellers to attribute famous sayings to famous people. Given all these sources of secondary material, it is understandable that much teaching attributed to Jesus in the gospels has nothing to do with magical practice.

Even sayings relevant to magic may not be presented as such, but may appear in contexts that conceal their original significance. Accordingly, we shall consider three types: sayings obviously relevant to magic (those on exorcism, the gift of the spirit, etc.), sayings that have parallels in magical texts, and sayings closely connected with notorious problems about Jesus' teaching. (These last may turn out to have magical significance, because problems are apt to result from distortion of embarrassing evidence, and magic was a cause of embarrassment.) The three groups often overlap—some of the teachings on

magical practices have parallels in magical texts, and both they and other
sayings with magical parallels lead to some of the major difficulties in exegesis
of the gospels.

Most of the teaching on exorcism has already been mentioned. Much is
presented in response to the charge that he cast out demons by "the ruler of the
demons" or "Beelzebul." He is made to reply: (1) It is impossible to cast out
one demon by another because if Satan were to act against himself his kingdom
would fall. The implication is: it will not, so the charge against me is false. (2)
It is impossible to cast out any demons by their ruler, because all demoniacs are
the property of this ruler, "the strong man," so none can be freed until the ruler
is bound (Mk. 3.27p.). (3) His opponents' followers also cast out demons, but
are not accused of practicing magic, so he should not be either (Lk. 11.19p.).
(This is important. How did Jesus differ from ordinary exorcists and so attract
the charge of magic?) Q added a saying: "If I cast out demons by the finger of
God, then the kingdom of God is in touch with you." We have just seen that
"the finger of God" was a power in magic; that the kingdom of God should be
identified (?) with the accessibility of such power is noteworthy.

The other teachings about exorcism attributed to Jesus—that the patient, those in charge of him, and the exorcist all need confidence, that for
some cases prayer is also required (Mk. 9.29), that exorcism should be done for
Jews, but may be done for gentiles (Mk. 7.27ff.), and that, for good public
relations, anyone should be permitted to use "the name of Jesus" in exorcising
(Mk. 9.39)—all these show practical experience and ideas expectable of a
first-century Jewish magician. So does the explanation of relapses—the expelled demon decides to return to its comfortable quarters and brings seven
friends (Mt. 12.43ff). The statements that control of demons is less important
than assurance of salvation (Lk. 10.20), and that some who exorcised and did
miracles in his name would not be saved in the end (Mt. 7.22f), show attempts
to belittle exorcism and subordinate magical powers to party membership and
"correct" behavior—the sort of thing we find in Paul.

It is strange that almost none of Jesus' teachings about healing have been
preserved—apart from the famous saying, "your trust has made you well."
Perhaps the early churches had less success with objectively determinable cures
than with exorcisms, and consequently less interest in the subject. So may
Jesus. Given ancient medical ignorance, the best one could do for most diseases
was go to bed and pray. Hence Christians were careful to report Jesus' teachings on prayer.

Prayer was a specialty of ancient magicians. An early Greek term for "a
man who can get what he wants from the gods"—who will later be called "a
magician"—is, "a pray-er," namely, one who can pray effectively. Hence
many defixions are prayers, many magical amulets have prayers inscribed on

them, and the magical papyri are made up chiefly of prayers and directions as to how these should be said; in other words they are evidence of magicians teaching their disciples how to pray, as Jesus and Apollonius are said to have done.

Most of the directions attributed to Jesus are within the magical tradition. We have mentioned his insistence on trust. Several of his sayings to inculcate trust have close magical parallels. He agrees with the magicians that "All things are possible to God," and, like the magicians, he claims to make his followers "friends" of his god. Consequently, they will get what they want. The promise, "Ask and it shall be given you," appears both in the gospels and in the magical papyri. Moreover, both fear that the god may be slow in attending to his friends' requests. Should this occur, both recommend persistence—particularly for the most important matter, getting a spirit. Luke strung together half a dozen sayings to prove that "even if ⟨God⟩ will not give a man ⟨what he asks, just⟩ because he is His friend, nevertheless ⟨if he shamelessly persists, God⟩ will, because of the shamelessness, get up and . . . give the holy spirit to those who ask him." Similarly, the magical papyri are full of prayers to get spirits, some of them very long and providing for repetition if not at first successful. Even Jesus' getting his god out of bed to wait on the petitioner has a close magical parallel! Against these sayings in Luke we have the more famous one found only in Mt. 6.7f.: "When you pray, don't repeat yourselves like the goyim, for they think they'll be heard on account of their verbosity. So don't be like them." This is suspect because it shows the hostility to gentiles often found in Matthew, and also his dislike of magical traits. Magical papyri also contain passages directing the magician to be brief when he speaks to the gods, and in them we find the explanation of the apparent contradiction—long spells may be needed when one is getting a spirit; after one has it, brief commands suffice. Accordingly, it is not impossible that the contradictory gospel traditions about Jesus' teaching on prayer derive from two aspects of his consistent magical practice.

Another consequence of that practice may have been his advice to his followers to pray in private (as magicians did) "to your hidden Father who sees that which is hidden." This is the magicians' "hidden, invisible One who sees all men," "according to the high priests" (*PGM* XII. 265, "According to the Egyptians ⟨he is⟩ *Phno* . . . , according to the Jews, *Adonaie Sabaoth*.") Another magician invoked Anubis-Hermes as "hidden bedfellow" (*PGM* XXIII.2), recalling Jesus' promise in John, "If one loves me . . . my Father will love him and we will come to him and dwell with him" (14.23).

Magical influence may also account for the preservation of a prayer remembered as that of Jesus. The magical texts are full of spells and prayers with famous "authors'" names: "Solomon's prayer to enchant a medium," "the prayer of Jacob" (to become an incarnate angel), etc. (*PGM* IV. 850; XXIIb; etc.) When we look at "the Lord's prayer" (all purpose) as it stands in Mt. 6.9ff. and Lk. 11.2ff. we find that:

The reference to a god as "father" and his location "in the heavens" are familiar in magical material.

"Hallowing" the Name in Matthew and Luke, and "glorifying" it in John mean the same thing—making the god's Name famous, demonstrating its power by miracles, obedience, etc., so that outsiders will know and revere it. For John this was Jesus' chief function; in his final prayer to the Father before the beginning of the passion Jesus says: "Father, . . . glorify your son that your son may glorify you . . . I have glorified you on earth completing the task you gave me . . . I have revealed your Name to the men whom you gave me . . . Keep them by your Name . . . When I was with them, I guarded them by your Name . . . and I have given them the glory that you gave me, that they may be one as we are one . . . I have revealed to them, and I reveal to them, your Name, that the love with which you loved me may be in them, and I in them" (Jn. 17). The thought here is closely related to that in many passages of the magical papyri which represent the magician as one who glorifies his god and reveals to his chosen followers the god's great Name. "Glorify me as I have glorified the Name of your son Horus!" (*PGM* VII. 504; cp. XXXVI. 165f.). "Tat, Tat, Tat . . . come . . . and reveal thyself to this boy here today . . . for I will glorify thee in heaven before Phre, I will glorify thee before the Moon, I will glorify thee on Earth," etc. "I am he whom you met under the holy mountain and to whom you gave the knowledge of your greatest Name, which I shall keep holy, communicating it to none save to your fellow initiates in your holy rites" (*PGM* XII. 92ff.). This last quotation shows that although magical texts generally agree with John in "glorifying" rather than "hallowing" the God and his Name, they are not unconcerned about its holiness, which is often mentioned. *The Eighth Book of Moses* in *PGM* XIII has as it subtitle "about the Holy Name," and in its climactic prayer the magician asks for deliverance from the laws of nature "because I have hymned thy true and holy Name." (XIII. 637f.)

"Thy kingdom come" has no clear magical parallel, it derives, of course, from Jewish eschatological thought. "Thy will be done" was a prayer used by magicians (*PGM* XII. 189), and "on earth as it is in heaven" expresses the most general objective of magical action: to change the natural order by influence of the supernatural (in this case, as often, the god's will). As the third-century philosopher and magician Iamblichus put it in his book, *On the Mysteries of the Egyptians* (II. 6), "Visitation by the gods ⟨as a result of magic rites⟩ gives us health of body, virtue of soul, purity of mind, and, in one word, the recall of all our faculties to their original principles. It also does away with what is cold and corruptible in us, increases what is warm and makes it more powerful and vigorous, and makes all things ⟨in us⟩ accord with the soul and the mind." An unknown Jewish magician expressed the same idea in more personal terms: "Fill me with wisdom; empower me, master; fill my heart with good things, master, *as an angel on earth*, as one become immortal, as one who has received your gift. Amen, amen."

"Give us today the food to carry us over to the next" brings us down to earth, to the real life of a vagrant performer—actor, magician, holy man or whatever—dependent from day to day on the contributions of the audience he would find in the next country town. The prayer's pathetic combination of magical pretension and genuine poverty argues for its authenticity; the paradox of the poor magician was ridiculed as typical by Lucian and Celsus.

This brings us to a major problem of New Testament criticism —that raised by Jesus' teaching about money. "Don't worry about tomorrow. Don't accumulate savings. It is easier for a camel to go through a needle's eye than for a rich man to enter the kingdom of God. So sell all you have, give ⟨the proceeds⟩ to the poor, and come, follow me." The authors of the gospels were already trying to tone these teachings down (therefore, they were not made up by the churches for which the gospels were written). Apologists have often explained that Jesus did not mean what he said. But these sayings perfectly fit their historical setting. "The poor" are Jesus and his followers. They were supported by contributions (Lk. 8.3). Jesus' prohibition of forethought did not prevent them from keeping a money bag (Jn. 12.6; 13.29). Even so they barely made ends meet, as the petition in the Lord's prayer shows. Accordingly, Jesus was contemptuous of wealth. Such contempt was a philosophic fashion of the time, also affected by Apollonius. It may have been sour grapes, but it was understandably popular—it comforted so many people of similar poverty.

Popularity is not edible. The survival of such a travelling company (a dozen men, with numerous hangers on) implies they had something to sell— an "act" of some sort that could be relied on to bring in contributions. The Roman author Apuleius (himself accused of magic) gives us in his book *The Golden Ass* (VIII. 27ff.) a good picture of another travelling company of holy men, devotees of the Great Mother, whose act was to dress themselves in exotic vestments and go about with the statue of the goddess, shouting, dancing, and playing music. When they came to a rich man's house they would throw themselves into a frenzy, dance like mad, bite and whip themselves, and slash their arms and legs with swords; one would be "filled with the divine spirit" and prophesy. And then they would take up a collection. No act, no collection. So what was the act of Jesus' company?

If we can trust the gospels, it was Jesus' miracles. Everything centered on him, the others were stage hands. Luke gives us a picture of their coming into Jericho. Everybody turned out to see the miracle worker; one man even climbed a tree. Jesus said to him "Zacchaeus, come down at once; I must stay at your house today." A miracle! He had never set eyes on me before, yet he knew my name at once! (But disciples had been "sent out before him into every town and village to which he was going to come" Lk. 10.1). So Zacchaeus, who just happened to be "rich," "received him ⟨and company⟩, rejoicing." No doubt the joy was mutual. A similar picture is given by the longer text of Mark: Jesus raised a young man from the dead, so "they went to the house of the young man, for he was rich." They stayed a week. That was a good week. At the end of it the young man came to Jesus in the evening "wearing a linen cloth over ⟨his⟩ naked ⟨body⟩, and remained with him that night, for Jesus taught him the mystery of the kingdom of God." Next morning Jesus and company left for Transjordan. Perhaps the lesson was not wholly satisfactory.

For some, however, it was. Mark makes Jesus refer to his disciples as "you ⟨to whom⟩ the mystery of the kingdom of God has been given," in contrast to "those outside" (Mk. 4.11f.). Similarly, the magician, given the god's secret name, keeps it "holy, communicating it to none save your fellow initiates in your holy rites" (*PGM* XII. 92ff.). The magician who has received the rite for getting a spirit is one who "has been thought worthy by the Lord God of this great mystery" that he is to "communicate to no one;" he is a "blessed initiate of holy magic." The rites for ascension to heaven are "transmitted mysteries for my only child ⟨for whom⟩ I desire immortality as an initiate" (*PGM* IV. 476f.; cp. 721ff.). To reveal "the holy mysteries" of the god's actions in magic is a sin (*PGM* IV. 2475ff.), and the ceremonies by which one is identified with a god are to be performed with the help of a "director of the mysteries" (*PGM* IV. 172).

Accordingly, it is not surprising that Mark believed Jesus "gave" his disciples "the mystery of the kingdom of God." That some such teaching was to be understood is indicated by the longer text's report of the youth's coming at night in the costume—a linen cloth over his naked body—that was standard for participants in magical rites, especially for boys to be possessed by spirits and made to see the gods. Canonical Mark reports that another young man in the same costume was with Jesus late at night at the time of his arrest (14.51). Nothing is said of what he was doing; we may suppose that he too was being taught "the mystery of the kingdom of God."

As to what Jesus' mystery could have been, the magical papyri give us a clue: A magician boasts that he is "the keeper of the keys of the three-cornered paradise of the earth, the kingdom" (*PGM* III. 541f.). Jesus is said to have promised the keys of the kingdom to Peter (Mt. 16.19) and to have promised the thief on the cross, "Today you will be with me in paradise" (Lk. 23.43).

Admittedly Paul thought the paradise to which either he or Jesus had been caught up was not on earth, but in the third heaven (II Cor. 12.2ff.). This would account for the Christian keys to paradise being "the keys of the kingdom of the heavens." The astronomic location of imaginary entities is liable to change, but the connection of paradise, kingdom, and power of the keys is striking, the more so because one of the peculiarities in Jesus' reported teaching, by which it differs radically from the apocalyptic predictions current in his time, was his claim that the kingdom of heaven was already accessible, and that he and some of his disciples were already in it. If he had the keys, why not? He promises his followers, "Ask and it shall be given you; seek and you shall find; knock and it shall be opened" (Mt. 7.7p.). We have noticed the magical parallels to "ask and it shall be given you" (above, p. 131). What the disciples are to "seek" is presumably what is hidden (i.e. the mystery); what "will be opened" can only be the kingdom of heaven—as Jesus is said to have promised Nathaniel, "You shall see the heaven opened and the angels of God ascending and descending on the Son of Man" (Jn. 1.51). Spells to open the heavens are numerous. Perhaps the closest to Jesus' promise is that already quoted from *DMP* X. 23ff.: "Open to me heaven, O mother of the gods! Let me see the bark of Phre ⟨the sun god⟩ descending and ascending . . . For I am Geb, heir of the gods." A related document is the "Mithras Liturgy" in which, at the spell of the magician who has become "the Son," the doors of the sun disc open and allow him to behold the realm of the gods within it (*PGM* IV. 587–635; compare IV. 959–973).

It is therefore possible that "the mystery of the kingdom" was a magical rite, by which initiates were made to believe that they had entered the kingdom and so escaped from the realm of Mosaic Law. This conjecture would explain a number of important points in Jesus' teaching and his followers' history that have long puzzled New Testament critics, but these points (which I have argued elsewhere) would take us too far from the purpose of the present chapter—to list those traits *in the gospels' picture* of Jesus that appear also in accounts of magicians or directions for magical practices.

Whatever the content of Jesus' mystery, he is said to have distinguished sharply between those who had received it and "those outside." Both he and Apollonius describe themselves as "shepherds," their followers as "the sheep," and outsiders/the wicked as "wolves" (Jn. 10.11ff.; *Life* VIII. 22). Jesus' hostility to outsiders goes further than Apollonius'. He can say, as an agent of the wrath of his god, "I have come to cast fire on the earth" (Lk. 12.49), as a malevolent magician says to the lesser gods, "I cast fury on you of the great gods of Egypt. ⟨Gods,⟩ fill your hands with flames and fire . . . cast it on the heart of (so and so)." Mark makes Jesus declare his purpose: "that seeing they may see and not perceive, and hearing they may hear and not understand." So too the magician of a defixion says, "afflict their intelligence, their mind, their senses, so that they may not understand what they do; pluck out their eyes that they may not see" (*DT* 242.55ff.).

Both Apollonius and Jesus, though they are said to have gone to temples and attempted to reform temple practices, are also said to have described them as dens of robbers. Worship is virtue, not sacrifice. However, in spite of these echoes of popular rationalism, both Jesus and Apollonius represent deification as the goal of their teaching. Apollonius declares himself "a man become divine by wisdom;" he teaches the wisdom of the Brahmans who declare themselves gods, and admires that of the magi, whom he declares divine. The Jesus of John assures his followers that they are united with him as he is with the Father. The union is of two spirits because for him, as for the magical papyri, "God is a spirit." But this spirit must be apprehended in a form. "Show me your true form" prays the magician, "for I am enslaved under your world, to your angel" (*PGM* XIII. 583f.). Jesus, too, reportedly believed in this "ruler of the world" (Jn. 12.31; *PGM* IV. 387), and promised his followers, as did the magicians, "You shall know the truth and the truth shall set you free" (Jn. 8.32). Jesus, like the deified magician, claims "I am the truth" (Jn. 14.6; *PGM* V. 148). His followers declare him "the image of the invisible God" (Col. 1.15; *DMP* V. 9f.), and assert that "No one has ever seen ⟨the highest⟩ God; the ⟨incarnate⟩ only-begotten god (i.e. Jesus) . . . has revealed Him" (Jn. 1.18), while Jesus himself is made to declare, "He who has seen me has seen the Father" (Jn. 14.9). For the gospel of John as for the magical papyri it is this vision of the truth, "the true form" of the god which "none of the gods can see" (*PGM* XIII. 580ff.), that sets one free from the ruler of this world.

This is the true, saving knowledge. Accordingly both Jesus and other magicians give thanks for this deifying revelation. "We thank thee with all our soul . . . ⟨thou⟩ who hast given us mind, speech, knowledge—mind that we may conceive thee, speech that we may call on thee, knowledge that we may know thee. We rejoice that thou hast revealed thyself to us. We rejoice that, while we are in our bodies, thou has deified us by knowledge of thyself" (*PGM* III. 591ff.). In this prayer from a magical papyrus we hear the voice of a church whose members, like the Jesus' followers, are "brothers" and "sisters" by virtue of their common participation in the spirit of their god. Jesus' thanksgiving is that of "the Son"—that "Son" we have met in the magical papyri, who is himself a god: "I thank thee, O Father, Lord of heaven and earth, that . . . thou hast revealed these things . . . All things have been given over to me by my Father, and no one knows the Son except the Father, and no one knows the Father except the Son and any to whom the Son may choose to reveal Him" (Mt. 11.25ff.p.).

Thus analysis of the teachings attributed to Jesus leads to the supernatural claims that closed the section on his miracles. His teaching turns out to be a consequence and extension of his miracles. The miracles won him his audience, gave his words importance, and made him an authoritative teacher (Mk. 1.27). His teaching is plausibly reported to have been the expression of this authority, this supernatural power that enabled him to set aside the Mosaic Law with a mere, "You have heard that it was said . . ., but *I* say ⟨something different⟩" (Mt. 5.21–45, cp. *Life* I. 17), and to assure his followers that "The Law and the prophets were ⟨valid⟩ until John" (the Baptist) and "among those born of women there is none greater than John;" "but from then ⟨John's time⟩ on the ⟨accessibility of the⟩ kingdom of God is proclaimed, and anybody can force his way into it," and "the least in the kingdom of God is greater than John!" (Lk. 16.16p.; 7.28p.). All minor elements of his teaching can be seen as expressions of this authority. We have considered only those with clear magical parallels. The most important role of magic for the study of his teaching is not its demonstration of these minor parallels, but its explanation of the authority, the power.

X

Consequently the most important magical parallel to the gospels is that to Jesus' life and legend as a whole. This we saw in the comparison of Jesus and Apollonius (above, pp. 85ff.), but even when Jesus' career does not parallel that of Apollonius, it is consistently paralleled by other magical material, and the parallels *are not haphazard*; they fit together. Taking the gospel material supported by such parallels, we get the following coherent, consistent and credible picture of a magician's career.

After undergoing a baptism believed to purge him of sin, Jesus experienced the descent of a spirit upon him — the experience that made a man a magician—and heard himself declared a god, as magicians claimed to be. Then "the spirit drove him out into the desert," a common shamanic phenomenon. After visionary experiences there, he returned to Galilee where his new spiritual power manifested itself in exorcism, in cures of types familiar in magic, in teaching, with magical parallels and authority, and in the call of disciples, who, like persons enchanted, were constrained to leave their families and belongings and follow him alone.

With these disciples he lived the predictable life of a travelling magician and holy man—a picaresque existence reflected, perhaps accidentally but not inaccurately, by the structure of the gospels. The company was supported by his success as exorcist and healer, which increased and was increased by his fame. His fame was such that other magicians began to use his name as that of a god in their exorcisms. Soon opposition developed. His neglect of Jewish law, especially as to fasting, purity, and the Sabbath, as well as his association with rich libertines ("tax collectors and sinners"), antagonized "the scribes" (Jewish notaries, lawyers and upper-schoolteachers) who collected, enlarged and disseminated a body of discreditable stories about him, including various charges of magic: he had raised John the Baptist from the dead and was magically identified with him; or, he did his miracles by control of the ruler of the demons, Beelzebul, and was identified with him.

Perhaps to counter these rumors, perhaps to extend his influence, perhaps for private reasons of which we have no evidence, he began to initiate his disciples into his own magical experiences. Such initiations are provided for in magical documents, but neither there nor in the gospels do we have more than hints of what went on. The synoptics describe the inner circle of disciples as those "to whom the mystery (initiation) of the kingdom of God has been given" and who can therefore receive further secret teaching, not given to "those outside." They say that "the twelve" were given power to exorcise. They tell of Jesus revealing himself in glory with two supernatural beings on "the mountain" in Galilee; and the longer text of Mark tells of a young man coming to Jesus by night, in the standard costume of an initiate, for instruction in the mystery. Canonical Mark (14.51) hints at a similar initiation by reporting that a young man in the same scanty costume was with Jesus on the night of his arrest. John (3.2ff.) has a similar story of a man coming to Jesus by night for secret instruction on how to enter the kingdom. He also reports that Jesus (or his disciples) baptized, and that Jesus instituted a rite of footwashing that cleansed his disciples and gave them a share in his lot. These are the data; as to what the ceremony—more likely, the sequence of ceremonies—was, we have no direct information.

We are better informed about another magical rite, the eucharist, that Jesus instituted to unite his disciples with himself, both in love and in body. Mark (followed by Matthew), Luke, and Paul give us at least partially independent, but closely similar accounts of the ceremony, while John, although he suppresses it, hints at it, interprets it, and echoes it in several places. The rite is a familiar type of magical ceremony in which the magician identifies himself with a deity, and identifies wine and/or food with the blood and/or body of this deity and of himself. The wine and/or food is then given to a recipient who by consuming it is united with him and filled with love for him. This rite is attributed to Jesus by the earliest and most reliable sources.

With the eucharist the gospels' account of Jesus' magical career virtually ends. While they all report that his claim to be a (son of) god was a factor in his prosecution, and John reports that he was also charged before Pilate with magic (18.30), it does not seem likely that these were the decisive charges. John's statement that the Jerusalem priests were motivated primarily by fear of a messianic uprising (11.48ff.), and the agreement of all the gospels that Jesus was executed as a would-be "King of the Jews," leave no doubt as to the cause of the crucifixion. While Jesus' magical powers may have led his disciples to believe him the Messiah, and may have persuaded him that they were right, that belief was not *in itself* a matter of magic. The fact that much magic is nonsense does not imply that all nonsense is magic; messianic nonsense was a different (more virulent) strain.

Jesus' resurrection, ascension, and miscellaneous post-resurrection activities belong to the psychopathic histories of his disciples. Those histories must have been shaped by their experiences with Jesus. What they saw after his death presumably reflected what they saw at his suggestion. However, our primary concern in this chapter has not been to determine what Jesus did, but to analyze the gospels' account of what he did and to point out the elements which correspond with magical material and which therefore, although preserved in the Christian stories of his life, provided evidence for a picture of Jesus the magician. This demonstration, now completed, has not been exhaustive. Many bodies of magical material, particularly in the miracle stories, have been indicated only briefly and in general; many additional details, particularly of the teachings, could be shown by probable arguments to have magical connections. Nevertheless, the picture presented has been full enough to be clear.

This picture is *not* based on hostile tradition about Jesus. The hostile tradition was traced and analyzed in chapters 3 and 4; in the present account it has appeared only insofar as the charges brought against him were events in his life and recorded as such by the gospels. The picture in this chapter has been drawn entirely from the gospels, the accounts of Jesus given by his own followers. We have merely read the gospels with some knowledge of ancient magical material and noticed what, in the light of that material, the gospel stories and sayings really say. The resultant picture obviously accords with the one given by the outsiders' tradition, which it commonly supplements rather than contradicts. That the two agree so often as to the facts reported and differ chiefly in their evaluation of these facts, is a strong argument for supposing the facts correct.

(A further piece of evidence may be worth adding here. After this book was finished and had gone to the publisher, I chanced on E. Becker, *The Denial of Death* (N.Y., 1973), and was amazed to find that Becker's picture of "the leader and his gang" in his chapter "The Spell Cast by Persons—The Nexus of Unfreedom" (pp. 127–158) agreed so closely with the preceding account of Jesus as magician that one might think it had been used as a source. That the gospel picture accords equally with the psychological type and with the magical data, seems to indicate the picture's veracity.)

~ 8 ~

What the Evidence Shows

I

The evidence presented in the preceding chapter was drawn from the gospels as they now stand. Therefore we have to ask some questions about its significance. In the first place, since Jesus was crucified about 30, and the gospels date from 70 to 100, how much of their evidence can be traced back towards his time, and how far? This question often arose in the preceding chapters, in regard to various details. Let us summarize the points already made.

All scholars recognize that the authors of the gospels used sources, and that when material can be assigned to a source its date must be moved back accordingly. Thus the source(s) of Q, the non-Markan material common to Matthew and Luke, is(are) usually thought to be at least as early as Mark; if this opinion be correct, material Mark and Q have in common will come from at least a generation earlier—from the time of Paul in the 50s; Paul was converted about four or five years after the crucifixion; he was in touch with Jesus' immediate disciples. However, even when the source of a story cannot be determined, close examination may show that some details have been added by the evangelist or some earlier editor, and that the story must therefore be earlier than the additions. Thus analysis of the story of Jesus' rejection in Nazareth showed that the saying, "A prophet is not without honor except in his home town" was an addition, because it interrupted the narrative, and that Mark's contradiction of the statement, "he was not able to do any miracle there" by adding "except that he healed a few sick, laying his hands ⟨on them⟩" was clearly secondary and apologetic.

Such apologetic material proved an important clue, since the things it tried to excuse or explain away were things that Jesus' followers would not have invented, but had to admit, or at least deny. But why were they mentioned at all? Evidently because Jesus' followers had to answer what their opponents were saying. Thus apologetic traits indicated the existence of charges about Jesus that the gospels were trying to answer. The charges must have been earlier than the answers. It seemed likely to suppose that they were not isolated accidents, but came from a body of hostile material. This supposition was confirmed when the accusations answered in the gospels by scattered apologetic passages turned out to fit together and form a coherent and credible account of Jesus the magician and his career. This did not prove the account true; as polemic, the total picture it gave was no less suspect than the gospels' apologetic answers. But the gospel answers did offer some indication of the truth of the individual accusations, since they reported things the authors of the gospels (or their sources) could not neglect and sometimes would not deny.

This evidence of an early date for the outsiders' tradition was confirmed by other facts: The tradition was closely related to stories of Jesus' early work in Galilee, stories that knew the names of the members of his family, the nicknames of his intimate disciples, the place names of Galilean villages. (Who in the outside world had even heard of Nazareth?) All these Galilean traits disappeared from the polemic tradition as it moved into the great world where no one was interested in such details. Similarly, the earliest accusations of magic made against Jesus—he had raised the Baptist from the dead, he had the demon Beelzebul—were specific and connected with the history and environment of his early ministry; they soon dropped out of use and never appear in later polemic where the charges are general and nameless (he was a *goes,* a "deceiver," etc.). Also, their picture of him does not accord with any earlier literary type, but only with the actual magicians of his time, as we know them from defixions, papyri and later literature; therefore, it was probably drawn from observation, not literary convention. The only demonstrable literary borrowings are from Old Testament stories of the prophets (including Moses), and these account for only a few miracle stories and some interpretive additions, not for the essential elements of the figure (see Appendix B).

Finally, this tradition was not an inference floating in air. It was attached by the gospels to a definite social class, the scribes. Analysis of the gospel references to hostile groups showed that those to the other main group, the Pharisees, were consistently secondary in material from the Galilean period (see Appendix A), but those to the scribes were original. These references reflect the interests and attitudes we should expect of the scribes (pious legalism), and the fact that the hostile tradition originated in the scribal class of Galilee explained the transmission of Galilean data to the scribes of Jerusalem and its development there. Accordingly it seems reasonable to conclude that the outsiders' picture of Jesus the magician, although it used material drawn from home town gossip, was principally shaped by the scribes during his work in Galilee.

II

This conclusion gives us some criteria by which to estimate the historical value of other elements in the gospels. Even if the picture was a caricature it must have had some points of resemblance to the original. Can these points be identified?

First, there were the miracles. They are presupposed by the outsiders' tradition—the charge "magician" results from an attempt to explain them, and even the stories that seem to deny Jesus' power to do miracles take for granted his reputation as a miracle worker. This is true of the story of his rejection in Nazareth as well as that of his refusal to give a sign (which may or may not be true to history, but, as the story of a challenge to a faith healer, is unquestionably true to life). Even the taunt at the crucifixion—"He saved others, himself he cannot save"—takes the miracles for granted, and can hardly be a creation of Christian propaganda. (Most likely it is part of the hostile tradition, introduced by the Christian storyteller for dramatic irony.)

We argued in chapter 2 that Jesus won his following primarily as a miracle worker and that if we begin with the miracles we can understand his authority as a teacher, his involvement in messianic speculation, and his ultimate crucifixion, but if we begin with the teaching, his role as a miracle worker and the consequent events and beliefs are unexplained. Of (literally) thousands of teachers of the Law recorded in rabbinic literature, none had a career similar to that of Jesus. He is a figure of a different social type.

Given his career as a miracle worker, it is not surprising that many miracle stories in the gospels show signs of repeated reworking, proof that they originated in early Christian circles and were handed down by long tradition. This has been demonstrated by form criticism and need not be argued again. Neither do we need to insist again on the Palestinian background of most of the miracle stories. That such stories circulated about Jesus in his lifetime cannot reasonably be questioned, nor can the likelihood that his disciples remembered and repeated them after his death. How much they grew by repetition, how much by invention, which of the details—or stories—reflect original facts, are questions often impossible to answer. The certain and important thing is the place in the earliest tradition of this *type* of story as evidence of the social type of the man.

III

A miracle worker is not necessarily a magician. The disciples of the scribes also cast out demons, and Jesus reportedly complained that they were not accused of doing so by Beelzebul, while he was (Lk. 11.19p.). Whether or not the report is true, the complaint reflects a difference that existed in his lifetime. He was in fact accused, while other exorcists—for instance, the one who demonstrated his powers before Vespasian—were admired as representatives of "our ⟨Jewish⟩ therapy." So there was in fact some difference, between him and them, that led to his being charged with magic. Therefore elements of the gospels that indicate what this difference was *may* be primitive.

The first difference alleged by the outsiders' tradition is that Jesus "had" a demon and did his exorcisms by this indwelling demonic power. Since this charge was not brought against the other exorcists, they must have been thought to effect their exorcisms by other means, presumably prayer to God, the use of spells, herbs, amulets attributed to Solomon, etc. Perhaps Jesus did not use such methods, but perhaps he did. The charge that he had a demon may have been based on other peculiarities—compulsive behavior, neglect of the Law, and claims to supernatural status. (Compulsive behavior was characteristic of demoniacs. For Jesus it is attested by the report that "the spirit drove him out into the wilderness" (Mk. 1.12) which, as we saw, is best explicable as a supposedly historical statement. (It did not serve Christian propaganda—both Matthew and Luke softened it—but it does agree with the pattern of shamanic behavior.) Even more important is the report that Jesus' family tried to seize him "because, they said, 'He is out ⟨of his mind⟩'" (Mk. 3.21). This surely comes from primitive polemic tradition—both Matthew and Luke deleted it. Mark probably included it because he found it in a summary of that tradition together with the immediately following charge of demonic possession (3.22) that he took over because he thought he had to answer it. In any event, both charges date from Jesus' lifetime and the one helps to explain the other.

Neglect of the Law is the theme of the stories of disputes with the scribes. That the disputes are with the scribes, as opposed to the later fashionable Pharisees, is evidence that the stories date before 70, and probably before 50 when the Jerusalem church began to be on good terms with its neighbors and to make many converts who were "zealots for the Law" (Acts 21.20). The general picture these stories give of Jesus is confirmed by the primitive polemic parodied in Q: "a gluttonous man and a winebibber, a friend of tax collectors and sinners" (Lk. 7.34p.). These early traditions about Jesus' behavior are supported strongly by the attribution to him of many antinomian sayings, but even more strongly by the extensive evidence for libertine Christian teachers already in the time of Paul. Where did this side of the movement come from, if not from Jesus? Finally, Jesus' rejection of the Law can be understood as a consequence and manifesto of his supernatural claims (discussed below). All of this is on the theological level. On the practical level it is easy to understand that a class of small town lawyers and teachers, who owed their prestige and income to the Law, would detest a fellow who publicly neglected it, would hate to see him attract large crowds, and would spread malicious charges to discredit him. Jn. 9.16,24 explicitly makes neglect of the Law (in this case, on Sabbath observance) "the Pharisees'" reason for refusing to attribute Jesus' miracles to God (and thereby implicitly attributing them to a demon).

Supernatural claims: In the early dispute stories, when Jesus' opponents complain of his neglect for the Law, he claims that he is a supernatural being on whom the Law is not binding. One claim which can be dated to his lifetime is that to be "the bridegroom" whose companions cannot fast "while he is with them." "The bridegroom" comes from the Song of Songs; second-century Jewish interpreters thought he was God. In discussion of the trial stories we saw that three various traditions represented Jesus' claim to be a (son of) god as a major point in the Jews' accusations against him; presumably it figured in the primitive polemic (above, pp. 39ff.)

This presumption is supported by the demonstrable antiquity of the story of the descent of the spirit that made him a (son of) god. Everyone agrees that this is prior to the legends of his having been sired by God (found only in Matthew and Luke), but Bultmann also observed that it contradicts John's theology and is preserved in John's text as an inconsistent fossil, presumably out of reverence for its established place in the belief of John's church. It also, as Bultmann again observed, contradicts the theology of Mark, who also must have taken it over from established tradition. A story that thus antedated not only the texts, but even the beliefs of both John and Mark, must have been very old. Are traces of the belief that the story expresses to be found in material that can be assigned to Jesus' lifetime? Indeed there are. The belief is the Christian equivalent of the outsiders' charge, "He has a demon" (*demon* and *spirit* were, in vulgar usage, interchangeable terms). If the outsiders' charges were already in circulation, it is hard to believe that the disciples would have made up a story that would justify them. We should therefore suppose either that the Christian story was the starting point, and the outsiders' attack a malicious interpretation of it, or, more probably, that both were independent, contemporary interpretations of Jesus' compulsive behavior and compelling powers. In either case the Christian story must be at least as early as the polemic, and must have originated during Jesus' activity in Galilee.

The same thing goes for the consequence of getting a spirit—the claim to be "a (son of) god". Commentators have read this expression as the trinitarian title it became, not the Aramaic phrase it originally was. Once its original meaning ("a god") is recognized, it accentuates the discrepancy between the miracle stories, in which Jesus appears as a god acting by his own power, and the gospel framework of these stories, that never bluntly calls him a god (except in Jn. 1.18) and seems at times deliberately to disguise his deity—to add traits emphasizing his human limitations, etc. This need not be taken to imply that the evangelists did not think Jesus a god. It may rather be a result of their effort to solve the literary problem of portraying that primitive paradox, the magician, the man who feels himself possessed of supernatural powers while remaining a man. Alternation between passionate assertion of divinity and pathetic acknowledgment of humanity is characteristic of the magical papyri. Observers see, understand, and therefore give predominance to the human side. This tendency would be reinforced by the evangelists' obligation to picture Jesus as a man, and even more by the strong trend in the early churches towards reconciliation with traditional Judaism. At all events, however the evangelic framework may be explained, the implications of the miracle stories are clear. They match the bridegroom saying, the reports of the accusations made to Pilate, and the baptism (and transfiguration) stories in pushing the date of Jesus' divinity back to his own lifetime. When so many independent lines of evidence point to a single conclusion, the conclusion seems likely.

IV

In discussing the story of the descent of the spirit we showed that its closest parallels are found in accounts of magical rites. Indeed it seems to be an abbreviated version of such a magical account—abbreviated to eliminate the magical traits. As such, it does not stand alone in the gospels. Fridrichsen, in *The Problem of Miracle in Primitive Christianity,* pointed out many similar passages. Sometimes it is clear that stories have been revised to get rid of magical details. The exorcism in Mk. 5 is a good example. According to Mark, Jesus makes the demon tell his name. This was standard magical practice; once you knew the name you could use it to order the demon out. But in Mark the exorcism proper has been deleted, so the question is useless. Even that was too much for Matthew; he deleted the question as well (8.29f.). Matthew's consistent deletion of magical traits has been demonstrated by Hull, *Hellenistic Magic,* 116ff. Such censorship left most references to magical procedure in the gospels scattered and isolated, one term here, another there. Consequently their true significance remained unrecognized until they were collected and explained by scholars in the present century. Now the consistency of their usage and function is clear and refutes traditional efforts to treat them as psychological observations or homiletic or dramatic elements. It has been established, by the work of Bauernfeind, Bonner, Eitrem, Fridrichsen, and others, that behind the present Jesus of the gospels there lurked, in Christian tradition, an earlier Jesus whose practices were much closer to those of Jesus the magician.

Consequently the many parallels demonstrated in the preceding chapter, between Jesus' practices and teachings and those of other magicians, carry with them a slight presumption in favor of authenticity. Even when allowance has been made for complicating factors—the narrators' love of the miraculous and a continuing, practical interest in magic in some Christian circles—it remains certain that the stronger tendencies of the tradition by which the gospel material was handed down were those hostile to magic. The prevailing temper, though far from rationalistic, was that of lower middle-class respectability and its commonplace structure of contradictions, "rational theology." Accordingly when magical traits appear in the gospels it is less likely that they have been added by the tradition than it is that they have survived from the earlier, lower-class, and more primitive form of the cult.

A conspicuous case is that of the eucharist, an unmistakably magical rite, the institution of which was reported by a tradition attributed to Jesus, that Paul "received" after his conversion within four or five years of the crucifixion. Substantially the same rite is reflected in more or less independent traditions known to Mark, Luke and John. In John's church the rite is still secret, he suppresses the story and discusses the miracle only by allusion. In all the sources we see it variously interpreted, moralized, and adjusted to Old Testament legend, by additions to the wording, by commentary, or by location in a secondary, theologically motivated framework. When such window dressing is stripped away, what remains is an absolutely primitive figure: a magician-god who unites his followers to himself by giving them his body and blood to eat and drink. Can there be any doubt as to which element is original, or where it came from?

There not only can be, there has been. Bultmann observed the inconsistency between the rite and the setting in which the synoptics place it—the setting calls for a passover meal (Mk. 14.12,16p.) which the eucharist clearly is not. Hence Bultmann leapt to the conclusion that the eucharist was a hellenistic rite that had replaced Jesus' original passover. But the eucharist is no more—and no less—"hellenistic" than was Jesus himself. It is a typical piece of the intercultural magic of the time, its closest analogues (which Bultmann ignored) being Egyptian (above, pp. 122f.). And the rite which Paul asserts was given him by tradition "from the Lord" (I Cor. 11.23) is clearly older than the passover framework, which is part of Paul's (and even more, of James') attempt to adjust Christianity to the Israelite tradition—to represent the Christians as "the true Israel," to equate either Jesus' death or the eucharist with the passover sacrifice; to show in one way or another, that Jesus and the details of his career were foretold by the prophets, and so on. All this is midrash, secondary interpretation, shown to be secondary by the facts: (1) it does not fit the original material, (2) different writers advance different and contradictory theories—even as to the date of the crucifixion—and (3) they all clutch at insignificant similarities in their desperate efforts to find anything to prop up their claims. Such defense is the most conclusive refutation. Accordingly while, as Bultmann saw, it is certain that the connection of the eucharist with the passover is secondary, it is also certain that the eucharist is the older element, the one derived from Jesus himself, and that the passover framework is the later addition. This accords with the common form-critical supposition that stories are usually older than the framework in which the evangelists have placed them. Common suppositions are not always correct, but the reversal of this one in the case of the eucharist should have called attention to the arbitrary nature of Bultmann's hypothesis.

This clear case should guide us in our judgment of others less certain. Though exceptions could occur, the later Christian tradition through which the gospel material came down was usually moralizing and respectable; it found magic embarrassing. Therefore the magical elements that remain in the text are likely to come from the earliest days of the movement, indeed, from its founder.

V

The reverse is true of "Judaizing" traits. Of course Jesus was a Jew, and so were all his disciples—presumably. The presumption is not certain; Galileans with pure Greek names like Philip are dubious. But even granting the presumption, the fact remains that nominal Judaism did not guarantee much knowledge or observance of Jewish law. The early polemic against Jesus tells us unequivocally that his neglect of "the Law" was sufficiently conspicuous to make him bitter enemies. If he practiced magic and claimed to be a god, as those enemies said he did, his private attitude towards the Law was probably even less reverent than that expressed in his public practice. There is little to indicate that his immediate disciples were much more observant than he. However, during the 40s when leadership of the Jerusalem church was taken over by his brother James, notorious for traditional piety, and the Jerusalem community improved its relations with the Pharisees, a similar development was taking place in the Aegean area from which most books of the New Testament come. This development was due to Paul. Before his conversion

Paul had been a Pharisee unfailing in his observance of the Law and so zealous that he persecuted the Christians (Phil. 3.5f., etc.). Conversion left him passionately convinced of his freedom from the Law, but he never lost the traces of his Pharisaic training. He proclaims that his only law is the will of Christ who lives in him (Rom. 8), but the indwelling Christ requires him to practice all the good, middle-class Jewish virtues, and to conceive of Christianity as a new "Israel" (Gal. 6.16).

With James and Paul as its two most influential figures, there is no doubt that Christianity between 45 and 60 swung far back towards conventional (and especially, toward Pharisaic) Judaism. Of the deposit this period left in the gospels, the more extreme expressions—for instance, the orders in Mk. 2.20 to require fasting, in Mt. 23.3 to obey all scribal and Pharisaic rulings—are readily recognizable, but much more is dubious. In general, this history of the tradition should make us suspicious of any gospel material that tries to square Jesus with the teachings of the Old Testament or the conventional Judaism of his time. Even more suspect are modern efforts to make him a rabbi or a prophet. We have remarked that the term "rabbi" did not acquire its modern sense until half a century or more after his death. Many outsiders, in his own time, did think him a prophet; a few gospel stories reflect this belief; more are designed to prove him greater than the prophets. However, as pictured in the gospels he obviously differs from the prophets, not only by being greater, but by being a different kind of figure, having a different relation both to God and to his followers. Appendix B shows the differences are so great that the gospel tradition cannot be explained by the supposition that the figure behind it was a prophet.

Therefore, in the gospels' picture of Jesus, prophetic traits, like Old Testament traits and Pharisaic traits, are *ipso facto* suspect. They are not necessarily false. Presumably Jesus did know something of the books now in the Old Testament, of the syagogue prayers and common pious practices of the Judaism of his time, and of the apocalyptic literature then popular. He may even have encouraged the belief that he was a prophet or messiah; perhaps he affected some appropriate traits. Matthew makes him go so far in this effort as to ride two donkeys at once; figuratively he may sometimes have tried to do so. If he did, it would probably be impossible now to distinguish authentic traits from the similar ones that Pauline and Jacobean Christianity have added to the stories about him. And even if the genuine traits could be distinguished, they would at best be of peripheral interest for any attempt to define the figure central to the gospel tradition. For that purpose, neither "prophet" nor "rabbi" nor "apocalyptic seer" will do. They simply do not account for most of the data, nor for its most important, central, and generative elements.

VI

If we look for a figure that could possibly account for the rise of the tradition preserved in the gospels, we find three pictures to guide us. One is the official portrait of "Jesus Christ, the Son of God," given by the gospels as they stand, one is the picture of "Jesus the magician" given by the hostile tradition, and the third is the primitive Christian picture of "Jesus the god" which, as we have seen, lies behind the present gospel portrait.

All three of these are expressions of propaganda and each is inherently incredible, since they all explain the phenomena of Jesus' life in terms of a mythological world of deities and demons that do not exist. The explanations must therefore be discarded, but what of the phenomena? Some of those reported are obviously inventions—walking on water, multiplying food, and the like are best explained not as "misunderstandings," but as fictions. As such, however, they are exceptional. Most of the miracles reported are possible, if stripped of the "explanations" that make them miracles. For example: Jesus could not cast out demons; there are none. But he could and probably did quiet lunatics, and the reports of "casting out demons" are merely reports of quieting lunatics (what observably happened) with built-in demonological "explanations." Again, he could not glow in the dark. But he could and probably did persuade himself and his disciples that he would appear in glory, and eventually they all "saw" (by hallucination) what they hoped to see.

The lines between inventions, exaggerations, misunderstandings, and true reports can rarely be drawn with complete assurance. For instance take the story that Jesus stilled a storm. He *may* have had such confidence in his own power as to order a storm to cease, and a storm *may*, by chance, have ceased when so ordered. The facts reported (first the order, then the cessation) *may* be true, as Herodotus said they were in the case of the magi; only the implied explanation ("the storm stopped because of his order") must be false. But the whole story may be a fiction. There is no way of deciding the question and, for our purpose, no need of deciding it. We are not trying to recover an exact record of the things done and words spoken by Jesus, but to determine what sort of things he did and said, what role he played in relation to his disciples and to the society around them. For this purpose the sort of stories made up about a man are often better evidence, more penetrating characterizations, than are exact reports of his actions (as Modigliani portraits are truer than passport photographs).

Besides accounting for the major traditions, the real Jesus must have been a figure of the social world of his time and have shared the notions then current about the supernatural and natural worlds. He can be described historically as "a Jew of the early first century, from Nazareth, who went for baptism to John, became famous in Galilee as a miracle worker and preacher, was arrested in Jerusalem by the priestly authorities, and was turned over to Pilate who, about A.D. 30, had him crucified as a would-be 'King of the Jews.'" Every point in this definition entails a set of circumstances that the real Jesus must have satisfied—in other words, he must have been the things any first-century Jew had to be.

The description, however, is not complete. It omits the things that made Jesus historically important. He was also, and no less historically, a Jew whose disciples saw him risen from the dead, believed him ascended into the heavens, expected him to return in glory as ruler of the world, and, while awaiting his return, formed the Christian Church, perpetuated the practice of the eucharist that he had begun, continued to tell stories of his life, miracles, and teaching, and developed these into the tradition from which the gospels were composed. And he was also, as said above, the cause of the neutral and hostile traditions we have surveyed. All these facts, too, entail sets of circumstances that the real Jesus satisfied, and that must be satisfied by any historical account of him. These are the (generally unnoticed) parameters within which the historical interpretation of the gospels must work. Let us try then, with these guidelines, to look at the most conspicuous features of the three portraits and see to what extent they reveal a common original. Since the individual points have already been discussed, we can simply present the results of the previous discussion.

VII

The gospels say that, like other "divine men", he was fathered by a god and born of a virgin. His opponents said he was the illegitimate son of a Galilean peasant woman by a Roman soldier named Pantera. The gospel stories and those of the opponents both appear towards the end of the century, but may be earlier. In the very early source of Mark 6 he is referred to simply as the son of his mother, Mary.

Matthew says he was taken to Egypt as an infant (for a grossly improbable reason) and as a small boy was brought to Nazareth. His opponents say he went to Egypt as a young man, looking for work, and learned magic there. The early elements of the gospels say nothing of his having been in Egypt, but contain accounts of many magical proceedings that have their closest parallels in Egyptian texts.

The rabbinic report that in Egypt Jesus was tattooed with magic spells does not appear in polemic material, but is cited as a known fact in discussion of a legal question by a rabbi who was probably born about the time of the crucifixion. The antiquity of the source, type of citation, connection with the report that he was in Egypt, and agreement with Egyptian magical practices are considerable arguments in its favor.

Another consideration in its favor is its close connection with the rabbinic report that he was "a madman"—that is, occasionally manic or hysterical. This also appears, as a known fact, in the same legal argument. The old source used by Mark attributed the same opinion to his family (3.21); both Matthew and Luke suppressed it. John reports the hostile opinion to discredit his opponents. The opinion is supported by gospel stories of Jesus' behavior that accord with phenomena observed in shamans and similar figures.

Mark reported that Jesus was baptized by John. Preserved accounts of his opponents' charges say nothing of this, but Matthew's attempt to "explain" the fact, and the fourth gospel's attempt to suppress it suggest that it did figure in polemic against him. In that event, the preservation of the report by all the synoptics argues for its truth.

The gospels' story of the descent of the spirit is matched by the outsiders' charge, "he has a demon." Here we have contrary evaluations of substantially the same supposed "fact." The gospels' myth of the descent of the spirit has several points in common with magical texts for much the same purpose—the heavens opened, the bird as a messenger or spirit, the result, that he is made "the Son." Such a group of agreements makes it seem that the gospel story came from a person whose imagination was shaped by knowledge of magical texts or ceremonies. Whether or not this person was Jesus is uncertain.

The synoptics report that the descent of the spirit was followed by a heavenly declaration that Jesus was "my Son." The invocation of the spirit in the "Mithras Liturgy" ends with the magician's claim to be "the Son." "The Son of the living God" was a power in the magical pantheon, as in the thought of some Christians (Mt. 26.63). The synoptics report that demoniacs repeatedly called Jesus a "son of god," and that after his miracles his disciples recognized him as such. The outsiders say his success in doing miracles enabled him to claim to be the son of a god. Again we have contradictory evaluations, and diverse mythological "explanations," of basic facts on which both parties agree, namely, that the miracles and the terms "son of god," meaning "god," and "the Son," the title of a supposed supernatural being, were closely connected.

Mark represents Jesus' claim to be "the Son" as a secret he reveals only in his confrontation with the High Priest (14.61f.). Q, however, reports that he claimed that only he, as "the Son," knew "the Father"—a claim that has striking magical parallels. In John he repeatedly claims to be "the Son" and similar supernatural entities, in terms that are sometimes found word for word in the magical papyri. Paul, a generation before Mark, commonly refers to Jesus as "the Son of God." The outsiders' tradition is unanimous in reporting that Jesus claimed to be a son of god, and in connecting the term or title with his miracles, and the gospels are unanimous both in connecting it with his miracles and in making Jesus' claim to it play an important role in the legal proceedings against him.

The many magical parallels to details in the stories of exorcisms and cures show that these stories have usually been shaped by knowledge of magical practices. It has been shown that such parallels were more conspicuous in the gospels' sources than they are in the present official portrait. Many of those that survived in Mark were eliminated by Matthew, and there are traces of similar censorship having been at work already in the composition of Mark. These parallels agree with the opponents' reports that Jesus did his miracles "by magic." In view of this evidence it seems probable that he did use magical methods, which may have worked for psychological reasons. Here the negative evidence is impressive. Legends of the gods credit them with impossible feats of surgery and wonders of all sorts, but the stories of magicians, the magical recipes in the papyri, and the gospel stories are all three limited, for the most part, to "miracles" that can be performed by suggestion. Both gospels and magical material would seem to reflect similar bodies of practice, and both depart from practice by exaggeration and wishful thinking, along similar lines and within similar limits.

The clearest evidence of Jesus' knowledge and use of magic is the eucharist, a magical rite of a familiar sort. The synoptics and Paul report the institution, but say little more; John suppresses the story of the institution, but puts in Jesus' mouth many sayings expressing and underlying idea—identification/union with his disciples—and these sayings have close magical parallels. We again come to the question: have the synoptics kept Jesus' teaching on this matter secret, or has John falsely attributed to him a body of teaching derived from magic? Here the evidence in favor of John is strong, for the rite presupposes the ideas with which he expounds it. The outsiders have heard only vague rumors of the eucharist and have maliciously misinterpreted whatever they heard. As we have seen, they were not interested in Jesus as a teacher, but as a miracle worker, so they tell us little of his teaching. Celsus' report of his eschatological preaching is exceptional.

Celsus pictures his vagrant career with a circle of disciples ("tax collectors and sailors of the worst sort") and his ultimate betrayal and execution; the general agreement of Celsus' account with the gospels, and its divergence from them in details, make it seem a partially independent witness for the reliability of the main outline of the life and passion narratives, and therefore important. Isolated parallels, even a considerable number of them, would not be significant if the elements paralleled did not fit together and give a coherent picture of a magician's life and work. These have done so.

Appendix A
The Pharisees in the Gospels

I. Most scholars believe that the material peculiar to Matthew or to Luke, although it may contain some old elements, is mostly late and to a considerable extent the work of the authors of these two gospels. It can therefore be used to show the interests and attitudes of their churches and their times, roughly the 80s of the first century. It contains many references to the Pharisees: Mt. *5.20; 23.2,15; 27.62;* Lk. 7.36; 11.37f., *53;* 13.31; 14.1, *3; 16.14;* 17.20; *18.10f.* Of these, the ones italicized are hostile. Therefore in the 80s the churches of Matthew and Luke were actively interested in and often hostile to the Pharisees. (Many of the "friendly" references in Luke, which represent Jesus as visiting and dining with Pharisees, serve as introduction to hostile sayings in which he rebukes or insults his hosts, so 7.36, compare 44ff.; 11.37f., compare 39ff.; 14.1, compare 11 and 24. It is also likely that these— probably false—reports that Jesus was invited to the homes and meals of Pharisees were reactions to the growth of Pharisaic influence on the diasporic Jewish community of which Luke's Christian-Jewish church was a part, and were intended to provide his fellow Christians with precedents that could be shown to their Jewish friends, to counter Pharisaic teachings that would exclude them. A little later—about 100 A.D. —the Pharisees introduced a curse on Christians into the daily prayer used in their synagogues; the introduction was intended to keep Christians out. The genuinely friendly references peculiar to Luke and Matthew may be relics from the period of good relations under James.)

II. It is also agreed that the interests of Matthew and Luke are indicated by the changes they made when using Mark. They often added references to the Pharisees: Mt. 9.34; 12.24; 15.12; 16.11f; 19.3 (See Metzger, *Textual Commentary,* on Mk. 10.2); 21.45; 22.34,41; Lk. 5.17,21; 7.39. All of these are hostile. This confirms the conclusion reached in section I, above. Of Mark's eleven references to Pharisees (all hostile), Matthew preserved all but three and Luke all but six (see note for references and discussion). This also confirms the conclusion of I: In the 80s the churches of Matthew and Luke were actively interested in and hostile to Pharisees.

III. In Q material both Matthew and Luke have many references to Pharisees, but the references do not occur in the same places. Usually only one version of the Q saying—most often Matthew's—refers to the Pharisees, and the version without the reference seems nearer the original, thus: Mt. 3.7 vs. Lk. 3.7; Mt. 23.13 vs. Lk. 11.52 (the original read, "scribes"); Mt. 23.26 vs. Lk. 11.41 (here Matthew's text seems better, but does not guarantee the reference to Pharisees); Mt. 23.27 vs. Lk. 11.44; Mt. 23.29 vs. Lk. 11.47. Lk. 7.30 vs. Mt. 11.32; Lk. 11.43 vs. Mt. 23.6; Lk. 19.39 vs. Mt. 21.14ff.(?—probably not parallel.). There are only two Q sayings in which a reference to the Pharisees occurs in both Matthew and Luke, namely, Mt. 23.23,25 ‖ Lk. 11.42 and 39 on tithing herbs and on cleaning utensils. Since both Matthew and Luke added references to the Pharisees in rewriting Mark, and introduced such references in their own material (above, sections I and II); it is presumable that most of these unparalleled references come from them, not from the source(s) of Q. All are hostile. This again confirms the conclusion of section I.

IV. In the passages cited above, "the Pharisees" has replaced "the scribes" in Mt. 9.34, 12.24, 21.45 (?, in Mk. the interlocutors—"the high priests and the scribes and the elders," were last specified in 11.27), 22.34f.,41 (compare Mk. 12.35); Lk. 19.39 (? compare Mt. 21.15). In even more instances "the Pharisees" has been added to "the scribes" (or "the lawyers" of Luke). Apparently the scribes declined in importance as opponents of Christianity while the Pharisees increased. With the rise of rabbinic Judaism they also declined in prestige *vis à vis* the Pharisaic rabbis. A second-century rabbinic text, romanticizing about the good old days, complains that "Since the fall of the temple ⟨rabbinic⟩ scholars have become like ⟨mere⟩ scribes" (*M. Sotah* IX.15).

V. The references to the Pharisees in Mark are as follows:

2.16. "The scribes of the Pharisees," a phrase found nowhere else in the New Testament; Mt. 9.11 has only "the Pharisees," Lk. "the Pharisees and their scribes;" compare Acts 23.9. Mark's source probably had only "the scribes," see IV, above.

2.18. "The disciples of John (and the Pharisees) were fasting and people say to him, 'Why do the disciples of John (and *the disciples of* the Pharisees) fast, and yours do not fast?'" The words in parentheses troubled both Matthew (9.14) and Luke (5.33) who changed the construction without succeeding to integrate the Pharisees. That the original contrast was between Jesus' disciples and those of the Baptist is suggested by the relation between Jesus' reply in Mark and the Baptist's comment in Jn. 3.29, where the Pharisees are not mentioned. Since the classic work of Albertz, *Streitgespräche,* scholars have recognized that the collection of stories about disputes between Jesus and Jewish authorities in Mk. 2.1–3.6 was cut from the same cloth as the similar collection in Mk. 12.13–37. The latter collection is composed of a series of stories, each setting Jesus off against a different group (see Smith, "Jewish Elements"). Removing the Pharisees from Mk. 2.16,18 we get a similar construction: The scribes criticize his forgiving sins and eating with sinners, the disciples of John fast and his disciples do not, the Pharisees (in verse 24, when the synoptics are at last unanimous) criticize *his disciples* for preparing food on the sabbath, and in 3.6, when he performs miracles on the sabbath, they plot with the Herodians to destroy him. We have seen that their cooperation with the Herodians dates from the 40s; a date after the crucifixion is also implied by the "prophecy" in 2.20, that Jesus' disciples shall fast after he is taken from them. That the questions often concern the actions of his disciples (not his own), or are put to them (not to him), accords with the date suggested for the composition of this complex.

2.24; 3.6. Probably from Mark's source, see the preceding paragraph.

7.1,3,5 "The Pharisees and some of the scribes coming from Jerusalem" see his disciples eating with unwashed hands. Both Matthew (15.12–14) and a late editor of Mark (in 7.3f) have added to the story comments that emphasize its offense to the Pharisees. In 7.5 "the Pharisees and the scribes" ask him why his disciples do not follow tradition. Jesus then attacks them for their neglect of scripture. Again it seems likely that Mark's source had only "the scribes," see section IV.

8.11ff. "The Pharisees" ask him for a sign, but his reply attacks the whole "generation," that is, the men of his times generally, not a particular party. The story circulated in various forms. In Mt. 12.38 it is asked by "some of the scribes and the Pharisees" (one important manuscript omits "and the Pharisees"), in Mt. 16.1 by "the Pharisees and Sadducees"; in Lk. 11.16 and 29; 12.54; and Jn. 6.30, the interlocutors are "the crowd(s)." This last form suits the reply and is probably original, for the introduction of the Pharisees see above, sections I-IV.

8.15 "Beware of the leaven of the Pharisees and the leaven of Herod." The connection of the Pharisees with a Herod again points to the persecution under Agrippa I, A.D. 41–44. Forty years later, neither Matthew nor Luke understood the saying. Both added false explanations and eliminated Herod (dead as an issue), but kept the Pharisees who were all too lively.

[10.2 These Pharisees got into Mark's text by contamination from Matthew's (19.3). See Metzger, *Textual Commentary*, 104, where the dissent by Metzger and Wikgren is supported by the evidence collected here. Matthew's addition of them in his own text was typical, see above, section II.]

12.13 Again the combination of Pharisees and Herodians, peculiar to the reign of Agrippa I (A.D. 41–44).

In sum, of the eleven references to Pharisees in Mark, it seems likely that only those in 2.24; 3.6; 8.15; and 12.13 came from his sources. The rest were probably added by Mark himself or his editors, and therefore date from about 75 or later. The addition of these references, and their hostility, shows a beginning of the polemic concern further developed by Matthew and Luke (above, sections I–III). It may be evidence that Mark should be dated somewhat later than 75, if this polemic is to be seen as a reaction to the increasing influence of the Pharisees and their followers in Jamnia (their center after the destruction of Jerusalem).

VI. It is noteworthy that neither Mark nor Luke attributes to the Pharisees any role in the passion story (for which Luke had another source besides Mark). In Luke they last appear at the entry of Jerusalem (19.39), in Mark they take part in the discussions in the city and ask the provocative question about tribute, which, however, Jesus parries (12.13); then they vanish. Matthew expands their role in the discussions (22.34), associates them more closely with the high priests in plotting Jesus' arrest (21.45), puts into Jesus' mouth, just at this time, a long diatribe against them (ch.23), and again associates them with the high priests in asking Pilate to have the tomb guarded (27.62); but he still gives them no part in the passion proper—the stories of the arrest, trial, and execution. On this point the agreement of the synoptics is practically decisive. Given the hostility to the Pharisees already apparent in Mark, and the demonstrated practice of adding references to them for polemic purposes to the gospel texts, it is incredible that, if any of the synoptic evangelists had heard anything of Pharisees participating in the actual proceedings against Jesus, he should not have reported it. Therefore Jn. 18.3, which shows them supplying Judas' forces for the arrest, is probably a hostile invention, and so are Jn. 7.32,45.47f. which show them managing an earlier attempt at arrest that failed because their agents were dazzled by a Johannine discourse—this must be John; no one save the author himself would have so high an opinion of his style.

John probably worked in the 90s, and the picture of the Pharisees given by the other passages of his work fits the position attained in Palestine, at that time, by rabbinic Judaism, and even better, the legend the Pharisees were trying to spread about their past dignity. It does not fit the facts of the situation before 70, as we know them from earlier sources. From earlier sources—mainly the Synoptics, the stories in Acts, and the course of events reported by Josephus (far more reliable than his comments)—it appears that the Pharisees before 70 were only one party among many and controlled neither the sanhedrin, nor the mass of the people, nor the majority of the synagogues (evidence for this and the following is presented in Smith, "Palestinian Judaism"). But in John they are practically a para-legal government. When the Baptist appears, it is they who send "priests and levites" to investigate his claims (1.19,24). When they learn that people are beginning to think Jesus the Messiah, they and the high priests send agents to arrest him, the agents report to both groups, and it is the Pharisees who call them to account and class themselves, in their comments, alongside "the rulers" (7.32,45ff.). When Jesus heals a blind man, the man is taken to them, not to the priests, for examination (9.13). When Jesus raises Lazarus the fact is reported to them, and they and the high priests call a meeting of the sanhedrin and discuss what should be done(11.46f.). Both they and the high priests issue orders that Jesus is to be apprehended and arrested (11.57). Indeed, "many of the rulers" who believed in Jesus were afraid to admit it because they feared the Pharisees, who could expel them from "the synagogue" (i.e. the Jamnia organization! 12.42, compare 9.22). They provide Judas with forces for Jesus' arrest (18.3). All this is utterly incompatible with what is known of first-century Pharisees before 70 (a devotional group, organized primarily to maintain a levitically pure table fellowship, but containing a few individuals of considerable political influence; see the evidence collected by Neusner, *Traditions,* and his conclusions, especially III.305f. and 312–319; see also the popular complaints about priestly rule before 70, in *B. Pesahim* 57a). John's picture does agree perfectly with the claims about Pharisaic influence made by

Josephus in the *Antiquities* (written, like John, in the 90s; Josephus knew almost nothing of these claims when he wrote the *War,* twenty years earlier); and the same picture is also found in later rabbinic material (*M. Middot* V.4; *Menahot* X.3; *'Ohalot* XVII.5; *Parah* III.7; *T. San.* VII.1; *Parah* III.8; *B. Pesahim* 88b; *Yoma'* 19a-b; *Niddah* 32b; etc.). Since the preceding list of anachronistic passages in John contains the great majority of the references to Pharisees in his gospel, and since none of those omitted contains any clear evidence of antiquity, it would seem that John's picture of the Pharisees reflects almost entirely the Jamnian Judaism of his own time and can never be used with confidence as evidence of Jesus' conflicts with members of the sect.

VII. This review of the gospels' references to the Pharisees has therefore left us with very little material that is likely to come from Jesus' lifetime. From Q we learn that Jesus *may* have ridiculed their neglect of moral obligations in favor of tithing herbs and cleaning utensils, from Mark, that they *may* have criticized him and his disciples for violating the Sabbath, and *may* have questioned him about giving tribute to Caesar. The saying about their leaven, since it connects them with a Herod, is not likely to be genuine. The Herod Jesus knew was in Galilee, and there is strong evidence that there were practically no Pharisees in Galilee during Jesus' lifetime. A generation later, when the great Pharisee Yohanan ben Zakkai lived there for eighteen years, only two cases were brought to him for decision; he reportedly cursed the country for hating the Law—it was destined to servitude. *Y. Shabbat* XVI.8 (15d, end). The story may be a legend—the curse looks like a prophecy *ex eventu* of the results of the later revolt—but at least the legend shows that the Pharisees remembered Galilee before 70 as a land where they had few followers. More important is the evidence of Josephus; it is clear from his *War* II. 569–646, and even more from his *Vita* (28–406 and especially 197f.), that as late as 66 Pharisees might be respected in Galilee for their legal knowledge (though Josephus' suggestion of this is suspect as part of his pro-Pharisaic progaganda), but they were certainly rare: the only ones Josephus encountered were sent from Jerusalem, and had been chosen to impress the Galileans by their rarity. Thus the synoptics' picture of a Galilee swarming with Pharisees is a further anachronism. John at least avoided this, his Pharisees all appear in Jerusalem, and Jesus goes to Galilee to get out of their reach (4.1ff.)

VIII. Finally, a further confirmation of our conclusion is to be found in the extreme poverty of the rabbinic tradition about Jesus, reviewed in chapter 4. The rabbis inherited the traditions of the Pharisees; among these traditions, it seems, there were none about Jesus. The lack can be explained in various ways, but the most natural and easiest explanation (and in view of the above evidence, the likeliest) is that few Pharisees encountered him and those few did not think their encounters memorable. How many members of the New York Bar left in their memoirs stories of their meetings with Father Divine?

Appendix B
Jesus vs. the Prophets

The gospels tell us that during Jesus' lifetime many outsiders and some of his early followers thought that he was a prophet, most often Elijah (whose return "before the coming of the great and terrible day of Yahweh" had been predicted at the end of the prophetic books of the Old Testament), or Jeremiah, or perhaps the "prophet like Moses" promised in Dt. 18.15,18 as a guide to the people (one through whom Yahweh would give oracular responses to everyday questions, so they would not have to consult magicians), or even Moses himself. When the gospels refer to these opinions they often correct them immediately—Jesus is *not* a mere prophet, he is the Messiah. Nevertheless, the extent and variety of the references show that the opinions were widely held, and the corrections show they came from a period prior to the gospels. Did Jesus perhaps share them? Did he think of himself as a prophet and try to act the part, as he conceived it, and is the data we have taken as evidence for the opinion that he was a magician actually evidence of his role as a prophet?

The textual evidence for the notion is weak. There are two passages in which he is made to speak of himself as a prophet (Mk. 6.4p.; Lk. 13.33b), but both are probably quotations of proverbs, and one, the saying "A prophet is not without honor except in his home town," is a late addition interrupting the story in which it is preserved (above, pp. 15f.).

The evidence from content seems stronger. The Old Testament stories of Elijah and Elisha do indeed present us with figures resembling the Jesus of the synoptics— men who receive a divine spirit that makes them miracle workers and revelators, and whose subsequent life is a series of miracle stories and revelations. Since we have gone through the gospels for material paralleled in the magical papyri, let us now compare the gospels with the stories of Moses, Elijah, and Elisha to see how the results tally. To facilitate the comparison we shall follow the outline used in chapter VII.

The Old Testament stories of Moses, Elijah, and Elisha contain nothing comparable to the coming of the magi. All three prophets have the spirit, or rather it "is on them" (II Kings 2.9,15; Num. 11.25). If it is the same as "the hand of Yahweh," Elisha is said to have induced its coming by listening to music. In contrast to the gospels and the magical papyri (above, pp. 96–103)(1) its coming is not preceded by a rite of purification, (2) it does not come down from heaven as a bird, nor is it heralded by one, (3) it does not make the recipient a son of god nor lead to his being worshiped as a god. The theme of identification with a god, central to the gospels and the magical papyri, is wholly absent from the Old Testament material on these prophets. Also absent is any notion of "the Son" as an independent supernatural being.

Jesus' going out to the wilderness follows the shamanic pattern, but may also have been inspired by Moses' and Elijah's experiences. The prophets go to meet Yahweh and/or receive his power, Jesus goes to meet Satan and overcome him. This may be coincidence, but we shall meet so many similar coincidences that this one must be noticed. Moses' forty day fast while receiving the Law is repeated by Elijah and Jesus (according to Q, but not Mark). The readers were probably expected to notice the parallels—and the difference. The notion common to the gospels and magical papyri, and basic to the temptation story, of a demonic "ruler of the world" is wholly unknown to the stories of the prophets.

Jesus' call of his disciples clearly parallels Elijah's call of Elisha, but again with a significant difference. The disciples drop everything and follow Jesus at once, as do persons enchanted by magicians (above, pp. 106f.); Elisha asks to say goodbye to his parents and goes back to offer a sacrifice. The contrast did not go unnoticed. Q told of a disciple who asked permission first to bury his father—one of the most sacred of legal duties—and was refused. The point? Jesus was more demanding, because holier, than Elijah, and his disciples more obedient than Elisha. Jesus' reported reply to the request was, "Let the dead bury the dead," that is, let the commandments of the Mosaic Law be carried out by those incapable of receiving the Life present in Jesus.

The exorcisms fundamental to Jesus' career and familiar in magical material are wholly absent from the stories of the prophets.

Cures were probably next in importance to exorcisms for Jesus' career, they are the concern of many stories of the gospels and of much magical material (especially amulets), but are rare in the stories of the prophets. Most of those reported are undoings of damage originally done by the prophets themselves, thus Moses first sends the plagues on Egypt, then calls them off (Ex. 7ff.), Elisha first has an army blinded, then has their eyes reopened (II Kings 6.18f). (These miracles are done by the prophets at Yahweh's direction or by Yahweh in response to the prophets' prayers, whereas Jesus and other magicians act by their own power.) Moses was told by Yahweh to set up a snake on a pole—much like Apollonius of Tyana's talismans—those who looked at it recovered from snake bite; Jesus gave his disciples immunity from snakes. Miriam's leprosy was healed by Moses' prayer, a leper in Galilee by Jesus' command (Num. 12.13; Mk. 1.41). Elisha treated a leper by telling him to go wash seven times in the Jordan; he did, and was cured after carrying out the prescription. Jesus told ten lepers to go to the priests; they did, and were cured on their way. The point: Jesus cured ten times as many as Elisha, and quicker. Cures for leprosy do not appear in the magical papyri, their appearance in the gospels may be due to a desire to show Jesus could do anything the prophets could, and do it better. On the other hand, some skin diseases are said to be causèd by hysteria and may therefore admit of miraculous cures. ("Leprosy" is not a specific term, it could be used for many disagreeable skin conditions.)

This handful contains all the cures attributed to the prophets. Of the many other afflictions cured by Jesus and the magicians—fever, ordinary blindness, lameness, paralysis, catalepsy, hemorrhage, wounds, and poison—the stories of Moses, Elijah, and Elisha say nothing. Whether or not the Israelite prophets were mainly healers, they do not conspicuously appear as such in the Old Testament and it is incredible that the Biblical accounts of them should have served as models for the great mass of the gospel healing stories.

It is equally incredible that they should have suggested the stories of Jesus' ability to command spirits and send them about, or into people. The prophets did nothing of the sort. At most we hear that Joshua "was full of the spirit of wisdom because Moses had laid his hands on him" (Dt. 34.9), and there are stories of Yahweh taking some of the spirit that was on Moses and putting it on the elders, and of Elisha getting twice as much spirit as Elijah had (not through Elijah's doing, he could not promise it) (Num. 11.24ff.; II Kings 2.9–15). These are a far cry from Jesus' giving Satan to Judas in a piece of bread or breathing his spirit into his disciples, both operations with magical parallels (above, pp. 110ff.). The prophets did have disciples and presumably were able to communicate their powers to them, but we hear even less of their training than we do of that of Jesus' disciples, and nothing of their master's "giving them authority" over demons or the like. Elisha sent his staff, by his assistant, to be laid on the mouth of a boy whom he hoped to revive, but this was mere fetishism; it gave no power to the assistant (and it didn't work; II Kings 4.31).

Again, the prophets do not forgive sins. The gospels say that the scribes were scandalized by Jesus' practice and asked, "Who can forgive sins, except God alone?" (Mk. 2.7). Their supposition ("Nobody!") reflects the Old Testament evidence which cannot have served as a model for this element of the gospels.

Prophecy was the prophets' long suit. As to specific predictions, including those of their own death (Dt. 32.50; II Kings 2.9f.), the stories of the prophets match those of Jesus and Apollonius and the promises of the magical papyri. Elijah and Elisha are also credited with "second sight"—knowledge of other people's thoughts and of events happening at a distance—as are Jesus and the magicians. By contrast, neither Moses, nor Elijah, nor Elisha appears in the Old Testament as a prophet of the end of the world. On "the Mosaic eschatological prophet" see the notes. Undoubtedly some sort of superprophet, most often Moses or Elijah, was expected to come as herald of the end of the world; Jesus was sometimes thought to be such a prophet (Jn. 6.14, 7.40; Acts 3.23) and the expectation has produced some elements of the gospels—notably their assignment to him of long apocalyptic sermons generally thought to be spurious. But as far as we know, nobody ever wrote anything like a "gospel"—a full account of the coming, miracles, career and consummation—of such an "eschatological prophet." Consequently it is not likely that the vague and contradictory expectations of such figures served as models for the gospels. As for the eschatological sayings that can plausibly be attributed to Jesus, the closest known parallels are the promises of the Syrian prophets reported by Celsus (above, p. 117). These differ essentially from all Old Testament and later Jewish apocalyptic prophecies by the fact that the speaker represents himself as a present god. So did Jesus and other magicians.

Both Elijah and Elisha raised boys (one each) from the dead by the drastic method of lying on top of them (Elijah three times, Elisha only twice) and praying to Yahweh (I Kings 17.21f.; II Kings 4.34f.). Jesus raised at least three persons, a girl by taking her hand, two young men by mere orders. This is clearly intended to show Jesus' superior power. (Apollonius touched the girl he raised and said a spell—*Life* IV.45.)

The stories of feeding the crowds in the desert also demonstrate Jesus' superiority (Mk. 6.32ff. p.; 8.1ff.p.). They are obvious imitations of II Kings 4.42ff., even to setting and dialogue. The point is that Elisha fed only a hundred, Jesus four or five thousand. Evidently some opponents countered by comparing Jesus to Moses who fed all the Israelites, so John gave up the claim to numerical superiority, made the feeding a symbol of the eucharist, and argued that Jesus was greater because the bread he gave was not corruptible, but was the bread of Life, his own body (Jn. 6.26–58).

Stilling storms and withering trees, in spite of their Old Testament parallels, are not attributed to Moses, Elijah, or Elisha, and, as we have seen, they do have magical parallels (above, p. 119). Moses turned water into poisonous blood (Ex. 7.20f.), Jesus turned it into wine (Jn. 2.1–11); was a contrast intended? Probably. Turning the Nile into blood was the first of the great plagues caused by Moses; John emphasizes that the turning of water into wine was the first of Jesus' great miracles (2.11). A contrast between the blood produced by Moses and that of the eucharist is not thereby ruled out—religious symbolism is not limited by either/or logic.

Moses divided the sea and walked through (Ex. 14.21ff.), Jesus simply walked over it (Mk. 6.48f.p.; Jn. 6.19)—another brilliant piece of one-upmanship, but not likely to have occurred to the evangelists had there not been a story of Jesus' walking on the water, as magicians were expected to (above, p. 120).

The miraculous escapes, sudden invisibility, etc., of Jesus and other magicians (above, p. 120) probably have nothing to do with the prophets. Something of this sort was once expected of Elijah, but he didn't vanish (I Kings 18.9ff.).

We have shown that the story of Jesus' transfiguration was primarily a story of a magical initiation, probably based on the disciples' recollection, and was itself transfigured (by identification of the supernatural beings as Moses and Elijah) into an allegory in which God the Father does away with the Law and the prophets and designates Jesus as the Son and sole guide of the Church (above, pp. 120ff.). The basic story had important similarities to stories of the prophets: both Moses and Elijah went alone to a mountain in the wilderness to meet Yahweh; Moses alone went up a mountain and into a cloud where God was; sometimes he took along companions to whom he revealed "the God of Israel." The same elements are found in stories of magical initiations and probably come from a common tradition of both magical and prophetic practice. This makes it impossible to be sure that the gospels' account of Jesus was influenced here by the stories of the prophets; it probably was. The report of his brilliance again shows one-upmanship: Only Moses' face shone, Jesus blazed all over, even his garments (Ex. 34.30ff.; Mk. 9.2f.p.). That the revelation of the Son replaces the giving of the Law, is the essential message of the redactor and is probably secondary.

There is nothing at all like the eucharist in the stories of the prophets. The attempts to equate the blood with that of the sacrifice of the covenant have already been shown to be antinomian inventions. They provided another opportunity for one-upmanship, made explicit by the Epistle to the Hebrews: Christ, the better High Priest, entered a better tabernacle, "not with the blood of bulls and goats, but with his own blood," to make a new and better covenant, etc. (Heb. 3.1–12.28; the quotation is from 9.12).

Elijah, Jesus, and Apollonius were taken up to heaven at the ends of their lives, Elijah in a fiery chariot. The story of Jesus' ascent is more like that of Apollonius or of the magician in "the Mithras Liturgy."

Moses, Elijah, and Elisha say almost nothing about the personnel and goings on in the world of spirits; contrast Jesus and the magicians (above, pp. 124ff.).

There is nothing in the prophets like the "I am" sayings of Jesus and the magicians, or the miraculous claims that are made in them.

The concern for one-upmanship has produced some pointed contrasts between the prophets and Jesus: Elijah called down fire on his enemies; the disciples proposed to do this but Jesus forbade it (II Kings 1.10ff.; Lk. 9.54f). Moral: Jesus was holier. Elisha got a bodyguard of angels from God: Jesus disdained to do so (II Kings 6.17; Mt. 26.53). Moral: Ditto.

Very little is said of the teaching of Elijah and Elisha. Moses is the mouthpiece through whom the Law is given; of his own teaching, apart from it, practically nothing can be discerned. Accordingly it is not worthwhile to compare the teaching of these prophets with that of Jesus. The supposition that Jesus might have cast himself as a prophet was based on the similarity of the prophets' miracles to his, and on his eschatological sermons. But the eschatological sermons are products of a late stage of evangelical invention; Moses, Elijah, and Elisha made no eschatological prophecies; and the similarity of the miracles turns out to be so rarely close and so often secondary that the prophetic model cannot be supposed a major factor in shaping the traditions behind the gospels.

Summing up the results of our comparison we find:

The story of the coming of the spirit and its consequences has magical, not prophetic sources.

The story of the retirement to the wilderness is of dubious background. It was adapted by Q to emphasize the difference between Jesus and the prophets: they got their authorization from the god of this world, Jesus overcame him.

The call of the disciples is also of dubious background. Q contrasted it with Elijah's call of Elisha, to Jesus' advantage.

The exorcisms are unparalleled in the stories of the prophets.

The cures are far more frequent than they are in stories of the prophets. Of all the gospel cures only the two healings of leprosy have close parallels in the stories of Moses, Elijah, and Elisha; these two were probably invented to show Jesus' superiority to the prophets.

Jesus' ability to command, send, and give spirits is unparalleled in the stories of the prophets.

His forgiving of sins is also unparalleled.

Jesus' particular prophecies (predictions) and "second sight" are equally paralleled by prophetic and magical sources. His eschatological sermons are most closely paralleled by those of the Syrian prophets reported by Celsus.

Jesus' raisings of the dead resemble those of Apollonius more closely than those of Elijah and Elisha; among the evangelists' many reasons for reporting them was perhaps a desire to show Jesus' superiority to the prophets.

The stories of feeding the multitude were modeled on the story of Elisha and intended to show Jesus' superiority to him.

The story of the miracle in Cana was modeled on a Sidonian cult legend, but so told as to show Jesus' superiority to Moses.

Stilling the storm and withering the fig tree have both magical and Old Testament connections, but do not come from the stories of Moses, Elijah, and Elisha.

Walking on the sea has a magical background, but is told to show Jesus' superiority to Moses.

The miraculous escapes, etc., come from magical tradition.

The transfiguration story reflects a magical rite but may also have been influenced by prophetic examples. It has been made over to show Jesus' superiority to the Law and the prophets.

The eucharist is a magical rite unparalleled in prophetic legends.

The ascension resembles magical examples more closely than it does Elijah's.

The sayings about spirits and their doings have magical rather than prophetic analogues.

The same is true for the "I am" sayings.

The desire to show Jesus' superiority to the prophets has produced two stories of his refusing to perform prophetic miracles (not calling down fire and not asking for an angelic bodyguard).

This list could be supplemented by another, of things a prophet should do and Jesus did not, but even by itself it suffices to refute the notion that the gospels' picture of Jesus was derived *mainly* from a prophet, or from the prophetic tradition. Jesus' fundamental activities—exorcisms and cures—are either unknown (exorcisms) or rare (cures) in the stories of the prophets. His getting the spirit had magical, not prophetic, analogues and consequences; so did his dealings with spirits and sayings about them, so did the majority of the miscellaneous miracles with which he was credited. He initiated his disciples and bound them to himself by magical rites unknown to the prophets, and his notions of their union with him and of his own divine nature are not prophetic but magical. Finally, the practice of telling stories about him so as to show his superiority to Moses and the other prophets explains why many stories have been told so as to parallel *and contrast with* Old Testament episodes. Such parallels-for-the-sake-of-contrast belong to the late, apologetic and propagandistic strata of the gospels, and reduce the amount of Old Testament material that can be assigned to the earliest stage of the tradition. While he was alive the important question was what he could do, not how he compared with the prophets. The latter became important a generation or so after his death when Jews and Christians got down to arguing about the relative merits of their respective heroes.

This conclusion both confirms and modifies the one reached in the body of the text from other considerations. The tendency of the mid-first-century tradition was not only to square Jesus with the teachings of the Pharisees, but also to demonstrate his superiority to the figures of the Old Testament. So Paul, often aggressively. For Matthew, more subtly, Jesus is "the fulfillment" of the Law (Mt. 5.17).

Notes

CHAPTER I

PAGE 1

A.D. 326: Eusebius, *Life of Constantine* III.66.
A.D. 333: H. Opitz, *Athanasius Werke* III.i.pp 66f., *Urkunde* 33.

PAGE 2

DECREES: Speyer, "Büchervernichtung," especially 141–147.
THEODORET: *Haereticarum fabularum compendium,* I.20 end.
'BY THE FOUR': A translation of *Diatessaron,* the Greek name for Tatian's gospel.
AGAINST THE CHRISTIANS: Harnack, *Porphyrius;* and "Fragmente."
JAMES: Oxford, 1924; often reprinted, but far from complete. Hennecke, *New Testament Apocrypha,* is fuller, but also omits much.
    GELASIUS: Preuschen, *Analecta* 155. I omit some thirty-five names of Christians listed as "heretics." The traditional attribution to Gelasius is probably false, but the work reflects the Italian ecclesiastical attitude about his time (Altaner, *Patrologie*[6] 427).

PAGE 3

    STUDY OF THE GOSPELS: See Schweitzer, *Quest.* The second German edition, *Geschichte,* reprinted with an added preface by Schweitzer as the sixth edition (Tübingen, 1951) is fuller than the English version and is the text cited in the present work.
    PAUL: Romans, I and II Corinthians, Galatians, Philippians, and Philemon are almost certainly genuine; I and II Thessalonians and Colossians are possibly genuine.
    GOSPELS: Commonly accepted dates are: Mark about 75, Matthew and Luke about 85, John about 95. The crucifixion is commonly dated about 30.
    CONTRADICTIONS BETWEEN GOSPELS: See any "synopsis" of the gospels, e.g. that of Aland.

PAGE 4

    HALLUCINATIONS: Of course this term is not used. The polite account is more like this: "They realized the higher truth of His enduring presence in their hearts, a presence now so vivid to them that they could see, and even touch Him, as He had been with them in the past, and would truly be with them forever." When a theologian talks of a "higher truth," he is usually trying to conceal a lower falsehood.
    JEWISH AND CHRISTIAN DOCUMENTS: The New Testament; the *Apocrypha and Pseudepigrapha* (ed. Charles); the Qumran manuscripts (many in Gaster, *Dead Sea Scriptures*), the *Mishnah, Tosefta,* and other early works of rabbinic literature, the works of Josephus and a few other

Jewish works in Greek literary forms (notably the early elements of the *Sibylline Oracles*). The fullest review of this literature is Schürer, *Geschichte* III, to be revised in Schürer-Vermes-Millar, *History*.

· MANY GODS: Cf. I Cor. 2.8; Lk. 22.53; Jn. 12.31; (cf. Lk. 10.18); Jn. 14.30; 16.11; etc.
THE DEMONS' AGENTS: II Thess. 2.8–12; II Cor. 11.14f.; Mt. 7.22f.
RULERS OF THIS AGE: I Cor. 2.8; etc. above; AVAILABLE AS HELPERS: *SHR*, throughout.
FOR WOMEN: Enoch 7.1.

PAGE 5

HARMFUL PROPHETS: I Kings 14.5–17; 17.1ff.; etc.
SORTS OF MESSIAHS: Smith, "Messianic Figures?"
ANTIPAS' OPINION: Mk. 6.14ff. Luke (9.7f.) doubted the story, but it is not beyond the superstitious fears of the times. For the translation "raised" rather than "risen" see below, pp. 34f.
JOSEPHUS' MISSION: Life 13–16. HIS PRIDE IN JEWISH MAGIC: *Antiquities* VIII. 46–49. HIS PROPHECIES: *War* III.351–355; 400–402. HIS EXEGESIS: War VI.312ff.
REPORTS OF JOSEPHUS' PROPHECY: Suetonius, *Vespasian* 5.6; Dio Cassius in Xiphilinus' *Epitome* 66.1.4.
SUCH PROPHECIES COMMON: Tacitus, *Histories* V.13.4: A few Jews were frightened by the prodigies that preceded the fall of Jerusalem, but "more were persuaded that it was foretold in the ancient books of the priests that at this very time the East should regain its strength and men sprung from Judea should rule." Suetonius, *Vespasian* 4.5: "Very prevalent throughout the whole East was an ancient and persistent opinion that it was fated that at this time men sprung from Judea should rule."
UNQUESTIONABLY: The proposition has been questioned, but the alternative explanations proposed—the theories of the "Christ myth school," etc.—have been thoroughly discredited.

PAGE 6

TRAJECTORIES: For method and applications see Robinson-Koester.
BUTLER: J. Butler, *The Analogy of Religion,* introduction, paragraph 3.
TROCMÉ: Philadelphia, 1975.

CHAPTER II

PAGE 8

BORN IN PALESTINE: Mt. 2.1; Lk. 2.6f. (both Bethlehem); Jn. 1.45f.; 7.41f., 52 (Galilee).
DATE OF BIRTH: Mt. 2.1, before the death of Herod the Great (4 B.C.); Lk. 2.2, during the census taken under Quirinus, governor of Syria, probably in A.D. 6. Both stories are legendary. Lk. 3.1f. dates the beginning of John the Baptist's activity in the fifteenth year of the emperor Tiberius (Aug. 19, A.D. 28 to Aug. 18, A.D. 29); 3.23 suggests that Jesus was about 30 when he was baptized. Jn. 8.57 makes Jesus' opponents say he was not yet 50.
GREW UP IN GALILEE: Jn. 1.45f.; 7.41f.,52; Lk. 2.39; 4.16; Mt. 2.22f.; 21.11; Mk. 1.9; the editors of Mk. 6.1p. thought Jesus' "home town" was in Galilee.
BAPTISM: The story cannot be a Christian invention; it shows the Master going to another prophet for sanctification. Hence Mt. 3.14f. tried to "explain" it and Jn. 1.29–34 suppressed it. Hence the essential report was probably true.
"CURES," OF HYSTERIA: McCasland, *Finger.*

PAGE 9

MATRIX: *Sitz im Leben.*

PAGE 10

AT ONCE WHEN HE CALLED, ETC.: This translates a half-Semitic, half-Greek construction; literally, "And at once he called them and, leaving . . . they followed." So Mt. 4.21f.; Wellhausen, *Evangelium Marci*²,8.

TEACHING REVEALS POWER: Mk. 1.22,27; Mt. 9.8. Starr, "Authority;" Hull, *Hellenistic Magic* 165; to Mark's public, "authority" meant a superhuman power to control demons and heal diseases.

CROWDS COME FOR MIRACLES: Mk. 5.14,18,22,24,27; 6.54ff.; 7.25,32; 8.22; 9.17; 10.13,50; etc.

PAGE 11

Q: From the German *Quelle,* "source." The abbreviation originally referred to the supposed, unknown source/s, but will here be used for the (known) common material.

CENTURION'S SLAVE: Lk. 7.1–10; Mt. 8.5–13.

BEELZEBUL CHARGE: Lk. 11.14f.; compare Mt. 9.32ff.; 12.22ff.; Mk. 3.22; Mt. 10.25.

Q'S ANSWER: Lk. 11.19f.; Mt. 12.27f.

MIRACLES ON THE SABBATH: Lk. 14.5; Mt. 12.11. The legal opinion implied is that a domestic animal fallen into a pit may be pulled out during the Sabbath. Cp. *B. Shabbat* 128b.

MIRACLES IN GALILEE: Lk. 10.13–15; Mt. 11.20–24.

REPLY TO THE BAPTIST: Lk. 7.18–23; Mt. 11.2–6.

PAGE 12

MATTHEW ON JESUS' WORK: Mt. 4.23ff.; again 9.35; 15.30f.; compare Mk. 1.28,32,34,39; etc.

JESUS SENT TO DO MIRACLES: Mt. 8.17 quoting Isaiah 53.4. Cp. Mt. 11.28.

PAGE 13

CROWDS CAME TO BE HEALED: Lk. 5.15; 6.18f.; this is also the implication of 13.14.

DEMONS' TESTIMONY AUGMENTED: Cf. Lk. 4.41 with its source, Mk. 1.34b.

REJOICING AT MIRACLES; Lk. 13.17; 18.43; 19.37.

WOMAN OF SAMARIA: Jn. 4.29. She was overstating the knowledge displayed by Jesus, and she had arrived at the messianic title only with his assistance (4.17ff.,25f.).

SPECIFIED "SIGNS": Jn. 4.46–54; 6.2–14; 9.1–16; 11.1–44,47; 12.17f.

UNSPECIFIED "SIGNS": Jn. 2.23; 3.2; 6.2; 7.31; 9.16; 11.47; 12.37; 20.30.

FOLLOWED BECAUSE OF SIGNS: Jn. 2.11,23; 3.2; 4.48, 6.2,14, 7.31; 9.16; 10.41; 11.47f.; 12.17f. Fortna, *Gospel*, thinks the miracles reported as signs, and the importance attached to them, derive from a much earlier gospel that John used as a source.

SIGNS PROVE HIM "SON": Jn. 2.11; 12.37ff.; 20.30f. Unworthy followers are reproached with the charge, "You seek me not because you saw signs but because you got a bellyful of the bread" (6.26). That after the feeding of the multitude unbelievers could still ask him, "What sign do you perform, that we may see and believe?" (6.30) is ironic evidence of their blindness.

CONCLUSION OF JOHN: Chapter 21 is thought to be a later addition; Brown, *John* II.1057; 1077–80.

PAGE 14

MIRACLES PROVE HIM MESSIAH: Mk. 10.47f. + 11.10; 15.31f; Lk. 7.18–23 and Mt. 11.2–6 (from Q); Mt. 12.15–21; 21.14ff.; Lk. 4.18–21; Jn. 1.48f.; 4.29; 7.31; 20.30f.

MIRACLES PROVE HIM SON OF A GOD: Mk. 3.11; 5.7; cf. 15.39; Mt. 14.33; Lk. 4.41; Jn. 1.49; 20.31. In the Q material he appears as "the Son" (of God, Mt. 11.27; Lk. 10.22). Although the title is not *explicitly* connected with his miracles, the connection is implied by the beginning of the verse, "All things have been given over to me by my Father," and by the following verse in Matthew ("Come unto me"). One Q passage, the temptation (Mt. 4.1–11; Lk. 4.1–13), thinks Jesus the Son of God, but attacks the connection of this title with his miracles. The attack presupposes the connection and is recognizedly apologetic; Fridrichsen, *Problème* 84ff.

RELIABILITY OF MIRACLE TRADITION: For a good critique of attacks on the gospel story in general, see Stanton, *Jesus.* Jesus' role as exorcist and healer is recognized by Böcher, *Christus* 71ff., 166f., etc., who answers recent attempts to deny it, 77f.

PALESTINIAN ORIGIN: Recent studies of the miracle stories arguing their Palestinian origin and recognizing the importance of miracles in the career of Jesus are van der Loos, *Miracles,* and Schille, *Wundertradition.* The linguistic, geographical, and cultural background of many of the miracle stories is specifically Palestinian: use of Aramaic, many Aramaisms in the text, knowledge of distances and small towns around the Sea of Galilee, many cultural traits (e.g. Jesus' attitude to the Syrophoenician woman), etc. The supposedly "hellenistic" traits found in the stories are worthless as evidence of place of origin because, like all the eastern Mediterranean littoral, Palestine, in Jesus' time, was profoundly hellenized.

REFUSAL TO GIVE SIGNS: Mk. 8.11ff.p.; compare Lk. 11.16; Jn. 6.30.

MATERIAL REPORTED TO ANSWER OPPONENTS: For this line of argument see Cadbury, "Rebuttal" and *Behind the Gospels,* though I disagree with some of his interpretations.

AKIBA: None of the later stories of his miracles is traceable to less than a century after his death.

YOUR TRUST HAS HEALED YOU: Mk. 5.34p.; 10.52p.; Lk. 7.50; 17.19; "faith" and "saved" are mistranslations, these are cures. Compare Mk. 2.5p.; 11.2p.; Mt. 9.29; 15.28; 17.20p.; 21.21p.

PAGE 15

SCANDAL IN PAUL: I Cor. 1.23; Gal. 5.11. In Rom. 9.32f. Paul identifies Jesus as "stone of scandal" (i.e. of stumbling) in Isaiah 8.14; this may be a piece of earlier Christian exegesis that he has taken over.

EXPLANATION OF REJECTION STORY: Bultmann, *Geschichte*[4] 30f. and *Ergänzungsheft* 9, thought it was invented to frame the saying; Cadbury, to show the unbelievers' resistance to grace ("Rebuttal" 101). Neither motive suffices to explain *invention* of such material by the followers of a man it might discredit.

JOHN 4.44: The Greek word *patris* can mean either "home town" or "home country."

PAGE 16

EMBARRASSING DETAILS IN MARK 6.1–6: On "the son of Mary," also altered by Matthew, and deleted by Luke and John, see below, pp. 26f.

PHARISEES NOT MIRACLE WORKERS: See Neusner, *Traditions.* (Fiebig, *Wundergeschichten,* completely misrepresents the material; see Smith, *Parallels* 81–84.)

PAGE 17

ROMAN INTERVENTIONS: Josephus, *War* II.66ff.; *Antiquities* XVIII.85ff.; XX.97f., 168–172, 188.

SOURCES OF THE PASSION STORY: It is commonly recognized that Luke used another source beside Mark, and John yet another. John's may have incorporated a variant form of an Aramaic document that also lay behind Mark. See Smith, *Clement* 158–163; 193f.; or, for a simpler account, *Secret Gospel* 56ff.

CRUCIFIED AS MESSIAH: Mk. 15.26; Mt. 27.37; Lk. 23.28; Jn. 19.19; Tacitus, *Annals* XV.44.

DATES OF PILATE: Josephus, *Antiquities* XVIII.33–35 and 89. Pilate's Roman title was "prefect," Levine, *Roman Caesarea* 19, n.126; E. Koestermann, *Tacitus* on *Annals* XV.44.

DATE OF CRUCIFIXION: The common date, about 30; is based mainly on the date of 28/29 for the Baptist's appearance (Lk. 3.1), and on the outline of Mark, which suggests that Jesus' public career lasted only one year. This date accords well with the chronology of Paul's career. Moreover, a reference to Jesus stands about midway in Josephus' account of Pilate's governorship (*Antiquities* XVIII.63f.), a passage corrupt but probably basically genuine.

NO RABBIS RESURRECTED: The passages commonly translated as statements that John the Baptist "has risen from the dead" (Mk. 6.14p.,16), probably mean he "has been raised," by necromancy. See below pp. 33ff. In any case, the Baptist was not a rabbi.

SCHOLARS' DISAGREEMENT: Kümmel, "Jesusforschung."

PAGE 18

THEAGENES OF THASOS: Pausanias VI.11.2–9; Plutarch, *Moralia* 811D; etc.
PHILIP OF CROTON: Herodotus V.47.2.
LUCIAN: *The Dream*, a parody of the famous story of "Hercules at the crossroads," but told partly in earnest—at least as encouragement for students of rhetoric.

PAGE 20

LUKE WROTE GAMALIEL'S SPEECH: This accounts for its historical inaccuracy: Judas was not "after" Theudas, but almost forty years earlier, Josephus, *War* II.118; *Antiquities* XVIII.4–10,23–25; XX.97f.
JUDAS OF GALILEE AND DESCENDANTS: Josephus, *War* II.433f., 442–448.
THEUDAS: Josephus, *Antiquities* XX.97f

CHAPTER III

PAGE 21

JOHN 9.29ff.: Compare 7.27, etc. John loves contradictions and dramatic ironies.

PAGE 22

PEOPLE MARVELED: Mk. 1.27; 2.12; 5.20; Mt. 9.33; 12.23; 15.31; Lk. 9.43; 11.14; Jn. 7.21.
FAME OF MIRACLES: Mk. 1.28,45; 3.8; 6.14; etc.; Mt. 4.24; 9.26,31; Lk. 7.17; Jn. 12.17f.; etc.
FEAR OF MIRACLES: Mk. 5.15; Mt. 9.8, Lk. 5.26; 7.16; 8.37. In Jn. 6.19f. the fear is mentioned only to have Jesus prohibit it, cp. I Jn. 4.18.
GENERAL ADMIRATION: Mk. 7.37; 11.8ff., Mt. 13.29–31, Lk. 11.27; 13.17; 23.41; Jn. 6.15; 12.12–19.
ENEMIES AFRAID: Mk. 11.18; 12.12; 14.1f.
DATE OF CRUCIFIXION: The gospels' dating is self-contradictory, theologically determined, and therefore untrustworthy. The "synoptic" gospels (Matthew, Mark, and Luke) equate the institution of the eucharist with the passover meal; John equates the death on the cross with the killing of the passover sacrifice (19.36; so does Paul: I Cor. 5.7). Accordingly, for Matthew, Mark, and Luke the passover must precede the crucifixion (Mk. 14.12–17p.) for John it follows (18.28).
CROWD'S REJECTION OF JESUS: Mk. 15.6–11; Mt. 27.15–21; Lk. 23.18f.; Jn. 18.39f.
CRUCIFIXION DEMANDED: Mk. 15.13f.; Mt. 27.22f.; Lk. 22.18–23; Jn. 19.15.
MOCKING ON CROSS: Mk. 15.29–32p. John omits.
TEACHER: Mk. 4.38; 5.35; 9.17; etc. Q, Mt. 10.24f.p. Mt. 8.19; 17.24; 23.8. Lk. 7.40; 11.45; 12.13; 19.39. Jn. 1.38; 3.2; 11.28; 13.13; etc.
RABBI: Mk. 9.5; 11.21; 14.45. Never in Luke nor, therefore, demonstrable in Q. Mt. 26.25; Jn. 1.38,49; 3.2; 4.31; etc.
EQUIVALENT TERMS: Mt. 23.8; Jn. 1.38; etc. The present meaning of *rabbi* (authorized authority on the law of that rabbinic organization which bestowed the title) developed only in the second century A.D.

STORIES OF LAWSUITS: Lk. 12.13f. (otherwise unknown, probably invented to introduce the teaching on avarice that follows it); Jn. 7.53–8.11. (Textually secondary, see Metzger, *Textual Commentary,* which is reliable on textual matters, not historical questions.)

PAGE 23

QUESTIONS INTENDED TO EMBARRASS: Mk. 2.18p.: Why don't your disciples fast? Mk. 2.24p.: Why do your disciples prepare food on the Sabbath? Mk. 7.5p.: Why don't your disciples wash their hands before eating? (No answer would have satisfied the questioners.) Three others try to put him on the spot: Mk. 12.14p.: Is it permissible to pay tribute to Rome? (If he said, "Yes," he would lose popular support, if "No," be denounced to the Romans.) Mk. 12.19–23p.: In the resurrection who will be the husband of a woman legally divorced and remarried? (an attempt to show that his teaching of the resurrection would lead to legal contretemps.) Jn. 8.5: Should a woman taken in adultery be stoned? (Capital punishment was unpopular, as shown by desperate efforts in rabbinic literature to get rid of the Old Testament prescriptions. Moreover, Jesus' mother was accused of adultery. However, if he said "No," he contradicted the Law.) These questions show no respect for his legal knowledge, and lead to no legal ruling; they are told to show his cleverness in escaping traps: "Give Caesar Caesar's and God God's," is not a legal principle; it brilliantly begs the question. That the resurrected are not married is not a legal principle, but an *ad hoc* revelation. "Let him who is without sin throw the first stone," pretends to be a legal ruling, but is unenforceable. Mk. 10.2p.: Is divorce permitted? was understood, by both Mark and Matthew, as an attempt to embarrass ("test") him. The questions added by Matthew (19.7,10) derive from later Christian discussion of Jesus' rule. Mk. 11.28p., about his authority, was probably not a legal question (see below, pp. 36f.); in any case he refused to answer.

CHRISTIAN INSTRUCTION: Jn. 4.19f., the woman of Samaria's (implicit) question— Which is the right place to worship, Gerizim or Jerusalem?—introduces "Jesus' prophecy" discrediting both, a prophecy invented after the destruction of Jerusalem. Mk. 10.17p. What shall I do to inherit eternal life? appears again in Lk. 10.25. In Jn. 6.28 this becomes: What shall we do to do the works of God? Mk. 12.28p.: Which is the chief commandment? All of these introduce Christian teaching. The Mk. 10 and Lk. 10 stories are expanded by secondary questions—Mk. 10.21f.p.: What must I do besides keep the commandments? Sell your property, give the proceeds to the poor, and follow me. Lk. 10.29: Who is my neighbor? answered not by a legal ruling, but by a parable that does not fit the question. (Logically it leads to the answer: Your neighbor is anybody who helps you, and *not* anybody who doesn't help you. But this conclusion is avoided by the comment in 10.37b which leaves the legal question in the air.)

QUESTIONS ABOUT DISCIPLES: So Mk. 2.18p.; 2.24p.; 7.5p.

QUESTIONS TO DISCIPLES: So Mk. 2.16p.; Mt. 17.24.

THE QUESTIONS' SOURCE: Mk. 2.1–3.6; 7.1–23; 10.2–12; 12.13–37. Mk. 12.13 is so related to Mk. 3.6 that at least these two sections seem to have come from the same document.

JESUS' ANSWERS: Mk. 2.8ff., he proves his right to forgive sins by doing a miracle; 2.17, he says he eats with sinners to save them (not a legal teaching); 2.19, he justifies neglect of fasting by claiming to be above the law; 2.25f., likewise for violation of the sabbath; 3.5f. he justifies his sabbath behavior by a miracle. Here we do get a legal rule (by implication), "It is permissible to do good on the sabbath;" but this is probably an interpolation, it interrupts the action. (Mk. 3.5 continues 3.3; 2.20ff., and 27f. are also glosses.) In Mk. 7 the disciples' practice is the point of departure, and the opponents' question is answered with abuse. In Mk. 10 and 12 the stories do arise from legal questions. However, two of the four (Mk. 12.1ff.,18ff.) are attempts to embarrass him. He answers by evasions. I have argued elsewhere that Jesus may have had a consistent position on legal questions (Smith, "Jesus' Attitude"), but if he did, it was part of his secret teaching, and is not plainly presented in the gospels.

RABBINIC TRADITION: See chapter IV.

HOSTILE CROWDS IN THE SYNOPTICS: Mk. 6.1ff.; the rejection in his hometown (Lk. 4.16ff. gives a different version). Mk. 5.17p. the Gerasenes ask him to leave because they fear his powers. (Mk. 5.40p. is dramatic irony, does not prove hostility, and does not affect the course of the action. Mk. 4.11f. does not indicate popular hostility.) In John there is confusion, the result of John's inconsistent revision and amplification of sources no longer clearly distinguishable. In some Johannine passages "the Jews" and "the world" are hostile to Jesus, and he to them, from the beginning: 1.10f.; 2.18; and often. Yet in 12.11 many Jews believe in him, in 12.42, many rulers. Moreover, John is full of statements that "many" or "crowds" believed or followed Jesus (2.23; 6.2ff.,14,24; 7.31; 8.30; 12.17ff.; etc.) and he often speaks of "many" or "crowds" in contrast to the Pharisees, high priests, or "Jews" (7.12f.,32,49; 12.11,42; etc.)

SAYINGS HOSTILE TO THE WORLD: Mk. 4.11ff.p.; 7.6p.; 8.34p.; 8.38; 9.19p.; 9.30f.p. ("Men" is a theological generalization of the small groups specified in 8.31 and 10.33; the saying has lost its original touch with history.) Q: Mt. 5.11f.p.; 7.13f.p.; 8.20p.; 10.16p.; 11.19p.; 11.21ff.p.; 12.39ff.p.; 23.35ff.p. Lk. 6.26; 12.56; 13.1–9; 17.25; 19.41ff. Mt. 11.20; 12.45; 22.14.

TAKE UP HIS CROSS: Mk. 8.34f.p.; Mt. 10.38f.p.

NO PERSECUTION BEFORE ARREST: The attempt on his life in Lk. 4.29 is known only to Luke and is probably fictitious; his miraculous escape is akin to those in Jn. 8.59 and 10.39. The plot against his life in Mk. 3.6 has no consequence before Mk. 12.13; the plot by Herod in Lk. 13.31 has none at all.

SALVATION NOW: Mk. 2.19; 4.11; 4.30ff.; 10.30; Lk. 7.28; 10.21f.; 11.52; 13.21; 16.16; 17.21; and the parallels to these. Thirty-four such passages are listed in my *Clement* 212f.

SALVATION FOR THE POOR. Mk. 10.31; Mt. 19.30; 22.10(?); Lk. 6.20f.,24f.; 14.23; 16.19–31; etc.

PAGE 24

CONTRAST BETWEEN POPULAR FOLLOWING AND HOSTILE GROUPS: Mk. 2.15f.; 3.20–22,31ff.; 11.18; 12 12,38; 14.2. Mt. 9.3,8; 9 33f.; 12.23f., 21.15; 22.33f, Lk. 12.1; 13.17; 19.47f. On John, see above, at the end of the note headed "Hostile crowds."

MT. 10.36: This is one of Matthew's Old Testament texts (Micah 7.6) and therefore dubious. However, Matthew put it into Jesus' mouth, and he may have done so because he knew from tradition that Jesus had been on bad terms with his family. Matthew wanted to excuse the fact as a fulfilment of prophecy.

MARK 3.31–4: Mk. 3.35 is a moralizing excuse. Luke 8.21 omitted the remark, but kept the excuse. Mt. 12.46–50 kept both.

HE WILL NOT GO UP TO JERUSALEM: Jn. 7.8. See Metzger, *Textual Commentary*. The reading "not yet" is an apologetic emendation.

PAGE 25

JESUS' BROTHERS' DESCENDANTS: Eusebius, *History* III.19f. quotes from Hegesippus the story of their interrogation and dismissal (by Domitian).

JESUS' BROTHERS' CAREERS: I Cor. 9.5; Gal. 2.9.

JESUS' BROTHERS AS WITNESSES FOR THE RESURRECTION: Mt. 28.10; I Cor. 15.7; Jerome, *De viris* 2, quoting the *Gospel according to the Hebrews*.

PILLARS OF THE CHURCH: The contrast between the importance of Jesus' family in the early Church and its unimportance in the gospels probably results from the fact that the family was most important in the Jerusalem church which made friends with the Pharisees and required public observance of at least the most conspicuous commandments of Mosaic law (Acts 15.1–29; 21.15–26; 23.6–10; Mt. 23.1f.). This Jerusalem church was ruined by the destruction of Jerusalem in 70, just before the gospels began to take final form. The family therewith lost much of its importance, and the compilers of the gospels did not include stories about its members.

MARK AND JESUS' MOTHER: She has often but improbably been identified with the second Mary of Mk. 15.40.

"WOMAN": Jn. 2.4; 19.26.

COMPANY AT CRUCIFIXION: Mk. 15.40f.; Mt. 27.55f. Contrast Lk. 23.49 as well as John. Since the Markan account is the least edifying and dramatic, it is the least likely to have been invented.

CANA STORY: See Smith, "Wine God," 815ff., on Achilles Tatius II.2.1–3.3.

PAGE 26

CHANGES IN MARK 6.3 AND PARALLELS: See the variants cited by Aland, *Synopsis,* and the editions of the Greek New Testament by Aland, Nestle, and Souter for Mk. 6.3; Mt. 13.55; Lk. 4.22; and Jn. 6.42.

TAMAR: Genesis 38.

RAHAB: Joshua 2 and 6.

RUTH: Ruth, chapters 1 and 3. "She uncovered his feet," and "spread your skirt over your serving girl," in 3.7 and 9 are euphemisms; "lay at his feet" in 3.8 and 14 may be.

BATHSHEBA: II Sam. 11 and 12.

PAGE 27

MATTHEW'S METHODS: See Stendahl, *School,* and compare Mt. 2.18, 4.15; 8.17; 12.17ff.; 13.35; 21.5.

DIVINE MEN: Holy teachers and miracle workers, supposedly of higher than human nature. See Smith, "Prolegomena," especially 179–188.

DIVINE FATHERS: Bieler, *Theios aner* I.22ff.

NAZARETH: Mk. 6.1–6p.; Lk. 4.16–30. Only Luke here identifies the home town as Nazareth, but Mk. 1.9 and Jn. 1.45 speak of him as coming from Nazareth. The infancy stories of both Matthew and Luke take him there (Mt. 2.23; Lk. 2.39,51); he is identified as the prophet or messiah "from Nazareth" by Mt. 21.11 and Acts 10.38; and Jn. 1.46 shows that the proverb, "Can any good come out of Nazareth?" was applied to him. Such a variety of evidence from all strands of the tradition is practically conclusive.

PAGE 28

MYTHOLOGICAL ADVERSARIES: For instance, Satan and other demons. Mk. 1.13; Mt. 4.1–11p.; Lk. 22.31; Jn. 13.2,27; etc.

FOLLOWERS OF THE BAPTIST: There are traces of rivalry between them and Jesus' followers, but the treatment of them is not openly unfriendly: Mk. 2.18 (cp. Mt. 9.14, rather an abbreviation than hostility); Mt. 14.12 (cp. Mk. 6.29); Lk. 11.1; in Jn. 3.26, they complain to the Baptist about Jesus' success. The Baptist is said to have sent his disciples to Jesus to ask if he were "the coming one" (prophet? messiah?), but this is presumably Christian propaganda (Mt. 11.2ff.p.). The purpose is, in part, to prove the Baptist's ignorance. On the other hand, "the coming one" is not a regular Christian title for Jesus and may have come from Baptist usage. (On Jn. 6.14 see Meeks, *Prophet-King.*)

HERODIANS VANISH: On the textual variant to Mk. 8.15, see Metzger, *Textual Commentary,* 98.

PAGE 29

HEROD ANTIPAS: Incestuous marriage and execution of John the Baptist, Mk. 6.17–28f.p.; Josephus, *Antiquities* XVIII, 109–119. He built a new city on a site unclean according to Pharisaic law (to keep the observant out?—*Antiquities* XVIII.36ff.) and in it a palace decorated with images of which the Pharisees disapproved (Josephus, *Vita* 65). For a recent discussion, see Hoehner, *Herod.*

ANTIPAS IN GALILEE: Luke says that Antipas was in Jerusalem as a visitor at the time of Jesus' trial and that Pilate sent Jesus to him for a hearing (23.7–12), but this story was probably invented to fulfil the prophecy Luke used it to fulfil in Acts 4.27. It also gave Luke an extra opportunity to make one of his favorite points: that all competent and unprejudiced authorities who examined Christian leaders found them guiltless (Lk. 23.4, 11,13ff.; Acts 16.35; 17.32ff.; 18.14ff.; 19.37ff.; etc.). The other gospels know nothing of such an examination, and would not have ignored it if it had occurred.

PHARISEES PRO-HERODIAN: *M. Sotah* VII.8; *B. Pesahim* 107b; *B. Ketubbot* 17a. The eulogy of Herod Agrippa I in Josephus, *Antiquities* XIX.328–337 probably represents the Pharisaic view.

HEROD AGRIPPA'S PERSECUTION: Acts 12.1ff.

MARK'S HERODIANS AN ANACHRONISM: Luke dropped them, compare 6.11 with Mk. 3.6, and Lk. 20.20 with Mk. 12.13. He often corrects or omits Mark's historical errors, for instance, the story of the Baptist's execution, and the name of Antipas' brother (it was Herod, not Philip; cp. Mk. 6.17ff. with Josephus, *Antiquities* XVIII.109–119 and 136ff. and Lk. 3.19f.). Both Matthew and Luke correct Mark's mistake about Herod's title; it was "tetrarch," not "king" (Mk. 6.14 vs. Mt. 14.1; Lk. 9.7). Matthew 12.9 dropped the Herodians of Mk. 3.6; their appearance in 22.16 may be due to early contamination from Mk. 12.13.

PHARISAIC PERSECUTION: I Cor. 15.9; Gal. 1.13,23; Phil. 3.4ff.; Acts 8.3; 9.1f.,21; 22.4; 26.10f.

JAMES' LEADERSHIP: Acts 21.18.

PHARISAIC PROTEST: Josephus, *Antiquities* XX.200ff. That the leaders of the protest were Pharisees is not stated but seems likely. Pharisees would doubtless have been glad of any excuse to depose a Sadducean High Priest, but that they chose to make an issue of a Christian's execution is noteworthy.

LEADERS DISPLACED OR DESTROYED: Eusebius, *History* III.5.3, says that the Christians of Jerusalem fled to Pella in Jordan before the outbreak of the war. But how many did so? Another tradition he reports (IV.5) kept the church at Jerusalem until the time of Hadrian (A.D. 134).

EXCLUSION OF CHRISTIANS: See the curse on them inserted into the rabbinic daily prayer, *B. Berakot* 28b–29a in uncensored texts, Strack, *Jesus* II, #21. The insertion was made in the time of Gamaliel II, who probably held power from about 80–120.

PAGE 30

MINOR GROUPS: Sadducees had no known connection with Galilee and have no importance in the gospels. (None, at least, as a group. Some of the leading priests were almost certainly Sadducees, but the gospels do not think the fact worth mention.) "Elders" appear only as associates of the high priests and/or scribes, except in Lk. 7.3 where they may be the elders of a synagogue. ("The tradition of the elders," in Mk. 7.3,5p. is not theirs; the phrase means, "our ancestral traditions.") "Rulers" is apparently non-technical and imprecise. The "commanders" of Lk. 22.4,52 are the officers in charge of the temple guard. None of these, nor any of the other minor groups that might be found, would, for our present purpose, reward discussion. On "lawyers" (for "scribes") see below.

SCRIBES NOT IN JOHN: Jn. 8.3 is part of an interpolation.

MATTHEW'S FAVORABLE REFERENCES (Q): Mt. 8.19; 23.34.

LUKE DELETED REFERENCES TO SCRIBES: So in 4.32 (cp. Mk. 1.22); 9.37 (cp. Mk. 9.14); 11.15 (cp. Mk. 3.22); 20.41 (cp. Mk. 12.35); also from Q material, compare Lk. 9.57 with Mt. 8.19, and Lk. 11.49 with Mt. 23.34. There are only three references to Jewish scribes in Acts (4.5; 6.12; 23.9), as against seven to Jewish elders, though in the gospels scribes appear much more often than elders.

SCRIBES IN LUKE'S SOURCES: So Lk. 15.2; 22.66; 23.10. 11.53 is dubious. In 6.7 and 20.19 he was using Mark, but his manuscripts (unlike ours) may have had "scribes."

"LAWYERS" FOR "SCRIBES": In Luke's peculiar material: 7.30; 10.25; 11.45f., 52(?); 14.3. 11.52 may possibly have come from Q, cp. Mt. 23.13; if so, Luke introduced the "laywers." The use in Mt. 22.35 results from contamination, see Metzger, *Textual Commentary* 59. The original limitation of the term to Luke's peculiar material indicates that it comes from a peculiar source; had Luke introduced it on his own he would have done so in all parts of his gospel.

"SCRIBES" REPLACED BY "PHARISEES": See Appendix A, #IV.

SCRIBES NOT A GROUP: Those who were members of the Jerusalem sanhedrin were part of a group, but as members of the sanhedrin, not as scribes.

PAGE 31

SCRIBES FROM JERUSALEM: Mk. 3.22; 7.1.

MARK 12.28ff.: Love God and love your neighbor. The scribal praise in Lk. 20.39 for Jesus' defense of resurrection was probably put together from Mk. 12.28 + 32, and is evidence of editorial economy rather than scribal attitude.

TRANSGRESSIONS OF LAW: Eating with publicans, etc., Mk. 2.16; Lk. 15.2; neglect of handwashing, Mk. 7.2; healing on sabbath, Lk. 6.7ff.; 14.3ff. (lawyers).

ATTACKS ON SCRIBES: Mt. 23 is a little summa compiled from various sources. Compare Luke's parallels.

CLAIMS TO SUPERNATURAL POWER: Forgiving sins, Mk. 2.6f.; rejection of prophetic pattern, Mt. 12.38f.; Mk. 11.27ff.p.; Messianic claims, Mt. 21.15f.; Messiah son of God, Mk. 12.35ff.p.

TEACHING WITH AUTHORITY: Mk. 1.22p., 27p.

MEANING OF "AUTHORITY": See Starr, "Authority," and, for examples, *PGM* IV.1949; XII.147; Mk. 3.15; 6.7; Mt. 8.9; 9.8; Lk. 12.5; 22.53; Acts 8.19; etc.

JESUS A MAGICIAN: Mk. 3.22p.; cf. Lk. 11.19p.; Mt. 10.25. The scribes were far from alone in this opinion, cp. Samain, "L'accusation."

"IDENTIFICATION CRISIS": See above, p. 19.

PAGE 32

SCRIBES' EXPLANATION OF JESUS: This same argument, from the contrast between human limitations and superhuman pretensions, will be used again by Celsus against Jesus, and again by Eusebius against Apollonius, see chapters IV and VI. Its basis is a form of the mind-body problem; the solution eventually adopted by the Church was the doctrine of the incarnation.

BEELZEBUL: This is the best attested form of the name. In rabbinic Hebrew, it would mean "Lord of the Fourth Heaven" (or "of the Jerusalem Temple," or "of the festival," *zebul* being ambiguous). Since Jesus' opponents would not have identified his demon with an admirable being, some ancient scholars changed it to *Beelzebub,* the name given by II Kings 1 to the god of the Palestinian city of Ekron, and rendered by some Greek translators as "the Lord of the flies" or "Baal the fly". For modern conjectures see Gaster "Beelzebul." Two likely possibilities are 1) that the name given was *Baalzebel,* "the Lord of manure," and this was changed by Christian tradition—both reference to dung in abuse of paganism and alteration of terms by vocalic changes were standard in rabbinic literature; 2) that the name was meaningless, an example of the "barbarous" names of demons which at this time begin to appear in magical texts and are there referred to as "Hebrew," Wünsch, *Fluchtafeln,* no. 1, line 12 and note.

REFLECTIONS OF THE SCRIBES' CHARGE: Mk. 3.22–30p.; 6.14ff.p.; 8.28p.; 9.38f.p.; Q: Lk. 11.19f.p.; Jn. 7.12,20; 8.48f.,52; 10.20f.,33ff.; 18.30; 19.7; Mt. 9.34; 10.25; 27.63; Lk. 4.23. These comparatively clear passages will be discussed in this chapter; chapter VII will show that many more are relevant to magical practice.

MARK 3.20–30 TAKEN OVER: By Mt. 12.24–32, and in large part by Lk. 11.15–22.

PAGE 33

"ONE WHO LEADS ASTRAY": Greek, *planos;* Jn. 7.12; Mt. 27.63.

WORSHIP OF ALIEN GODS: So the Hebrew, *mesit,* M. *Sanhedrin* VII.4,10; cf. Dt. 13.7.

SAMAIN: "L'accusation," 456ff. See further below, p. 54, in the note on Justin, *Dialogue* 108.2.

"DOER OF EVIL" = MAGICIAN: *Codex Theodosianus* IX.16.4; *Codex Justinianus* IX.18.7 citing Constantius; compare I Peter 4.15 and Tertullian, *Scorpiace* 12.3. Selwyn, *I Peter,* understood 4.15 correctly and cited Tacitus' use of *malefica, Annals* II.69, end.

"SON OF A GOD" = "GOD" = MAGICIAN: See chapter VII.

JESUS THOUGHT THE BAPTIST: Mk. 6.14ff.p.; 8.28p.

PAGE 34

JESUS DISTINGUISHED FROM THE BAPTIST: Mk. 1.9p.; Jn. chs. 1–3 (3.24 seems intended to contradict the tradition found in Mk. 1.14p.).

"HAS BEEN RAISED": Mk. 6.14. The Greek *egegertai,* commonly translated "has risen," can also mean "has been raised." On the translation "by him," for the Greek *"en autoi"* see below.

ORIGEN: *Commentary on Mt.* X.20.

THE BAPTIST THOUGHT ELIJAH: Mt. 11.14 (which Origen cites) and 17.12f. Origen's interpretation is that of Lk. 1.17.

THE WISE SAID NOTHING: What the others said is collected by Taylor, *Mark,* p. 309.

KRAELING: "Jesus," 147ff. The account given in the text tacitly corrects some difficulties in Kraeling's position.

CHRISTIANS IN SMYRNA: *The Martyrdom of Pionius* 13 (Knopf, *Märtyrerakten*). For the use of spirits of the dead to compel demons, see *PGM* no. IV, lines 1911ff.; no. LVII, line 6. On the role in necromancy of persons untimely dead, see Bidez-Cumont, *Mages,* vol. I, pp. 180–186, who trace the practice to the fifth century B.C.

SPIRITS OF DEAD AS SERVANTS: *DT* nos. 22, 25, 26, 28–35, 38, 234, 235, 237–240, etc.

PRAYER TO HELIOS-IAO-HORUS: "Iao" is a Greek form of "Yahweh" common in the magical papyri. "Yahweh" is the name commonly misspelled in English Bibles as "Jehovah." The prayer is in *PGM* IV.1948ff.

BY HIM ⟨I.E. BY HIS ORDERS⟩: Greek, *en autoi. En* instrumental is used here to indicate the person by whose order or under whose authority an action is performed, so Mt. 9.34; 12.24; etc.; Blass-Debrunner-Funk, *Grammar,* section 219.

SIMON THOUGHT TO BE JESUS: Irenaeus, (ed. Harvey), I.16.1: "He who appeared among the Jews as 'the Son.'"

SIMON'S SPIRIT: *Clementine Recognitions* II.13.1f.

PAGE 35

THE ALIEN EXORCIST: Mk. 9.38–40; Lk. 9.49f.; the words in parentheses are found only in Mark.

THE POWER OF NAMES: This sort of magical thinking permeates the New Testament, see for examples, Jn. 17.6,26; 20.31; Acts 3.6,16; 4.12,30; etc. I Cor. 1.13ff.; Phil. 2.9f.; Heb. 1.4; James 5.14; Apoc. 2.13; 3.12; 14.1; 17.3; 19.12,16; 21.12ff.; 22.4. The classic study is that by W. Heitmüller, *"Im Namen Jesu,"* Göttingen, 1903.

PAGE 36

HIGH PRIESTS MENTIONED FIRST: Mt. 26.57 is not truly an exception; the High Priest is mentioned first as representative of the group. True exceptions are Mk. 8.31p.; Lk. 20.19; and Acts 6.12. "The rulers" of Acts 4.5 are probably the high priests, whose leaders are later specified individually; 4.5 has shaped 4.8. The "general" in charge of the temple takes precedence in Acts 5.24 because he is the official immediately concerned with the situation. Otherwise the high priests take first place in more than forty passages.

MEANING OF "HIGH PRIESTS": Schürer, *Geschichte* II.274ff.

ROLE OF PRIESTS IN THE PASSION: Arrest: Mk. 14.1,10,43,47p.; Mt. 27.3,6; Jn. 11.46f.,57; 18.3,10,12. John's report that the Pharisees cooperated in the plot and the arrest is an anachronism. Even in John they disappear after the arrest (18.3). Interrogation: Mk. 14.53–64p.; Lk. 22.66; Jn. 18.12,24. Handing over: Mk. 10.33p.; Mk. 15.1p. (Lk. 23.1 refers to 22.66). Prosecution: Mk. 15.3,11,13f.(?)p.; Lk. 23.4f.,13f.,21,23; Jn. 19.6.

GUILT SHIFTED: To "the crowd," Mk. 15.13f.(?),15p.; to "the people," Mt. 20.25; to "the Jews," Jn. 18.31,38ff.; 19.7,12,14f.

PASSION PROPHECIES: Mk. 8.31p.; 9.31p.; 10.33f.p.; cf. Lk. 17.25; 24.7,46. The root from which this thicket grew was probably an apocalyptic saying like that in Lk. 9.44b.

PRIESTS IMMEDIATELY PLOT TO KILL JESUS: Mk. 11.18; Lk. 19.47; 20.19; Mt. 21.45; Jn. 7.32,45; 11.46f.,57.

JOHN REPORTS PLOTS AGAINST JESUS: 5.18; 7.1,19,25,30; 8.37; 11.8,50; etc.

PAGE 37

PRIESTS' QUESTION FOLLOWS MIRACLE: Mk. 11.27; Mt. 21.23; Luke has suppressed the miracle, probably because he did not want Jesus to refuse to state the source of his *miraculous* powers. He has not, however, connected the question closely with the attack on the market; instead he has inserted a report of Jesus' "teaching daily . . . and preaching the Gospel" (!—19.47f.; 20.1) and has thereby made the question refer to his authority as a teacher, an apologetic interpretation.

"AUTHORITY" IN MARK: Above, pp. 10 and 31.

YAHWEH HAS SENT ME: Is. 6.8f.; 48.16; 61.1; Jer. 25.17; 26.12,15; 42.21; Ezek. 2.3f.; 3.5ff.; etc.

JESUS' CLAIM TO BE SENT BY GOD: Mk. 9.37p. (apparently not known to Matthew, who would never have omitted it); Q: Lk. 10.16p.; compare Jn. 13.20. Also Jn. 3.17,34; 5.36ff.; 6.29,57; 7.28f.; 8.42; 10.36; 20.21; etc.

OUTSIDERS THOUGHT HIM A PROPHET: Mk. 6.15p.; 8.28p.; Mt. 21.11,46; Lk. 7.16; 24.19 (Cleopas does not yet realize Jesus' true nature); Jn. 4.19; 7.40; 9.17. BECAUSE OF HIS MIRACLES: Mk. 6.14 indicates that 6.15 is an attempt to explain the miracles; so, therefore, is 8.28; Lk. 7.16; 24.19 ("powerful in deed" refers to the miracles); Jn. 4.19; 9.17 (both responses to miracles).

OUTSIDERS WERE WRONG: Mk. 8.29p.; Lk. 24.25ff. (correcting 24.19ff.); Jn. 4.25f.; 7.40; 9.35ff.—all of these correct the Johannine passages cited in the preceding note.

IN THE SYNOPTICS JESUS NEVER CLAIMS TO DECLARE YAHWEH'S WORD: Luke makes the claim for him (5.1) and makes him make it by implication (8.11f., contrast Mk. 4.14; 8.21, vs. Mk. 3.35; 11.28 unparalleled). Evidently this was all he could do. John was less inhibited (17.14; also 3.34; 8.47; 14.10; 17.8) and is less credible.

PAGE 38

PRIESTS BRIBED JUDAS, ETC.: Mk. 14.10,43,53p. Lk. 22.52. Jn. 18.3 says nothing of the bribe, but gives Judas more troops—the Roman cohort, no less!

INTERROGATIONS AND TRIALS: Discussion of these is endless; for a sampling of recent apologetics see Bammel, *Trial.* Sanhedrin by night: Mk. 14.53–72p.; high priests: Jn. 18.13–24; sanhedrin by day: Mk. 15.1p.; Lk. 22.66–71; Pilate: Mk. 15.2–15p.; Lk. 23.1–7,13–25; Jn. 18.28–19.16; Herod: Lk. 23.8–11.

PILATE'S RELUCTANCE INCREDIBLE: Pilate's record is known from Josephus *War* II. 169–77; *Antiquities* XVIII. 55–64, 85–89. He was notoriously brutal in putting down political disturbances and insensitive to Jewish opinion. If he found an accused man innocent, it is unlikely that he would have hesitated to release him for fear of offending the Jews; that he should have hesitated to execute a man he thought a messianic pretender, is incredible. Therefore, the theatrical scenes set off by his alleged hesitation are Christian polemic against the high priests or, in Matthew and John, the Jews.

PRIESTS' VACILLATION: Compare Mk. 11.18p.; Jn. 11.46–53; etc.; with Mk. 14.55p.

DESTRUCTION OF THE TEMPLE: Mk. 14.58p.; 15.29p.; Jn. 2.19ff.; Acts 6.14. John tries to excuse the saying by allegorizing it (2.21f.), another sign that it was a genuine embarrassment.

PAGE 39

PENALTY FOR BLASPHEMY: *M. Sanhedrin* VII.4f.; etc.

COMBINATIONS OF TITLES EDITORIAL: Thus, for instance, Matthew added both "Son of Man" and "Son of God," as official titles, to the story of Peter's confession; in Mark, Peter said only that Jesus was the Messiah. Compare Mt. 16.13 with Mk. 8.27, and Mt. 16.16 with Mk. 8.29. The agreement of Lk. 9.18ff. with Mark leaves no doubt as to the original text.

SON OF GOD USUALLY RELATED TO MIRACLES: Mk. 3.11, exorcism; 5.7p., exorcism; 15.39p., after the supernatural signs that accompanied Jesus' death; Mt. 4.3,6p., the devil demands miracles; 14:33 the disciples' inference from Jesus' walking on the sea; 16.16, the revelation given through Peter (see vs. 17); 27.40,43 the mocking of Jesus' inability to perform a miracle; Lk. 1.35 the angel's prediction of his birth; 4.41 exorcism; see also Mk. 1.11p., 9.7p., the voices from heaven; Mt. 11.27p., only the Son knows the Father. ("The Son" who does not know the date of the end, in Mk. 13.32p., is probably the Son of Man from 13.26p.) These facts are overlooked in van Iersel, *Sohn.*

SON OF GOD NOT COMMONLY MESSIANIC: This has been overlooked because of the orthodox supposition that each title implies all the others, so "the Son of God" is *ex officio* Messiah, Son of Man, etc. He may have been all of these for the final editors of the gospels, but the amazing consistency with which the different titles appear separately, each in contexts of a different sort, in the stories and sayings from which the gospels were put together, indicates their earlier independence. There is nothing *per se* messianic in the exorcisms of Mk. 3.11; 5.7p. (Mt. 8.29 gives the Son of God an eschatological role unknown to his original), Lk. 4.41 (Luke has added a messianic explanation lacking in his source, Mk. 1.34); nor in the centurion's confession, Mk. 15.39p.; nor in the temptations to make bread from stones, or fly through the air (Mt. 4.3,6p.; Ps. 91 is not necessarily messianic; it was most widely used as a magical prophylactic text, see Haupt, "Maccabean," 275ff.; *PGM* P17, P19); nor in Mt. 14.33, the disciples' worship, nor in the taunt in Mt. 27.40. Even in Lk. 1.35 the description "Son of God" results from divine paternity; it was not implied by the messianic dignity prophesied in 1.32f. and had to be predicted separately. The voices from heaven in Mk. 1.11p., 9.7p., say nothing about messiahship unless we suppose that "my beloved, in you I take delight" is to be understood as a reference to Is. 42.1, which the beginning of the verse makes dubious. There is no reference to Ps. 2 in these texts nor in II Pet. 1.17; that such references were introduced by the tradition behind the *Ebionite Gospel* and Justin Martyr (*Dialogue* 88.3,8; 103.6) shows secondary messianic interpretation, begun already in Mk. 9.11ff.p. In Mark especially, the transfiguration cannot have been understood as a revelation of the messiahship, since Mark made Peter's confession precede it (8.29). This so troubled Schweitzer that he proposed to reverse the sections (*Geschichte* 426ff.)! What the transfiguration revealed was more than a messiah, it was a son of God. Similarly Mt. 11.27p. is not merely non-messianic, but anti-messianic; salvation is here. Thus the only passages in which "Son of God" is equated with "Messiah" by its immediate context are editorial, Mk. 1.1 and 14.61f.p.; Mt. 16.16 (see the note before last) and probably 27.43 (more of the same).

PAGE 40
JESUS' DENIAL OF SECRET TEACHING: Jn. 18.20. An untrue answer, if we are to believe Jn. chapters 3,4,7,13ff.; etc.

PAGE 41
"DOER OF EVIL" = "MAGICIAN": Above, p. 33 and note.

PAGE 42
MATTHEW'S ADDITION: Mt. 27.43; the quotation is from a slightly variant text of the messianic Ps. 22.8. Matthew again conjoins the titles of Jesus used in his own church and in his opponents' propaganda. See above, in the notes on combinations of titles and "Son of God."
"THAT MAGICIAN": Greek, *planos*. literally "deceiver." See above, p. 33 and notes.

CHAPTER IV
PAGE 45
JOSEPHUS ON JESUS: "The Slavonic Josephus" is now generally recognized to be spurious.
JOSEPHUS AND RABBINIC JUDAISM: See Smith, "Palestinian Judaism," and the forthcoming work on Josephus' *Vita* and *War II* by S. Cohen.

OPINIONS OF ANT. XVIII.63f.: See Feldman, Josephus, *Antiquities* vol. IX, pp. 573ff. and add Moreau, *Témoignages* 11ff.

PAGE 46

CHANGES IN ANT. XVIII.63f.: "Sophist" (*sophistes*) for *sophos* ("wise"); "impiety" (*t'asebe*) for *t'alethe* ("truth"); add Greek for "who said that" and "they asserted that"; "pretended prophets" (*pseudopropheton*) for *theion propheton* ("divine prophets"). The other bracketed words are implied by the Greek text.

RABBINIC STORIES ABOUT JESUS: All rabbinic texts on Jesus have suffered more or less in manuscript tradition and many have been deleted entirely from most current editions and manuscripts. I have used chiefly the collection by Strack, *Jesus*.

ARREST OF R. ELIEZER: *T. Hullin* II.24 B. *'Abodah Zarah* 16b–17a; *Midrash Qohelet Rabba'* I.8.3. On these see Neusner, *Eliezer* I.400–403, and the literature cited there; II.199, 203f.,365ff. In 365ff. Neusner points out that the oldest source *(T.)* does not specify the sayings; only the later versions pretend to know that a legal ruling was involved and to be able to identify it. One might add that the ruling specified is suspicious because of the frequent use of references to excrement in rabbinic abuse of opponents. Further, the ruling is not given in the same form in *A.Z.* 16f. and *Qoh.R.* I. 8.3, and appears in both only as a conclusion drawn from a statement explicitly attributed to Jesus. The original form of this statement was probably that in *Qoh.R.*, "From filth they came, and to filth they shall return," perhaps with the citation of Micah 1.7. The story is in the main credible; rabbinic tradition would never have invented such a tale about Eliezer had there been no basis for it. For legal aspects of the case, see Lieberman, "Roman" 20ff.(=76ff.), who would date it about 107/108. However, his evidence is not conclusive and Eliezer, one of the leading figures of the first generation at Jamnia, was probably about fifty in A.D. 70.

PAGE 47

PANTERA'S GRAVESTONE: *CIL* XIII.ii.1.7514; reproduction in Eisler, *Iesous*, plate XLV.

ELIEZER ON JESUS: On *T. Yebamot* III.3f., and *B. Yoma'* 66b, see Lieberman, *Tosefta*, vol. VI, p. 24. The passages are deliberately obscure and their reference to Jesus is uncertain. Equally uncertain is the reference of the statement of Rabbi Simeon ben 'Azzai' (c. 100–130): "I found in Jerusalem a genealogical scroll and in it was written, 'So-and-so is a bastard (born) of adultery.'" (*M. Yebamot* IV.13; *B. Yebamot* 49b).

ELIEZER ON BEN STADA: *B. Shabbat* 104b, *T. Shabbat* XI.15; *J. Shabbat*, XII.4 (13.d), *B. Sanhedrin* 67a. The spelling *Stara*, not *Stada*, is defended by Lieberman, *Tosefta*, III.179f., as better attested by manuscript tradition; but the manuscript evidence is limited, late, and full of corruptions, while the pun in *B. Sanhedrin* 67a, is most easily explained by supposing the name was pronounced *Stada* in the third century. Pumbeditha, a Babylonian town, was a center of rabbinic studies. On tattooing and magic see Lassally, "Amulette," 130ff., whose evidence tends to confirm the rabbinic report. Also Dieterich, *Mithrasliturgie* 252, note to p. 165. The rabbinic reference to "cutting" rather than "tattooing" may refer to the practice of cutting and rubbing foreign matter into the cuts to produce raised scars. We shall henceforth use "tattooing" to refer to any way of permanently marking the flesh.

THE ORIGINAL BEN STADA: *T. Sanhedrin* X.11; *J. Sanhedrin* VII.16(25c–d); *J. Yebamot* XVI.5(15d). In *B. Sanhedrin* 67a the penalty is changed by assimilation to the story of Jesus, and becomes crucifixion ("hanging") on the eve of the passover.

MARKS ON JESUS' BODY: This is overlooked by Lieberman in his argument against the reference; see the note before last. Weaker arguments are advanced by Schoeps, "Simon Magus," whose case is vitiated by his almost total neglect of the gospel evidence for polemic against Jesus. In favor of the identification see Rokeah, "Ben Stara'." For tattoo marks, etc., on slaves and adherents of gods as signs of divine ownership, see Lietzmann on Gal. 6.17, who recognizes that Paul appeals to his marks as to an amulet, for magical protection, and cites parallels.

PAGE 48

JESUS POSSESSED: Jn. 7.20; 8.48,52; 10.20; etc.

LUKE'S INFANCY NARRATIVE: Lk. 2.22–39; cf. Leviticus 12.

MATTHEW'S PROPHECY: Mt. 2.15; quoting Hosea 11.1. For Matthew's practice of finding prophecies to suit his purposes, see above, p. 27 and note.

BEN DAMA AND ISHMAEL: T. *Hullin* II.22f.; parallels in *J. Shabbat* XIV.4(14d, inf.); *J. 'Abodah Zarah* II.2 (40d); *B. 'Abodah Zarah* 27b; *Midrash Qohelet Rabba'* I.8.3. In *B. 'Abodah Zarah* the name of the healer's village has been changed to identify him with the man who talked with R. Eliezer a generation earlier; the peculiar name is the more likely reading. The "fence" is the set of para-legal rules that must be observed to keep one far from transgression of a rule of the Law itself.

THE CURSE IN DAILY PRAYER: *B. Berakot* 28b–29a; *J. Berakot* V.3(9c); *T. Berakot* III.25; an early text in Strack, *Jesus*, p. 31.

PAGE 49

GRANDSON HEALED BY MAGICIAN: *J. 'Abodah Zarah* II.2(40d); *J. Shabbat* XIV.4 (14d); *Midrash Qohelet Rabba'* X.5.

JESUS STONED: *B. Sanhedrin* 43a. The leading astray is also interpreted as introducing the worship of alien gods, but false prophecy was originally a distinct offense.

THREE CHARGES: Dt. 13.2–6, false prophecy; 13.7–12, inciting to apostasy; 18.9–13, magic.

JESUS AND JOSHUA BEN PERAHYA: *B. Sotah* 47a; *B. Sanhedrin* 107b; cp. *J. Hagigah* II.2(77d); *J. Sanhedrin* VI.13(23c). The addition is at the end of the *'En Ya'aqob* version of the *Sotah* story.

JOSHUA B. PERAHYA'S MAGIC: Neusner, *History* V.218–43, cites the evidence.

CURSE ON RESURRECTION BY NAME: R. Simeon ben Laqish in *B. Sanhedrin* 106a. For the later belief see the mediaeval Jewish lives of Jesus.

"IF THE WHORE'S SON TELLS YOU": *Midrash Pesiqta' Rabbati*, ed. M. Friedmann, Vienna, 1880, folia 100b–101a. Braude, *Pesikta Rabbati*, p. 422, tactfully refrained from understanding the reference.

R. ABBAHU'S SAYING: *J. Ta'anit* II.1, end (65b). The word translated "regret" literally means "loathe," but the sense is probably, "He will loathe himself for having said it," or, "He will loathe the claim because of the penalty it entails."

PAGE 50

JESUS' CLAIM TO GO UP TO HEAVEN: Jn. 3.13, 6.38,42,58,62; II Cor. 12.2–5, where the man Paul knew is probably Jesus; the hymns in Phil. 2.5–11 and I Tim. 3.16 are best understood as references to Jesus' claim. See Smith, *Clement*, 237–248.

JESUS DISGRACED HIMSELF: *B. Berakot* 17a–b; *B. Sanhedrin* 103a,end. Of the four names in *B. Berakot* 17b, three correspond with three of the four in *M. Sanhedrin* X.2. If the fourth of each should therefore be identified, *M. Sanhedrin* X.2 would tell us that Jesus, in the late second century, was nicknamed Balaam and denied a place in the world to come.

SUPPOSED RABBINIC REFERENCES TO JESUS: Passages like *B. Shabbat* 116a–b (the story of 'Imma' Shalom and the "philosopher" who cited Mt. 5.17), and *B. Sanhedrin* 106b (the heretic who told Rabbi Hanina' he had seen, in an account of "Balaam the lame", that Balaam was 33 years old when " Pinhas the robber" killed him) are not demonstrations of rabbinic tradition, but merely evidence the rabbis' knowledge of the gospels or other Christian documents (in the latter case, perhaps Lk. 3.23). At most, "the lame" may come from rabbinic tradition; but does it refer to Jesus? To take "Pinhas the robber" as a nickname for Pontius Pilate is difficult, because Pinhas (ancestor of the priestly line, and a distinguished murderer, see Num. 25.1–15) was a national hero.

THE MESSIAH, THE SON OF GOD: Mt. 16.16; 26.63; Mk. 1.1 (MSS. B,D,etc.); 14.61; Jn.

11.27; 20.31; Acts 8.37 (Latin, Syriac, Coptic MSS.); II Cor. 1.19; Heb. 3.6; I Jn. 1.3; 3.23; 4.15; 5.20; II Jn. 3.

CHRESTUS' RIOTS: Suetonius, *Life of Claudius* 25.4.

PAUL IN ROME: Acts 28.22. The date is fixed by the fact that Paul was sent to Rome by Festus shortly after Festus took over the governership of Palestine in 60.

SUETONIUS ON PERSECUTIONS: *Life of Nero* 16.2, written shortly after 122. A more general translation, "a new and maleficent superstition" is also possible, but begs the question, Why was the cult thought maleficent? This question is answered by the magical significance of *malefica*; see above, p. 33 and the note on "doer of evil" *(maleficus)*.

PAGE 51

TACITUS ON PERSECUTIONS: *Annals* XV.44.3–8. In preferring the spelling "Christiani," I follow Syme, *Tacitus* II.469. For other points of detail see the commentary of E. Koestermann, Heidelberg, 1968, pp. 253ff. As noted above, Pilate was not a procurator, but a prefect.

PAGE 52

RULER OF THE EARTH: Lucan, *Pharsalia* VI.697; Hippolytus, *Refutation of All the Heresies* X.14,15,19,20,21, etc., compare the "God of this aeon" acknowledge by Paul, II Cor. 4.4, and "the ruler of this world," in Jn. 12.31.

LUCAN'S WITCH: *Pharsalia* VI.706–711. "Sing these hymns" means "recite these spells." For cannibalism compare Tibullus I.5.49ff., Horace, *Epodes* 5; Philostratus, *Life* VIII.5; etc. For gods of magicians charged with cannibalism see *PGM* IV.2594f., Selene is said "to drink ⟨human⟩ blood, . . . to eat ⟨human⟩ flesh;" also 2483,2656f.. On human sacrifice and cannibalism in ancient magic and mystery cults (including Christianity), see Henrichs, *Phoinikika,* 28ff. Particularly impressive is the fact that Pliny the elder, praising the Romans for their prohibition of magic, refers to magical rites as "atrocities, in which killing a man was an act of utmost piety, and even eating one, most salubrious," *Natural History* XXX.13 (end); cf. XXVIII.6. Lucan might be dismissed as a rhetorician, but Pliny expresses the best informed legal opinion of Nero's time, and Horace, although a satirist, pictures the sort of thing that was thought to go on, and doubtless did.

SING A HYMN: The same words as those meaning "recite a spell," in the preceding note.

PAGE 53

RELIABILITY OF PLINY'S LETTER; See the commentary by Sherwin-White, *Letters,* 691ff., a whitewash.

EVOKING A CRIMINAL: On the supposed power, and the importance in magic, of the spirits of condemned criminals, see above, p. 34. Most gods were thought to belong to the heavenly and good world, demons to the underworld and the powers of evil. Men might become either gods or demons, but most became demons. For Christians accused of having raised Jesus, a condemned criminal, by necromancy, see *The Martyrdom of Pionius* 13.

THE CHRISTIANS' OATH: An oath of secrecy was commonly a part of the ceremony in the mystery cults, and such oaths were frequent in magic. See Henrichs, *Phoinikika* 37–44.

THE SORTS OF CHRISTIANITY: See the evidence in Smith, *Clement* 262ff.; *Secret Gospel* 115–134.

ATTESTATION OF THE GOSPELS: The dramatic date of the *Dialogue against Trypho* is 133/4, but the actual date is after 150. The first reference to the canonical gospels is made by a Phrygian bishop named Papias. Since the preserved evidence is Christian we should have expected reference to the gospels considerably before references to their opponents.

PAGE 54

JEWISH REPRESENTATIVES: Cp. *Dialogue* 117.3 "The Son of God . . . whose name the high priests and teachers of your people have made contemptible and scandalous through all the world."

THE QUOTATION FROM JUSTIN: *Dialogue* 108.2; abbreviated in *Dialogue* 17.1. The last phrase might also be rendered, "those who confess (Jesus to be) Christ and teacher and Son of God." For *planos,* "deceiver," meaning "magician" see above, p. 33, and add as further evidence *Dialogue* 69.7, and Vettius Valens, *Anthologiae* book II, chapter 16, Hermes with Ares (ed. Kroll, p. 74, line 18). In II Jn. 7 *planos* is used of the Antichrist, the arch-magician, compare II Thess. 2.9–11; *Didache* 16.4; *Sibylline Oracles* III.63ff. (Simon Magus).

CHRISTIAN ORGIES: *Dialogue* 10.1 and often elsewhere; such stories were widespread and lost nothing in the telling. See the famous parody, Tertullian, *Apology* 8.

MATTHEW'S GRAVE ROBBERY: Mt. 27.62–66; 28.4,11–15.

JUSTIN ON JEWISH CURSING: *Dialogue* 93.4; 95.4; 96.2; 133.6; etc.

PAGE 55

JUSTIN ON JESUS' REPUTATION: I *Apology* 30. Note that Justin thinks the title "Son of God" was given to Jesus *because of his miracles.*

ACCUSATIONS OF MAGIC: *Dialogue* 69.7; see the note above on *Dialogue* 108.2. Also *B. Sanhedrin* 43a, above, p. 49.

QUADRATUS: Quoted in Eusebius, *Ecclesiastical History* IV.3.2.

CONTRASTED MIRACLES: Compare the imitation in Irenaeus, *Against All Heresies* II.49.2f. (ed. Harvey).

CHARGES OF IMMORALITY: *Dialogue* 17.1,3; 35.1; 108.2; 117.3. For the connection of magic with libertinism see Smith, *Clement* 237–263; *Secret Gospel* 115–131.

"GODLESS" TEACHING: Justin deals with the question at length, *Dialogue* 50–57, but as usual does not specify the Jewish criticisms.

REFUTATION BY CRUCIFIXION: I *Apology* 13.4; 22.3; *Dialogue* 10.3; etc.

JEWS FORBIDDEN TO READ GOSPELS: *Dialogue* 38.1; *T. Hullin* II.20, and parallels: Christian books are forbidden as "books of magic." Nevertheless, Justin supposed Trypho *had* read a gospel, or at least a book of Jesus' sayings, *Dialogue* 18.1.

PAGE 56

LUCIAN'S NOTION OF CHRISTIANITY: Betz, *Lukian* 9. Perhaps Lucian had in mind Aristophanes, *Clouds,* 423ff., where the dupe being initiated into the wicked mysteries of Socrates must undertake to acknowledge no god other than the trinity: Chaos, the Clouds, and the Tongue.

JESUS AS LAWGIVER: On the reported ruling about a prostitute's gift, see above, p. 46 and notes. Galen's reference to the "laws for which no reasons are given" in the schools of Moses and Jesus (*De pulsuum differentiis* II.4) is probably later than Lucian's work.

PAGE 57

"A SYRIAN FROM PALESTINE": Palestine was considered a part of Syria.

JEWS FAMOUS AS EXORCISTS: Josephus, *Antiquities* VIII.46.

PAGE 58

CELSUS: See Chadwick, *Origen,* xxivff. Andresen, *Logos,* identifies as Celsian some material that escaped Chadwick's notice. Against the notion that Celsus' work belongs to a class of "Exposures of Frauds" represented by Lucian's *Alexander, Peregrinus, Menippus, Philopseudes,* (Mette, "Oinomaos 5"), it must be said that the "class," a discovery of modern literary criticism, was not an entity known to ancient thought, and the works assigned to it are so diverse that no detailed conclusions about the content of any one can be drawn from knowledge of the others.

CELSUS' BEGINNING: Origen, at the end of his preface, states that in the first section of his work (before I.28ff.) he does not adhere to the order of Celsus' text, so it is not certain that his first item on Jesus was also Celsus' first. However, from Origen's comments ("First . . . next . . . after this . . ." etc.) it seems to have been so.

JESUS' MOTHER'S HUSBAND: So I.28, twice; in I.32 he is her fiancé, perhaps because of Origen's memory of Matthew's story.

PANTHERA: I.32. Unless Celsus was using rabbinic material, which is not likely, this name must have come to him from non-rabbinic Palestinian tradition. The earliest source that now preserves it is the Palestinian story of Rabbi Eliezer (above, p. 46).

MAGI: Celsus wrote "Chaldaeans" instead of "magi," doubtless a blunder as Origen supposes (I.58), and probably due to Matthew's story that the magi came because they saw his star (II.2). The Chaldaeans were astrologers *par excellence.* Origen was nit-picking; the equation of Chaldaeans with magi was common: see Lucian, *Menippus* 6. Philostratus, *Life* I.26 locates the magi in Chaldaea (Babylon).

ONLY TEN DISCIPLES: I.62; II.46. Since II.46 is emphatic about the limitation, the words "or eleven" in I.62 may have come from Origen, not Celsus.

PAGE 59

CELSUS ON THE DISCIPLES: *Against Celsus* I.62; compare II.46. Andresen, *Logos* 12f.

ARGUMENTS APPEALING TO JEWS: II.1 Why have you left the law of our fathers? II.7 Many of Jesus' actions were profane. II.28 The Old Testament prophecies could be applied to others more plausibly than to Jesus. II.29 They do not accord with Jesus' career. II.32 His actual birth was incompatible with royal ancestry. Etc.

JEWISH CHRISTIANS WHO KEPT SOME OF THE LAW: They are known from many documents, especially the *Clementine Homilies* and *Recognitions.*

PAGE 60

JESUS THOUGHT AN ANGEL: II.9,44; V.52 (which makes it impossible to understand "angel" as meaning merely "messenger," that is, "prophet"). See, however, Andresen, *Logos,* 102f. who would see in this the reflection of an equation with Hermes, appropriate for a necromancer.

CELSUS CLAIM TO OTHER INFORMATION: II.13. Origen's suggestion (that there was *no* information except that in the gospels) was false.

JESUS CRUCIFIED BETWEEN BANDITS: The correct translation of the word generally rendered "thieves," Mk. 15.27; Mt. 27.38,44.

CELSUS' PASSION STORY: Origen's claim in II.10 that Celsus had no source for his statement that Jesus "hid himself" was a slip, Jn. 8.59; 12.36.

EUSEBIUS ON PANTHERA: *Eclogae propheticae* III.10, on Hosea 5.14; 13.7.

EPIPHANIUS ON PANTHERA: *Panarion,* Heresy 78.7.

PAGE 61

LATER CHRISTIANS ON PANTHERA: See the passages collected by Strack, *Jesus,* 11*ff.

MANDAEANS: See Drower, *Mandaeans,* and Rudolph, *Mandäer.*

JESUS AND SIMON MAGUS: Hippolytus, *Refutation of all Heresies* VI.19, Simon said it was he who had appeared "to the Jews as Son, in Samaria as Father, and to the other peoples as Holy Spirit."

SAMARITAN MATERIAL: See for example, the review by Ben Hayyim, in *BO* 23(1966)185ff. of Macdonald, *Memar.* The best sources for Simonian opinions of Jesus are the *Clementine Homilies* and *Recognitions,* but their "Simon" draws mainly on the canonical gospels.

THE PEREIRE CRUCIFIXION: See Derchain "Darstellung" 109ff. and the brief description, with pictures, in Delatte-Derchain, *Intailles,* no. 408 (p. 287). (The Constantia gem and others of its type are later.)

PAGE 62

BRITISH MUSEUM GEM 231: See Derchain, "Darstellung," and Bonner, *Studies* 226.

THE PALATINE GRAFFITO: See the description, comments, and bibliography by K. Parlasca in Helbig, *Führer,* II.861ff. no. 2077. Cf. H. Solin, *Graffiti del Palatino* I, 1966, 209ff.

THE HEAD A DONKEY'S: The ears are not long, but the artist was no artist. Donkey, rather than horse, is determined by the religious and magical associations.

YAHWEH DONKEY-HEADED: Josephus, *Against Apion* II.8off.; Tacitus, *Histories* V.3f.; Epiphanius, *Panarion, Heresy* 26.10; etc.

SETH: See Bonnet, *Reallexikon* 702ff. The donkey replaced the original Seth animal (whatever it was) especially in magical practice, ibid. 714.

IAO WITH A DONKEY-HEADED GOD: For example, British Museum no. G 294, with *Sabao* on the face and *Iao Sabao* (miswritten *Sasao*) on the reverse. *Sabao(th)* is a transliteration of the Hebrew word commonly translated "of hosts" in the title "the Lord of hosts." A donkey-headed deity associated with *Adonai* (a Jewish substitute for the name *Yahweh*) is prominent on curse tablets of about A.D. 400 from Rome, see Wünsch, *Verfluchungstafeln* (though many of its conclusions have been challenged). Procopé-Walter, "Iao," collected much evidence of the identification, but neglected the social background.

THE CARTHAGE GRAFFITO: Tertullian, *Ad nationes* I.14; *Apology* XVI.12. *Onokoites* is formed as *arrenokoites*. Since *arrenokoites* means "a man who beds with men," *onokoites* should mean "a man who beds with donkeys." In this case, however, the god himself is a donkey, therefore the meaning is presumably "a donkey who beds with men," namely, with his worshipers. This makes the compound's first element subject rather than object of the implied verb, but authors of graffiti were no more observant of grammatical than of ethical proprieties and, in any event, the subect—object relation was uncertain. Anubis is addressed as "secret bedfellow" in *PGM* XXIII.2.

BESTIALITY AND MAGIC: For example, in the canons of the council of Ancyra, 16 ("Isidore" and Dionysius Exiguus understood *qui tempestatem patiuntur* as demoniacs). This belief was developed in medieval and later witchcraft. Almost the *sine qua non* of a witch was an animal "familiar" (all too familiar!).

THE MONTAGNANA CRUCIFIX: Bettini, "Crocifisso-Amuleto."

PAGE 63

THE MEGARA CURSE: Wünsch, *Fluchtafeln*, no. 1. The restorations are defended by Wünsch in the notes; so is the interpretation of *abraikos* as *hebraikos*.

THE CARTHAGE CURSE: Wünsch, *Fluchtafeln*, no. 4.

PGM III.420: *PGM* no. III is "Papyrus Mimaut" = Louvre, Pap.gr. no. 2391, written shortly after A.D. 300. In this and the following papyri the line cited is that in which the name of Jesus occurs.

PGM IV.1233: *PGM* IV is "the Paris magical papyrus" = Bibliothèque Nationale, Supp. gr. 574, written between 300 and 350 A.D. This spell (in Coptic, like the preceding) probably came from a Jewish-Christian gnostic source. The great majority of the material in the manuscript is pagan.

PGM XII.192: Leiden, Gr. p. J. 384, A.D. 300–350.

PAGE 65

JOSEPHUS KNEW JESUS' MESSIANIC CLAIMS: *Antiquities* XVIII.63f., *if* our emendation of the text (above, p. 46) be correct.

PAGE 66

CHRISTIAN PROMISCUITY: Minucius Felix, *Octavius* (a Christian apology written about A.D. 200), chapter 9.2f. makes a pagan say of the Christians: "They recognize each other by secret signs and objects, and love each other almost before they meet. Among them religion constantly joins with itself, as it were, a sort of lust, and they commonly call each other brothers and sisters, so that even ordinary debauchery may be made incest by the use of the sacred name." He goes on to report cannibalism and incestuous orgies, and worship of an ass-headed deity, genitalia, a crucified criminal, and the cross. All this is a straw structure set up to be knocked down, but it probably does reflect common gossip.

COMMUNITY OF WIVES: For instance, Clement of Alexandria, *Stromateis* III.xviii.105.2–108.2.

CANNIBALISM, INCEST, ETC.: Above, pp. 52f. Further, of the magi, Clement of Alexandria, *Stromateis* III.ii.11.1; Catullus, *Carmina* 90; Bardesanes in Eusebius, *Praeparatio Evangelica* VI.10.16; Sextus Empiricus, *Outlines of Pyrrhonism* III.205.

PORPHYRY ON THE EUCHARIST: Harnack, *Porphyrius,* Fragment 69, from Macarius Magnes III.15.

JESUS AN ANGEL: *Against Celsus,* II.9.44; V.52. Celsus probably got the notion from Christian circles, where it was rather widely held, see Barbel, *Christos.*

CHAPTER V

PAGE 68

JEWISH CONQUESTS IN PALESTINE: Schürer-Vermes-Millar, *History* I.207–228.

SEMITIC PAGANISM: This has been almost wholly neglected in Palestine. For neighboring countries see Teixidor, *Pagan God.*

EGYPTIAN AMULETS IN PALESTINE: See the finds from Ascalon, Athlit, Sebastia, etc., in the Palestine Archaeological Museum, *Gallery Book, Persian, Hellenistic, Roman, Byzantine Periods* (1943), nos. 790–802, 813, 838–42, 946–58, etc.

PERSIAN INFLUENCE IN JUDAISM: Smith, "Second Isaiah" (monotheism); Bousset, *Religion*[3] 478–520 (demonology, eschatology, etc.)

GREEK GOVERNMENT OF GALILEE: Schürer-Vermes-Millar, *History,* I.217f.; 240ff.

PAGE 69

SPIRITS OF THE DEAD AS BEGGARS: Lattimore, *Themes* 132f., 230–234.

NO CLEAR LINE BETWEEN MAGIC AND RELIGION: So Pfister, "Kultus," 2108, sec. 4: "I can see no difference in principle between men's beliefs about magical, and their beliefs about cultic acts. Means and objectives are the same, so are the basic forms of thought and belief." Pfister repeated this (with different wording) in "Epode," 325; Nock cited and supported it in "Paul and the Magus," 169.

SAME MEANS AND GOALS IN MAGIC AND RELIGION: Nock, "Paul and the Magus" 170f. Necromancy was practiced at Greek oracles, Hopfner, "Nekromantie" 2232. (His statement that the spirit of the deceased was expected to appear only in a dream is contradicted by the implications of Plutarch, *De sera* 555c; *Cimon* VI.6[482].) *Defixio* was public in the temple of Demeter in Cnidus, *DT* p. 5 (against Audollent's interpretation). Official burning of wax images of public enemies, *SEG* IX(1938)no.3, lines 44ff., on which Nock, "Paul and the Magus" 170f. Compare, however, Dušanić, "Horkion," who thinks the text an ancient forgery. Even if he is correct, it shows what the ancients thought possible. See further Pfister, "Epode."

IMPRECATORY PSALMS: 35; 58; 59; 69; 109; 141; etc. See Nikolsky, *Spuren.*

PETITIONARY PRAYERS IN PGM: For instance, XII.104ff.,183ff. ("Give me what you will"!),238ff.,244ff.,301ff. All these from one papyrus; many could be added from the others.

PAGE 70

GOETEIA AND SHAMANISM: See Burkert, *"Goes."*

EQUATION OF "SOPHIST" AND "GOES": Plato, *Sophist* 234a–235a; *Statesman* 291c,303c; *Meno* 80a–b; *Symposium* 203d; Gorgias, *Helena* 10–14. See de Romilly, *Magic and Rhetoric.*

BOTH USED OF JESUS: *Sophist:* Josephus, *Antiquities* XVIII.63f.(?); Justin *I Apology* 14.5 (denial indicates usage); Lucian, *Peregrinus* 13. *Goes:* Celsus in Origen, *Against Celsus* I.71; II.32,49; VIII.41; etc.

GOES = "BEGGAR," ETC.: Burkert, *"Goes"* 51, n. 74.

PLATO'S PENALTY FOR GOETEIA: *Laws,* Book X, 909a–e.

JOSEPHUS' GOETES: *War* II.261ff.; *Antiquities* XX.97,167ff.,188.

PAGE 71

MAGI A PRIESTLY CLAN: Kent, *Old Persian* 201, on *magu*.

MAGI INTERPRET DREAMS, ETC.: Herodotus I.107f.,120,128; VII.19,37.

MAGI IN FIFTH CENTURY DRAMA: Sophocles, *Oedipus Tyr.* 387; Euripides, *Orestes* 1497.

MAGEIA AND GOETEIA: Gorgias, *Helen,* 10, reading *hamartemata.* On Greco-Roman magic generally see Hopfner, "Mageia," and Hubert, "Magia." Hull, *Hellenistic Magic* is a good elementary introduction to problems the author did not recognize.

MAGIAN ENDOGAMY: Xanthos of Lydia, *Magika,* in Clement of Alexandria, *Stromateis* III.ii.11.1. Jacoby, *FGrHist* III.C.no.765, fragment 31, would limit Xanthos' report to the relations with mothers. If he is right, Clement's statement shows how the story grew.

PLINY "THE ELDER": Died in the eruption of Vesuvius, A.D. 79; uncle of "the younger" (above, p. 52). The following quotation comes from his *Natural History* XXX.14–17.

PAGE 72

BURDEN TO THE PROVINCES: They had to house, feed, and transport him and his train. The visit was in A.D. 65–66.

NERO GAVE HIM A KINGDOM: He crowned him King of Greater Armenia. Suetonius, *Nero* 30.4, says Nero also spent 8,000 gold pieces a day on his support and gave him more than a million when he left. A gold piece was worth about 160 dollars; this in terms of the amount of bread it would buy. It was worth 1600 *asses,* and bread, in Nero's Italy, cost about 3 *asses* a pound (Frank, *Survey* V.144f.) Bread now costs about 30 cents a pound, so the value of the *as* (the basic Roman coin) was about 10 cents. The equivalents given in most reference works have been outdated by inflation, as this one soon will be.

MAGIC INCAPABLE OF PRODUCING EVIDENCE: This sense of *intestabilis* is dictated by the point of the story, that Tiridates could not teach Nero magic because magic does not work and therefore is not teachable (vs. Ernout and Bostock).

PLUTARCH'S ACCOUNT OF THE MAGI: *Isis and Osiris* 46 and 47 (369d–370c). A recent commentary is Griffiths, *Plutarch's De Iside.*

PERSIAN ESCHATOLOGY IN OLD AND NEW TESTAMENTS: Notably in Daniel, Mark 13p, and the Apocalypse, but also in many shorter elements. See also the Jewish intertestamental literature, notably I Enoch.

PAGE 73

PHILO OF BYBLOS: Quoted by Eusebius, *Praeparatio Evangelica* I.10.52. For *to physikon* meaning "magic" see Liddell-Scott-Jones, *Greek English Lexicon, physikos* III.

THE HAWK-HEADED GOD: Philo specifies Chnum (*Kneph*) and Agathos Daimon (I.10.48,51), but the anguipede is more likely; see Delatte-Derchain, *Intailles,* nos. 1–38, 52–89,126,223.

MAGI TEACHING ON MORALS: Diogenes Laertius I.7, from Sotion of Alexandria, an older contemporary of Jesus.

MAGI PRACTICE CANNIBALISM: Pliny, *Natural History,* XXVIII.6; XXX.13.

LUCIAN'S MENIPPUS. Chapters 3–10. This is a parody of a typical story of conversion to the true religion or philosophy; compare Justin, *Dialogue,* introduction, and see Nock, *Conversion* 107ff.

MAGI ARE CHALDEANS: A common erroneous equation; see above p. 58 and note. Lucian perhaps knew better and used the error to demonstrate his dupe's ignorance.

HONEY, MILK, CHOASPES WATER: Honey mixed with milk was used for oblations to the gods of the underworld, Odyssey X.519, etc. The (by Lucian's time) ancient emperors of Persia were supposed to have drunk only water from the river Choaspes.

PAGE 74

HERCULES, ULYSSES, ORPHEUS: All were famous for visits to the underworld. The cap was part of Ulysses' customary costume, the lion skin belonged to Hercules, the lyre to Orpheus. Since "Menippus" had been the name of a notorious satirist, the intent is clear.

THE "DIVINE MAN": See Hadas-Smith, *Heroes,* and Smith, "Prolegomena." The objections raised by Tiede, *Charismatic Figure,* will be answered in a forthcoming article in the *Mélanges M. Simon.*

MIRACLES WITHOUT SPELLS THE CRITICAL TEST: Philostratus, *Life* VII.38. A similar position is defended by the Christian author of Pseudo Justin, *Answers to the Orthodox* 24.

SPIRITS OBEY MERE ORDERS: Compare PGM I.181ff. and Lk. 7.6–10. Also *PGM* IV.199f.; etc.

PAGE 75

PAUL CLAIMED UNION WITH JESUS: Rom. 8.9ff.; Gal. 2.20; etc. Compare *PGM* I.179f.; III.470ff.; XIII.791ff.

RITES TO MAKE THE SOUL DIVINE: *PGM* I.20f.; III.600; IV.215f., 475ff.; etc.

THE FORMULATION OF THE LAW ON MAGIC: Berger, *Dictionary* 550, on *Lex Cornelia de sicariis.*

PAULUS' COMMENTARY: *Sententiae receptae Paulo tributae* XXIII.15–18, in Baviera, *FIRA* 409f. The last sentence of the passage here translated has been thought a later addition.

PAULUS DECLARED AUTHORITATIVE BY CONSTANTINE: Berger, *Dictionary* 701, on *Sententiae Pauli.*

PAGE 76

PAULUS ON PROPHETS AND ASTROLOGERS: *Sententiae receptae Paulo tributae* XXI, in Baviera, *FIRA* 406f.

CONSTANTINE'S COMPROMISE: *Codex Theodosianus* IX.16.3. The correct date is probably May 23,318, Seeck, *Regesten* 62 and 166.

THE REVERSAL REVERSED: Ammianus Marcellinus XXIX.2.26,28; in general, Barb, "Survival."

PAGE 77

RABBIS ON MADMEN AND MAGICIANS: *T. Terumot* I.3 and parallels (cp. Mk. 5.2ff.p.); *B. Hagigah* 3b,end; cp. *B. Sanhedrin* 65b,end; *J. Terumot* I.1(40b).

ELIADE ON SHAMANS: *Shamanism* 236. For ancient analogues see Hanse, *Gott* 30–38.

PAGE 78

'OBOT THOUGHT SPIRITS OF THE DEAD: For example, Koehler-Baumgartner, *Lexikon* 19f. Contrast Dt. 18.11 which explicitly distinguishes between consulting *'obot* and "inquiring of the dead."

'OBOT OBJECTS OF WORSHIP: Lev. 19.31; 20.6; II Kings 23.24; Isaiah 19.3.

A GOD RISING FROM THE EARTH: I Sam 27.13. The present Hebrew text has "gods" (the verbal form is plural), but the text used by the third-century B.C. Greek translators had the singular. The plural is probably an apologetic revision to prevent any suggestion that Yahweh appeared. Hebrew has no indefinite article.

RABBINIC PASSAGES ON 'OBOT: *Sanhedrin* 65b, where some opinions identify *'obot* and (spirits of) the dead. The parallel in *J. Terumot* I.1(40b) calls them demons (*shedim*).

PAGE 79

"FALSE PROPHET" = "MAGICIAN": Acts 13.6; Fascher, *Prophetes,* 182–198; Wetter, *Sohn,* 73–81.

RABBINIC PASSAGES ON SOLOMON AND DEMONS: *B. Gittin* 68a–b; the midrashim on Song of Songs and Ecclesiastes.

"THE LORD, THE HIGHEST GOD, SABAOTH:" *TSol,* "original text" I.7.

AMULETS WITH DIVINE NAMES: "The Lord" (= *Adonai*), *Sabaoth,* and the Greek forms of Yahweh (*Iao, Iaoe,* etc.) are banal, see the indices of Delatte-Derchain, *Intailles.* "The highest god" (*hypsistos*) appears in Bonner, *Studies* 308, no. 328.

SOLOMON'S FALL: *TSol* "original text" XXVI and parallels.

SOLOMON PARALLELED WITH JESUS: Berger, "Messiastraditionen," gives much evidence of this.

CHAPTER VI

PAGE 81

EXORCISMS CAUSED CHARGES: Mk. 3.22p; Mt. 9.34; Lk. 11.19f.p.

QUADRATUS: Above, p. 55 and notes.

JUSTIN'S OPPONENTS: *I Apology* 30; *Dialogue* 69.7 (Trypho).

CELSUS' CHARGE: Origen, *Against Celsus* I.38; further I.6,68,II.49. Dunn, *Jesus* 70.

"SON OF GOD" CONNECTED WITH MIRACLES: Above, p. 39 and note.

MIRACULOUS CLAIMS AND DEMONIC POSSESSION: Jn. 8.51f. 10.17–20. (In Jn. 7.20 the charge is perhaps vulgar abuse.)

SIMON MAGUS: Acts 8.9–24, especially 8.10.

PAGE 82

SIMON, JESUS, AND THE BAPTIST: *Clementine Homilies* II.23, contrast *Clementine Recognitions* II.7–8, probably revised out of respect for the Baptist.

SIMON'S SUCCESS: Justin Martyr, *I Apology* 26.3 says, "almost all the Samaritans, and a few in other ethnic groups, worship (Simon) as the First God" (this about A.D. 150). For Simon's success in Rome, *I Apology* 26 and 56.

CLAIM OF DIVINITY EVIDENCE OF MAGIC: *Against Celsus* I. 69–71; cp. Jn. 8.51f.

"IMPIETY" ETC.: *Against Celsus* I and II throughout; VII.53; etc.

JESUS TAUGHT DUALISM: *Against Celsus* VI.42.

WE SHOULD NOT BE DECEIVED: I follow Wifstrand's emendation.

PAUL ON THE ANTICHRIST: II Thess. 2.3–12.

ANTICHRIST A MIRACLE WORKER: For example, *Didache* 16.4.

PLUTARCH ON THE MAGI: Above, p. 72 and notes. There were Persian elements in the Christian figure, see Bousset, *Antichrist*.

PAGE 83

CELSUS ON JESUS AND GOETES: *Against Celsus* I.68.

JESUS' MIRACLES NOT USUALLY CONNECTED WITH TEACHING: Exceptions: Lk. 5.10* the miraculous draught of fishes confirms his call of the apostles. Mk. 1.44p; Lk. 17.14p* lepers, for healing are told to obey the Mosaic law. Mk. 2.10p*, healing a paralytic proves his power to forgive sins. Mk. 3.4f.p; Lk. 13.15f., 14.3ff healings on the sabbath prove the permissibility of doing good on it. Mk. 9.29* exorcism of demoniac boy proves need of prayer. Mt. 11.5p* Jesus' miracles prove him "the coming one". Mt. 17.27* the coin in the fish's mouth proves the advisability of paying taxes. Besides these, many miracle stories prove the need of trust (*not* "faith") for healing. In four stories about sayings Jesus is made to refer to his miracles as evidence for his teachings (Lk. 4.21*; Mt. 11.21,23p*; 12.28p; 12.39p*). Prophecies have been omitted since they could not, when (or, if) uttered, have been perceived as miracles. In the starred items above either the miracle is clearly fabulous or its connection with the teaching clearly secondary. The rest, if true, would show that Jesus knew his miracles required trust, used them to prove his right to neglect the sabbath, but required beneficiaries who were not of his immediate circle to observe the Mosaic law. He saw them as evidence that the kingdom was at hand, and perhaps as fulfilment of prophecy. Whatever his moral teaching, they had little recorded part in it.

DISTINCTIONS OF JESUS' MIRACLES: *Reality*: Irenaeus II.49.3; Origen, *Against Celsus* II.51; but the transfiguration seems to have been a vision, Mk. 9.8p. *Permanence*: Quadratus; Papias, as cited in Preuschen, *Antilegomena* 94; Irenaeus II.49.3; but apparently some of Jesus' exorcisms did not last, either, Lk. 11.24ff.p. *Not tricks nor demonic*: Irenaeus II.49.2f.; Origen, *Against*

Celsus I.6; II.51; Arnobius, *Adversus Nationes* I.43ff.; but Jesus is said to have used phrases in barbarous languages (Mk. 5.41; 7.35), and the story that he compelled a demon to tell its name (Mk. 5.9) suggests that he used the name to order it out. *Helpful and gratis*: Irenaeus II.49.2f.; Origen, *Against Celsus* II.51; *Clementine Homilies* II.34; Arnobius, *Adversus Nationes* I.43ff.; but the exorcisms and cures performed by other magicians were also helpful, and Jesus and his twelve companions evidently lived on "contributions," Jn. 12.6. *Greater than others*: Irenaeus II.49.2f. *Prophesied*: Justin, *I Apology* 30; Irenaeus II.49.3; Tertullian, *Against Marcion* III.3; this is the argument on which Christian authors most often insisted; it is now generally recognized to be false. *They produced conversions*: Irenaeus II.49.3; Origen, *Against Celsus* II.51; III.33–35. The argument that the success of Christianity proves the truth of its claims has been weakened by the greater success of communism.

PAGE 84

THE TEACHINGS OF THE MAGI: Above, pp. 72f. and notes.

APOLLONIUS OF TYANA: For the following account see Philostratus, *Life,* ed. Conybeare (outline and comments in Hadas-Smith, *Heroes* 196ff.), the letters attributed to Apollonius (in Conybeare, vol. II), Eusebius' reply to Hierocles (also in Conybeare II), and the testimonia collected in Speyer, "Bild" and Petzke, *Traditionen* (on which however see Speyer's review, *JAC* 16 [1973]133f.)

PAGE 85

SIMILARITIES BETWEEN APOLLONIUS AND JESUS: This list of similarities should not be seen as a denial of differences: The miraculous element in the preserved tradition about Jesus is greater than in that about Apollonius; Jesus was not himself an ascetic; the libertine element in his practice and in his teaching for his initiates, as opposed to outsiders, is lacking in Apollonius (except for two alleged slanders, *Life* I.13; Philostratus, *Lifes of the Sophists* II.5[570]); Apollonius did not share Jesus' eschatological expectations, nor Jesus Apollonius' philosophical views; Apollonius' followers thought him a "divine man"—the indwelling supernatural power was his own; this view of Jesus appears in the gospels—most clearly in John and in the synoptics' birth stories—but they also represent him as possessed of "the holy spirit," an originally outside power. Many other differences will surely occur to readers anxious to find them.

APPEARANCES AFTER DEATH: Apollonius' appearance to the doubting youth (*Life* VIII.31) is paralleled not only by Jesus' to Thomas (Jn. 20.26ff.), but also by Jesus' to Paul (Acts 9.3ff.). For a further appearance of Apollonius, in later legend, see *Historia Augusta, Aurelian* 24.3–6.

"LIFE OF APOLLONIUS": The exact title is, "The (things) about Apollonius the Man of Tyana."

PAGE 86

PHILOSTRATUS' SOURCES: *Life* I.2f. For Moiragenes see Miller, "Moiragenes," and Chadwick, *Origen* 356, n.3.

CARACALLA'S PATRONAGE: Dio Cassius LXXVII.18; Philostratus, *Life* VIII.31 end.

PYTHAGOREAN FICTIONS: So Speyer, "Bild" 50ff. The stories were not made up by Philostratus; he was an enthusiast for pure Greek culture and disapproved of orientalizing.

LITERARY PROBLEM LIKE GOSPELS: Especially Luke, who refers to the "many" earlier attempts to write accounts of Jesus' work, 1.1.

SIMILARITIES OF LITERARY FORM: Again, to state the similarities is not to deny the differences. For instance, the narrative frame of the *Life* is much fuller than that of the gospels, the exotic travel sections from "Damis" are relatively coherent narratives, as is the account of dealings with Vespasian in Alexandria. In other sections, notably I.8–15; IV.1–35; VI.35–43, the incoherence and consequent resemblance to the gospels is more conspicuous. Obviously, different sorts of material have been used in these different sections.

PAGE 87

EVIDENCE OF MAGICAL POWERS: *Life* I.2; IV.43end; VIII.23; IV.10,18f.,25; etc.

SEXUAL IRREGULARITIES: *Life* I.13. Such charges were the stock in trade of ancient polemics, no doubt because they were often true. Therefore, they are particulary difficult to evaluate.

THE HIEROPHANT AT ELEUSIS: *Life* IV.18; for the translation of *ta daimonia* compare IV.43end; VIII.23.

THE PRIESTS OF TROPHONIUS AND THE WATCHMEN IN CRETE: *Life* VIII.19,30 end.

ACCUSATIONS TO DOMITIAN: *Life* VII.11,20; VIII.5. References to some of these charges also appear in Apollonius' *Letter* 8, but its authenticity is dubious. That he was thought a god is stated in *Letter* 44.

EUPHRATES DID NOT STRIKE HIM: V.39; compare *Clementine Recognitions* II.11, where the rod goes right through the magician without hurting him. Conybeare's "skill at single-stick" is a misinterpretation.

PAGE 88

THE MURDER OF DOMITIAN: Dio Cassius LXVII.18; the divergence from Philostratus' *Life* VIII.26, shows independent traditions.

DIO ON CARACALLA: Dio LXXVII.18end. The Greek term translated "in the strict sense of the word" may also mean "careful and precise" or "thoroughly trained, perfected;" but the hostility of the context seems to indicate the less favorable sense. Perhaps the influence of this passage persuaded a glossator to add, in the previous one, after the reference to Apollonius, "this man was a Pythagorean philosopher, and, indeed, a *goes*."

ALEXANDER SEVERUS' CHAPEL: *Historia Augusta, Severus Alexander* 29.2; plausible but dubious.

ORIGEN ON APOLLONIUS: Origen, *Against Celsus* VI.41.

PAGE 89

PORPHYRY ON APOLLONIUS VS. JESUS: *Harnack, Porphyrius*, nos. 4 (= Jerome, *De psalmo LXXXI*, end) and 63 (Macarius Magnes III.1); cf. nos. 46, 60.

APOLLONIUS' TALISMANS: Speyer, "Bild" 56f.

EPIC LIFE OF APOLLONIUS. *Suidae Lexicon*, ed. Adler, under Soterichos.

HIEROCLES: Governor of Bithynia, in N.W. Asia Minor, at the time he wrote. He later rose to be Prefect of Egypt. See Seeck, "Hierokles 13." On his comparison of Apollonius and Jesus, see below.

APOLLONIUS THOUGHT MERELY A MAN: This was not wholly true; Apollonius was also worshiped as a present deity: *Letter* 44, *Life* VII.21; VIII.5; etc.; Eunapius, *Lives of the Sophists* 454 middle, 500end.

LACTANTIUS' REPLY TO HIEROCLES: *Divinarium Institutionum* (henceforth *Div. Inst.*) V.2.12–3.26.

WORSHIP OF APOLLONIUS AND JESUS: *Div. Inst.* V.3.14f. The cult of Apollonius as (an incarnation of) Herakles was established in Ephesus, but Apollonius was almost certainly worshiped by the Pythagoreans and probably still had his own cult in Tyana.

LACTANTIUS' ARGUMENT FROM PROPHECY: *Div. Inst.* V.3.18–21; now generally discredited.

PAGE 90

EUSEBIUS' REPLY TO HIEROCLES: Conybeare, *Philostratus* II.484ff., entitled, *The Treatise of Eusebius the Son of Pamphilus, against the Life of Apollonius of Tyana written by Philostratus, occasioned by the parallel drawn by Hierocles between him and Christ*. The original title has been lost. Henceforth, *On Philostratus*.

JESUS A COMPANION OF GOD: Eusebius was not quite orthodox in his opinions about "the Son of God;" he thought him inferior to "God the Father."

EUSEBIUS' ARGUMENTS AGAINST APOLLONIUS: The main ones used to prove him a *goes* will be found in chapters 10, 11, 14, 15, 17f., 22, 23, 24f., 26, 27, 29, 31, 35, 37, 39, 40.

EUSEBIUS' PRIMARY ARGUMENT AGAINST APOLLONIUS' DIVINITY: *On Philostratus* 5–7. Eusebius conveniently overlooked the fact that Jesus got relatively little attention during the first century after his death.

EUSEBIUS' BELIEF IN MAGIC: See, for example, his proposed explanations of Apollonius' miracles, *On Philostratus* 31, 35.

PAGE 91

CRITERIA TO PROVE APOLLONIUS A MERE MAN: Inconsistency: On Philostratus Chs. 10, 11, 14, 22, 24f., 29. Ignorance: Chs. 14, 15, 24, 29, 37. No miracles before visiting Brahmans: Ch. 23. Flattery and deception: Ch. 39, and often.

CRITERIA TO PROVE APOLLONIUS A MAGICIAN: Materials and purposes: Chs. 10, 22. Association with magicians: Chs. 11, 17f., 22, 27, 40. Recognition and control of demons: Chs. 23, 26. Necromancy: Chs. 24f. Accusations of magic: Chs. 26, 40. Predictions: Ch. 31. Cures: Ch. 31. Other miracles: Ch. 35. Magical devices: Ch. 40. Peculiarity of accusations: Ch. 40.

CHAPTER VII

PAGE 94

$320,000: That is, 50,000 silver pieces (denarii), worth 64 asses each. See the notes to p. 72.

CHRISTIANS ACCUSED OF MAGIC: For example, Hippolytus, *Philosophumena* VI.7ff., 39ff.; VII.32; IX.14ff.; X.29. Compare Origen, *Against Celsus* VI.40; etc.

CHRISTIAN MAGICAL PAPYRI: Greek: *PGM*, vol. II, nos. 1 to 24; Coptic: Kropp, *Zaubertexte*.

EXAGGERATION OF MIRACLES: For example, Matthew, taking over Markan miracle stories, sometimes doubled the persons cured: Mt. 8.28ff. (vs. Mk. 5.1ff.); 9.27ff. and 20.29ff. (vs. Mk. 10.46ff.).

MINIMIZING THE MIRACULOUS: Fridrichsen, *Problème*. Hull, *Hellenistic Magic* 116-141, has shown that this tendency is particularly strong in Matthew. Compare the preceding note. That contrary tendencies are conspicuous in the same gospel shows how complex the problem of tradition is.

PAGE 95

CLEMENT ON GNOSTIC PRAYER: *Eclogae propheticae* 15 (ed. Stählin-Früchtel, III.141).

ENCOURAGEMENT FOR FAITH HEALERS: Mk. 11.23p.; Lk. 17.6; "confidence" is commonly mistranslated "faith," but the Markan form of the primary saying shows that the "faith" in the parallels means "confidence."

TRANSLATIONS IN MAGICAL TEXTS: For example, *PGM* XXXVI.315ff. where the Coptic command "Open for me, open for me, bolt," is immediately translated. Similarly, Coptic papyri translate Greek formulae, see the passage cited by S. Eitrem, *Papyri* I, p. 116.

PAGE 96

THE MAGI AND TIRIDATES: Dio Cassius LXIII.5.2; Dio says they returned by a route "in which they had not come" (LXIII.7.1). This resembles Mt. 2.12, "They returned by another road," but the resemblance is probably coincidental. The statement in Dio reports historical fact; the one in Matthew reflects magical convention: after a meeting with a supernatural being you should go home by a different road, *SHR* I.5 end.

MAGI INITIATED NERO: Pliny, *Natural History* XXX.17, quoted above, pp. 71f.

JESUS THE SUPREME MAGUS: This interpretation develops that of Origen, *Against Celsus* I.60 (where the *magoi*, though distinct from the Chaldaeans, are unmistakably magicians). See also Chrysostom, *Homilies on Matthew* VII.1 and 3; VIII.1 (for the antithesis to the Jews). So Clarke, "Rout"; contrast Hengel-Merkel, "Magier" (ignorant conjectures).

BETHLEHEM VS. NAZARETH: The prophecy, Micah 5.1ff.; the fact, Mk. 1.9; Mt. 21.11; Lk. 4.16; Jn. 1.45f.; Jn. 1.45f. proves the contradiction was a source of embarrassment.

ADOLESCENT PRECOCITY FROM DIVINE MAN: See Bieler, *Theios aner* I.33ff.

OMISSION OF RITUAL: This was facilitated by the tendency of oral tradition to abbreviate. Such factors are complementary. Rabbinic literature customarily omits references to ritual in reporting both magical operations and miracles performed by holy men; Blau, *Zauberwesen* 32f.

PAGE 97

SPIRIT IDENTIFIED: Mt. 3.16; Lk. 3.22; The charge is in Mk. 3.22, answered in 23–30. That "the Holy Ghost" belongs to demonology rather than to angelology is recognized by Böcher, *Christus* 19, 27, 40, etc.

JN. 1.32ff.: John's remodeling also served his purpose of subordinating the Baptist and making him testify to Jesus.

BAPTISM THE BEGINNING: So in many lines of Christian tradition: Mk. 1.1ff.p.; Lk. 16.16p.; Jn. 1.6; Acts 1.22; 10.37; 13.24.

STORIES OF WAYS TO GET SPIRITS: Preisendanz, "Paredros," is not satisfactory. It extends the meaning of *paredros* to include almost any sort of supernatural helper and obscures the distinction between conjuring a demon for a single operation and getting one as a permanent assistant. The word *paredros* commonly refers to a permanent assistant.

JESUS EVOKED THE BAPTIST: Above, pp. 34f. and notes.

PAGE 98

SIMON'S SPIRIT: *Clementine Recognitions* II.13. (The author did not believe this explanation, but claims that Simon did, III.49.)

JESUS MAINLY A HEALER: This supposes that the stories selected by the gospels represent approximately the range of those that circulated in Jesus' lifetime. In fact, the selection is surely biased in Jesus' favor. Stories of persons blinded, struck dead, etc., presumably circulated about him as they did about his disciples (Acts 5.5, 10; 13.11; I. Cor. 5.3ff.; I. Tim. 1.20), but the only thing of that sort that has been preserved is the blasting of the fig tree (Mk. 11.12ff., 20ff.p.).

BAPTIST THEORY DROPPED: We hear nothing more of it after the two references in Mk. 6.14ff.; 8.28, and their transcriptions by Matthew and Luke—a reason for thinking Mark's report of it comes from early tradition.

OMISSIONS IN TRANSLATION: In this section there are considerable gaps in the text due to breakage of the papyrus. I have followed Preisendanz' restorations in the readings, and the example of the evangelists in shortening the text by omission of much of the ritual.

IN FRONT OF HIS BODY: Preisendanz thought, "in the middle (of the roof)," but when a star stands "in the middle of the roof" a few lines later, the roof is specified, and a different construction is used.

ANGEL: Or "messenger"—the original meaning is "messenger," but in imperial times the word has come to mean "supernatural being," so that the "angel" here is the "god" in the sentence after next. The magical papyri often use "angel," "spirit," "demon," and "god" as interchangeable.

KISS HIM: Compare Judas' recognition of Jesus, Mk. 14.45p.

PAGE 99

KNOW, THEREFORE: Reading *ginoske toi* for *ginosketai* and *hon* for *ho*.

THE LORD OF THE AIR: This spirit is identified as "the ruler (*aion*) of this world" in Ephesians 2.2.

RECEIVE THIS MYSTERY: Compare Mk. 4.11, "To you ⟨his close associates⟩ has been given the mystery."

⟨YOU⟩ WILL NOT GO INTO HADES: Compare Peter on Jesus, Acts 2.31.

ALL THINGS SUBORDINATE TO THIS GOD: I Cor. 15.27.

ONLY YOU WILL SEE OR HEAR HIM: So Paul's Jesus, Acts 22.9; 26.14; versus 9.7.

PAGE 100

JESUS' BAPTISM: Mk. 1.9. On its historicity see above, in the notes on pp. 8 and 97.

RITES TO GET SPIRITS: *PGM* I.1–42; and XIa, perhaps also IV.1717–1870; and XII. 14–95 in which statuettes of Eros are animated. Note I.39f. where the god will speak to his host (in bed) "mouth to mouth," as the writer of II Jn. 12 and III Jn. 14 will speak to his disciple. Did the writer of the epistles think, like Paul (Gal. 2.20) that he was an embodiment of Christ and therefore a god to his disciples?

IRENAEUS ON MARCUS: *Adversus haereses* I.vii.2 (ed. Harvey).

SON OF GOD AND MESSIAH: Luke justified "Messiah," which means "anointed," by reference to the sequel of the baptism; God anointed Jesus with the spirit (Acts 10.38; cf. 4.18). Clearly homiletic reflection.

"SON OF GOD" NOT A COMMON MESSIANIC TITLE: Dalman, *Worte* 223. For the continuing argument see van Iersel, *Sohn,* 3–26; Pokorný, *Gottessohn,* especially pp. 27–42. The fact is clear.

"SON OF GOD" COMMONLY CONNECTED WITH MIRACLES: Above, p. 39 and notes.

PAGE 101

JESUS' MIRACLES RARELY ATTRIBUTED TO SPIRIT: Jesus makes the claim in reply to his enemies in Mk. 3.29p. and Mt. 12.28; Mt. 12.18 and Lk. 4.18 contain biblical verses supporting it, contributed by Matthew and Luke; Luke's prefatory remarks in 4.1,14 represent the victory over the temptation and the ministry in Galilee as the work of the spirit, and in 10.21 he represents Jesus' secret knowledge as the work of the spirit. None of these references occurs in a story of a particular miracle. The *only* gospel story in which a single, specific miracle is *perhaps* attributed to Jesus' spirit is that of the healing of the paralytic in Mk. 2.1ff., where 2.8 *might* be taken to mean that Jesus, "by his ⟨familiar⟩ spirit," knew his opponents' thoughts. Matthew and Luke omitted the reference to the spirit. In Lk. 7.8 the centurion evidently supposes Jesus will send a spirit to heal his son, but this is the opinion of an ignorant outsider.

OPPONENTS ATTRIBUTE JESUS' MIRACLES TO DEMONS: Mk. 3.22p.; Mt. 9.34; 10.25 (by implication); 12.26p.; cf. Jn. 8.48,52; 10.20. These observations, and those in the preceding note, correct my former opinions ("Aretalogy," and *Clement* 219f.).

"SON OF GOD" IN GRECO-ROMAN USAGE: Smith, "Prolegomena," 179ff. On Origen, *Against Celsus* VII.9, see below p. 117.

PALESTINIAN PAGANISM: Above, pp. 68 and 77ff. and notes; further, Smith, *Parties,* especially chapter IV.

"SONS OF GOD" = "GODS": Dt. 32.8,43 (LXX); Ps. 29.1; 89.7; Job 1.6; 2.1; Dan. 3.25.

SYNOPTICS NEVER CALL JESUS "GOD": John is less inhibited and calls him "Only Begotten God" (a title) as distinct from "God" (the Father), 1.18; see Metzger, *Textual Commentary.* Most English translations follow inferior texts.

APOLOGETIC LINE IN BIRTH STORIES: The allegation of divine paternity, as opposed, for instance, to mere vindication of Jesus' legitimacy (that would also have been possible within the generous limits of evangelic veracity).

DMP X.23ff.: Repeated in XXVII.1ff. Compare Jn. 1.51, where Jesus promises a disciple, "You shall see the heavens opened and the angels of God ascending and descending on the Son of Man." For the Son's intercession before the Father on behalf of his creatures, see Hebrews 7.25. On having/getting/becoming a god, in magical and other texts, see Hanse, *Gott.*

PAGE 102

YOUR NAME IS MINE: Phil. 2.9f.; James 2.7; Rev. 3.12; 14.1; 22.4.

I AM YOUR IMAGE: Phil. 2.6; II Cor. 3.18.

I KNOW YOU, AND YOU ME: Jn. 17.25; Gal. 4.9; I Cor. 13.12.

THE WORLD RULER: The "Pantokrator"—an epithet of Yahweh frequent in the LXX.

LORD OF LIFE: Jn. 11.25; Acts 3.15; Eph. 4.18; I Jn. 5.20; Rev. 11.11; Ecclesiasticus 23.1,4 LXX.

RIGHTEOUSNESS NOT TURNED ASIDE: Ps. 118.142 LXX; Is. 51.6,8 LXX.

WHO HAST . . . TRUTH: Jn. 14.6,17; 15.26; 16.13; I Jn. 4.6; 5.6.

GOD'S NAME/SPIRIT ON GOOD MEN: Is. 42.1 = Mt. 12.18; Is. 61.1 = Lk. 4.18; Num. 6.27.

GOD TO ENTER THE ORANT: II Cor. 1.22; Gal. 4.6; Eph. 3.17; etc.

IAO ABLANATHANALBA: Iao is Yahweh, the Israelite god; Ablanathanalba is a magical palindrome (word that can be read backwards) of uncertain meaning. For the idea of the preceding sentence, compare Acts 1.8; 10.38; I Cor. 5.4; II Cor. 12.9.

PGM IV.475–830: Often misnamed "the Mithras liturgy." The technique for ascent into the heavens, here presented, was known in a widely variant form in Judaism. See my "Observations," 142ff., and *Clement* 238ff.

A E E I O U O: The Greek vowels, often taken as representing the essential elements of the world, but also used as a resonant "magical" word to excite the celebrant. Most magical terms will henceforth be reduced to three dots.

"I SURPASS THE LIMIT": Reading *proucho t(on) horon* for *procho proa*, but the letters may be magical gibberish.

PAGE 103

JESUS' ASCENT TO HEAVEN: After death, Acts 1.9; before, see Smith, *Clement* 243ff.

HOLY SPIRITS IN MAGICAL PAPYRI: I.313; III.8,289,393, 550, IV.510; XII.174; etc

THE SON OF THE LIVING GOD: *DMP* XX.31ff. "The living god" is a familiar Old Testament figure (Joshua 3.10; Hosea 2.1; Ps. 42.3,9; etc.) who had a great success in the New Testament (Matthew, Acts, Paul, the Pastorals, Hebrews, I Peter, and the Apocalypse). Mt. 26.63 makes the High Priest use him in conjuring Jesus to declare his identity, and Peter in Mt. 16.16 identifies Jesus as "the Son of the living God." Nevertheless, "the living god" could equally well be Osiris, and the spell in the Demotic papyrus begins by identifying the magician with a group of Egyptian deities, so it seems safest to suppose that both "the living god" and "the son" were international magical personalities. In *PGM* XXXVI.10,15f. the magician declares himself the son of the god Typhon-Seth (who was often identified with Iao, see above, p. 62).

BIRD AS MESSENGER: See also Psellus, *On the Work of Demons* 15 (ed. Boissonade, p. 24), cited below, in the notes to p. 121.

PAGE 104

NEW TESTAMENT PARALLELS TO PGM IV.154ff.: Mk. 1.10; II Cor. 10.4; Jn. 15.15; Mt. 16.19; I Cor. 2.8; II Cor. 3.18; Phil. 2.6; Acts 3.16; Jn. 5.18.

NO OTHER SIMILAR EVIDENCE: Compare Bultmann, *Geschichte*[4] 263ff. Bultmann concluded from Mk. 14.61 that the story reports Jesus' election as Messiah—in spite of the fact that it does not mention the Messiah. He paid no attention to the peculiar usage of "son of god" nor, of course, to its Semitic meaning. Because Dalman reported that in *rabbinic* literature "the spirit" cannot be used for "the holy spirit" without some distinctive addition, Bultmann supposed that the same was true in Jesus' time and circles (neglecting Num. 11.25ff.; I Kings 22.21; Hosea 9.7; etc.). Hence, the story must have come from his favorite data dump—"the hellenistic community." He explained it mainly from Acts 10.38: Since it was believed Jesus had been made Messiah (i.e. "anointed") by being anointed with the spirit, and since baptism was supposed to give the spirit, the appointment of Jesus as Messiah was located at his baptism and the story of that event was told to suit this purpose. (Christians however—and Acts with special emphasis, 19.1–7—*denied* that the Baptist's baptism gave the spirit!) Finally Bultmann does notice that "Mark, as a hellenistic Christian of the Pauline sort, already saw Jesus as the preëxistent Son of God" (p. 270) and that the story of the baptism seems to contradict this, but he thinks Mark was so dumb that he never noticed the difficulty *(ibid)*. Admittedly, one must be careful not to exaggerate the intelligence of the blessed evangelist, but when he included material that seems to contradict his own views we may charitably suppose he did so under some compulsion, most likely because he found it in an authoritative source, or knew it as a revered element of oral tradition. (That he was not willing to follow tradition all the way is shown by his avoidance of Jesus' complete deification.)

ELIADE'S REPORT: *Shamanism* 108, cf. 64f., etc. Ordeals 33–66; spirits/animals 88–95.

POSSESSOR/POSSESSED: Above, p. 32. Cf. Jn. 7.20 versus 8.48; Mk. 3.21 versus 22. Midrash Sifré, sec. 318 end, on Dt. 32.17, says, "What is the common practice of a demon? It enters into a man and compels him."

THE LOST TEMPTATION LEGEND: So Bultmann, *Geschichte*[4] 270.

MARK'S STORIES TO BE SUPPLEMENTED: Smith, *Clement* 446; *Secret Gospel* 15.

PAGE 105

FLYING THROUGH THE AIR: As the Son of Man, equated by Christians with the Messiah, is to come. Mk. 13.26p.; Dan. 7.13.

FREE FOOD: A favorite feature of "the days of the Messiah." Lk. 6.21; Irenaeus V. xxxiii.3 end, ed. Harvey; Ps. 22.27; 72.16; Enoch 10.19.

WORLD CONQUEST: Apoc. 19.11–20.6; Is. 42.4; 45.1–14; Ps. 72.8–11. The facts in this and the two preceding notes were overlooked by Fridrichsen, *Problème* 85ff.

Q.E.D.: This fallacy is of the "undistributed middle term" type, that is, even if we grant the premise (all who rule the world must be magicians), it does not follow that all who become magicians will rule the world. The devil might default.

EITREM'S OBSERVATIONS: "Versuchung" 9ff. For flying magicians he cites Maspéro, *Contes* 37; *PGM* XIII.284f. (add I.119; XXXIV.9); Lucian, *Lover of Lies* 13; the *Actus Petri cum Simone,* end; Philostratus, *Life* III.15,17; VI. 10f.; Iamblichus, *De mysteriis* III.4. For changing stones into bread, the stories of Cinderella and the magicians of Egypt (Ex. 7.12) exemplify similar transformations, and the stone, wooden, and pottery "food" commonly found in Egyptian tombs was to be changed into real food for the dead by magical ceremonies, see Smith, *Egypt* 29, 67, 95f. Christians made the magician Simon claim to perform these miracles and use them as proof of his supernatural (magical) powers, *Clementine Recognitions* II.9; III.47; *Homilies* II.32.

MAGICAL USE OF PSALM 91: "Versuchung" 11ff.; *PGM* 17.15; T2 verso; Schrire, *Hebrew Amulets* 127f., 133.

SERVICE BY DEMONS/ANGELS: "Versuchung," 14. on Mk. 1.13p., citing as examples of demons serving magicians, magical texts now in *PGM* V.164ff.; XII.40,48f.

EITREM ON FASTING AND KINGSHIP: "Versuchung" 15ff. His passages for fasting actually refer only to keeping oneself in a state of ritual purity, and possibly to abstaining from meat and fish. Lk. 4.2 is explicit, Jesus "ate nothing." Similarly, Eitrem's passages on political power say only that magic will make one *"a friend of"* rulers, "great" and "glorious," etc. (This is interesting. The magical texts are not entirely products of free, wishful thinking, but show awareness of actual limitations of the magicians' circumstances.)

FASTING IN *PGM:* I.235; III.334,412,427.

NO FASTING IN MARK: Mk. 1.13. That Mark says Jesus was in the wilderness "forty days" does not imply fasting. "Forty days" (or "years") is an Old Testament locution for "a long time."

FORTY-DAY FASTS: Mt. 4.2p.; Ex. 24.18; 34.28; Dt. 9.9,25; I Kings 19.8.

KINGSHIP IN THE *PGM:* XXIIb, "A Prayer of Jacob," records (not quite accurately) that the god addressed gave "the kingdom" to Abraham, but it asks only for direction, wisdom, power, a heart full of good things, the status of an earthly, immortal angel (i.e. a Jewish "divine man"). *PGM* III.540f. identifies "the kingdom" with "the three-cornered paradise of the earth," and says the magician has the key to it. All other "kingdoms" in *PGM* are supernatural (XIII.187,509; cf. IV.263; V.448. Similarly, *DT* 22.43f.,46f.; again 24; 29; 30; etc.). Most uses of "king" refer to gods. Human kings appear in nine instances as patrons, in four as proposed subjects of magic, and in four as magicians (IV.243,255,1928; XII.202), but in three of these last instances they are legendary figures, and in none is there any suggestion that they became kings by practicing magic.

THE GOD OF THIS AEON: Lk. 4.6f.p.; II Cor. 4.4.

PAGE 106

THE CHALLENGING TEMPTATIONS: Mt. 4.3p., 6p.; "*If* you are the Son of God," perform this (proposed) miracle. (The difference between the first two and the third in the Matthaean order argues for the originality of that order against Luke's).

APOLLONIUS' ATTRACTION OF FOLLOWERS: Philostratus, *Life* I.19; IV.1,17,31f., 47; V.21; VIII.21f.; etc.

LOVE CHARMS: *PGM* VII.973ff.; XV.3. *DMP* XXI.27–43.

JESUS' FOLLOWERS WHO LEFT HOME, ETC..: Mk. 10.29p., cf. Lk. 14.26p.

CONVERSION BY LOVE SPELLS: *PGM* LXI.29f., cf. IV.327f., 2757ff.; XIXa.53f.

PAGE 107

EX-DEMONIACS AMONG JESUS' FOLLOWERS: Lk. 8.1ff.; Mk. 15.40p.; Lk. 23.55. Spells to bring women to men and vice versa are very common. *PGM* IV.1716ff.; VII.300ff.; XIII.238f.; etc. The men whom Apollonius saved from demons became his disciples, *Life* IV.20 end, 25; VI.28 (the same Menippus).

SPELLS ETC., FOR EXORCISM: *PGM* IV.1227f., 2170, 3007ff.; V. 96ff.; XIII. 242ff.; XXXVI. 275ff. *Cyranides* (ed. de Mély-Ruelle) p. 47, lines 22ff.; 69.26f.; 71.9f.; 101.1f.,14f.; 103.9; 111.10; 112.2. Tamborino, *Daemonismo* 18f.

EXORCISM IN PHILOSTRATUS, LUCIAN, CELSUS: Philostratus, *Life* III.38; IV.20.25; Lucian, *Philopseudes* 16 (quoted above, p. 57). Lucian's words just prior to the section quoted imply that such figures were common, as do Origen's, *Against Celsus* I.68 (quoted above, p. 83).

JESUS' EXORCISTIC SKILL: Mk. 7.24ff.p.; 5.8ff.p. The relation of the Marcan exorcism stories to magic was demonstrated by the classic study of Bauernfeind, *Worte*, and has been studied in much detail by Böcher, *Christus*, supported by the material collected in his *Dämonenfurcht*.

SPELLS ETC. FOR CURES: *PGM* I. 190; VII. 193ff., 218ff., 260ff.; XII. 305f.; XIII. 244ff.; XVIIIa; XX; XXIIa; XXXIII. *DMP* XIX; XX. 1ff., 28ff.; XXIV. 27f.; *Verso* IV. 1off.; V; VI (?); VIII–XI; XX; XXXIII. Cf. *SHR* I. 1; II. 6; II. 12.

AMULETS FOR CURES: Bonner, *Studies*, thinks "perhaps most" amulets are medical, p. 21. Pp. 51–94 of *Studies* are devoted to "Medical Magic."

CURES IN LITERARY MATERIAL: Philostratus, *Life* III.38ff.; IV.1,10; VI.43; Lucian, *Philopseudes* 11,18f. *J. Sabbat* XIV.4(14d); *B. Sanhedrin* 101a; *Cyranides* (ed. de Mély-Ruelle) II.0.6 (p. 69,26f.); III.ψ.2 (p. 101, 14f.); Pliny, *Natural History* XI.203; XXI.166,176; XXII.20,50,61; XXIV.156ff.; etc.

CURES VS. EXORCISMS: The attempt of Böcher, *Christus* 70ff., to represent all healings as exorcisms, is refuted by the fact that the gospels do not do so. We must not impose theoretical clarity on evangelic confusion.

"PLAGUE AND FEVER FLEE" ETC.: Bonner, *Studies*, no. 111, p. 271 and plate V; discussion, 67f.

FEVERS CAUSED BY DEMONS: *PGM* IV.1528ff., 1541ff., 2487ff., 2930f.; VII.472,990f.;

XII.479ff.; XVI.4f.; XIXa.50; etc. These all come from love charms; fever was thought to be a customary symptom of love (Theocritus II.85), but also in maleficent magic demons are adjured to cause fever, *PGM* XIV.25f.

DISEASES ARE DEMONS: Sophocles, *Philoctetes* 758ff.(cp. Lk. 11.24ff.!); Philostratus, *Life* IV.10. Further examples in Tamborino, *Daemonismo* 63ff.

JESUS' CURES: For psychosomatic afflictions see the material cited in the preceding notes on "cures." For wounds: Lk. 22.51; *DMP Verso* IV.10ff.

SNAKES, SCORPIONS, POISONS, PANACEAS: Snakes: Lucian, *Philopseudes* 11f.; *PGM* I.116f.; XIII.249f.,261; *DMP* XX.1ff(?); Tzetzes on Aristophanes, *Plutus* 885; Plato, *Republic* 358b; *Euthydemus* 289e,f. Suetonius, *Augustus* 17; Aelian, *De Natura Animalium* XVI.27; A. Gellius XVI.11; Pliny, *Natural History* VII.14; XXIX.19ff.; Orpheus, *Lithica* 405ff. (ed. Abel); Scribonius Largus 163ff. Scorpions: *PGM* VII.193ff.; *DMP* XX.1ff.; Heim, *Incantamenta*, nos. 74,242f.; Bonner, *Studies* 77f. Schneider's index to Pliny has four columns under "scorpione." Their stings were ideal for magical treatment because, while extremely painful, they are not usually fatal, and, whatever is done, the patient is likely to get better, which proves the power of the remedy. Poisons: *PGM* VIII.33; XIII.253; XXXVI.256ff.; *DMP* XIX.10ff. Panaceas: *PGM* IV.922,2170ff., 2517,2699ff.; VII.370ff.; VIII.32ff.; XII.258ff.; XIII.1048ff.; Bonner, *Studies* 95f.

PAGE 108

MARK'S TEMPORAL SEQUENCE: The argument for this opinion was set forth by Schmidt, *Rahmen*. New evidence for extensive parallels between Mk. 6.32–15.47 and Jn. 6.1–19.42 (Smith, *Clement* 158–163; *Secret Gospel* 56ff.) casts doubt on Schmidt's position.

THE FAUSTUS STORIES: Schmidt, "Stellung."

PAGE 109

OVER 200 GOSPEL MIRACLES: I have a list of 232 that omits all parallels in Matthew and Luke to Mark's miracle stories, all parallels in Luke to Matthew's, and almost all *general* sayings about future rewards and punishments—sayings the evangelists probably thought were prophecies, but well within the prophetic powers of the average preacher. Indirectly, of course, everything reported of Jesus is miraculous for the gospel writers since he is a living miracle—a deity present in a man. Consequently, an exact enumeration of his miracles, as of those of Apollonius and Moses, involves many difficult decisions. Hence the figures given in the text are approximate.

124 MIRACLES OF MOSES: Including his prophecies, but excluding "And God/the Lord said unto Moses" at the beginnings of laws.

THE RULER OF THE DEMONS: Mk. 3.22p.; Mt. 9.34.

ONE DEMON BY ANOTHER: Eusebius, *On Philostratus* 26 ("as they say").

PORPHYRY ON SERAPIS: In Eusebius, *Praeparatio evangelica* IV.23.1.

THE CENTURION'S SPEECH: Lk. 7.6ff.p. On Jesus' "authority" and its magical parallels see above, pp. 10, 31, 34 and notes. The classic expression is Milton's: "Thousands at His bidding speed / And post o'er land and ocean without rest" *(Sonnet on His Blindness)*.

PAGE 110

DEFIXIONS: The largest collections are *DT* and *IG* III.iii.

"EULAMON, RECEIVE," ETC.: *DT* no. 156. Cf. nos. 155,161,163,248, etc. *PGM* V.334f.

"PUT . . . INTO JUDAS' MIND: Jn. 13.2; "heart" for "mind" is common in biblical material.

"AFTER ⟨HE HAD EATEN⟩": Jn. 13.27; the translation, with interpretive addition, follows Bauer, *WB*[5], under *meta* B.3 (col. 1009).

PAGE 111

"SPELL SAID TO THE CUP" ETC.: *PGM* VII.643ff.; the same notion underlies 385ff., 620ff.,970ff.; *DMP* XV. 1ff.,21ff.; XXI.10ff.; etc.

DEMONS EATEN WITH SACRIFICES: So I Cor. 10.14ff. The theory appears also in Porphyry and the *Corpus Hermeticum*, see Bousset, "Dämonologie" 153ff.

ORIGEN'S COMMENT: Quoted as "Origen" in "Aquinas," *Enarrationes* on Jn. 13.27.

ONE WHO "HAD EATEN" HIS "BREAD": Ps.41.10, cited in Jn. 13.18, at the beginning of the scene. The similarity to the basic idea of the eucharist (to be discussed later) has led several scholars to suppose that the bread given Judas was from the eucharist, and that Satan's consequent possession of him was an example of the "judgment" with which Paul threatens those who take the eucharist unworthily (I Cor. 11.29), cf. Brown, *John* II.575, on the verse. Brown rightly questions the notion; it is in fact impossible, because the spirit in the eucharistic bread is that of Jesus, not Satan.

"NOW, NOW! QUICK, QUICK!": Above, p. 110 and note. Further *PGM* I.262; III.35, 85,123; IV.1924,2037,2098; VII.248,254,259,373,410,993; etc.

MAGIC IN FAMILY QUARRELS: Gordon, "Bowls" 324, text B, lines 6f.; more examples in Yamauchi, *Mandaic . . . Texts* 17f. For "dividers" see *PGM* III.164; VII.429; XII.365; *DMP* XIII.1ff.; *DT* 68f.; etc.

"GOD, WHO SMITEST THE EARTH" ETC.: *PGM* XII.365ff. This is not unique; compare the similar formula in 455ff.

PAGE 112

GIFT OF JUDAS TO SATAN?: Böcher, *Christus* 55, thinks the gift of the sop to Judas was "a giving over (of Judas) to Satan."

THE SPIRIT OF TRUTH: Jn. 14.16f.26; 15.26; 16.13f.

OTHER INVOCATIONS AND SENDINGS OF SPIRITS: *PGM* IV.858ff.; VII.628ff.; XII. 114ff.,317ff.; XXXVI.353ff. Bell-Nock-Thompson, *Magical Texts*, Recto V.13, "Come to me, Lord of truth."

PAGE 113

BLOW AWAY DISEASES: Origen, *Against Celsus* I.68; compare Böcher, *Christus* 103f.

THE GOD OF THE HEBREWS: *PGM* IV.3019ff. "Thoth" is an Egyptian god, "Iaba" is probably a poor transliteration of "Yahweh," and "Iae" and "Aia" are permutations of "Iao," the Greek name for Yahweh.

ON BLOWING SPIRITS: Tambornino, *Daemonismo* 81; 102; Dieterich, *Mithrasliturgie*[3] 116f.; Eitrem, *Demonology*[?] 47, note 4. Cf. *PGM* II.84, Apollo blows prophecies into seers.

THE TWELVE DISCIPLES: Mk. 3.14f.p.; 6.7ff.p. The apparent contradiction between "to be with him" and "to send them out" in 3.14 is more famous than real.

ALEXANDER'S TRAINING: Lucian, *Alexander* 5, quoted above, p. 88.

APOLLONIUS' STUDIES: Philostratus, *Life* I.26,40; III.13–49.

"DO THIS WITH AN . . . EXPERT": *PGM* IV.172, quoted above, p. 103.

PAGE 114

BOYS AS MEDIUMS: Examples cited above, p. 112, and below, p. 121, and notes.

THE GIFT OF HEALING: Lk. 9.1p.; 10.9p. These Q verses are probably reflected by the additions, Mt. 10.1b and Mk. 6.13b.

THE NAME OF JESUS: The basic book is still Heitmüller, *Im Namen Jesu*. The connection of prayer "in the name of Jesus" with exorcism "in the name of Jesus" is rightly noticed by Böcher, *Christus* 133.

MK. 6.14: The sequel to 6.7–13. The question is not one of historical accuracy, but of Mark's notion of cause and effect, as evidence for his notion of the formula used in the exorcisms and cures.

SHAKING DUST OFF SHOES: To bring a curse. Compare the shaking out of clothes in Nehemiah 5.13; Acts 18.6. The legal explanation offered by Strack-Billerbeck, *Kommentar,* on Mt. 10.14 is an anachronism; the law is second century.

JESUS' NAME IN EXORCISM: Mk. 9.38f.p.; Acts 19.13; *PGM* IV.3020; etc.

ABRAHAM, ISAAC, JACOB: Their names appear together as part of the Hebrew name of God in *PGM* XIII.976; they are often used, together and individually, in spells: VII.315; XII.287; etc.

MOSES AND SOLOMON: "I am Moses your prophet," *PGM* V.109. *DMP* verso XII.5f. speaks of the "longing . . . a bitch feels for a dog, the longing that the god, the son of Sopd (?), felt for Moses going to the hill of Ninaretos," probably from a legend telling of Moses' initiation. Moses' magical reputation is attested by Pliny, *Natural History* XXX.11, and by the half dozen magical texts attributed to him in *PGM* VII.619; XIII.3,21,343,382f.,724, 731f.,970,1057,1077. Solomon probably appears as the deity "Salama" in *PGM* XII.80; XXVIIIa2 and b6; demons are conjured by his seal in IV.3040; rites, spells and many magical books were attributed to him (IV.85off.; etc.) His name is often used on amulets.

NO HISTORICAL PAGANS NAMED IN SPELLS: The nearest approach is an invocation of "Subterranean Amphiaraos" in *PGM* IV.1446 as an underworld hero—which he was; "Theseus" in IV.2779 has been thought a constellation.

THE KEYS GIVEN PETER: Mt. 16.19a. Matthew's interpretation of the verse by associating it with the authority to "bind" and "loose" (16.19b)—that is, to declare acts, objects, or persons legally permitted or tabu—is mistaken; one does not "bind" or "loose" with keys, one "locks out" or "admits." Matthew was probably misled by Jesus' curse on the scribes because they "locked up the kingdom of heaven in men's faces" and neither went in themselves nor permitted others to enter (Mt. 23.13, from Q, also misunderstood by Lk. 11.52). They did this by making the requirements for purity (that had to be met before one could approach the kingdom) more and more severe, and their ability to change the purity laws was based on their power "to bind and to loose," which Matthew's tradition conceded them (23.2f.). Hence the mistaken connection of Mt. 16.19a and 19b. That 19b was originally an independent saying is shown by its independent appearance in Mt. 18.18 where its disciplinarian-legal significance is clear. It has nothing to do with magical binding, though Jesus is said to have claimed the power (Mk. 3.27, to be discussed below).

KEYS HELD BY MAGICIANS: *PGM* IV.189 (above, p. 103); the keys of the underworld appear in IV.341,1465ff.,2293 (in a magician's control), 2335; VII.785. Michael has the keys of the kingdom of heaven in the *Greek Apocalypse of Baruch* 11.2. See also Wortmann, "Texte" I.10f.; Delatte-Derchain, *Intailles* 90 and no. 294; Wortmann, "Kosmogonie" 102 and citations there.

PAGE 115

FORGIVENESS OF SINS: Mk. 2.5ff.p.; Lk. 7.47; Jn. 20.23. (On Mt. 16.19b and 18.18, see the note before last; here they are irrelevant.)

JOHN'S BAPTISM: Mk. 1.4p. The word commonly translated "remission" also means "forgiveness" and comes from the same root as the word translated "forgiven" in the stories about Jesus. On the Baptist and his rite, see Smith, *Clement* 205ff.; *Secret Gospel* 90ff.

DID JESUS BAPTISE? For evidence that he continued to use the rite, see Smith, *Clement* 209ff.; *Secret Gospel* 93f.; John says he did baptise (3.22,26; 4.1, contradicted in 4.2); the synoptics say nothing.

TRUST IN HIS POWER: Mk. 2.5p., commonly mistranslated "faith."

FORGIVENESS MANIFESTS JESUS' DIVINE POWER: This was "corrected" by a glossator who added Mk. 2.10 (a parenthetic interruption) to attribute this power to "the Son of Man on earth" (so Boobyer, "Mk. 2.10a"). There is no evidence that in Jewish circles the Messiah was expected to forgive sins (Strack-Billerbeck, *Kommentar* I.495). The claim here has resulted from an attempt to avoid the earlier Christian claim that Jesus was a god.

FORGIVENESS INDEMONSTRABLE: Mark, or one of his sources, was aware of this objection and therefore placed the story of forgivenss of sins in the story of the cure of a paralytic; the cure provided an objective (if not strictly consequential) "proof" that the sins were forgiven; see Taylor, *Mark* 197.

JESUS' KNOWLEDGE OF OTHERS' THOUGHTS: Mk. 2.8p.; Lk. 7.39f.; Mt. 12.25p.; Mk. 8.16f.p.; Lk. 9.47; Mk. 12.15p.; Mt. 23.5 (?); Jn. 6.15,26,70; 8.37,40; etc. OF OTHERS' FUTURES AND PASTS: Mt. 17.25; Mk. 9.33; Jn. 1.42,47ff.; 4.17f.,29; 7.19; 9.3; 21.18.

PAGE 116

SPELLS TO KNOW OTHERS' THOUGHTS, ETC.: Above, p. 99. Further examples, besides the following, are *PGM* III.459; XIa.25; XIII.611f.; 710ff. (to know your own prehistory).

MIND READING BY APOLLONIUS: Philostratus, *Life* I.10; II.39; IV.10,20,25f.; V.24,42; VI.3; etc. BY THE INDIAN SAGES: Philostratus, *Life* III.16ff.

TRICKS TO READ SEALED LETTERS, ETC.: Lucian, *Alexander* 19ff.; Hippolytus, *Refutation* IV. 28,34.

DIRECTIONS FOR DIVINATION: *PGM:* I.173ff.,328; II.1ff.; III.187ff.,345,424ff., 698; IV.1ff.,52ff.; etc. *DMP:* I.1ff.; IV.1ff.,21ff.; V.3ff.; VI.1ff.; IX.1ff.; etc. *SHR:* I.3,5; IV.1f.; V.

MAGICIANS' PROPHETIC POWERS: Apollonius: Philostratus, *Life* I.12; IV.4,18,24; V.11,24,30; VI.32; etc. Lucian, *Alexander,* throughout.

JESUS' KNOWLEDGE OF DISTANT EVENTS: Mk. 5.39p.; 6.48 (?); 7.29; Lk. 5.4ff.; Jn. 1.48; 4.50; 11.11,14. Apollonius' performance was more spectacular, Philostratus, *Life* VIII.26; also IV.3; V.30; VI.27. Compare *PGM* I.189.

JESUS' PREDICTIONS: Mk. 2.20p.; 8.31p.; 9.31p.; 10.29ff.p.,33f.p., 39p.; 11.2f.p.; 14.8f.p.,13ff.p.,18ff.p.,25,27ff.p.,72p. Such material increases greatly in the other gospels; for further passages and parallels to them see Smith, *Clement* 225. Apollonius: see the note before last, and add *Life,* VII.38,41; VIII.5,30. With Lk. 5.4ff. compare Iamblichus, *Life of Pythagoras* VIII(36).

OMNISCIENCE: Philostratus, *Life* I.19; VII.14 (Apollonius); III.18 (Brahmans); Jn. 16.30.

REPORTS OF IGNORANCE: Mk. 5.9; 6.38; 11.13; etc; Philostratus, *Life* VI.13; VII.30; etc. Eusebius overlooked this parallel.

PAGE 117

PROMISES OF REVELATORY SPIRITS: Jn. 14.26; 16.13,23; *PGM* I.312ff. (cited above, p. 99); I.175ff. (above, p. 112); etc.

CELSUS' PROPHETS A PARODY: So Chadwick, *Origen* 402f. and note 6.

ESCHATOLOGICAL PROPHECY COMMON: Josephus, *War* II.258ff.; *Antiquities* XVIII.85, 118; XX.168ff.

PAGE 118

GODS CURE SURGICAL CASES: For example, the cures recorded on the wall of the temple of Asclepius in Epidaurus, *IG* IV² .i, nos. 121–2.

PROTECTIVE LAYING ON OF HANDS: Mk. 10.13p.; Böcher, *Christus* 83.

DEMONS SUPPLYING FOOD: *PGM* I.103,110; Suidas, under *Pasēs*; Philostratus, *Life* IV.25; etc. The legend told by Plutarch, *Numa* 15, comes nearer the gospel story, but is not close.

PAGE 119

STILLING STORMS: *Pythagoras:* Iamblichus, *Life of Pythagoras* XXVIII (135); *Empedocles:* Clement of Alexandria, *Stromateis* VI.iii.30 (ed. Stählin-Früchtel II.445). *Magi:* Herodotus VII.191, above, p. 71; Pliny, *Natural History* XXXVII.142,155. *For agriculture: Codex Theodosianus* IX.16.3, above, p. 76. *Not in PGM* (XXIX has been thought to be a spell for fine weather, but is said by Page, *Papyri* III.431, to be a sailor's song. Why not both? *PGM* I.120ff. promises a paredros who will "solidify . . . the sea . . . and restrain the sea-running foam," but says nothing of storms). *Apollonius' talismans*: Pseudo Justin Martyr, *Answers to the Orthodox* 24. See also *PGM* II, p. 242, line 31.

MAGICIANS' POWERS TO HARM: Rites designed for any sort of damage desired are *PGM* III.1ff.; IV.2241ff.,2624ff.; VII.429ff.; *SHR* I.2.

SPELLS TO WITHER, CONSUME, ETC.: *PGM* XXXVI.246ff. *DT* 155b.11; 250a.23f; 270.18. Withering trees was an accomplishment of some African magicians (Pliny, *Natural History* VII.16).

OLD TESTAMENT WITHERING OF THE WICKED: Num. 12.12; I Kings 13.4; Ezek. 17.9f.; Hos. 9.16; Zech. 11.17; Ps. 129.6.

JESUS = "THE HOLY ONE": Smith, *Parallels* 152ff.

PAGE 120

THE DIONYSIAC FESTIVAL: Achilles Tatius II.2.1–3.3. See Smith, *Wine God*. The similarities in wording are to Jn. 4.11,14; 6.55.

WALKING ON WATER: *PGM* I.121. XXIX is dubious (see p. 119, note, on stilling storms); so is XXXIV.

BECOMING INVISIBLE OR INTANGIBLE: Lk. 4.29f.; 24.31; Jn. 7.30,44; 8.20,59; 10.39; 12.36(?).

SPELLS FOR INVISIBILITY/ESCAPE: *Invisibility:* *PGM* I.102,222ff.,247ff.; V.488; VII.620ff.; XII.160ff.; XIII.234ff., 267f.; XXIIa.11f; etc.; compare Plato, *Republic* 359d,f.; Pliny, *Natural History* XXXVII.165. *Escape: PGM* I.101,196ff.; IV.2145ff.: V.488; XII.160ff.,279, etc. Note *PGM* XII.173f. where the magician says after escaping, "I thank thee, Lord, that the holy spirit, the only begotten, the living one, has released me."

PAGE 121

DISGUISED GODS REVEAL THEIR TRUE FORMS: *Homeric Hymn to Demeter* 268f.; Plutarch, *Isis and Osiris* 16(357c); Judges 13.19; Tobit 12.6ff.; Pfister, "Epiphanie," with many examples.

MOSES ON SINAI: Ex. 20.21; 24.1–18; etc. When Moses came down his face was still shining (Ex. 34.29ff.); Jesus was seen blazing with glory.

THE MOUNTAIN IN GALILEE: The references in Mt. 28.16 to "the mountain (in Galilee) of which Jesus had told them," and in II Peter 1.18 to "the holy mountain" suggest that other stories about this mountain, and perhaps reverence for some Galilean mountain as a holy place, may have survived for a while in some early Christian circles. Perhaps this—and the desire to equate Jesus with Moses—explains why Matthew located the first Q sermon on "the mountain" (5.1); Lk. 6.17 puts it on a plain, probably Q's setting. Matthew's "Judaizing" traits are notorious (23.2f.).

LIBERATION BY JESUS: Gal. 5.1. Jesus' divinity frees us from the Law because he, as a god, is free from the Law, and we can share in his nature and freedom, being united with him by baptism and the eucharist.

GOING UP A MOUNTAIN TO MEET GODS: *Apollonius:* Philostratus, *Life* III.13; the Brahmans were living gods (III.18; etc.). *The kings of Babylon and Tyre:* Is. 14.13ff.; Ezek. 28.12ff. Compare also Psellus, *On the Work of Demons* 15 (ed. Boissonade, pp. 23ff.); a pagan prophet captured in Thessaly said "he had been initiated into demonic arts by a vagrant Libyan 'who took me up by night into a mountain and told me to eat of some plant. Then he spat into my mouth and rubbed some ointments around my eyes and so enabled me to see a company of demons, from whom I perceived something like a crow fly down and enter my mouth. And from that time to the present I am moved to prophecy whenever, and about whatever things, the (power) that moves me wishes.'"

JEWISH ASCENTS INTO THE HEAVENS: *I Enoch* 14.8ff.; 71; *II Enoch* 3–10; *Ascension of Isaiah* 7–9.

TRANSFIGURATION NOT AN ASCENT INTO HEAVEN: These considerations lead me to doubt my former interpretation of the transfiguration story as the reflection of an experience of ascent into the heavens (*Clement,* 243f.). The other evidence presented there persuades me that Jesus did practice "ascent," and communicated his hallucinations to some of his disciples who consequently shared his belief that they had entered the Kingdom of God and were above the Law. But I now suppose that the transfiguration story reports only an experience preparatory to this final initiation, teaching about which will have been reserved, as in Judaism, for oral instruction to chosen disciples, one at a time. *M. Hagigah* II.1 limits it to one disciple at a time, and that one, "only if he is a scholar and naturally gifted to understand (such things)."

SPELLS TO MAKE GODS APPEAR: In *The Eighth Book of Moses, PGM* XIII.710ff.; cf. I.1ff., 42ff.,263ff.; II.82ff.; III.305f.; VII.727ff.; etc. In many such spells the magician himself is identified as a god. That one god might need the service or information of another was commonly supposed in antiquity (as it is in Christianity when the Father is represented as needing the service of the Son to redeem mankind; Milton, *Paradise Lost* III.203–343).

MAGICIAN LETS DISCIPLE SEE GODS: *PGM* IV.172,732ff.; V.1ff. *DMP* XXIX (note especially line 30); there are many rites of this sort.

PROPHETS → ANGELS → GODS: *II Enoch* A 22.8ff.; 37; *Ascension of Isaiah* 7.25; 9.30; the Hebrew word "gods" is translated "angels" by the Septuagint in Pss. 8.6; 97.7 (LXX 96.7); 138.1 (LXX 137.1); etc. For pagan gods identified as angels see Bietenhard, *Welt* 108ff. and *SHR* throughout (many examples). For the common equivalence of "angel" and "god" in magical usage, see above, in the note on "angel," on p. 98.

PAGE 122

TABERNACLES: Mk. 9.5p. The common supposition that these are *sukkot*—the temporary dwellings for the feast of "tabernacles"—does not fit the facts: (1) There is no reference in the context to the feast. (2) The *sukkot* were originally places to spend the night, but it is not clear that Jesus and company stayed overnight, and if they did three *sukkot* would not have sufficed for the six of them (counting Moses and Elijah). Subsequently the *sukkot* became mainly places in which to eat, but it was customary for all members of a group to eat together, so one would have been enough (and there is no suggestion of eating in the story). (3) The Israelites were commanded to make *sukkot* for *themselves;* but the tabernacles are to be made for the three deities only.

THE THEOLOGY OF THE TRANSFIGURATION STORY: The scene is polemic against Judaizing Christianity, compare Galatians. That Peter proposes making the tabernacles may reflect Peter's role in the diaspora as a leading representative of a moderately Judaizing position.

THE INTERRUPTED SÉANCE: A classic example is Burns' *Tam O'Shanter.* For others see Del Rio, *Disquisitionum* II.xvi, pp. 162ff.

MAGICAL ANALOGUES TO THE EUCHARIST: *PGM* VII.385ff.,970ff.; *DMP* XIII.17ff.; Verso XXXII.1ff.; etc. *PGM* VII.620ff. is that from *The Diadem of Moses.*

PAGE 123

JOHN'S EUCHARISTIC DISCOURSE: Jn. 13.34; cf. 14.20; 6.56ff.

THE NEW TESTAMENT EUCHARISTIC TEXTS: Mk. 14.22–24; Mt. 26.26–28; Lk. 22.19–20; I Cor. 11.24–25. On the abbreviated text that is found in some old manuscripts of Luke, see Metzger, *Textual Commentary,* on Luke 22.17–20.

JESUS IN FOLLOWERS AND THEY IN HIM: Jn. 6.56 (as a result of the eucharist); 14.20.

PAGE 124

GOD TO COME TO MAGICIAN'S HOUSE: *PGM* I.2f.,38ff.,85ff.,168f.; III.575f.; *DMP* IV.20; XVIII.25ff.; etc.

GOD SHARES MAGICIAN'S BED: *PGM* I.2f. Compare the charge against the Christians' god, above, p. 62 and note.

JESUS' MIRACLES AFTER DEATH: Survival and post mortem appearances, *PGM* I.178ff.; above p. 85 and note (Apollonius); invisibility and transformations, pp. 120f.; going through locked doors, *PGM* XII.16off.,279; XIII.327ff.,1064ff.; XXXVI.311ff.; immunity from snakes and poison, above, p. 107 and note; gift of the spirit, pp. 113, 117.

ASCENT INTO THE HEAVENS: Smith, *Clement* 238ff. *Apollonius*: Philostratus, *Life* VI.11 end, he attributed it to the Brahmans; he claimed it himself (III.51), and was credited with it by legend (VIII.30 end). *In the papyri*: *PGM* IV.475ff., especially 537ff.; the introduction is quoted above, p. 102.

JESUS' ASCENT BEFORE DEATH: Phil 2.5–11; I Tim. 3.16; and Jn. 3 are all discussed in Smith, *Clement* 243ff.; briefly in *Secret Gospel* 110. Add, perhaps, II Cor. 12.2ff. The man Paul knew may have been Jesus.

"TODAY . . . IN PARADISE": Lk. 23.43. Techniques to enable a magician to take an initiate with him into the other world are hinted at by the papyri (*PGM* IV.732ff.), parodied by Lucian, *Menippus* (quoted above, pp. 73f.), and described later in *Hekalot Rabbati*.

"WHEN A SPIRIT HAS GONE OUT": Mt. 12.43ff.p. The opinion was current already in Sophocles' time, *Philoctetes* 758ff.

PAGE 125

ASCENTS BY GOETES AND SHAMANS: On *goetes* see above, p. 70 and notes; on shamans, Eliade, *Shamanism*, 181ff.

JESUS' "I AM" SAYINGS: Jn. 6.35,41; 8.12,18,23; 10.7,9,11; 11.25; 14.6; etc.

LUCIAN, ALEXANDER 18: This is Alexander of Abonuteichos speaking for his god, Glycon. See Weinreich, "Alexandros," 145f.

PAGE 126

PARALLELS OF DETAIL: These details have been studied especially by Bauernfeind, *Worte*, Bonner, "Traces," Deissmann, *Light*[2], and Eitrem, *Demonology*[2]. Many were noticed incidentally by other scholars, most of whose observations have now been collected by Böcher, *Christus*, with a full bibliography of the German works on the subject.

GENERAL WORLD VIEW: Böcher, *Christus* 16ff.

"THE HIGHEST GOD": *Testament of Solomon* 1.7; 11.6; *PGM* IV.1067f.; V.46; XII.63,71; Mk. 5.7p.; Acts 16.17; Lk. 1.32,35,76; 6.35. The superlative supposes comparison.

RULER OF DEMONS/THIS WORLD: Mk. 3.22p.; compare Jn. 12.31; 14.30; 16.11; I Cor. 2.6,8 "the ruler of this world/age"; *Testament of Solomon* 2.9; 3.5; etc. *DT* 22.24; 25.12; 26.15f.; etc; *PGM* IV.387; VII.788,880; XII.115; XIII.166,477; etc.

DEMONS CAUSES OF DISEASES, ETC.: So throughout *Testament of Solomon*. For gospel and other parallels see above, p. 107 and notes.

DEMONS ARE DEAF, DUMB, ETC.: Mk. 9.25; Lk. 11.14; *DT* 22.24; 26.15f.; 29.14; etc.

DEMONS ARE DISEASES: Above, p. 107 Böcher, *Dämonenfurcht* 152ff.

ANGELS MAINLY HELPERS: Hull, *Hellenistic Magic* 94, who thinks Matthew in this respect stands closer to Jewish apocalyptic literature, Luke closer to magical material, as exemplified by *Testament of Solomon* and *Tobit*. The treatment of the angels in *SHR* supports his distinction between the types of material.

DEMONS ENTER VICTIMS: Mk. 5.12f.p.; 9.25f.p.; Lk. 11.24ff.p.; Philostratus, *Life* III.38; IV.20; Lucian, *Philopseudes* 16; Josephus, *Antiquities* VIII.45ff.; compare Pseudo Aristotle *De Mirabilibus Auscultationibus* 180.

MULTIPLE DEMONS, OFTEN SEVENS: Lk. 8.2; 11.26p.; Apoc. 1.4,20; 3.1; 4.5; 5.6; 8.2; etc. *Testament of Solomon* 8.1ff.; King, *Gnostics*[2] 57, fig. 3; Dalton, *Rings*, no. 59; *PGM* IV.663ff.; VIII.46.

DEMONS SPEAK AND ACT THROUGH VICTIMS, CAUSE HARMFUL ACTS, ETC.: Mk. 1.23f.p.,34p.; 3.11; 5.2ff.p.; 9.17f.,22p.; Philostratus, *Life* III.38; IV.20; Lucian, *Philopseudes* 16.

PAGE 127

MEN "LED"/"DRIVEN" BY DEMONS: Mt. 4.1; Lk. 4.1; cf. Mk. 1.12; I Cor. 12.2.

DEMON/AFFLICTION CALLED A "WHIP": Mk. 3.10; 5.29,34; Lk. 7.21; *PGM* XVIIa.25; *Aeschylus, Prometheus* 681f.; Eumelus, Fr. 10 (ed. Kinkel) = Scholion Veneti 454 on *Iliad* VI.131.

BINDING AND LOOSING: Mk. 7.35; Lk. 13.15.; Acts 2.24 (*not* Mt. 16.19; 18.18, where the terms have their technical, Jewish legal sense). *PGM* IV.231ff.; V.320ff.; VII.438; XII.380ff.; XV.2; XXXVI.156ff.,259. *DT* 49,64–68,70–73, etc.

LOOSING PEOPLE; BINDING DEMONS: Mk. 3.27p.; *PGM* IV.1246,2327,2861,2904; XXXVI.143.

JESUS PROMISES GOOD SPIRITS: Mk. 13.11p.; Lk. 21.15; compare Jn. 14.26; *PGM* I.306–314; III. 571–581; IV.499–515, 1120ff.; XIII.795–819; *SHR* 2.10. *The paraclete*: Jn. 14.26; etc. *On Paul*: Smith, *Clement* 213ff.,237,248ff.; *Secret Gospel* 97–114.

JESUS' "POWER": In Greek, *dynamis*. The word is found in this sense for Jesus' supernatural power in Mk. 5.30, but more often in Luke. Hull, *Hellenistic Magic* 105ff., thinks it evidence of magical influence on Luke's thought, and points out the importance of the concept in Egyptian magic (evidence collected by Preisigke, *Gotteskraft*) and the similar use in *Testament of Solomon* (often), and in *PGM* (he cites XXXV.25; XXXVI.312) and Bell-Nock-Thompson, *Magical Texts*, p. 254, line 9 (= *PGM* LXI.9). In the New Testament the most clearly magical use is that in Mark. Luke, although he takes this over (8.46), specifies in two of his four other uses that the power is not Jesus' (in 4.14 it is the Spirit's, in 5.17 the Lord's). These two specifications were probably intended to obscure Jesus' claim to divinity by disguising him as a prophet—a man of the spirit, or man of God. The original miracle stories probably never represented Jesus' miracles as the work of "the spirit" (above, p. 101 and notes), nor as the work of a god ("the Lord") distinct from Jesus.

JESUS' "AUTHORITY": In Mark, this customarily means "supernatural power" (Starr, "Authority") as it does in *PGM* I.215f.; IV.1193f.; XII.147; XVIIa.5 (*exousia* and *dynamis* used together as synonyms, as in Lk. 4.36 and 9.1). Above, pp. 10, 31, 34, 37, 109 etc.

HIS POWER WORKED AUTOMATICALLY: Mk. 5.30p.; cf. 3.10; 6.56p. Other magicians were thought to be able to enchant a person they touched (*PGM* VII.980; etc.), but the fetishistic notion of a power that works automatically appears mainly in stories of magical stones and plants (where it is common; Preisigke, *Gotteskraft*).

PREPARATORY PERIODS: Six days before the transfiguration (Mk. 9.2p.; Lk. 9.28 has "eight"); four days before the raising of Lazarus, Jn. 11.39; six days before his initiation (the longer text of Mark as quoted by Clement; Smith, *Clement* 452; *Secret Gospel* 17); two or three before the resurrection (Smith, *Clement* 163, n. 8).

PRAYER (AND FASTING?): Mk. 9.29 (and variant); Jn. 11.41f. *PGM* IV.3007ff.; V.96ff. and often. Luke much increased Jesus' praying and fasting (Böcher, *Christus* 114f., 133); perhaps this was also part of his attempt to disguise the deity.

"THE FINGER OF GOD": Lk. 11.20; *PGM* Ostraka 1; McCasland, *Finger*.

DEMONS' PERCEPTION OF JESUS' POWER: Mk. 1.23f.p.; 3.11; 5.6f.p.; 9.20p.; compare the cry from the tomb when Jesus approaches it in the longer text of Mark, Smith, *Clement* 106f. and 156f.; *Secret Gospel* 16 and 55; Philostratus, *Life* III.38.

CALLING BY NAME: Bauernfeind, *Worte* 16ff.; 25; etc. Böcher, *Christus* 88f. *PGM* IV.870ff. (by magician); and often.

DEMONS' ENTREATIES: Mk. 5.7,10,12pp.; Philostratus, *Life* IV.20,25; *Testament of Solomon* II.6; etc.

DEMONS' BARGAINING: Mk. 5.12f.; Maspero, *Stories* 178f.; compare *Testament of Solomon* II.6; VI.5–10.

EXORCISM AT A DISTANCE: Mk. 7.29p.; Mt. 8.13p.; Jn. 4.50; Acts 19.12; compare Mk. 5.27f.p.; 6.56p.; Philostratus, *Life* III.38; Lucian, *Philopseudes* 12. Remote control of demons is presupposed by invocations and spells to send demons, to give dreams, to bring lovers, etc.; these are innumerable.

PAGE 128

MAGICAL DETAILS CONSISTENT: This is proved by Hull, *Hellenistic Magic* 73–86.

DEMONS QUESTIONED: Mk. 5.9p.; Lucian, *Philopseudes* 16; Philostratus, *Life* IV.25; *PGM* IV.3037ff.

DEMONS "MUZZLED": Mk. 1.25p.; 4.39; compare *DT* 15.24; 22.42; 23.2; 26.30; cf. Rohde, *Psyche* 604. On silencing demons in general, Böcher, *Christus* 130.

A WORD IS ENOUGH: Mk. 1.25f.p.; 2.11f.p.; etc. Mt. 8.8p.; 8.16; Philostratus, *Life* III.38; IV.20,25. Böcher, *Christus* 86f.

SHORT ORDERS PREFERRED: Mk. 4.39; 5.41p.; 7.34; Jn. 11.43; etc.; Philostratus, *Life* IV.20; Delatte-Derchain, *Intailles*, nos. 280,307. Compare the rabbinic command to stop menses: *qom mezobek, B. Shabbat* 110b.

FOREIGN WORDS IN MAGIC TEXTS: "Be opened" in Coptic *PGM* XXXVI.315ff., in Hebrew Mk. 7.34 (not Aramaic, Rabinowitz "'Be Opened'"); a command in Aramaic Mk. 5.41: All three are translated by the texts that quote them. Eitrem, *Papyri* 116, cites a similar example of a Greek formula quoted and translated in a Coptic spell. On "barbarous terms" generally, Böcher, *Christus* 89f.

"I COMMAND YOU": Mk. 1.27p.; 9.25; Lk. 8.25; *PGM* I.254; VII.332; etc.

SPIRIT "SUBJECTED": Lk. 10.17,20; *PGM* I.273; IV.3080f.; V.164; XIII.744; etc.

ANGER, SNORTING, ETC.: Anger: Mk. 1.41 (variant reading); Lucan, *Pharsalia* VI.725ff.; Philostratus, *Life* IV.20. Snorting/fuming: Mk. 1.43(?); Jn. 11.33,38; Bonner, "Traces," 175f. followed by Eitrem, *Demonology*[2] 52; Lieberman, *Tosefta, Part V* (1962) 1363, note to p. 80.

SIGHING/GROANING: Mk. 7.34; PGM IV.2494; VII.768; Bonner, "Traces," 172ff.; Eitrem, *Demonology*[2] 54; Böcher, *Christus,* 45, 85. Against Taylor's denial of the ritual significance of these parallels, see Hull, *Hellenistic Magic* 149, n. 61.

REBUKES/THREATS/PRAYERS: Mk. 9.29; Lk. 4.39; Jn. 11.41f.; Lucian, *Philopseudes* 16; *PGM* IV.1246f.; 2248ff.; Lucan, *Pharsalia* VI.725ff.; etc.

BRIEF PRAYERS: See the examples cited in the preceding note. For short formulae, see *PGM* XIII.243 (only say the secret name); Bonner, *Studies* 182f.; 310, no. 339.

DON'T REPEAT YOURSELVES: Mt. 6.7. *PGM* IV.2085f. recommends a paredros because "he immediately accomplishes the assigned tasks, with all facility, without ⟨requiring⟩ any rigmarole."

TOUCHING: Unspecified, Mk. 1.41p.; fingering, Mk. 7.33; taking hold of, Mk. 1.31p. and often. Philostratus, *Life* III.39; IV.45; Eitrem, *Demonology*[2] 42ff. *PGM* IV.2164; VII.980; etc. On "the finger of God" see the note above.

THE MAGICIAN'S HAND: Eitrem, *Demonology*[2] 41ff.; Smith, *Clement* 109f.; Böcher, *Christus* 80ff.

SPITTLE: Mk. 7.33; 8.23; Jn. 9.6; Heim, *Incantamenta* 489 (citing Pliny, *Natural History* XXVIII.35ff.; etc.); Blau, *Zauberwesen* 68, n. 2 (citing *T. Sanhedrin* XII.10; *B. Shebu'ot* 15b; etc.); *PGM* III.420ff.; Lucian, *Menippus* 7; Psellus, *On the Work of Demons* 15 (cited above, p. 121, note); Bonner, "Traces" 171; Eitrem, *Demonology*[2] 56ff.; Böcher, *Christus* 102.

COMMANDS NOT TO RETURN: Mk. 9.25; Josephus, *Antiquities* VIII.47; Philostratus, *Life* IV.20.

JESUS' EXPLANATION OF RETURNS: Lk. 11.24ff.p.

SPELLS ETC. TO PREVENT RETURN: *PGM* IV.1254,3015, as interpreted by Eitrem, *Demonology*[2] 33, n.1.

PROHIBITION OF SPEAKING: Mk. 1.44p.; 7.36; 8.26(?); Mt. 9.30; *PGM* II.24; V.399; VII.440,726,1011,1025f.; VIII.67; XXIIb.33. *M. Berakot* V.1; etc.

CURE THOUGHT EXPULSION: Lk. 4.35; Deissmann, *Light*[2] 256ff. and 260, n. 1, comparing *PGM* IV.3013.

DEMON GIVES PROOF OF DEPARTURE: Mk. 5.13p.; Josephus, *Antiquities* VIII.48; Philostratus, *Life* IV.20.

PATIENT GIVES PROOF OF CURE: Mk. 2.11f.p.; Jn. 5.8f.; Lucian, *Philopseudes* 11 end.

PAGE 129

JESUS AS HOLY MAN: For magicians as holy men see *PGM* IV.1115–1137; V.417; VII.808; XVIIb.22. Apollonius is only the best known example (after Jesus).

JESUS' TEACHING AUTHORITATIVE: I. Cor. 7.10; 9.14; 11.23ff.; I Thess. 4.15 (?).

SPIRIT OF JESUS IN EARLY CHRISTIANS: Gal. 2.20; I Cor. 6.17; 12.8–13; II Cor. 3.17.

ATTEMPTS TO DISTINGUISH: I Cor. 7.10,12. But what of I Cor. 14.37?

BARE COLLECTIONS OF SAYINGS: *The Gospel according to Thomas;* much of the source(s) of Q was evidently like this.

SPURIOUS SAYINGS IDENTIFIED: Especially by Bultmann, *Geschichte*[4].

FAMOUS SAYINGS GIVEN TO FAMOUS PEOPLE: So Jesus was credited with the 'golden rule' (of which the negative form is found in *Tobit* 4.15 and *B. Shabbat* 31a) and with the saying, "The healthy don't need a doctor, the sick do" (Mt. 9.12p., a proverb attributed to several philosophers, see Wettstein, *NT,* on the verse).

PAGE 130

CAN SATAN CAST OUT SATAN: Mk. 3.23ff.p.; this implicitly anti-eschatological saying was the nucleus to which the collections of other sayings on the same subject in Mark and Q were attached; it therefore must be very early, and it contradicts the general eschatological expectations of later gospel material. Why, then, was it preserved? Perhaps because it was genuine. Eusebius overlooked it in making the same charge against Apollonius, *Against Hierocles* 26.

THE FINGER OF GOD: Lk. 11.20p. Matthew was embarrassed by the magical connotations of "the finger" and changed it to "the spirit." On his minimization of magical traits see Hull, *Hellenistic Magic* 116ff.

CONFIDENCE NECESSARY: Mk. 9.23; Mt. 15.28; 17.20p.; the Greek word *(pistis)* here meaning "confidence" or "trust" is often in these passages mistranslated "faith." That it means "trust" in Jesus' supernatural power, not "belief" in any doctrine, is shown by Jesus' permission of exorcisms performed "in his name" by strangers on whom he imposed no requirement of belief, Mk. 9.39.Lk. 7.50 shows the same principle extended to forgiveness of sins (cp. Mk. 2.5) perhaps conceived as release from the power of demons, and Mk. 11.22f. shows it was thought to hold for other miracles, too.

SUBORDINATION OF MAGIC: Paul had other problems than exorcism, but the principle by which he dealt with them is the same which appears in these sayings; compare I Cor. 8.9; 10 entire; 12 entire. Miracles ("powers") and healings rank below apostolate and prophecy in his list of spiritual gifts, 12.28ff.; exorcism is not mentioned at all (presumably it was a subclass of "healings"). Yet Paul was credited with exorcisms, Acts 16.18.

YOUR TRUST HAS MADE YOU WELL: Commonly mistranslated, "Your faith has saved you." See the note above on "confidence." The word here is again *pistis.* Mk. 5.34p.; 10.52p.; Lk. 17.19; compare Mt. 9.29.

PRAY-ER: *Areter: Iliad* 1.11,94; 5.78 (honored as a god!).

PRAYERS ON AMULETS: Bonner, *Studies* 254, no. 7; 255, no. 15; 263, nos. 57,59; 278f., no. 156; 285, no. 192; etc.

PAGE 131

TEACHING DISCIPLES TO PRAY: Lk. 11.1; Philostratus, *Life* IV.19,40.

ALL THINGS POSSIBLE TO GOD: Mk. 10.27p.; 14.36; *PGM* XIII.713 "All things are possible to this god."

FOLLOWERS MADE FRIENDS OF THE GOD: Jn. 15.9–16; compare 14.21,23; 16.26f.; Lk. 11.5ff. *PGM* I. 171ff.: "Thus you will be a friend of the powerful angel" (who was called "god of gods" eight lines earlier), 190f.: "Having the god as a friend you will be worshiped as a god."

ASK AND IT SHALL BE GIVEN YOU: Mt. 7.7p.; Mk. 11.24p.; Jn. 14.13f.; 15.7; 16.24.
PGM IV.777f.: "Ask the god whatever you wish and he will give it you;" 2172: "When you ask,
you shall receive." On the independence and early common source of the gospel passages see
Dodd, *Historical Tradition* 350f.

PERSISTENCE RECOMMENDED: Lk. 11.5–13; again 18.1ff. "that they should always keep
praying and not give up."

REPETITION RECOMMENDED: *PGM* III.272ff.; VII.912,917; LXXII.27ff. Compare
IV.2901ff.; IV.2441–2620, instead of recommending repetition, provides three different
spells. Variants are plentiful.

GETTING THE GOD OUT OF BED: Lk. 11.8 = *PGM* IV.369f. The magician tells his spirit,
"Just get yourself up from your rest . . . and" (do as you're told).

HOSTILITY TO GENTILES IN MATTHEW: Only Matthew makes Jesus forbid the apostles to
go to the gentiles, 10.5. The prohibition was rescinded, perhaps by a redactor, in 28.19.

MATTHEW'S DISLIKE OF MAGIC: Hull, *Hellenistic Magic* 116ff.

CONTRADICTION EXPLAINED: *PGM* I.181ff. A striking example is *PGM* XIII, in which
ceremonies and prayers to learn the name of the god fill most of 230 lines, and are followed by
two dozen directions, averaging about four lines each, for miracles to be done by mere pronouncement of the name with, at most, some simple rite or short spell.

YOUR HIDDEN FATHER: Mt. 6.6, literally, "to your Father, the ⟨god⟩ in the hidden ⟨place⟩
. . . looking into what ⟨is⟩ hidden."

PAGE 132

GOD AS "FATHER": Matthew's "our" results from adaption to public, community use; Luke
has only "Father." *PGM* LXI.62; IV.548; XXIIb.1ff.; I.304; IV.1182,1918; etc.

"IN THE HEAVENS": *DT* 22.46f.; 24.27f.; 29.31; etc. Philostratus, *Life* VI.11end,19;
PGM III.259,262; IV.1061,1178; VII.555; XII.106,261; XV.15; XXIIa.18; etc.

"HALLOWING" GOD'S NAME: Strack-Billerbeck, *Kommentar*, on Mt. 6.9.

"TAT, TAT, TAT." ETC.: *DMP* XVII.1ff.; again V.15ff.; VII.11ff. "Tat" is the Egyptian
god, Thoth.

GOD'S NAME(S) "HOLY": *PGM* III.570,624; IV.870ff., 1005, 3071; compare XII.398.

PAGE 133

"AN ANGEL ON EARTH": *PGM* XXIIb.23ff., conclusion of "the Prayer of Jacob." My
italics. The doubling, "Amen, amen," recalls that attributed to Jesus by John, 1.51; etc. (two
dozen other instances).

FOOD TO CARRY US OVER: Lk. 11.3p.; the common translation "our daily bread" is
probably wrong. "Give us today our . . . bread" (that is, "our food") is clear, but the rare word
epiousion that describes the bread would hardly have been used for so common a meaning as
"daily." The suggestion given in the text modifies that in *ThWb* on *epiousios*.

THE POOR MAGICIAN: Lucian, *Philopseudes* 15end; Origen, *Against Celsus* I.68. To make the
magician the Son of God makes the problem more acute; Christain attempts to answer it led to
the doctrine of kenosis.

JESUS ON MONEY: Mt. 6.19–34; Mk. 10.17–25p.; Lk. 12.33; etc.

TONING DOWN: Mark blunted the needle saying by adding hope for an exception—the
magical principle, "all things are possible to God" (10.27; above, p. 131 and note); Matthew
limited the sale order to those who wished "to be perfect" (19.21); etc.

JESUS' POVERTY: There are no reliable stories of *large* contributions during Jesus' lifetime.
Lk. 19.8 is suspect because it is exemplary and known only to Luke.

APOLLONIUS ON MONEY: Philostratus, *Life* I.13,35; II.7; V.40; Jesus had less to lose and
was more extreme.

THE SIZE OF JESUS' COMPANY: Mk. 15.41p.; Lk. 8.2; 23.55; Acts 1.13f.

PAGE 134

ENTRANCE OF JERICHO: Lk. 19.1ff. It need not be supposed that the story is true; the important thing is that Luke *thought* it was true, in other words, to him it seemed the sort of thing that happened.

LONGER TEXT OF MARK: As quoted by Clement of Alexandria, Smith, *Secret Gospel* 16f.; *Clement* 452, with commentary, 111ff.

THEY STAYED A WEEK: Compare the *Didache* 11.4ff.: "Any apostle who comes to you should be received as the Lord. But he is not to remain more than one day and, in case of necessity, a second. If he remains for three days, he is a false prophet," etc.

MK. 4.11f.: See Smith, *Clement* 117f.,178ff.; *Secret Gospel* 78f. One detail needs correction: I was mistaken in supposing, in *Clement* 183 end, that the use of *edidaske* with *mysterion* in the longer text probably results from a corruption. It may; but there are many passages in which *didaskein* and cognates are used of magical rites and mysteries, for instance, *PGM* IV.750,1872; Herodotus II.171; Dionysius Hal., *Roman Antiquities* I.68; Porphyry, *On Abstinence* IV.16; *Chaldean Oracles* (ed. des Places) no. 224.1.

PGM XII.92ff.: The giving of the name was associated with a "holy mountain" as was Jesus' revelation of his true nature before his disciples, see above, pp. 121 and 132.

GREAT MYSTERY . . . BLESSED INITIATE: *PGM* I.127ff., "initiate" translates *mystes*, one who has received a mystery (*mysterion*).

CLOTH OVER NAKED BODY: *PGM* III.706ff.(?); IV.88,170ff.,3095; *DMP* III.13; XXVIII.6, XXIX.23 (?). In all these passages the word for "linen cloth" designates the same peculiar kind of cloth as that specified in Mk. 14.51 and the longer text. Contrast Böcher, *Christus* 107f.

PAGE 135

KINGDOM ACCESSIBLE: Smith, *Clement* 211f.; *Secret Gospel* 94f.

SPELLS TO OPEN HEAVEN: *PGM* IV.1180; XII.324; XIII.327ff.; LXII.29.

POINTS ARGUED ELSEWHERE: *Clement*, 201–266, summarized in *Secret Gospel* 78–138.

"THOSE OUTSIDE": Mk. 4.11, cf. I Cor. 5.12; Col. 4.5; I Thess. 4.12; Bauer, *WB*[5], under *exo*.

"I CAST FURY ON YOU": *DMP* verso XII.11–XIII.1ff.; compare verso XXII.16.

"SEE AND NOT PERCEIVE": Mk. 4.12p.; 8.17f.; Jn. 9.39; 12.40.

PAGE 136

DT 242.55ff.: For *apoknizo* meaning "pluck," see *PGL*.

VISITS TO TEMPLES: Mk. 11.15ff.p.; Jn. 2.14ff.; Philostratus, *Life* I.16; IV.2,24, etc.

"DENS OF ROBBERS": Mk. 11.17p., compare Jn. 2.16; Apollonius, *Letters* LXV.

VIRTUE VS. SACRIFICE: Mt. 9.13; 12.7; Jn. 4.23, Apollonius, *On Sacrifices* (in Eusebius, *Praeparatio Evangelica* IV.12f.) and *Letters* 26,27.

APOLLONIUS CLAIMS DIVINITY: Philostratus, *Life* VIII.7.vii,end; Conybeare mistranslates.

BRAHMANS CLAIM DIVINITY: Philostratus, *Life* III,18; compare VI.11end.

MAGI DECLARED DIVINE: Apollonius, *Letters* XVIf.

UNION WITH JESUS: Jn. 10.14f.; 11.25f.; 15.4–10,14ff.; 17.3–26.

GOD IS A SPIRIT: Jn. 4.24; *PGM* I.96f.; III.8; etc.

"BROTHERS" BY COMMON SPIRIT: *PGM* IV.1113ff., especially 1135f.; compare Rom. 8.12ff.

LORD OF HEAVEN AND EARTH: So Helios, *PGM* IV.640f.

ALL THINGS GIVEN ME: *PGM* V.109f.

CHAPTER VIII

PAGE 140

REJECTION IN NAZARETH: Above, pp. 15f. on Mk. 6.1–6.

PAGE 141

ACCUSATIONS FORM COHERENT PICTURE: Above, pp. 27f., 31ff., 42ff.

SCRIBAL ORIGIN OF POLEMIC TRADITION: Above, pp. 30f.

PAGE 142

HE SAVED OTHERS, HIMSELF HE CANNOT: Mk. 15.31p.
PALISTINIAN ORIGIN AND DEVELOPMENT OF MIRACLE STORIES: Above, pp. 9f., 14, 32 and notes. Schille, *Wundertradition,* has settled this.

PAGE 143

THE ADMIRED EXORCIST: Josephus, *Antiquities* VIII.46.
METHODS OF APPROVED MAGICIANS: Josephus' acquaintance, see preceding note. Magic was thought praiseworthy by some rabbis; in the third century Rabbi Yohanan even maintained that expertise in magic should be required of every member of the governing rabbinic assembly (*B. Sanhedrin* 17a,end).
ON MK. 1.12f.: Above, pp. 104ff.

PAGE 144

LIBERTINISM IN EARLY CHRISTIANITY: Smith, *Secret Gospel* 111ff., 121–131; *Clement* 248ff., 254–263.
THE PRESENT BRIDEGROOM: Mk. 2.19p. An addition to the story justified the introduction of fasting after his death. Jesus is again identified as "the bridegroom" by an independent tradition in Jn. 3.29.
"THE BRIDEGROOM" = GOD: *Midrash Shir Hashshirim Rabbah,* introduction, section 11end, and *passim.*
DESCENT OF SPIRIT, PRIOR TO JOHN: Bultmann, *Johannes*[10] 64 (end of n. 8 of p. 63) and p. 65 with no. 3.
ALSO PRIOR TO MARK: Bultmann, *Geschichte*[4] 270.
"DEMON" AND "SPIRIT" SYNONYMOUS: For instance, *TSol* III.7.

PAGE 146

EUCHARIST NOT A PASSOVER MEAL: Of attempts to prove it a passover meal, Jeremias' *Abendmahlsworte* is easily funniest.
BULTMANN'S CONCLUSION: *Geschichte*[4] 286.

PAGE 147

CHRISTIANITY THE TRUE ISRAEL: Rom. 9.6ff.; Gal. 6.16. Examples of the following interpretive gameplans have all been pointed out in the preceding chapters.
JAMES NOTORIOUSLY PIOUS: Hegesippus in Eusebius, *Church History* II.23.

PAGE 148

PAUL'S PHARISAIC MORES: Smith, *Clement* 256 ff. and 263 ff., abbreviated in *Secret Gospel* 132.
RIDING TWO DONKEYS: Mt. 21.7, to fulfil one of Matthew's misinterpreted prophecies (Zechariah 9.9).

NOTES TO APPENDIX A

PAGE 153

MARKAN PHARISEES OMITTED BY MATTHEW OR LUKE: Both lack the reference in Mk. 7.3, a gloss on Mark that was not in their manuscripts. In Mt. 9.14, versus Mk. 2.18, the question of fasting is asked only by the disciples of the Baptist; this, too, may reflect the original text of Mark. Mk. 8.11 is in a large section of Mark—6.45–8.26—that Luke wholly omitted. Was it in his manuscript? In 20.20 Luke substituted "persons pretending to be righteous" for the "Pharisees" of Mk. 12.13. Luke in his parallels to Mk. 2.18; 3.6; and 7.5; and Matthew in his parallel to 7.5, keep the clear references to Pharisees, but omit the term as pleonastic.

NOTES TO APPENDIX B

PAGE 158

JESUS THOUGHT A PROPHET: Mk. 6.15p.; 8.28p. (Matthew adds another candidate, Jeremiah); Mt. 21.11,46; Lk. 7.16; 13.33; 24.19; Jn. 4.19; 6.14; 7.40; 7.52; 9.17; Acts 3.23; possibly Mk. 6.4p.

ELIJAH: Mk. 6.15p.; 8.28p.; compare Malachi 3.23f.; Ben Sira 48.1–11.

THE PROPHET LIKE MOSES: Jn. 6.14; 7.40; Acts 3.22f. The Old Testament probably anticipated a series of prophets, one in every generation, but this did not prevent misunderstandings (on which see Meeks, *Prophet-King,* and Teeple, *Prophet*). That the prophets are to substitute for magicians is stated clearly in Dt. 18.9–14.

MOSES: Acts 7.35–40 looks as if it came from a sermon on Jesus; if so it has now been revised to refer to the "historical" Moses.

NOT PROPHET BUT MESSIAH: Mk. 8.28f.p.; Lk. 24.19,25ff.; Jn. 4.19.25ff.; 9.17,36f.

"THE HAND OF YAHWEH": II Kings 3.15. With "the hand of Yahweh" compare "the finger of God" with which Jesus was thought to perform his exorcisms, above, p. 127.

PAGE 159

RECIPIENT NOT MADE A GOD: In Ex. 7.1, where Yahweh says to Moses, "I have made you a god to Pharaoh," "god" means "source of oracular responses," as shown by the following phrase, "And Aaron . . . shall be your prophet." "Prophets" were officials regularly attached to oracles, by whom the responses were read out. The statement thus replies to the preceding sentence. (Moses' objection that he is not a good speaker).

NO OLD TESTAMENT PROPHET IDENTIFIED WITH A GOD: In Philo's *Life of Moses* Moses becomes the incarnate Law and image of God (I.27,158,162); but Philo's *Life of Moses* in this and other important respects shows the influence of pagan aretalogies. See Hadas-Smith, *Heroes* 129ff.

GOING TO THE WILDERNESS: Mk. 1.12f.p., above, pp. 104ff.; Ex. 3.1f.; I Kings 19.8f.

FORTY DAY FAST: Ex. 34.28; Dt. 9.9; 10.10; etc.; I Kings 19.8; Lk. 4.2p.

CALL OF DISCIPLES: Mk. 1.16ff.p.; 19f.p.; 2.14p.; Lk. 5.8ff.; I Kings 19.19ff.

REQUEST TO BURY FATHER: Lk. 9.59f.p. For the legal duty see Strack-Billerbeck, *Kommentar,* on Mt. 8.21.

PROTECTION FROM SNAKES: Num. 21.9; Lk. 10.19. For Apollonius' talismans, see Nau, *Apotelesmata,* and *CCAG* VII(1908)175ff.

GO WASH AND BE HEALED: II Kings 5.10; Lk. 17.14. The "go wash and be healed" motif appears again in Jesus' cure of a blind man, Jn. 9.7, where it may or may not echo Kings; it is familiar in folklore. Edelstein, *Asclepius,* I, nos. 423,37; 804.15; Weinreich, *Heilungswunder* 132; Böcher, *Christus* 98; etc.

PAGE 160

HYSTERIA AND SKIN DISEASES: Burkill, "Healing."

"SECOND SIGHT": I Kings 21.18; II Kings 1.3; 5.26; etc.

NO ESCHATOLOGICAL PROPHECY: The nearest approach is Dt. 28–30, but this is not a prophecy of the End. After Israel's punishment comes repentance, pardon and restoration; then life will go on as before.

"THE MOSAIC ESCHATOLOGICAL PROPHET": This shadowy figure is an inference of modern criticism from the Old Testament prophecy of the return of Elijah and promise of a prophet like Moses, and from a sprinkling of references in Jewish and Christian literature from 200 B.C. to A.D. 200 that expect the coming of one or the other, or a similar figure, to introduce the End. See above, notes on Elijah, Prophet like Moses, and Moses; add for example, *Testament of Levi* 8.15; *Testament of Benjamin* 9.2, variant reading. These prophets are a subspecies of the amazingly mixed crop of "messianic" and similar figures this age produced, see Smith, "Messianic Figures?"

JESUS' APOCALYPTIC SERMONS: Mk. 13; Mt. 10.17–42; 24–25; etc. It is not denied that these contain some early sayings.

NO LIFE OF AN ESCHATOLOGICAL PROPHET: Note that the lives of Moses by Philo and Josephus do not present him as an eschatological figure. It should be needless to specify that no account of the career of an eschatological prophet *has been preserved.* The important thing is that, so far as we know, *none ever existed.* To argue on these questions from accidents of preservation is a waste of time; see, for example, H. Kee, "Aretalogies" 2,32,37,etc.

PAGE 161

JESUS RAISINGS OF THE DEAD: Mk. 5.41p. (hand); Lk. 7.14f. (order); Jn. 11.43f. (order). (However, in the parallel to Jn. 11.43f. in the longer text of Mark—Smith, *Clement* 452; *Secret Gospel* 17—Jesus raises the youth by taking his hand, probably a sign that this was an earlier form of the story).

TRANSFIGURATION STORY: Originally the story may have been a cautionary tale for initiates, to warn them against speaking in the ceremony, and the fault of Peter may not have been what he said, but that he spoke at all. If so, he probably said no more than the first sentence of his present speech (Mk. 9.5b) to which the rest is a non sequitur that has always puzzled commentators.

PROPHETS ON MOUNTAINS: Ex. 3.1; 20.21; 24.9ff.,13,15f.,18; etc.; I Kings 19.8ff.

PAGE 162

ASCENTS TO HEAVEN: II Kings 2.11; Acts 1.9 Philostratus, *Life* VIII.30end; *PGM* IV.475–731, the introduction is quoted above, p. 102.

DIFFERENCES BETWEEN JESUS AND THE PROPHETS: This list could easily be supplemented with another, from the things that a prophet should do and Jesus did *not.* See above, p. 37.

List of Scholarly Works
and Editions Cited

Aland, *Synopsis* = K. Aland, *Synopsis of the Four Gospels, Greek -English Edition*, 2 ed., N.Y. 1976

Albertz, *Streitgespräche* = M. Albertz, *Die synoptischen Streitgespräche*, Berlin, 1921

Altaner, *Patrologie*[6] = B. Altaner, *Patrologie*, 6 ed., Freiburg, 1960

Andresen, *Logos* = G. Andresen, *Logos und Nomos*, Berlin, 1955 (*AKG* 30)

"Aquinas," *Enarrationes* = *Divi Thomae Aquinatis Enarrationes, quas Cathenam vere aureum dicunt, in Quatuor Evangelia*, Venice, 1567

Audollent, *DT*, see *DT* in *Abbreviations*.

Bammel, *Trial* = *The Trial of Jesus* (Moule Festscrift), ed. E. Bammel, London, 1970 (*SBT*, Series II, 13)

Barb, "Survival" = A. Barb, "The Survival of Magic Arts," in *The Conflict between Paganism and Christianity in the Fourth Century*, ed. A. Momigliano, Oxford, 1963, pp. 100ff.

Barbel, *Christos* = J. Barbel, *Christos Angelos*, Bonn, 1941 (*Theophaneia* 3)

Bauer, *WB*[5] = W. Bauer, *Grieschisch-Deutsches Wörterbuch zu den Schriften des Neuen Testaments*, 5 ed., Berlin, 1958

Bauernfeind, *Worte* = O. Bauernfeind, *Die Worte der Dämonen im Markusevangelium*, Stuttgart, 1927 (*BWANT* 3 F., H. 8)

Baviera, *FIRA* = J. Baivera, *Fontes Iuris Romani antejustiniani, pars altera, auctores*, Florence, 1940

Bell-Nock-Thompson, *Magical Texts* = H. Bell, A. Nock, H. Thompson, *Magical Texts from a Bilingual Papyrus*, London, 1931 (from *PBA* XVII)

Berger, *Dictionary* = A. Berger, *Encyclopedic Dictionary of Roman Law*, Philadelphia, 1953 (*TAPS* NS.43.2)

Berger, "Messiastraditionen" = K. Berger, "Die königlichen Messiastraditionen des Neuen Testaments," *NTS* 20(1973)1ff.

Bettini, "Crocifisso-Amuleto" = S. Bettini, "Un Crocifisso-Amuleto onocefalo," *Nuovo Didaskaleion* 1(1947)60ff.

Betz, "Jesus"=H.D. Betz, "Jesus as Divine Man," in *Jesus and the Historian* (Colwell Festschrift), ed. F. Trotter, Philadelphia, 1968, 114ff.

Betz, *Lukian*=H.D. Betz, *Lukian von Samosata und das Neue Testament*, Berlin, 1961 (*TU* 76)

Betz, *Paraklet*=H.D. Betz, *Der Paraklet*, Leiden, 1963 (*AGSJUC* II)

Bidez-Cumont, *Mages* = J. Bidez and F. Cumont, *Les Mages hellénisés*, Paris, 1938, 2 vols.

Bieler, *Theios aner* = L. Bieler, *Theios aner*, Vienna, 1935–6, 2 vols.

Bietenhard, *Welt*, = H. Bietenhard, *Die himmlische Welt im Urchristentum und Spät-judentum*, Tübingen, 1951 (*WUNT* 2)

Blass-Debrunner-Funk, *Grammar* = F. Blass and A. Debrunner, *A Greek Grammar of the New Testament*, tr. R. Funk, Chicago, 1961

Blau, *Zauberwesen* = L. Blau, *Das altjüdische Zauberwesen*, Budapest, 1898 (in *Jahres-bericht der Landes-Rabbinerschule in Budapest, 1897–8*)

Böcher, *Christus*, = O. Böcher, *Christus Exorcista*, Stuttgart, 1972 (= *BWANT* 96)

————, *Dämonenfurcht* = O. Böcher, *Dämonenfurcht und Dämonenabwehr*, Stuttgart, 1970 (= *BWANT* 90)

Bonner, *Studies* = C. Bonner, *Studies in Magical Amulets*, Ann Arbor, 1950 (*U. of Michigan Studies, Humanistic Series* 49)

————, "Traces" = C. Bonner, "Traces of Thaumaturgic Technique in the Miracles," *HTR* 20(1927)171ff.

Bonnet, *Reallexikon* = H. Bonnet, *Reallexikon der ägyptischen Religionsgeschichte*, Berlin, 1952

Boobyer, "Mk. 2.10a" = G. Boobyer, "Mk. 2.10a and the Interpretation of the Healing of the Paralytic," *HTR* 47(1954)115ff.

Bousset, "Dämonologie" = W. Bousset, "Zur Dämonologie der späteren Antike," *ARW* 18(1915)134ff.

Bouché-Leclercq, *Histoire* = A. Bouché-Leclercq, *Histoire de la divination dans l'an-tiquité*, Paris, 1879–1882, 4 vols.

Bousset, *Antichrist* = W. Bousset, *The Antichrist Legend*, tr. A. Keane, London, 1896

————, *Religion*[3] = W. Bousset, *Die Religion des Judentums im späthellenistischen Zeital-ter*, 3ed., ed. H. Gressmann, Tübingen, 1926 (*HBNT* 21)

Boyce, *History* = M. Boyce, *A History of Zoroastrianism*, Leiden, 1975 (*Handbuch der Orientalistik* I.VIII.i.2.2A)

Braude, *Pesikta Rabbati* = W. Braude, tr., *Pesikta Rabbati*, New Haven, 1968, 2 vols. (Yale Judaica Series 18)

Broadhead, *Persae* = H. Broadhead, *The Persae of Aeschylus*, Cambridge, 1960

Brown, *John* = R. Brown, *The Gospel according to John*, N.Y., 1966–1970, 2 vols.

Bultmann, *Ergänzungsheft*, see Bultmann, *Geschichte*[4]

————, *Johannes* = R. Bultmann, *Das Evangelium des Johannes*, 10ed., Göttingen, 1941

————, *Gesshichte*[4] = R. Bultmann, *Die Geschichte der synoptischen Tradition*, 4 ed. with *Ergänzungsheft*, Göttingen, 1958 (*FRLANT* 29). English translation, *The History of the Synoptic Tradition*, tr. J. Marsh, 2ed., Oxford, 1968

Burkert "*Goes*" = W. Burkert, "*GOES.* zum griechischen 'Schamanismus'," *RMP*, NS 105(1962)36ff.

Burkill, "Healing" = T. A. Burkill, "Miraculous Healing in the Gospels," *CAJM* 19(1973)99f.

Cadbury, *Behind the Gospels* = H. Cadbury, *Behind the Gospels*, Pendle Hill, Pa., 1968 (*Pendle Hill Pamphlet* 160)

————, "Rebuttal" = H. Cadbury, "Rebuttal. A Submerged Motive in the Gospels," in *Quantulacumque* (Lake Festschrift) ed. R. Casey, London, 1937, 99ff.

Chadwick, *Origen* = H. Chadwick, *Origen: Contra Celsum*, Cambridge, England, 1953

Charles, *Apocrypha and Pseudepigrapha* = R. Charles, ed., *The Apocrypha and Pseudepigrapha of the Old Testament*, Oxford, 1913, 2 vols.

Clarke, "Rout" = W. Clarke, "The Rout of the Magi," in *Divine Humanity*, London, 1936, 41ff.

Conybeare, *Philostratus* = Philostratus, *The Life of Apollonius of Tyana, The Epistles of Apollonius, and the Treatise of Eusebius*, tr. F. Conybeare, London, 1912, 2 vols. (*Loeb Library*)

Dalman, *Worte* = G. Dalman, *Die Worte Jesu I*, 2 ed., Lepzig, 1930

Dalton, *Rings* = O. Dalton, *Catalogue of the Finger Rings, Early Christian . . . and Later* (British Museum), London, 1912

Deissmann, *Light*² = A. Deissmann, *Light from the Ancient East*, tr. R. Strachan, 2 ed., N.Y., 1927

Del Rio, *Disquisitionum* = M. Del Rio, *Disquisitionum Magicarum Libri VI*, Venice, 1606, 3 vols.

Delatte-Derchain, *Intailles* = A. Delatte, P. Derchain, *Les intailles magiques gréco-égyptiennes*, Paris (Bibliothèque Nationale, Cabinet des Médailles et Antiques), 1964

Derchain, "Darstellung" = P. Derchain, "Die älteste Darstellung des Gekreutzigten," in *Christentum am Nil*, ed. K. Wessel, Essen, 1963, 109ff.

Dieterich, *Mithrasliturgie*³ = A. Dieterich, *Eine Mithrasliturgie*, 3 ed., ed. O. Weinreich, Leipzig, 1923

Dodd, *Historical Tradition* = C. Dodd, *Historical Tradition in the Fourth Gospel*, Cambridge, England, 1963

Drower, *Mandaeans* = E. Drower, *The Mandaeans of Iraq and Iran*, (reprint) Leiden, 1962.

Duchesne-Guillemin, *Religion* = J. Duchesne-Guillemin, *La Religion de l'Iran ancien*, Paris, 1962 (*Mana* I.3)

Dunn, *Jesus* = J. Dunn, *Jesus and the Spirit*, Philadelphia, 1975

Dušanić, "*Horkion*" = S. Dušanić, "The *horkion ton oikisteron* and Fourth Century Cyrene," to appear in the papers of the VIIe Congrès Internationale d' Epigraphie grecque et latine.

Edelstein, *Asclepius* = E. and L. Edelstein, *Asclepius*, Baltimore, 1945, 2 vols. (*Publications of the Institute of the History of Medicine*, Johns Hopkins U., Second series, II)

Eisler, *Iesous* = R. Eisler, *Iesous basileus ou basileusas*, Heidelberg, 1928–30, 2 vols.

Eitrem, *Demonology*[2] = S. Eitrem, *Some Notes on the Demonology in the New Testament*, 2 ed. revised, Oslo, 1966 (*SO, Suppl.* 20)

———, *Papyri* = S. Eitrem, *Papyri Osloenses I*, Oslo, 1925

———, "Versuchung" = S. Eitrem, "Die Versuchung Christi, mit Nachwort von A. Fridrichsen," *NTT* 25(1924)2 Hefte, 2ff.

Eliade, *Shamanism* = M. Eliade, *Shamanism*, Pantheon Books, 1964 (*Bollingen Series* 76)

Fascher, *Prophetes* = E. Fascher, *Prophetes*, Giessen, 1927

Feldman, Josephus, *Antiquities* = Josephus, *Antiquities*, ed. L. Feldman, vol. IX, London, 1965 (*Loeb Library*)

Fiebig, *Wundergeschichten* = P. Fiebig, *Jüdische Wundergeschichten des neutestamentlichen Zeitalters*, Tübingen, 1911.

Flemington, *Doctrine* = W. Flemington, *The New Testament Doctrine of Baptism*, London, 1948

Fortna, *Gospel* = R. Fortna, *The Gospel of Signs*, Cambridge, 1969 (*SNTS Monograph Series* 11)

Frank, *Survey* = T. Frank, ed., *An Economic Survey of Ancient Rome*, Baltimore, 1933–1940, 6 vols.

Fridrichsen, *Problème* = A. Fridrichsen, *Le problème du Miracle dans le Christianisme primitif*, Paris, 1925 (*EHPR* 12). English translation, *The Problem of Miracle in Early Christianity*, tr. R. Harrisville and J. Hanson, Minneapolis, 1972

Gaster, "Beelzebul" = T. Gaster, "Beelzebul," *IDB* I.374

———, *Dead Sea Scriptures* = T. Gaster, *The Dead Sea Scriptures*, 3 ed., N.Y. 1976

Gollancz, *Book of Protection* = H. Gollancz, ed., *The Book of Protection, being a collection of charms . . . from Syriac MSS.*, London, 1912

Goodspeed, *Index* = E. Goodspeed, *Index apologeticus*, Leipzig, 1912

Gordon, "Bowls" = C. Gordon, "Aramaic Magical Bowls in the Istanbul and Baghdad Museums," *ArOr* 6(1934)319ff.

Grégoire, "Thraces" = H. Grégoire, "Thraces et Thessaliens," *Bulletin de l'Académie Royale de Belgique*, Classe des lettres, 5ᵉ série, 35(1949)159ff.

Griffith-Thompson, *Demotic* = F. Griffith and H. Thompson, *The Demotic Magical Papyrus of London and Leiden*, London, 1904–1908, 3 vols. (All references are to vol. I.)

Griffiths, *Plutarch's De Iside* = J. Griffiths, *Plutarch's De Iside et Osiride*, University of Wales, 1970

Hadas-Smith, *Heroes* = M. Hadas and M. Smith, *Heroes and Gods*, N.Y., (Harper & Row), 1965 (*Religious Perspectives* 13).

Hanse, *Gott* = H. Hanse, *Gott Haben*, Berlin, 1939 (*RGVV* 27)

Harnack, "Fragmente" = A. von Harnack, "Neue Fragmente des Werks des Porphyrius gegen die Christen," *Sitzungsberichte*, Berlin, 1921, 266ff.

———, *Porphyrius* = A. von Harnack, *Porphyrius 'Gegen die Christen,'* 15 *Bücher*, Berlin, 1916 (*Abhandlungen*, Berlin, 1916.1)

Haupt, *Maccabean* = P. Haupt, "A Maccabean Talisman," *Florilegium . . . M. de Vogué*, 1909, 271ff.

Heim, *Incantamenta* = R. Heim, *Incantamenta magica graeca latina,* Leipzig, 1892 (Offprint from *Supplementa Annalium Philologicorum* 19)

Heitmüller, *"Im Namen Jesu"* = W. Heitmüller, *"Im Namen Jesu,"* Göttingen, 1903 (*FRLANT* 2)

Helbig, *Führer* = W. Helbig, *Führer durch die öffentlichen Sammlungen . . . in Rom,* 4 ed., ed. H. Speier, Tübingen, 1963–1972, 4 vols.

Hengel-Merkel, "Magier" = M. Hengel and H. Merkel, "Die Magier aus dem Osten," in *Orientierung an Jesus* (J. Schmid Festschrift), ed. P. Hoffman, Freiburg, N. D. (c. 1970), 139ff.

Hennecke, *Neutestamentliche Apokryphen*[3] = E. Hennecke, *Neutestamentliche Apokryphen,* ed., W. Schneemelcher, Tübingen, 1959–1964, 2 vols. English translation: *New Testament Apocrypha*, tr. A. Higgins et al., Philadelphia, 1963–1966, 2 vols.

Henrichs, *Phoinikika* = A. Henrichs, *Die Phoinikika des Lollianos*, Bonn, 1972 (*PTA* 14)

Hoehner, *Herod* = H. Hoehner, *Herod Antipas*, Cambridge, England, 1972 (*SNTS Monograph Series* 17)

Hopfner, *"Mageia"* = T. Hopfner, *"Mageia,"* *RE* 14(1928)301ff.

——, "Nekromantie" = T. Hopfner, "Nekromantie," *RE* 16(1935)2218ff.

Hubert, *"Magia"* = H. Hubert, *"Magia",* Daremberg-Saglio, III.2.1494ff.

Hull, *Hellenistic Magic* = J. Hull, *Hellenistic Magic and the Synoptic Tradition*, Naperville, Ill., 1974 (*SBT* Second Series 28)

van Iersel, *Sohn* = B. van Iersel, *'Der Sohn' in den synoptischen Jesusworten,* Leiden, 1961 (*SNT* 3)

Jacoby, *FGrHist*, see *FGrHist* in "Abbreviations"

Jaeger, *Aristotle* = W. Jaeger, *Aristotle,* tr. R. Robinson, 2 ed., Oxford, 1948

James, *Apocryphal* = M. James, ed., *The Apocryphal New Testament*, Oxford, 1924

Jebb, *Sophocles* = R. Jebb, ed., *Sophocles,* Cambridge, England, 1883–1896, 7 vols.

Jeremias, *Abendmahlsworte* = J. Jeremias, *Die Abendmahlsworte Jesu*, 4 ed., Göttingen, 1967

Kee, "Aretalogies" = H. Kee, "Aretalogies, Hellenistic "Lives," and the Sources of Mark, in *Colluquy 12* ed. W. Wuellner, Berkeley, (The Center for Hermeneutical Studies) 1975, 1ff.

Kent, *Old Persian* = R. Kent, *Old Persian,* 2 ed., New Haven, 1953

King, *Gnostics*[2] = C. King, *The Gnostics and their Remains,* 2 ed., London, 1887

Knopf, *Märtyrerakten* = R. Knopf, *Ausgewählte Märtyrerakten,* 4 ed., 1965

Koehler-Baumgartner, *Lexikon* = L. Koehler and W. Baumgartner, *Hebräisches und aramäisches Lexikon zum Alten Testament*, Leiden, 1967ff., 2 vols. to date.

Koestermann, *Tacitus* = E. Koestermann, *Cornelius Tacitus Annalen*, Heidelberg, 1963–68, 4 vols.

Kraeling, "Jesus" = C. Kraeling, "Was Jesus accused of Necromancy?" *JBL* 59(1940)147ff.

Kropp, *Zaubertexte* = A. Kropp, *Ausgewählte koptische Zaubertexte,* Brussels, 1930–1931, 3 vols.

Kümmel, "Jesusforschung" = W. Kümmel, "Jesusforschung seit 1950," *ThR* 31(1966)15ff. and 289ff.

Lassally, "Amulette" = O. Lassally, "Amulette und Tätowierungen in Ägypten," *ARW* 29(1931)130ff.

Lattimore, *Themes* = R. Lattimore, *Themes in Greek and Latin Epitaphs*, Urbana, reprint, 1962

Le Moyne, *Sadducéens* = J. Le Moyne, *Les Sadducéens,* Paris, 1972

Levine, *Roman Caesarea* = L. Levine, *Roman Caesarea*, Jerusalem, 1975 (*Qedem* 2)

Lieberman, "Roman" = S. Lieberman, "Roman Legal Institutions," *JQR* 35 (1944)1ff. (=*Texts and Studies*, N.Y., 1974, 57ff.)

———, *Tosefta* = S. Lieberman, *Tosefta Ki-fshutah*, N.Y., 1955ff., 9 vols. to date.

Lietzmann, *Galater* = H. Lietzmann, *An die Galater,* 3 ed., Tübingen, 1932 (*HBNT* 10)

Lipsius-Bonnet, *Acta* = R. Lipsius and M. Bonnet, *Acta Apostolorum Apocrypha*, Leipzig, 1891–1903, 2 vols in 3.

van der Loos, *Miracles* = H. van der Loos, *The Miracles of Jesus*, Leiden, 1965 (*SNT* 9)

McArthur, *Search* = H. McArthur, *In Search of the Historical Jesus*, N.Y., 1969

McCasland, *Finger* = S. McCasland, *By the Finger of God*, N.Y., 1951

Macdonald, *Memar* = J. Macdonald, *Memar Marqah*, Berlin, 1963, 2 vols. (*Beihefte zur ZAW* 84)

Maspéro, *Contes* = G. Maspéro, *Les Contes populaires de l'Égypte ancienne*, Paris, 1882 = Maspero, *Stories* = G. Maspero, *Popular Stories of Ancient Egypt*, tr. A. Johns, revised by G. Maspero, reprint, New Hyde Park, N.Y., 1967

Meeks, *Prophet-King* = W. Meeks, *The Prophet-King*, Leiden, 1967 (*SNT* 14)

Mette, "Oinomaos 5" = H. Mette, "Oinomaos 5) Von Gadara," *RE* 17(1937)2249ff.

Metzger, *Textual Commentary* = B. Metzger, *A Textual Commentary on the Greek New Testament*, N.Y., 1971

Miller, "Moiragenes" = J. Miller, "Moiragenes 1" *RE* 15(1932)2497.

Moreau, *Témoignages* = J. Moreau, *Les plus anciens témoignages profanes sur Jésus*, Brussels, 1944

Nau, *Apotelesmata* = F. Nau, ed., *Apotelesmata Apollonii Tyanensis*, in *Patrologia Syriaca* 2(1907)1372ff.

Neusner, *Development* = J. Neusner, *Development of a Legend*, Leiden, 1970 (*Studia post-biblica* 16)

———, *Eliezer* = J. Neusner, *Eliezer ben Hyrcanus, the Tradition and the Man*, Leiden, 1973, 2 vols. (*SJLA* 3 and 4)

———, *History* = J. Neusner, *A History of the Jews in Babylonia*, Leiden, 1964–1970, 5 vols. (Vol. I, corrected reprint, 1969) (*Studia post-biblica* 9, 11, 12, 14, 15)

———, *Traditions* = J. Neusner, *The Rabbinic Traditions about the Pharisees before 70*, Leiden, 1971, 3 vols.

Nicolsky, *Spuren* = N. Nicolsky, *Spuren magischer Formeln in den Psalmen*, tr. G. Petzold, Giessen, 1927 (*Beihefte ZAW* 46)

Nilsson, *Geschichte* = M. Nilsson, *Geschichte der griechischen Religion,* 2 ed., Munich, 2 vols., 1955–1961 (*Handbuch der Altertumswissenschaft* V.2)

Nock, *Conversion* = A. Nock, *Conversion*, Oxford, 1933

————, "Paul and the Magus" = A. Nock, "Paul and the Magus," in *The Beginnings of Christianity*, ed. K. Lake et al., Part I, vol. 5, London, 1933,164ff. (=*Essays on Religion and the Ancient World*, ed. Z. Stewart, Cambridge, Mass., 1972, 308ff.)

Page, *Papyri* = D. Page, *Select Papyri*, vol. III, London, 1941 *(Loeb Library)*

Petzke, "Frage" = G. Petzke, "Die historische Frage nach den Wundertaten Jesu," *NTS* 22(1976)180ff.

————, *Traditionen* = G. Petzke, *Die Traditionen über Apollonius von Tyana und das Neue Testament*, Leiden, 1970 *(SCHNT 1)*

Pfister, "Epiphanie" = F. Pfister, "Epiphanie," *RE Suppl.* 4(1924)277ff.

————, "Epode" = F. Pfister, "Epode," *RE Suppl.* 4(1924)323ff.

————, "Kultus" = F. Pfister, "Kultus," *RE* 11(1922)2106ff.

Pokorný, *Gottessohn* = P. Pokorný, *Der Gottessohn*, Zürich, 1971

Preisendanz, "Paredros" = K. Preisendanz, "Paredros 2" *RE* 18(1949)1428ff.

Preisigke, *Gotteskraft* = F. Preisigke, *Die Gotteskraft der frühchristlichen Zeit*, Berlin, 1922 *(Papyrusinstitut Heidelberg, Schrift 6)*

Preuschen, *Analecta* = E. Preuschen, *Analecta*, Freiburg i.B., 1893 *(Sammlung ausgewählter kirchen-und dogmengeschichtlicher Quellenschriften 8)*

————, *Antilegomena* = E. Preuschen, *Antilegomena*, 2 ed., Gieszen, 1905

Procopé-Walter, "Iao" = A. Procopé-Walter, "Iao und Set," *ARW* 30(1933)34ff.

Rabinowitz, "'Be Opened'" = I. Rabinowitz, "'Be Opened,'" *ZNW* 53(1962)229ff.

Resch, *Agrapha* = A. Resch, *Agrapha*, 2 ed., Leipzig, 1906 *(TU, NF 15.3/4)*

Riccobono, *FIRA* = S. Riccobono, *Fontes Iuris Romani antejustiniani, pars prima, leges*, 2 ed., Florence, 1941

Robinson-Koester, *Trajectories* = J. Robinson, H. Koester, *Trajectories through Early Christianity*, Philadelphia, 1971

Rohde, *Psyche* = E. Rohde, *Psyche*, 8 ed., tr. W. Hillis, London, 1925

Rokeah, "Ben Stara" = D. Rokeah, "Ben Stara Is Ben Pantera," *Tarbis* 39(1970)9ff. (in Hebrew)

de Romilly, *Magic and Rhetoric* = J. de Romilly, *Magic and Rhetoric in Ancient Greece*, Cambridge, Mass., 1975

Rudolph, *Mandäer* = K. Rudolph, *Die Mandäer, I. Prolegomena: Das Mandäerproblem*, Göttingen, 1960

Samain, "L'accusation" = J. Samain, "L'accusation de magie contre le Christ dans les Évangiles," *Ephemerides Theologicae Lovanienses* 15(1938)449ff.

Sanders, "11 QPsᵃ Reviewed" = J. Sanders, "The Qumran Psalms Scroll (11 QPsᵃ) Reviewed," in *On Language, Culture, and Religion* (E. Nida Festschrift), edd. M. Black and W. Smalley. The Hague; 1974, 79ff.

Schille, *Wundertradition* = G. Schille, *Die urchristliche Wundertradition*, Stuttgart, 1967 *(AT 29)*

Schmidt, *Rahmen* = K. Schmidt, *Der Rahmen der Geschichte Jesu*, Berlin, 1919

————, "Stellung" = K. Schmidt, "Die Stellung der Evangelien in der allgemeinen Literaturgeschichte," in *Eucharisterion* (Gunkel Festscrift), Göttingen, 1923, 2 vols., II.51ff.

Schneider, *Index* = O. Schneider, *In C. Plini Secundi Naturalis Historiae Libros Indices*, Gotha, 1857, 2 vols., reprint, Hildesheim, 1967.

Schoeps, "Simon Magus" = H. Schoeps, "Simon Magus in der Haggada," *HUCA* 21(1948)257ff.

Schrire, *Hebrew Amulets* = T. Schrire, *Hebrew Amulets*, London, 1966

Schürer, *Geschichte* = E. Schürer, *Geschichte des jüdischen Volkes im Zeitalter Jesu Christi*, 3–4 ed., Leipzig, 1901–1911, 4 vols.

Schürer-Vermes-Millar, *History* = E. Schürer, *The History of the Jewish People in the Age of Jesus Christ*, vol. I (edd. G. Vermes and F. Millar), Edinburgh, 1973

Schweitzer, *Geschichte*[6] = A. Schweitzer, *Geschichte der Leben-Jesu-Forschung,* 6 ed., Tübingen, 1951

————, *Quest* = A. Schweitzer, *The Quest of the Historical Jesus*, London, 1910

Seeck, "Hierokles 13" = O. Seeck, "Hierokles 13," *RE* 8(1913)1477.

————, *Regesten* = O. Seeck, *Regesten der Kaiser und Päpste,* Stuttgart, 1919

Selwyn, *I Peter* = E. Selwyn, *The First Epistle of St. Peter*, London, 1946

Shaked, "Qumran" = S. Shaked, "Qumran and Iran: Further Considerations," *IOS* 2(1972)433ff.

Sherwin-White, *Letters* = A. Sherwin-White, *The Letters of Pliny*, Oxford, 1966

Smith, "Good News" = J. Smith, "Good News Is No News: Aretalogy and Gospel," in *Christianity, Judaism, and Other Greco-Roman Cults,* (M. Smith Festschrift) ed. J. Neusner, Leiden, 1975, 4 vols., I.21ff.

Smith, "Aretalogy" = M. Smith, "The Aretalogy Used by Mark," in *Colloquy* 6, ed. W. Wuellner, Berkeley, (The Center for Hermeneutical Studies), 1973, 1ff.

————, *Clement* = M. Smith, *Clement of Alexandria and a Secret Gospel of Mark*, Cambridge, Mass., 1973

————, "Jesus' Attitude" = M. Smith, "Jesus' Attitude Towards the Law," in *Papers of the Fourth World Congress of Jewish Studies*, Jerusalem, 1967, 241ff.

————, "Jewish Elements" = M. Smith, "The Jewish Elements in the Gospels," *Journal of Bible and Religion* 24(1956)90ff.

————, "Messianic Figures?" = M. Smith, "What Is Implied by the Variety of Messianic Figures?" *JBL* 78(1959)66ff.

————, "Observations" = M. Smith, "Observations on Hekalot Rabbati," in *Biblical and Other Studies,* ed. A. Altmann, Harvard, 1963, 142ff.

————, "Palestinian Judaism" = M. Smith, "Palestinian Judaism in the First Century," in *Israel*, ed. M. Davis, N.Y., 1956, 67ff. reprinted in H. Fischel, ed., *Essays in Greco-Roman and Related Talmudic Literature*, N.Y., 1977, pp. 183ff.

————, *Parallels* = M. Smith, *Tannaitic Parallels to the Gospels,* Philadelphia, 1951 (*JBL* Monograph Series VI), corrected reprint, 1977

————, *Parties* = M. Smith, *Palestinian Parties and Politics that Shaped the Old Testament*, N.Y., Columbia University Press, 1971

————, "Prolegomena" = M. Smith, "Prolegomena to a Discussion of Aretalogies," *JBL* 90(1971)174ff.

————, "Second Isaiah" = M. Smith, "II Isaiah and the Persians," *JAOS* 83 (1963)415ff.

————, *Secret Gospel* = M. Smith, *The Secret Gospel*, N.Y., (Harper & Row), 1973

————, "Wine God" = M. Smith, "On the Wine God in Palestine," *Salo W. Baron Jubilee Volume*, Jerusalem, 1975, English section, 815ff.

Smith, *Egypt* = W. Smith, *Ancient Egypt as represented in the Museum of Fine Arts, Boston*, 4 ed., Boston, 1960

Speyer, "Bild" = W. Speyer, "Zum Bild des Apollonius von Tyana," *JAC* 17 (1974)47ff.

————, "Büchervernichtung" = W. Speyer, "Büchervernichtung," *JAC* 13 (1970)123ff.

Stanton, *Jesus* = G. Stanton, *Jesus of Nazareth in New Testament Preaching*, Cambridge, England, 1974 (*SNTS Monograph Series* 27)

Starr, "Authority" = J. Starr, "The Meaning of Authority in Mark 1.22," *HTR* 23(1930)302ff.

Stendahl, *School* = K. Stendahl, *The School of St. Matthew*, 2 ed., Uppsala, 1969 (*ASNT* 20)

Strack, *Jesus* = H. Strack, *Jesus, die Häretiker, und die Christen, nach den ältesten jüdischen Angaben*, Leipzig, 1910 (*Schriften des Institutum Judaicum in Berlin*, 37)

Strack-Billerbeck, *Kommentar* = H. Strack and P. Billerbeck, *Kommentar zum Neuen Testament aus Talmud und Midrash*, Munich, 1922–1961, 6 vols.

Syme, *Tacitus* = R. Syme, *Tacitus*, Oxford, 1958, 2 vols.

Tambornino, *Daemonismo* = J. Tambornino, *De antiquorum daemonismo*, Giessen, 1909 (=*RGVV* VII.3)

Taylor, *Mark* = V. Taylor, *The Gospel according to St. Mark*, London, 1952

Teeple, *Prophet* = H. Teeple, *The Mosaic Eschatological Prophet*, Philadelphia, 1957 (*JBL Monograph Series* 10)

Teixidor, *Pagan God* = J. Teixidor, *The Pagan God*, Princeton, 1977

Tiede, *Charismatic Figure* = D. Tiede, *The Charismatic Figure as Miracle Worker*, Missoula, Montana, 1972

Trocmé, *Formation* = E. Trocmé, *The Formation of the Gospel According to Mark*, tr. P. Gaughan, Philadelphia, 1975

————, *Jésus* = E. Trocmé, *Jésus de Nazareth vu par les témoins de sa vie*, Paris, 1971. English translation: *Jesus as Seen by His Contemporaries*, Philadelphia, 1975

Weinreich, "Alexandros"=O. Weinreich, "Alexandros der Lügenprophet," *NJB* 47(1921)129ff. (= *Ausgewählte Schriften I*, Amsterdam, 1969, 520ff.)

————, *Heilungswunder* = O. Weinreich, *Antike Heilungswunder*, Giessen, 1909 (*RGVV* VIII.1)

Wellhausen, *Evangelium Marci*[2] = J. Wellhausen, *Das Evangelium Marci*, 2 ed., Berlin, 1909

Wetstein, *NT* = J. Wetstenius, ed., *Novum Testamentum graecum*, Amsterdam, 1751–2, 2 vols.

Wetter, *Sohn* = G. Wetter, *Der Sohn Gottes*, Göttingen, 1916

Wortmann, "Kosmogonie" = D. Wortmann, "Kosmogonie und Nilflut," *BJ* 166(1966)62ff.

————, "Texte" = D. Wortmann, "Neue magische Texte," *BJ* 168(1968)56ff.

Wünsch, *Fluchtafeln* = R. Wünsch, *Antike Fluchtafeln*, Bonn, 1912 (*Kleine Texte* 20)
——, *Verfluchungstafeln* = R. Wünsch, *Sethianische Verfluchungstafeln aus Rom*, Leipzig, 1898
Yamauchi, *Mandaic . . . Texts* = E. Yamauchi, *Mandaic Incantation Texts*, New Haven, 1967 (*American Oriental Series* 49)

Abbreviations

AGSJUC = *Arbeiten zur Geschichte des Spätjudentums und Urchristentums*
AKG = *Arbeiten zur Kirchengeschichte*
ArOr = *Archiv Orientální*
ARW = *Archiv für Religionswissenschaft*
ASNT = *Acta Seminarii Neotestamentici Upsaliensis*
AT = *Arbeiten zur Theologie*
B = *Babylonian Talmud*
BO — *Bibliotheca Orientalis*
BJ = *Bonner Jahrbucher*
BWANT = *Beiträge zur Wissenschaft vom Alten und Neuen Testament*
CAJM = *Central African Journal of Medicine*
CCAG = *Catalogus codicum astrologorum graecorum*
CIL = *Corpus Inscriptionum Latinarum*
DMP = *The Demotic Magical Papyrus of London and Leiden,* vol. I, ed. F. Griffith and
     H. Thompson, London, 1904.
DT = A. Audollent, *Defixionum Tabellae*, Paris, 1904
Daremberg-Saglio = C. Daremberg and E. Saglio, edd., *Dictionnaire des antiquités
     grecques et romaines,* Paris, 1877–1919, 6 vols. in 10
EHPR = *Etudes d'histoire et de philosophie religieuses*
FGrHist = F. Jacoby, *Die Fragmente der griechischen Historiker*, Berlin and Leiden,
     1922–1958, 15 vols. (vols. 1 and 2 corrected reprints, 1957)
FRLANT = *Forschungen zur Religion und Literatur des Alten und Neuen Testaments*
HBNT = *Handbuch zum Neuen Testament*
HTR = *Harvard Theological Review*
HUCA = *Hebrew Union College Annual*
IDB = *Interpreter's Dictionary of the Bible*
IG = *Inscriptiones Graecae*
IOS = *Israel Oriental Studies*
J = *Jerusalem Talmud* = *Palestinian Talmud*
JAC = *Jahrbuch für Antike und Christentum*
JAOS = *Journal of the American Oriental Society*

JBL = Journal of Biblical Literature
JQR = Jewish Quarterly Review
M = Mishnah
NF = Neue Folge
NJB = Neue Jahrbücher für das klassische Altertum
NS = New Series
NTS = New Testament Studies
NTT = Norsk Teologisk Tidsskrift
PBA = Proceedings of the British Academy
PGL = A Patristic Greek Lexicon, ed. G. Lampe, Oxford, 1961
PGM = Papyri graecae magicae, 2 ed., edd. K. Preisendanz and A. Henrichs, Stuttgart, 1973–1974, 2 vols.
PTA = Papyrologische Texte und Abhandlungen
RE = Paulys Real-Encyclopädie der classischen Altertumswissenschaft, Neue Bearbeitung, edd. G. Wissowa et al.
RGVV = Religionsgeschichtliche Versuche und Vorarbeiten
RMP = Rheinisches Museum für Philologie
SBT = Studies in Biblical Theology
SCHNT = Studia ad Corpus Hellenisticum Novi Testamenti
SEG = Supplementum Epigraphicum Graecum
SHR=*Sefer ha-Razim (The Book of Secrets)*, ed. M. Margalioth, Jerusalem, 1966 (This is cited by heavens and their subdivisions, thus "I.5" means "First heaven, fifth camp")
SJLA = Studies in Judaism and Late Antiquity
SNT = Supplements to Novum Testamentum
SNTS = Studiorum Novi Testamenti Societas/Society for New Testament Studies
SO = Symbolae Osloenses
T = Tosefta
TAPS = Transactions of the American Philosophical Society
ThR = Theologische Rundschau
ThWb = Theologisches Wörterbuch zum Neuen Testament, edd. G. Kittel et al, Stuttgart, 1933–1973, 9 vols.
Thesaurus = Thesaurus Graecae Linguae, edd. C. Hase, G.de Sinner, T. Fix, Paris, 1865, 9 vols.
TS = Texts and Studies
TSol = The Testament of Solomon, ed. C. McCown, Leipzig, 1922.
TU = Texte und Untersuchungen
WUNT = Wissenschaftliche Untersuchungen zum Neuen Testament
ZAW = Zeitschrift für die alttestamentliche Wissenschaft
ZNW = Zeitschrift für die neutestamentliche Wissenschaft